ISRAEL,

JORDAN,

AND

PALESTINE

ASHER SUSSER

# ISRAEL, JORDAN, AND PALESTINE

## The Two-State Imperative

A Crown Center for
Middle East Studies Book

BRANDEIS
UNIVERSITY PRESS
Waltham, Massachusetts

Brandeis University Press
An imprint of University Press of New England
www.upne.com
© 2012 Brandeis University
All rights reserved
Manufactured in the United States of America
Designed by Doug Tifft and Michelle Grald
Typeset in Quadraat OT by Integrated Publishing Solutions

University Press of New England is a member of the Green Press
Initiative. The paper used in this book meets their minimum require-
ment for recycled paper.

For permission to reproduce any of the material in this book, contact
Permissions, University Press of New England, One Court Street, Suite
250, Lebanon NH 03766; or visit www.upne.com

The Crown Center for Middle East Studies at Brandeis University is
committed to producing balanced and dispassionate research regarding
all aspects of the contemporary Middle East. In addition to publishing
basic research in the form of books and monographs, the Center provides
timely analysis in the form of Middle East Briefs. The Center's activities
also include conferences, seminars, and workshops. Visit www.brandeis
.edu/crown

Library of Congress Cataloging-in-Publication Data
Susser, Asher.
Israel, Jordan, and Palestine : the two-state imperative / Asher Susser.
p.   cm
"A Crown Center for Middle East Studies Book."
Includes bibliographical references and index.
ISBN 978-1-61168-038-6 (cloth : alk. paper)—ISBN 978-1-61168-039-3
(pbk. : alk. paper)—ISBN 978-1-61168-040-9 (ebook)
1. Arab-Israeli conflict—1993—Peace.   2. Arab-Israeli conflict.
3. Pacific settlement of international disputes.   4. Palestine—
International status.   I. Title.
DS119.76.S87 2011
956.9405'4—dc23                                         2011034876

5 4 3 2 1

# CONTENTS

# MAPS

## ACKNOWLEDGMENTS

I owe a special debt of gratitude to my colleagues at the Crown Center for Middle East Studies at Brandeis University, where I spent the 2009–2010 academic year on sabbatical from my home institution, Tel Aviv University, as a Visiting Senior Fellow on the Myra and Robert Kraft Chair for Arab Politics. Above all, I am deeply indebted to my friend and colleague of many years, Professor Shai Feldman, the Judith and Sidney Swartz Director of the Crown Center, who made my sabbatical at Brandeis possible and who was so instrumental in making it a most enjoyable and productive year. Professor Feldman, Nadir Habibi, the Henry J. Leir Professor in the Economics of the Middle East; Kanan Makiya, the Sylvia K. Hassenfield Professor of Islamic and Middle Eastern Studies; Senior Fellows Professors Yezid Sayigh and Khalil Shikaki; Dr. Naghmeh Sohrabi, the Assistant Director for Research; and Jonathan Snow, a PhD candidate at the Crown Center, all read the first draft of the manuscript and offered their learned critique, from which I benefited enormously. Their comments, queries, and criticisms were invaluable.

I am equally indebted to my friends and colleagues of many years from Tel Aviv University, Professors Itamar Rabinovich and Meir Litvak, experts on this subject second to none, who read the manuscript and made many extremely knowledgeable and insightful suggestions. I am similarly indebted to another prominent and prolific historian of the Arab-Israeli conflict, Professor Neil Caplan of Concordia University in Montreal, who also read the manuscript and offered equally important suggestions. I, of course, am solely responsible for any errors of fact or judgment that remain.

I am most thankful to Haim Gal, the director of the Arabic press archive at the Moshe Dayan Center for Middle Eastern Studies at Tel Aviv University, and to his very competent assistant, Michael Barak, who were indefatigable in their searches on my behalf for the Arabic materials that I needed for this project. I am also most grateful to the extremely helpful, painstaking, and devoted staff of Brandeis University Press and the University Press of New England, and especially to Debra Hirsch Corman, Phyllis Deutsch, Amanda Dupuis, Sylvia Fuks Fried, and Lori Miller, who all invested much thought, time and effort into bringing this project to completion. Last but not least, my sincere thanks go to the always efficient administrators of the Crown Center, Kristina Cherniahivsky, the Associate Director, and Marilyn R. Horowitz, the Senior Department Associate, whose daily input always helped to make things actually happen.

*Asher Susser*
August 2011

## PREFACE

Speaking of Palestinian statehood could have various possible meanings. It could mean one single state in the area between the Mediterranean and the River Jordan or Western Palestine that would replace Israel. It might refer to a two-state solution in which a Palestinian state in the West Bank and Gaza would coexist with Israel, more or less in its pre-1967 boundaries. It could even mean a Palestinian state on the East Bank of the Jordan River that would be established instead of the Hashemite Kingdom of Jordan. Historically, the area referred to as Palestine, though not always quite clearly delineated, included large swaths of territory on both banks of the Jordan. In fact, at different points in time, the Zionist movement or parts of it, the Jordanian monarchy, and the Palestine Liberation Organization (PLO) have all claimed the entire territory from the Mediterranean Sea to the Syrian-Iraqi desert, that is, both banks of the River Jordan, or the entire area of the British Mandate for Palestine (including Transjordan), as their patrimony. In the early years of the Zionist enterprise, immediately after the First World War, Zionist territorial aspirations reached across the River Jordan, as far as the Hijaz Railway, and even beyond. The Zionist right regarded both banks of the river, including all of Transjordan, as part of the Jewish homeland all along until they finally conceded in the mid-1960s. Some on the Israeli far right still believe so to this day.

In the late 1940s, King Abdallah of Jordan sought to include all the territory west of the river in his realm and to offer the Jews autonomy under the Hashemite crown. After the foundation of the PLO in 1964, the shoe was largely on the other foot. The first chairman of the PLO, Ahmad al-Shuqayri, in his numerous clashes with King Husayn of Jordan in the mid-1960s, denied that Jordan had any right to exist. Jordan, Shuqayri said, was a colonial creation that had no historical foundation. It had been unjustifiably carved out of historical Palestine, which stretched from the Mediterranean to the Syrian and Iraqi deserts. Similarly, the PLO under Yasir Arafat, when immersed in conflict with Jordan in the early 1970s, claimed that there was no historical justification for the separation of Jordan from Palestine, as the two countries were essentially one unit.

Between 1948 and 1967 Jordan controlled the West Bank, which was formally annexed to the kingdom in 1950. Aside from the snippet of Gaza under Egyptian military administration, Palestine was essentially divided between Jordan and Israel, and Palestine as a political entity ceased to exist. Some on the Israeli right presently argue that the Kingdom of Jordan, once part of historical Palestine, should be replaced by the state of Palestine, while all of Palestine west of the Jordan River should be incorporated into Israel. And there are also those, Palestinians and others, who argue that Israel as presently constituted, as the state of the Jewish people, should cease to exist and ought to be replaced by one single unitary or binational Palestinian state that will span the entire territory of Western Palestine from the Jordan River to the Mediterranean Sea.

In recent years, two valuable works have been written on the subject by two preeminent scholars. The renowned Israeli historian Benny Morris wrote *One State, Two States: Resolving the Israeli/Palestinian Conflict* (Yale University Press, 2009), and Hussein Ibish, the noted Washington-based Arab scholar and Senior Fellow at the American Task Force on Palestine, wrote *What's Wrong with the One-State Agenda? Why Ending the Occupation and Peace with Israel Is Still the Palestinian National Goal* (American Task force on Palestine, 2009). Morris discusses the history and the goals of the Palestinian national movement and of the Zionist movement, considers the various one-state and two-state proposals made by different trends in the two movements, and assesses the practicality of various proposed solutions. Ibish discusses the various arguments made by the supporters of the one-state agenda, explains their shortcomings, and concludes by suggesting an effective strategy for the Palestinians.

This study, building upon these two important predecessors, seeks to go beyond them by expanding upon the analysis of the historical evolution of the one-state and the two-state ideas among both Israelis and Palestinians; by exploring more extensively the causes for the repeated failure to actually obtain a two-state solution; by providing an in-depth analysis of Jordan's role and positions on the questions at hand and whether there still is any form of "Jordanian option"; by engaging in a more detailed discussion of the one-state argument as put forward by its various protagonists; and by providing, in conclusion, an updated analysis of the two-state imperative as it presently unfolds through the initiative taken by the Palestinian Authority under President Mahmud Abbas and his prime minister, Salam Fayyad.

This study, therefore, discusses the evolution and the fate of the one-state idea during the British Mandate and then moves on to examine the development of Palestinian and Israeli positions toward the one-state and the two-state paradigms for the resolution of their conflict. It elaborates upon the various restrictions and conditions that both Israelis and Palestinians have woven into their conceptions of the two-state solution and seeks to explain why this two-state solution has been so elusive thus far, despite the fact that it has been accepted in principle by both parties.

The study seeks to examine the positions of the three key players, Israel, Jordan, and the Palestinians, on the various options for a solution, the underlying assumption being that it is the local actors who are going to have to make the decisions on their future relations. The relationship cannot be forged on the basis of an intellectual exercise, however logical and appealing it may seem, if the parties themselves do not find it acceptable. Nor can the solution, if there is to be one at all, be imposed on the parties by external powers.

The failure to implement the two-state paradigm has given renewed vitality and relevance to the one-state alternative. Had the two-state solution been implemented during the Oslo process in the 1990s, as initially envisaged, it is highly unlikely that the one-state alternative would ever have been proposed. The study makes a critical examination of the recent development of the one-state agenda at a time when the two-state idea has been losing traction, with the foundering of the Oslo process.

The evolution of Jordan's historical role in Palestine is also examined, as is the measure to which, in the present circumstances of apparent stalemate between Israelis and Palestinians, the Jordanians might be coaxed into renewed direct involvement in the affairs of the West Bank or, alternatively, to what extent the ideas of a Jordanian-Palestinian federation or confederation are still relevant. And finally, the study suggests possible avenues to pursue in peacemaking, considering the historical evolution of the conflict and the experience that has been acquired thus far in the "peace process."

# INTRODUCTION

The failure to achieve a peaceful solution between Israel and the Palestinians based on two independent states, Israel and Palestine, has given rise
to the recently more salient support for the one-state idea. This notion suggests that instead of two states there should be one single state spanning the
entire territory of Western Palestine from the Jordan River to the Mediterranean Sea. For Hamas, in principle, it would have to be an Islamic state, in
which the Jews, if they remained, would become a tolerated minority in a
Sharia-dominated polity. For Palestinian secularists and their like-minded
Western supporters, at least in theory, it ought to be a unitary, secular, democratic state, where Muslims, Jews, and Christians would be fully equal in one
undivided, non-ethnic, civic nation-state.

A civic national identity is defined by "a common loyalty to a territorially
defined state and rooted in a set of political rights, duties, and values shared by
the citizens of that state, regardless of their ancestry and of the non-political
(e.g. linguistic, religious, etc.) aspects of their cultural heritage." The United
States is often referred to as the quintessential civic nation, based on such a
civic national identity. For a long time in the social science typology, this civic
nation was contrasted with the ethnic nation, whose identity was based on the
principal of kinship. Members of the ethnic nation shared "a myth of common
descent" and were "bound to one another by putative ties of blood, not just by
juridical categories and/or ideological affinities. Their sense of kinship is both
manifested in and reinforced by distinctive cultural attributes (such as language and/or religion) that they have in common with one another and that
mark them apart from those who do not share their national identity."[1]

The association of peoples' identities with fixed cultural markers rather
than with their residence and membership in an existing territorial unit, so the
critics of ethnic nationalism argued, led to the discriminatory tendencies often
associated with ethnic nationalism. If national identity was construed as an

inherited quality, it would appear by definition to be less liberal, tolerant, and inclusive than civic nationalism, whose criteria for membership could theoretically be met by any resident of the nation-state's territory. Any individual could choose to subscribe to a common set of principles. Conversely, ethnic nationalism (such as ethno-cultural German, Greek, or Jewish nationalism) was considered intolerant of both individual rights and cultural diversity because of its preoccupation with ascriptive qualities that could not be freely acquired nor voluntarily relinquished.[2]

The discussion about Israel and Palestine is therefore also part of this wider debate in the social sciences on the virtues and vices of civic and ethnic nationalism, where a Jewish Israel alongside an Arab Palestine is often deemed to be a negative example of ethnic nationalism, as opposed to the one-state solution founded on the ostensibly more liberal and inclusive civic nationalism.

However, the dichotomous presentation of civic nationalism as inherently liberal, democratic, and tolerant—that is, "good nationalism"—as opposed to the intrinsically exclusionary and potentially repressive ethnic nationalism—that is, "bad nationalism"—is somewhat out of date. It has been superseded in recent years by a considerably more nuanced approach, in which "civic" is never entirely so, and elements of "ethnic" are associated with it, just as "ethnic" is hardly ever quite as "un-civic" as suggested in the extreme typology.

As Craig Calhoun has pointed out, the contrast of "ethnic to civic nationalism, organic to liberal, Eastern to Western is so habitual today that it is hard to recall that it was invented. Like nationalism itself, it seems almost natural, a reflection of reality rather than a construction of it. But while the distinction does grasp important aspects of modern history and contemporary politics, it does so in a specific way, shaping evaluations and perceptions, reinforcing some political projects, and prejudicing thinkers against others."[3]

Moreover, the theoretical distinctions are actually quite blurred. There are civic elements in ethnic-leaning nations, just as there is "kinship imagery" in civic frameworks of nationhood. As Aviel Roshwald has noted, "It is difficult to imagine how a purely civic nation-state could retain its social and political cohesion in practice, particularly if its political culture was informed exclusively by principles of liberal individualism. . . . For any democratic polity to function . . . its members must have some sense that they are bound together as a community of fate, not just a club of like minded individuals." People have died for God and country, but it was hardly likely they would hurl themselves into a hail of bullets "on behalf of the American Dental Association." The citizens of a polity "based on the popular sovereignty principle must feel that the state is the public expression of who they are." And in satisfying that sense of communal identity the polity "ceases to be a purely civic nation-state." Or alternatively, an avowedly ethnic nation-state that was aware of the potential alienation of minority groups and was therefore willing to find various ways of accommodating or compensating them, while simultaneously upholding civil rights of all individual citizens regardless of ethnicity, would actually be preferable to a state that actively suppressed minorities in the name of a supra-ethnic ideal. France, for example, a civic-leaning nation state *par excellence*, applies pressure on cultural minorities to assimilate "into a supposedly universalistic French civilization" at a time when these government-defined norms "cannot be viewed as neutrally universalistic, for they are themselves the outgrowths of a specifically European and French cultural heritage."[4]

Even in the United States, the most civic-leaning and inclusive of nations, where ethnic heritage is preserved and even favored over complete assimilation, there are certain limitations on the state's tolerance of diversity. A certain degree of "*pro forma* doctrinal and symbolic conformity with perceived national norms is seen as a precondition for reaping the full political benefits of American ethno-racial tolerance." Ethnic lobbies therefore feel obliged to trumpet their unswerving loyalty to America and their belief in what are regarded as American social and political values.[5]

Another version of the one-state concept, aside from the unitary civic or ethno-national model, is the binational state. Binationalism, as the term itself suggests, is not based on the concept of either the civic nation-state or the ethnic nation-state. Rather it is founded on the mutual and symmetric recognition of the national rights of the ethno-cultural peoples that combine to make up the society of a heterogeneous state, which may or may not have a dominant majority group or may even have no majority group at all. Such a state is made up of groups who have agreed on a power-sharing formula for their divided society, famously defined by Arend Lijphart as consociationalism. The system is characterized by four main principles: the formation of a grand coalition government representing all major linguistic, ethnic or religious groups; a measure of cultural autonomy for each of the component groups; proportionality in political representation and civil service appointments; and minority veto power over vital minority rights and autonomy.[6]

This form of power-sharing is "a set of principles that, when carried out through practices and institutions, provide every significant identity group or

segment in a society representation and decision-making abilities on common issues and a degree of autonomy over issues of importance to the group."
The overarching idea is that by sharing power, political, economic, territorial,
and military, between the different segments of society, a system of accommodation is created to reduce insecurities and thus minimize the likelihood of
conflict.[7]

Discussing the one-state idea, whether of the unitary or the binational
models, naturally gives rise to the question of their applicability to the Israel-
Palestine arena. To what extent do the Jewish Israelis and the Arab Palestinians
possess a mutually accepted historical narrative, ideological affinity, common
loyalty, and shared values that would allow them to participate in the construction of a shared polity of any type, unitary (civic or ethno-national) or consociational? Do these two peoples constitute a community of fate, that is, do they
possess a sense of shared interest and destiny? Do they share a will to accommodate to an extent that would override their ethnic separateness, their history
of hostility and mistrust, and their religious, linguistic, and cultural differen-
tiation? Or, alternatively, could these differences be mitigated within a consociational model of binationalism?

## Stating the Case

The areas of today's Middle East that form Jordan, the West Bank and Gaza,
and Israel have been tied together by geography, demography, history, and
politics since time immemorial. The political destinies of Jordan, Israel, and
Palestine as modern political entities have been inextricably linked since the
very day of their creation, and in constantly alternating ways they remain so
until the present.

Various ideas on the future relationship between Israel, Jordan, and Palestine have evolved over the years. In 1947 the United Nations proposed the partition of Palestine into two states, one Jewish and one Arab. After the 1948
War, Israel acquiesced in Jordan's incorporation of the major remnant of Arab
Palestine, the West Bank, into the Hashemite Kingdom. Jordan's control of
the West Bank ended in 1967, and in recent years the dominant paradigm for
an Israeli-Palestinian settlement has been based on the partition of British
Mandatory Palestine into two independent states.

Proposals envisaging a federation or confederation between Jordan and Palestine or between Israel, Jordan, and Palestine have also been raised at different

times since 1967. Others have, on occasion, gone so far as to propose arrangements predicated on the removal, destruction, or disappearance of the polity of one or two of the other of these three parties concerned. Presently the international consensus, as it was in the 1940s, is still for an Israeli-Palestinian settlement based on partition and the establishment of two independent states, Israel and Palestine. This is also the formula consistently supported by most Israelis and, in most polls, by a majority of Palestinians in the West Bank and Gaza.

The central thesis of this study is that during various phases of the twentieth century, Israelis, Palestinians, and Jordanians have developed cohesive collective identities, which have all too frequently violently collided with each other. The situations of conflict have only tended to further entrench these three particular identities, each defined against their respective competitive "Others."

Each one of these three peoples aspires to self-determination in an independent state of its own, aspirations that remain to a large degree contradictory and are, more often than not, at the expense of one another. Their mutual acceptance is grudging at best, and achieving stable agreement between them has proved to be a very tall order.

However, the notion that these peoples, since agreement between them is so hard to obtain, should somehow be thrust together and/or assimilated in one shared political entity, whereby any one of these distinct collective identities might stand to lose or would even be expected to relinquish its inherent right to self-determination and collective self-expression, is not likely to provide a stable solution. On the contrary, one binational or unitary state for Israelis and Palestinians, or a Jordanian state that should be made to give way to Palestine, would most probably set the stage for interminable intercommunal conflict and bloodshed.

## The Historical Setting

Jordan and Israel have been intimately tied together through the Palestinian problem for decades. It is virtually impossible to discuss Jordanian-Israeli relations in isolation from the Palestinian context, one cannot fully comprehend the Israeli-Palestinian interaction if one ignores the Jordanian component, and likewise Jordanian-Palestinian relations are inexplicable if detached from the Israeli input. Both recent and more distant history and present-day demographic realities link these three protagonists together, perhaps considerably more than they would really want to be. Jordan is home to a Palestinian population that quite possibly constitutes more than half of the kingdom's total of some six million and probably outnumbers the Palestinians in the West Bank and Arab Jerusalem combined. Moreover, the special ties linking the Arab populations on both banks of the Jordan River are anything but new, nor are they solely a consequence of the Arab-Israeli conflict and the birth of the Palestinian refugee problem.

The lay of the land has contributed to the merger of the peoples on both banks of the river since the earliest of times. Three rivers flow from east to west on the East Bank of the Jordan into the Jordan Valley, carving the East Bank into three distinct geographical segments: the Yarmuk in the north, on what today forms the border between the states of Syria and Jordan; the Zarqa in the center, flowing from its source near Amman into the Jordan Valley; and the Mujib in the south, which flows into the Dead Sea. In their flow westward, these rivers cut through the hilly terrain of the East Bank creating deep ravines and gorges, more difficult to cross than the Jordan River itself, which is easily traversed during most times of the year. Historically it was far less challenging for people and goods to travel along the east-west axis across the Jordan rather than along the more daunting routes on the north-south axis.

It followed naturally that political, administrative, economic, social, and family ties developed more intensively between the East and West Banks of the Jordan than between the northern and southern parts of the East Bank. Towns like Salt and Karak on the East Bank, which are part of the present-day Hashemite Kingdom of Jordan, were more intimately connected through a web of historical, family, and commercial ties with their sister towns on the Palestinian West Bank, Nablus and Hebron respectively, than they were to each other. In the administrative divisions of both banks of the Jordan River in biblical times, then again in the Roman era, at the time of the Arab conquest, thereafter under the Ottomans, and finally with the initial formation of the British Mandate for Palestine, large areas on both banks of the river were united in the same provinces. Over extended periods of time, from antiquity to the modern era, the Jordan River was not the administrative boundary between them.

Eugene Rogan quotes a Damascene visitor to the East Bank town of Salt who had written in 1906 that economic migrants from Nablus had flocked to the town in such great numbers, for trade, construction, and government employment, that "it could almost be called 'Nablus the Second.'"[8] Some Salti families were originally from other parts of Palestine, like Nazareth for example. Karak and Hebron had similarly close ties. The Majalis, one of the most powerful tribes in Jordan and time-honored stalwarts of the Hashemite monarchy, hail from the southern town of Karak. But the origins of the family are actually from the environs of the Palestinian West Bank town of Hebron, from whence they immigrated to Karak, as merchants, in the mid-seventeenth century. With the passage of time "a succession of brilliant political leaders [was] able to raise the tribe from a virtually powerless position to that of the leading power of the region and a mover in the whole of Transjordan." Karak traded much with Hebron and Jerusalem, and it was also a tradition in Karak to reserve a seat for a Hebronite on the municipal council.[9] Other Transjordanian towns had Palestinian connections of their own. The northern town of Irbid, usually noted for its links to Damascus, also had its share of families whose origins were in northern Palestinian towns, such as Safed.[10]

Upon their occupation of Palestine at the end of the First World War, it was hardly surprising for the British to observe that "Palestine is politically and economically closely interested in all that passes beyond the Jordan." The two areas were "economically interdependent" and "Palestine has ever looked to Transjordania for surplus supplies of cereals and cattle." The development of the two areas, therefore, ought to be "considered as a single problem."[11] With all the above in mind, it made perfect sense for the British to include both banks of the Jordan within the boundaries of their mandate for Palestine.

## Borders and States in British Mandatory Palestine

In 1921 the British decided that the territory of the East Bank of the Jordan River, though part of the Palestine Mandate, would become the Emirate of Transjordan and would develop into an independent Arab state. The Zionist project would, therefore, be restricted solely to Palestine west of the river. Thus carved out of the Mandate for Palestine, Transjordan was to be intimately associated with the Palestinian question from its very inception, and it remained part of the Palestine Mandate until granted independence in 1946. The emirate was placed by the British in the hands of the Hashemite prince, or emir, Abdallah. He was the son of the illustrious Husayn ibn Ali, the sharif of Mecca, who had launched the Arab Revolt, in cooperation with the British, against the Turks during the First World War.

At the end of the war, the Hashemites, led by Abdallah's younger brother

Faysal, were ensconced in Damascus, from where they ruled over the short-lived Arab Kingdom of Syria, which lasted until July 1920. Faysal was then unceremoniously ejected by the French, who had come to claim their zones of influence, as agreed with their British counterparts in the notorious Sykes-Picot Agreement of May 1916. After Faysal's ouster, the French took Syria, but Transjordan, which was part of the British zone of influence, was no longer governed as a province of Faysal's kingdom, as it had been hitherto, and the British were in a quandary about its dispensation. When Abdallah came up north from the Hijaz to Transjordan in late 1920, ostensibly on his way to Damascus to coerce the French to reinstate the Hashemites, a solution to the British uncertainty about Transjordan had just presented itself.

After talks in Jerusalem between Abdallah and the British colonial secretary, Winston Churchill, Abdallah agreed in early April 1921 to remain in Amman as the prospective ruler of Transjordan and abstain from pursuing his initial objective of confronting the French in Syria. But during the talks with Churchill, even before the boundaries of Transjordan had finally been drawn, Abdallah repeatedly requested of Churchill to have Palestine included in his realm. Churchill turned him down,[12] but Abdallah never gave up.

It was agreed that Abdallah would take control of Transjordan for an initial trial period of six months. He undertook to prevent both anti-French and anti-Zionist agitation to the best of his ability, and he was promised a British stipend in return.[13] Abdallah could hardly remain on his seat of power in Amman without British support. It goes without saying, therefore, that he also accepted the British Mandate for Palestine, of which his emirate was a part.

Acceptance of the British Mandate was not to be taken lightly. It also meant acquiescing in the Zionist enterprise, which the British were committed to foster in terms of the mandate they had obtained for Palestine from the League of Nations. The Arabs of Palestine never accepted the mandate precisely because of its Zionist agenda. Thus, from the outset, the emir of Transjordan was at loggerheads with the embryonic Arab nationalist movement in Palestine and its first leader, the mufti of Jerusalem and chairman of Palestine's Supreme Muslim Council, Hajj Amin al-Husayni. Concurrently, potential common cause between the emir, the British, and the Zionists was already in the making. This was not a question of ideology, just plain and simple pragmatism.

Abdallah was not enamored with his swath of desert in Transjordan. Likened to a canary in a cage, for Abdallah Transjordan was but a stepping-stone to greater prizes in Syria, Iraq, or Palestine.[14] He envied his younger brother

Faysal, who received the throne of Iraq, seated in Baghdad, a glorious city of antiquity and capital of the Abbasid Caliphate, in the land of the great rivers of the Tigris and the Euphrates. Abdallah, on the other hand, was quartered in Amman, the dusty and almost desolate remains of Roman Philadelphia, at the time a nondescript Circassian village of some two thousand souls, not even quite reaching the banks of the Zarqa, a stream of which hardly anyone had ever heard. The country was sparsely populated. It had a literacy rate of about one percent, and "high civilization" needless to say "was undeveloped."[15] Just a few months after his arrival, Abdallah declared in the summer of 1921, in his obviously frustrated anguish, that he had "had enough of this wilderness of Trans-Jordania. . . ."[16] Abdallah sought expansion, and Palestine was definitely an option.

## Zionists, Hashemites, and the Arabs of Palestine

The Arab Rebellion that erupted in Palestine in April 1936 was to become a critical turning point in the history of the triangular relationship between the Hashemites, the Zionists, and the Arabs of Palestine. Clashes between Arabs and Jews spread rapidly throughout the country in the hitherto most-sustained Arab opposition to the British Mandate and the Zionist enterprise. Palestinian educator and diarist Khalil al-Sakakini called it a "life-and-death struggle" of the Arabs of Palestine for their country. David Ben-Gurion, the chairman of the Jewish Agency and independent Israel's first prime minister, observed that the Arabs of Palestine were fighting a war against dispossession that could not be ignored.[17]

Indeed it was not ignored. The Jews of Palestine now realized more fully than ever before that if it was a Jewish state in Palestine that they really desired, they would have no choice but to fight a strident Arab nationalist movement to obtain it. The British appointed a royal commission to ascertain the causes of the rebellion and to make recommendations for a way out of the Palestinian conundrum. The commission, headed by Lord William Robert Peel, former secretary of state for India, arrived in Palestine in November 1936. After some seven months of deliberation and enquiry, the commission produced its report in July 1937.[18] To this day, seventy years hence, the Peel Commission's report remains one of the most thorough and brilliantly insightful documents ever written on the Palestine problem.

The report noted that "an irrepressible conflict has arisen between *two na-*

*tional communities* [emphasis added] within the narrow bounds of one small country." The British had come a long way from the formulations of the Balfour Declaration. The Balfour Declaration had recognized only the Jews as a people with national rights, regarding the Arab population as no more than the "existing non-Jewish communities in Palestine," who had civil and religious, but not national, rights.[19] It was the Arab Rebellion that had imposed new modes of thinking about Palestine, coercing both the British and the Zionists to recognize the Arabs in Palestine as a national entity.

It was now more readily apparent that there were *two* national communities in Palestine, one Arab and one Jewish, and both equally deserved to exercise their right to self-determination. But, the report observed, the lesson of the rebellion was "plain, and nobody . . . will now venture to assert that the existing system offers any real prospect of reconciliation between the Arabs and the Jews." The obligations that Britain undertook toward the Arabs and the Jews had proved to be irreconcilable. "To put it one sentence," the Peel Commission concluded, "we cannot—in Palestine as it now is—both concede the Arab claim to self-government and secure the establishment of the Jewish National Home."[20] The commission, therefore, recommended that the country be partitioned into two states, with the Arab part adjoined to the Hashemite Emirate on the East Bank.

Syria was Abdallah's obsession until his dying day. But it was a political mirage, "a sad catalogue of wishful thinking" never to materialize. Despite all of his intrigue in Syria, and his pleading and maneuvering with the British, they never had the slightest intention of installing Abdallah in Damascus. At best, they treated him with patronizing disinterest. At times they were irritated or embarrassed by his machinations, which only complicated their relations with some of their other Arab allies.[21]

Palestine, on the other hand, was no obsession. It was primarily about realpolitik and rational state interest. Considering the historical ties between both banks of the Jordan River, whatever occurred west of the river had immediate ramifications for the East Bank. He who ruled Transjordan could only ignore events in Palestine at his peril. Transjordan's links to Palestine were, therefore, naturally strong. Many of Abdallah's cabinet ministers and civil servants hailed from Palestine. More significantly, the three most prominent prime ministers of his entire reign were of Palestinian origin: Ibrahim Hashim from Nablus, Tawfiq Abu al-Huda from Acre, and Samir al-Rifa'i from Safed.[22]

Abdallah always meddled in Palestinian politics, constantly courting the enemies of Hajj Amin al-Husayni. Palestinian Arab society was deeply divided between two rival camps: Hajj Amin and his allies, the Husaynis, and their opponents, the Nashashibis, otherwise known as the "opposition" (al-mu'arada). Abdallah and the Husaynis were to become mortal enemies. This was not a personal feud nor a tribal vendetta. These were conflicting political interests at play, and they carried over to future generations. Abdallah's grandson, King Husayn, would thus be similarly entrapped in conflict in later years with the founder of the Palestine Liberation Organization (PLO), Ahmad al-Shuqayri, and with his successor at the helm of the Palestinian movement, Yasir Arafat.

As Hajj Amin was the bête noire of both the Hashemites and the Zionists, it made sense for Abdallah to forge close ties with the Jews. Abdallah's links to the Jewish Agency were both political and financial. Though the emir accepted money from the Zionists, it would be wrong to infer that his relative moderation was simply bought. The Zionists and Abdallah had many genuine common interests. Moreover, Jewish financial assistance granted Abdallah a much-needed measure of leeway in his overly dependent relationship with his British patrons and with some extra means to manipulate East Bank local politics too. Thus in 1936, during the Arab Rebellion in Palestine, money was liberally disbursed to tribal leaders in Transjordan and also spent on relief work, as a way of keeping people in distressed areas quiet. It was not unknown that "some of Abdallah's largesse came from the Jewish Agency."[23]

The emir Abdallah, just as he had accepted the British Mandate, supported partition too. It would seem to have been the eminently sensible thing for him to do. Considering his most impressive territorial gain, coupled with the political exclusion of his nemesis, Amin al-Husayni, who had fallen out of British favor with the outbreak of the rebellion, the annexation of Arab Palestine to his realm was hardly an offer he could refuse. But in so doing he was not only accepting Arab Palestine as part of Transjordan, he was also acquiescing to Jewish statehood in the other parts of the country. That was an unforgivable concession, completely at variance with the Arab consensus, and, in the eyes of other Arabs, a betrayal of their cause in Palestine. Abdallah was vilified by all and sundry. The partition proposal was soon dropped by the British, because of the unrelenting Arab opposition. But the initial foundations had been laid for eventual partition, for Jordanian preeminence in Arab Palestine, and for the postponement of Palestinian independence that would last for decades.

# 1

## BETWEEN BINATIONALISM
## AND PARTITION

The debate on partition and, in its present reincarnation, the discourse on the pros and cons of the one-state or two-state solution go back to the earliest days of the conflict in British Mandatory Palestine. Some of the original assumptions of the Zionist founding fathers were flawed. The first was that with the issue of the Balfour Declaration by Great Britain in support of a Jewish national home in Palestine, in November 1917, and the conquest of Ottoman Palestine by the British in the closing phases of the First World War, the Jews of Eastern Europe would choose in great numbers to immigrate to Palestine. On the eve of the Paris Peace Conference at the end of the war, Zionist leader Chaim Weizmann envisaged a land that would be made available for the settlement of "four or five million Jews." In their "immediate post-1918 euphoria" Zionist leaders anticipated "70,000 to 80,000 immigrants annually."[1]

Such a pace of immigration would have made the Jews the majority within a decade in the sparsely populated land of Palestine, whose indigenous Arab population at the time hardly reached seven hundred thousand. The territorial desiderata that the Zionists initially put forward to the British were determined far more by geography, resources, and perceived natural boundaries than by demography, which they apparently assumed was not going to pose a real problem.

Not only did they demand all of what became Palestine of the British Mandate, but they also set their sights on southern Lebanon up to the Litani River, and eastward across the Jordan up to the line of the Hijaz Railway, and even beyond. Indeed, in the early years of the Zionist enterprise after the First World War, the Zionists claimed both banks of the river for themselves. Even after the creation of the Emirate of Transjordan on the East Bank, the Zionist right continued to demand the creation of a Jewish state with a Jewish majority on both banks of the Jordan River,[2] a demand that they only "quietly buried" in the mid-1960s.[3]

However, the Zionists were soon to find out to their profound dismay that the great majority of Jews leaving Eastern Europe preferred immigration to the affluent, liberal democratic West, in Europe and especially in North America. This was far more attractive than the trials and tribulations of settling in the rugged terrain of the uncertain and potentially dangerous frontier of Palestine.

Another flawed assumption was that the Arabs of Palestine would eventually acquiesce to the Zionist project. After all, so the Zionists really believed, it would bring the Arabs the material benefit of Western-style modernity and the capital and progressive enterprising spirit of the Zionists, which would raise the standard of living of the indigenous Arab population. Ben-Gurion was stunned when, in his first meeting with the Palestinian leader Musa al-Alami, in March 1934, Alami gave short shrift to Ben-Gurion's exposé on the benefits of Zionism to the Arabs. Alami retorted to the effect that he would rather have the country remain poor and desolate for another hundred years, until such time as the Arabs would be capable of cultivating and developing it themselves, than to have the Zionists take it over.[4]

## The First Binationalists

The failure to rapidly establish a Jewish majority and the force of Arab opposition drove some on the Zionist left (Brit Shalom and subsequently the Ihud and Hashomer Hatza'ir movements) to support a binationalist solution, that is, a state that would be equally Jewish and Arab. First voiced in the mid-1920s, the idea, though never supported by more than a small minority, remained a disproportionately influential part of the internal Zionist debate[5] until the UN partition resolution of 1947. Palestine, the binationalists argued, was a country of two nations, and therefore, it should become "a bi-national state, in which the two peoples will enjoy totally equal rights as befits the two elements shaping the country's destiny, irrespective of which of the two is numerically superior at any given time." Majority status was not essential for Brit Shalom. On the contrary, they argued, striving for a Jewish majority only instilled fear in the Arabs and exacerbated the conflict.[6]

In 1930 Brit Shalom published a memorandum calling for "the constitution of the Palestine state . . . composed of two peoples, each free in the administration of their respective domestic affairs, but united in their common political interests, on the basis of complete equality." Some in Brit Shalom even urged the Zionists to restrict Jewish immigration and assuage the Arabs by declaring their "desire to remain a minority."[7]

In the immediate aftermath of the 1929 disturbances, which culminated in the destruction of the Jewish community in Hebron, when the Jews of Palestine were still reeling from shock, even Ben-Gurion gave some consideration to a version of the binational idea. These were most trying times for the Jews, when the entire future of the Zionist enterprise seemed to be hanging by a thread. In the face of mounting Arab opposition, Britain was on the verge of adopting a far more hostile and restrictive policy toward the Jewish national home. To preempt the imposition of an undesirable British plan, Ben-Gurion proposed that in the longer run a federal state should be established in Palestine, based on a formula of parity in government, national cantons, and the end of the British Mandate. His ideas were unpopular even in his own party, Mapai, and they were rejected. Even so, general ideas on eventual parity in government with the Arabs still remained in the party's platform until 1937.[8]

The fortunes of the Zionist enterprise improved dramatically with the large-scale immigration from Europe in the 1930s. The resultant regeneration of the power and self-confidence of the Jewish community washed away any remnants of binationalist thinking among mainstream Zionists. Mainstream thinking was by then predominantly in favor of independent statehood and partition.

By the mid-1930s Brit Shalom had essentially ceased to exist, but a few years later, in 1942, the Ihud Association was founded as its ideological successor.[9] Like Brit Shalom, Ihud was willing to accept perpetual minority status with special constitutional protection for the Jews of Palestine. The catastrophic predicament of the Jews in Europe forced the binationalists onto the defensive in the face of mounting criticism by mainstream Zionists, who condemned their conciliatory position on immigration. In response, the binationalists adapted their program to correspond with both the Jewish tragedy in Europe and newly prevalent ideas in Britain and the Arab world on Arab unity. They proposed a binational state in Palestine as part of a regional federation that would enjoy the protection of the Western powers. The binational state would be based on demographic equality at first. It could eventually become a Jewish majority state, with the agreement of the Arabs of Palestine. The Palestinian Arabs, the binationalists believed, would be less concerned about being engulfed by the Jews if and when they were part of a greater Arab federation. Binationalism, they argued, was preferable to partition. A small Jewish state established in part of Palestine against the wishes of the Arabs "would be forced to live by the sword," and its long-term survival would always be in doubt.[10]

The problem with binationalism was obviously not its well-intentioned drive for fairness and peace, but its feasibility. There was something fundamentally naïve about the idea. It did not enjoy much support among either the Jews or the Arabs. "This was an instance of the idealist's hope for the abstract . . . without much regard for the concrete tendencies."[11] As Jewish immigration increased and tension and violence mounted in the 1930s, it became abundantly clear that the Jews and Arabs of Palestine simply did not have the elementary common political interests to make binationalism a reality. As Alexander Cadogan, a British Foreign Office official concluded at the time, the dream of binationalism was "pure eyewash."[12] Those who were willing to commit to a permanent Jewish minority were unable to find a mechanism that would ensure the security and well-being of the Jewish community in the Arab-majority state. Nor did they know how to finesse the problem of Arab-Jewish power sharing as equals, when the Jews were only a minority.

Some suggested that the mandatory power serve as an indefinite protectorate to ensure that the majority would not subjugate the minority. Thus in the name of protecting the rights of both Jews and Arabs, they produced the unintended consequence of denying national independence to both peoples.[13] Others believed in the gradual creation of a Jewish majority but could not find Arab partners who would agree to any Jewish immigration at all. With the passage of time, matters only got worse as immigration continued and Arab political consciousness developed and deepened and with it emerged an ever more determined and well-articulated rejection of the Zionist enterprise.

Even so, the Marxist Hashomer Hatza'ir movement did not lose faith in their version of binationalism, seeking throughout the 1930s and 1940s to establish a "bi-national socialist society in Palestine." But they believed simultaneously in the unhindered advancement of the Zionist enterprise, the eventual achievement of a Jewish majority, and governmental parity irrespective of the numerical ratio between the two peoples. Indeed, for Hashomer Hatza'ir, a Jewish majority was a precondition for the creation of the binational socialist society that they envisaged. In due course, they believed, the class solidarity of the workers would overcome the national alienation between Jews and Arabs.[14] These ideas, needless to say, had virtually no Arab takers either. Two Arabs, Fawzi Darwish al-Husayni and Sami Taha, neither of whom had any substantial political or intellectual standing, were assassinated (Husayni in November 1946 and Taha in September 1947) for apparently exhibiting a readiness to cooperate with Jewish binationalists.[15]

After all, from the Arab point of view, why should they share a land they believed was entirely theirs as equals with a minority of foreigners, particularly if these new immigrants strove to become the majority under the protection of the binational idea? After the Second World War, Hashomer Hatza'ir accepted the inevitability of partition, and though they never formally relinquished binationalism as an ideal, in practice they joined the Zionist consensus on Jewish statehood.[16]

A variation of the binationalist theme was cantonization. According to this idea, the country would be divided into autonomous Arab and Jewish cantons united in one federal state under the British Mandate. Cantonization was thoroughly discussed by the Peel Commission, which rejected the idea as impractical, as it went nowhere to satisfy the intense desire of both Jews and Arabs for national self-government. Moreover, the commission noted, the old uncertainty as to the future destiny of Palestine would remain to intensify the antagonism between the parties. The commission concluded that cantonization presented most, if not all, of the difficulties presented by partition, "without Partition's one supreme advantage—the possibility it offers of eventual peace," based on two states.[17]

After Britain's decision in early 1947 to hand the Palestine question over to the UN, the UN Special Committee on Palestine (UNSCOP) set out to study the problem and to recommend a solution. The binationalists presented a written statement to UNSCOP calling for a UN trusteeship for an agreed transitional period, under which an undivided binational Palestine would be established. During the period of trusteeship, Jewish immigration would continue until numerical parity was reached with the Arabs. Thereafter immigration would be agreed upon by Arabs and Jews, in terms of their binational constitution.[18] The only thing that united the Zionist mainstream and the Arabs on these ideas was their total and unremitting rejection of the binationalist proposals.

UNSCOP also considered this and other varieties of the binational solution (including cantonization, federation, or confederation) and rejected them all as unfeasible. The Zionist position presented to UNSCOP dismissed the alternatives to partition, arguing that none of them had the advantages of partition, "which is final, clear-cut, and well-formed."[19] Essentially this was the view adopted by the UNSCOP majority. The new reality that emerged in the wake of the 1947 UN partition resolution and the establishment of Israel in May 1948 brought an end to the discussion of binationalism, which had been trumped by the two-state solution, at least for the meantime.

## The Triumph of Partition

For the mainstream Zionists, the quintessential issue was not binationalism but to create a majority community in all, or at least part, of Palestine. It made no sense for the Zionists to have a so-called "national home" in a territory where they would be just another Jewish minority the likes of which already existed all over the diaspora. After all, from the Herzlian political Zionist point of view, the solution to the Jewish problem could only come about if the Jews would finally escape their deplorable minority predicament through Jewish sovereignty in a state they could call their own. But the Arabs had no intention of passively agreeing to become a minority in a country where they had been the majority for centuries. They did not feel any compulsion to have that change because Jews were being oppressed in Europe. As they made clear very early on, they would resist the Zionist enterprise to the bitter end. The Arabs were prepared only to grant the Jews minority rights, but no more. As Arthur Ruppin, one of the Zionist enterprise's key figures, explained, what the Jews really needed from the Arabs, they could not get, and for what they could get, they had no use. "For minority rights the Jewish people would not invest its blood and capital in the building of Palestine."[20]

Unable to muster a majority in all of Palestine, faced with relentless Arab resistance, and opposed to binationalism as both undesirable and unrealistic, the Zionists were forced to finally acquiesce in the partition of the country into two separate political entities. In fact, even before the country was partitioned territorially, it was governed by the British on the basis of a de facto ethnic partition due to the incapacity and unwillingness of the Arabs and the Jews to cooperate. From the outset, disagreement between Jews and Arabs prevented the British from creating a unified political community in Palestine embracing both peoples.

The administration of Palestine foreshadowed ethnic partition. Each community had its own governing institutions as the communities also developed their own separate economies and political, cultural, and social institutions. From quite early on in the mandate, the British were inclined to assign Jewish and Arab officials to posts where they would be required to deal mainly with members of their own ethnic groups. There was also a tendency for the delineation of administrative districts to similarly reflect relative ethnic preponderance.[21]

The critical turning point toward territorial partition came in the 1930s. The

clouds of impending disaster about to befall the Jews of Europe began to ac-
cumulate in the early 1930s with the rise of the Nazis to power in Hitler's Germany and vicious anti-Semitism in Poland. Though nothing as horrific as the
Holocaust could have been foreseen, Jews in ever-increasing numbers sought
to escape from Europe. Accordingly, the number of immigrants to Palestine
was suddenly and dramatically on the rise.[22] The Arab population was genuinely disturbed by the possibility of being overwhelmed by a Jewish majority,
and they rose in rebellion.

Even though the Peel Commission's partition plan offered the Jews less
than 20 percent of Palestine, the majority opinion in the Zionist movement
was to accept partition. Partition recognized the principle of Jewish statehood,
and considering the extreme sense of urgency in respect to the plight of the
Jews in Europe, any sovereign sanctuary was better than none. According to
the partition plan, one area would become a new British Mandate for the Holy
Places and would include an enclave of Jerusalem and Bethlehem, with a corridor to the sea via the towns of Lydda and Ramle and terminating at Jaffa. A
second area, encompassing much of the Coastal Plain as far south as Majdal,
the Valley of Jezreel, and the Galilee, would become an independent Jewish
state. The rest of Palestine, the Negev, the West Bank and the Gaza area, and
the southern Coastal Plain, would be united with Transjordan to form an independent Arab state under the Hashemite crown.[23]

Though partition was accepted by the Zionists, the decision was finally
made only after fractious internal debate. By the time of the Peel Commission,
in early 1937, both Ben-Gurion and Weizmann were ardent supporters of partition, which for Ben-Gurion had become a "cornerstone for a new Zionist
policy." However, even convincing his own party, Mapai, not to mention the
Zionist movement as a whole, was no foregone conclusion. Initially all the
Zionist parties in Palestine, including Mapai, rejected the Peel scheme.[24]

At the Twentieth Zionist Congress held in Zurich in August 1937, Ben-
Gurion convinced the majority by making the following main arguments: the
principle of partition ought to be accepted; the Peel proposal need not be endorsed as it stood, but rather should serve as a basis for negotiation with the
British to improve their plan; a small Jewish state was better than none and
would provide an essential sanctuary for the Jews who were in awfully dire
straits in Germany and Poland; and the small state could be the basis for expansion at some later stage.[25] The fact that the British proposal included an
exchange of population, which meant transferring a significant part of the

Arab population out of the Galilee to the proposed Arab state (some voluntarily and others compulsorily), made the proposal more acceptable to many
of the Zionist delegates. Eventually Ben-Gurion won the day at the Zionist
Congress by the handsome margin of 299 to 160.[26]

The Arabs of Palestine, however, adamantly rejected the idea of partition. In
the late summer of 1937, the Arab Rebellion was renewed with a vengeance.
On September 26, Lewis Andrews, the acting district commissioner of the
Galilee, was killed by Arab assailants. The Palestinian leadership, the Arab
Higher Committee (AHC), headed by Hajj Amin al-Husayni, was outlawed,
and warrants were issued for the arrest of its members. Hajj Amin first went
into hiding and subsequently, in mid-October, managed to slip out of the
country by boat to Lebanon.

From then onward, the recognized Palestinian Arab leadership functioned
in exile. The absence of their leadership, and its inherent illegitimacy in the
eyes of the powers that be, would haunt the Palestinians for decades, giving
their Zionist and Hashemite rivals a built-in advantage. This Palestinian hand-
icap was only finally overcome with the signing of the Oslo Accords and the
return of the Palestinian leadership to the homeland in the early summer of
1994, for the first time in nearly sixty years.

In the face of Arab rejection, at the end of 1938, after yet another commission of inquiry, the British retreated from the idea of partition, arguing that it
was unworkable. They summoned a conference of Arab and Zionist representatives in London in February 1939, which ended, as expected, in failure. In
"proximity talks" of an earlier era, in which Arabs and Jews talked not to each
other but to the British alone, a few weeks of fruitless negotiations ensued. At
the conclusion of this dialogue of the deaf, an exasperated British government
issued a new White Paper in May 1939.

The rebellion had run out of steam by then, and as the clouds of war collected over Europe it made sense for the British to try and satisfy the Arabs,
who were of immeasurably greater strategic and economic importance than
the Jews of Palestine and their supporters in the diaspora. The White Paper
severely limited Jewish immigration to Palestine, restricted land sales to Jews,
and promised independence to Palestine within ten years. In such circumstances, independence could only have meant an independent Arab state, in
which the Jews would have been relegated to the unenviable and untenable
position of a permanent minority. Needless to say, had this White Paper ever
been fully implemented, Jewish statehood would never have come to pass.

But the outbreak of war in Europe with its catastrophic consequences for European Jewry reconfigured the political context of the Palestine problem. Arab opposition and the other political realities in Palestine were obscured and forced into the background by the plight of the Jews in Europe, and the inner logic of partition resurfaced again. But Jewish and Arab positions remained irreconcilable. The Jewish Agency insisted on partition, while the Arabs would have nothing less than Arab majority rule and independence in all of Palestine.

By now British energy and interest for the intractable conflict in Palestine had been exhausted. Once Britain had decided to finally part with India, the jewel in the crown of the empire, the passage to India, of which Palestine was an essential link, had lost its inherent strategic value. In February 1947, unable to impose a solution of their own, His Majesty's government decided to hand the issue of Palestine over to the UN. The General Assembly established yet another committee to study the conundrum—UNSCOP.

In September, after having traveled to Palestine, the majority on the committee recommended partition. On November 29, 1947, the UN General Assembly passed Resolution 181 endorsing the plan to partition Palestine into two states, one Jewish and one Arab, with Jerusalem and Bethlehem and their holy places as an international enclave, to remain under UN supervision.

For the Jews, the UN resolution was a historic achievement. The international community had endorsed the principle of Jewish statehood and thus fulfilled the fundamental ambition of the Zionist enterprise. For the Arabs, however, partition was unacceptable. The Arabs in Palestine had boycotted UNSCOP, which they felt was biased in favor of the Zionists. Informally, however, various Arab spokesmen did put forward the Arab position rejecting partition and binationalism, calling for an independent unitary Arab state in all of Palestine. The Arab position had already been submitted in a detailed paper to the Anglo-American Committee of Enquiry, which had preceded UNSCOP, in early 1946.[27]

The paper, "The Arab Case for Palestine," one of the most comprehensive exposés of the Arab position, showed no concern for the recent suffering of the Jews of Europe and their urgent need for relief, nor did it concede that the Jews had any valid historical claim to, or association with, Palestine. The Arabs of Palestine argued in no uncertain terms that "the whole Arab people is unalterably opposed to the attempt to impose Jewish immigration and settlement upon it, and ultimately to establish a Jewish state in Palestine." They could not

Map 1. The UN partition of Palestine, 1947

acquiesce in the subjection of "an indigenous population against its will to alien immigrants, whose claim is based upon a historical connection which ceased effectively many centuries ago. Moreover they form the majority of the population; as such they cannot submit to a policy of immigration which if pursued for long will turn them from a majority into a minority in an alien state; and they claim the democratic right of a majority to make its own decisions in matters of urgent national concern."[28]

Furthermore, in the Arab view, the Arabs of Palestine, which was geographically "part of Syria," belonged "to the Syrian branch of the Arab family of nations; all their culture and tradition link them to the other Arab peoples." But the Zionist presence and ambitions had cut them off from the other Arab states, retarded their advance to independence, and prevented their full participation in the affairs of the Arab world to which they naturally belonged, thus undermining the "traditional Arab character" of Palestine. Any settlement to be attained in Palestine would have to "recognize the fact that by geography and history Palestine" was "an inseparable part of the Arab world." Palestine should be a unitary Arab state, as the majority of its citizens were Arabs. Decisions on such matters as immigration and land sales should be taken democratically in accordance with the wishes of the majority.[29]

As irrevocably opposed as the Arabs were to Zionism, they were "in no way hostile to the Jews as such." The Jews in Arab Palestine would not suffer as the minority and would enjoy full civil and political rights in the country (a contention that Jews, needless to say, would find unconvincing after years of fierce conflict). They would be able to maintain their own cultural institutions and could also enjoy municipal autonomy in the districts "in which they are most closely settled." However, the idea of partition was inadmissible for the same reasons of principle as the idea of establishing a Jewish state in the whole country. As unjust as it was, in their view, to impose a Jewish state on the whole country, it was equally unjust to impose it on any part of the country. A binational state based on parity was hardly any better and was rejected for "denying the majority its normal position and rights." There were also "serious practical objections to the idea of a bi-national state, which cannot exist unless there is a strong sense of unity and common interest overriding the differences between the two parties."[30] There was obviously no such common interest or sense of unity between Jews and Arabs in Palestine.

The Zionist enterprise, from the Arab point of view, was in total contradiction to the right of the Palestinian Arabs to self-determination and unfairly denied them the capacity to exercise that right just like other Arab nations. The Zionist enterprise had been imposed on the Palestinian people against their will and as such was unquestionably illegitimate in the eyes of the Arabs. This position was to remain the backbone of the Palestinian case for decades to come.

After the publication of the UNSCOP recommendation, the Arab Higher Committee, the formal representative Palestinian Arab leadership, rejected the idea of partition, since a "consideration of fundamental importance to the Arab world was that of racial homogeneity. . . . It was illogical [to introduce] an alien body into the established homogeneity [of the Arab world], a course which could only produce new Balkans. . . . The Arabs . . . would lawfully defend with their life blood every inch of the soil of their beloved country."[31]

# 2

## THE PALESTINIANS AND
## THE TWO-STATE IDEA

*A Guide for the Perplexed*

After the Palestinians had finally lost the war of 1948, Jordanian and Iraqi forces were in control of the West Bank, and Israel was in control of the rest of Mandatory Palestine, except for the Gaza Strip, which was under the control of the Egyptian army. All the same, the Arab Higher Committee and the Palestine National Council, meeting on October 1, 1948, in the city of Gaza, declared the independence of Palestine. With the entire country occupied by Israel and various Arab armies, declaring the independence of Palestine may have seemed ridiculous. But it was a calculated act of defiance and a historical rejection of what had come to pass.

The Palestinian leadership proclaimed the "*full independence of the whole of Palestine*" and then announced the formation of the "All-Palestine Government" (emphasis added).[1] The decision to form such a government had been taken by the Arab League in late September with the objective of safeguarding the Arab claim to sovereignty over the whole of Palestine.[2] This implacable refusal to accept either partition or the results of the 1948 war was to be a position of principle that guided Palestinian politics and policies for generations to come.

In practice, the All-Palestine Government was an empty vessel and continued to exist in name only, with offices in Cairo, until Abd al-Nasir closed them down in 1959.[3] As the Palestinians in the 1950s were still recovering from the shock of defeat and dispersal, they looked to the Arab states and especially to the Egypt of Abd al-Nasir for salvation. In the late 1950s and early 1960s, the "revival of the Palestinian entity" was supported by the Arab League. The revival was led by competing initiatives of Egypt and Iraq to establish some form of rejuvenated Palestinian national representation, albeit under the auspices of the Arab states. Simultaneously, but independently of the Arab initiative, various Palestinian groups, the most important of which was Fatah, began to or-

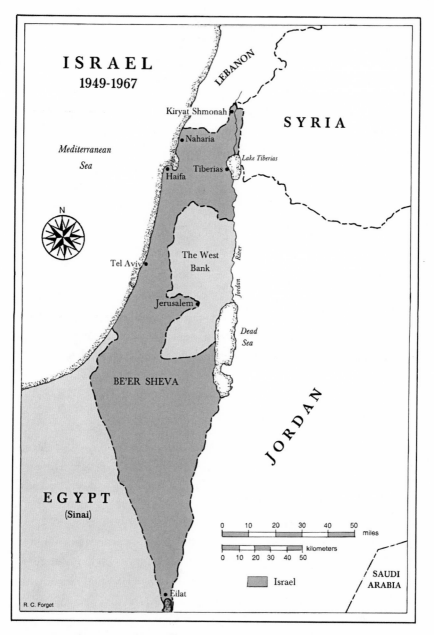

Map 2. Israel after the 1948 war

ganize clandestinely. This was an effort to create new representative Palestinian organizations that would lead the struggle for national liberation, uncon-
trolled by the Arab states.

In May 1964 the Palestine Liberation Organization (PLO) was established in
accordance with an Arab League resolution. The PLO's first chairman was a
Palestinian political activist named Ahmad al-Shuqayri, a refugee and the de-
scendant of a notable Palestinian family originally from Acre, in what had become Israel in 1948. The PLO in its original form was very much under the
thumb of Abd al-Nasir, but after the Arab debacle in 1967, the organization
was completely restructured. It was taken over by Fatah, which had launched
its armed struggle against Israel in January 1965 and had already begun to
overshadow the PLO prior to the war in 1967. By 1968 the PLO had been transformed into an umbrella organization of Palestinian fighting organizations
spearheaded by Fatah, under the leadership of Yasir Arafat, who became the
leader of both Fatah and the PLO.

The PLO, as its name suggested, sought to liberate Palestine and to create a
unitary Arab state in all of Palestine, which had been the objective of the Palestinians since the advent of the British Mandate. The Charter of the PLO, as
originally formulated in 1964 and amended in 1968, rejected all that had come
to pass under the mandate and since the UN partition resolution and the establishment of Israel. The PLO thus followed in the footsteps of its predecessors and did just as the All-Palestine Government and the Arab Higher Committee had done before.

The PLO Charter defined Palestine as "the homeland of the Arab Palestinian people" and as "an indivisible territorial unit [wahda iqlimiyya]." The partition of Palestine and the establishment of Israel were "null and void," as were
the Balfour Declaration, the British Mandate, and all that ensued from them,
regardless of the passage of time. They were all equally illegitimate and inconsistent with the right of the Palestinian people to self-determination. Zionism
was "fascist and Nazi in its methods," and intimately linked to imperialism.
Thus the objective of the PLO was to "eliminate [tasfiya] the Zionist presence"
in Palestine.[4]

Struggling for the liberation of Palestine and the creation of a unitary Arab
state raised the question of what was to become of the Jewish population of
Israel. The PLO Charter of 1964 was somewhat vaguer on the issue than the
generally more radicalized charter of 1968. According to the 1964 charter,
"Jews who were of Palestinian origin [min asl Filastini] would be regarded as

Palestinians" provided they were committed to live peacefully and loyally in Palestine. It was not quite clear what "of Palestinian origin" meant. This could have been understood to mean all Jews born in Palestine at any time. The amended charter of 1968 clarified that only those Jews who were resident in Palestine prior to "the beginning of the Zionist invasion," which in PLO parlance meant the Balfour Declaration of 1917, would be regarded as Palestinians.[5] This essentially excluded the great and ever-increasing majority of Jewish Israelis, who would not be entitled to citizenship in the new state.

The question of the fate of the Jewish community had already been discussed during the mandate. The answers provided then by Palestinian representatives were not uniform and thus gave rise to serious uncertainty as to the fate of the Jews in the event of the creation of an Arab state in Palestine. When Hajj Amin was questioned on this issue by the Peel Commission in January 1937, he was evasive. In one answer he said that the Jews would have complete freedom as natives of the country. But when asked directly whether the Arab state "could assimilate and digest the Jews," his answer was "no." On whether some of them would consequently have to be removed, he was only prepared to say that the matter should be left to the future.[6]

"The Arab Case for Palestine" that was presented to the Anglo-American Committee in early 1946 noted that those Jews who had already entered Palestine and who "had obtained or shall obtain Palestinian citizenship by due legal process will be full citizens of the Palestinian state."[7] When the Arab Higher Committee rejected partition in late 1947, it similarly referred to "all genuine and law-abiding nationals,"[8] who would enjoy civil rights in the Arab state of Palestine. These were both formulations designed to exclude the many thousands of Jews who had immigrated to Palestine illegally, against the rules and regulations of the British Mandatory power, or had yet to obtain citizenship. On the other hand, these definitions did suggest that the large majority of the Jews in Palestine would be able to remain.

However, Arab positions on the issue were inconsistent. In September 1946 the Arab governments (without Palestinian approval) proposed to the British government the formation of a unitary independent Arab state in Palestine, in which the Jews would have representation in the government and the legislature that would not exceed one-third. The Arab Higher Committee protested vociferously, rejecting the proposal and insisting that the proportion of Jewish representation not exceed a ratio of one to six. This corresponded to the Jewish-Arab ratio that had existed before 1918 and suggested that only Jews who had lived in Palestine before the British Mandate would be eligible for citizenship in the Arab state.[9] In essence, this was the stand carried over into the PLO Charter as revised in 1968.

In the ideal world of the PLO in its formative years, the objective was clear and absolute. History had to be rolled back until all that had been created under the auspices of the British Mandate in Palestine was completely undone. All of Palestine was to be an Arab state, and the great majority of the Jews who presently lived there would be expected to leave.

## Setbacks in Jordan and Lebanon: Prelude to Political Change

In the real world, however, PLO policies over the years were dictated by regional shifts in the balance of power and the PLO's political fortunes far more than by the wording of the PLO Charter. When the charter of 1968 was written, the PLO was safely ensconced in its optimal autonomous base of operations in Jordan. In Jordan the PLO could mobilize the huge Palestinian population of the kingdom on behalf of the struggle and wage operations against Israeli targets from Jordan's very long and rather porous border with Israel. This was the mythical heyday of the fida'iyyun, and the PLO was at a high point that has never been fully re-created since. Partition, compromise, and a two-state solution with Israel were all out of the question. Negotiations were therefore unnecessary and unacceptable, and as the charter stressed, "armed struggle was the only way to liberate Palestine."[10] But the PLO's dogmatic single-mindedness would not last.

In the first years of the Israeli occupation of the West Bank, in the late 1960s, Palestinian intellectuals such as Aziz Shahada and Muhammad Abu-Shilbaya and some of the mayors of the larger towns, such as Hamdi Kan'an from Nablus and Muhammad Ali al-Ja'abari from Hebron, toyed with the idea of creating a Palestinian entity or state alongside Israel. Neither Jordan nor the PLO was interested in any local initiatives in the West Bank that might have undermined their influence. Israel had no interest in a Palestinian state either, and the disparate initiatives of the various activists in the West Bank came to naught.[11] But the idea of a Palestinian state alongside Israel, and not instead of it, had been placed on the Palestinian national agenda.

In September 1970, when the Jordanians finally came to the conclusion that the armed PLO presence had become an intolerable threat to the kingdom, they crushed the fida'iyyun in a prolonged multistaged offensive, which eradicated the Palestinian military presence in the country by the summer of 1971. The rout in Jordan was the "end of a myth." It "represented a defeat of the strategy of people's war championed by the various guerrilla groups since 1967, and posed a fundamental challenge to their professed aims, political programs, and organizational structure."[12] The armed struggle as the one and only strategy for the liberation of Palestine, without the Jordanian stronghold, was an unrealistic proposition. Lebanon was a poor second best to Jordan as a base of operations, and in the wake of the limited gains of the Arab armies in the October War of 1973 against Israel, the PLO was ready to engage in a serious reassessment of the organization's strategy and policies.

Gradually a consensus emerged in Fatah that the October War had created new realities in the region that had to be recognized. As Salah Khalaf, one of the founding fathers of Fatah, put it, the Middle East peace process was moving forward, and it was not enough to simply say no. Absolute rejection of some version of two states was no longer feasible, and the PLO had to adopt a policy that would block Jordan and make sure that the West Bank did not revert to King Husayn.[13]

In June 1974 the quasi-parliamentary body of the PLO, the Palestine National Council (PNC), approved a new political program that included the first major departure from the absolutist formulations of the PLO Charter. The charter had initially called for the complete liberation of Palestine in one fell swoop, by an act of war. According to the new PNC resolutions, "the PLO would struggle by all means, in the main by armed struggle [that is, not only armed struggle] to liberate Palestinian land and to establish the people's national, independent, fighting authority on any part of the land of Palestine that would be liberated. This would require a greater change in the balance of power in favor of our people and its struggle." Indeed such a shift in the balance of power would have to take place, as the PLO would not accept "any plan for a Palestinian entity the price of which would be recognition, peace or secure boundaries [for Israel] or conceding the national right or the denial of our people's right of return or its right to self-determination on its national soil."[14]

This meant that the PLO would be willing to establish a national authority in the West Bank and Gaza, alongside Israel, at least temporarily, as the result of a negotiation, as a phase toward the liberation of all of Palestine. This, of course, would not entail the recognition of Israel or the making of peace with it. That is, more or less, the position presently assumed by Hamas.

The radicals, the so-called rejectionists of the time, warned that this strategy might in fact culminate in the recognition of Israel. In their analysis, this phased strategy could be blocked halfway (marhaliyya masduda) if concessions were made to Israel in the interim. Israel would have to be coerced to go further, and that could only be achieved by the use of force.[15] In the end the rejectionists were proved right, primarily because the required shift in the regional balance of power, in favor of the Arabs in general and the Palestinian struggle in particular, did not materialize. On the contrary, as of the mid-1970s, contrary to the post–October War expectations, the regional balance of power shifted inexorably in Israel's favor.

In November 1977 President Sadat launched his unprecedented peace initiative with Israel leading to the conclusion of a peace treaty between Egypt and Israel in March 1979. The peace between the most powerful of Arab states and Israel revolutionized the Arab-Israeli conflict and left the Palestinians almost entirely to their own devices in the fight with Israel. Israel has not had to fight a full-scale war against any Arab state for nearly forty years. In 1982 Israel crushed the PLO forces in Lebanon and compelled them to evacuate their last autonomous redoubt on Israel's border. In their hour of need, the Palestinians obtained virtually no assistance from their Arab brethren, aside from a limited measure of Syrian intervention, which had more to do with Israel confronting Syrian forces in Lebanon, rather than the other way round.

The 1982 war in Lebanon was another dramatic turning point in the history of the Palestinian national movement, gradually shaping the reality that eventually coerced the PLO to acquiesce to a two-state solution. As the PLO suffered yet a further severe setback, the organization's regional and international standing was in commensurate decline. The war had an immense effect on the PLO, which lost the territorial base of its state-in-exile, its headquarters, and the bulk of its military infrastructure. The loss of the "Fakhani Republic," as the state-within-a-state in Lebanon came to be known (named after the suburb of Beirut where the PLO headquarters were located), was a severe blow to the "neopatrimonial system of political control managed by Arafat." The loss of its territorial base also removed a main pillar of the mainstream PLO leadership's diplomatic strategy.[16]

In the meantime, as a direct consequence of the Lebanon debacle and PLO disarray, the center of gravity of Palestinian politics began to shift toward the West Bank and Gaza. The Palestinians under Israeli occupation, while still very loyal to the PLO, could hardly expect to be liberated by an organization that was still not recognized by the United States and other Western powers, nor by an armed struggle that could no longer be effectively waged from the depths of the diaspora and that had virtually no affect on the regional balance of power.

The prevalent despair was at the root of the outbreak of the first Intifada in December 1987, which rapidly transformed the West Bank and Gaza into the core of the Palestinian national endeavor. The PLO and the people in the West Bank and Gaza reversed roles. If for decades the people in the occupied territories had been the passive bystanders to the armed struggle waged by the PLO from without, the PLO now became the passive bystander to the civilian uprising waged by the people from within. The PLO, which had hitherto enjoyed political and moral superiority as the vanguard of the struggle, now had to show deference to the people in the occupied territories, who "manned the trenches," so to speak, on the new front line.

The people in the West Bank and Gaza who had previously been the disciplined recipients of the political diktats of the PLO now demanded a voice of their own, not to challenge the PLO, whose leadership they accepted virtually without question, but to have a say in the organization's decision-making process. For decades the PLO had fought to achieve three main objectives: to promote and preserve the Palestinian national identity; to prevent any Middle East settlement from which the PLO would be excluded; and to delegitimize Israel. The Intifada was manna from heaven for the PLO, as it achieved all three objectives more effectively than a quarter of a century of armed struggle had ever done.

The Intifada reestablished the PLO's inter-Arab and international credentials, reaffirmed its representative stature, and essentially saved the organization from the doldrums of oblivion in the aftermath of its expulsion from Lebanon. For the people in the West Bank and Gaza, the immediate objective was to liberate themselves from Israel's occupation. As they waged their struggle, they expected the PLO to make the necessary decisions to transform their trying campaign into tangible and meaningful political gain. In practical terms, this meant advancing toward formal acceptance by the PLO of a Palestinian state alongside Israel.

It was doubly important for the PLO to listen to the voices from within the occupied territories to maintain its representative role and to avoid losing ground to Hamas, which was exploiting the Intifada to make inroads at the PLO's expense. The fact that King Husayn of Jordan disengaged from the West Bank in July 1988 added to the pressure on the PLO to prove its diplomatic mettle. In the PLO leadership, there were those who were concerned that if the organization did not launch a courageous initiative, the people of the West Bank and Gaza might launch an initiative of their own, or worse still, the Jordanians would exploit PLO inertia to return to the arena themselves.[17] The predominant view in the PLO was that the Intifada provided an opportunity for political and diplomatic gain that had to be exploited before the uprising ran out of steam.[18]

It was against this background that the PNC convened in Algeria in November 1988 to make a series of momentous decisions that were designed to set the stage for a peace process that, for the first time ever in PLO decision making, would formally support a two-state solution. The PNC issued two historic documents: the Palestinian Declaration of Independence, which was based on the UN partition resolution of 1947, and the PNC's Political Statement, which endorsed UN Security Council Resolution 242 of 1967. The PLO had adamantly rejected both resolutions in the past, and the albeit cryptic acceptance of them now broke new ground. The acceptance, however historic, was simultaneously equivocal and fraught with tortuous mazes of interpretation.

## The Convoluted Acceptance of Two States

The Declaration of Independence noted, "Despite the historical injustice inflicted on the Palestinian Arab people resulting in their dispersion and depriving them of their right to self-determination, following upon UN General Assembly Resolution 181 (1947), which partitioned Palestine into two states, one Arab, one Jewish, it is this Resolution that still provides those conditions of international legitimacy that ensure the right of the Palestinian Arab people to sovereignty and national independence."[19]

Thus, while this document accepted the partition resolution and a two-state solution, the inherent injustice of partition remained unaltered in the Palestinian national narrative. Rashid Khalidi has argued that the Declaration of Independence was "the first official Palestinian recognition of the legitimacy of the existence of a Jewish state."[20] But the text does not lend itself to such a charitable interpretation. Moreover, in later years Palestinian leaders flatly refused to recognize Israel as a Jewish state, which they could have done with no difficulty had Khalidi's interpretation been correct.

Though the partition resolution provided international legitimacy for the future independent Palestinian state, the resolution did not thereby become historically just. The resolution would ensure the right of the Palestinians to sovereignty and national independence, which could be attained in any part of Palestine, but it was not interpreted as having endorsed the Palestinians' right to self-determination, which in Palestinian parlance could only be satisfactorily addressed in the land of Palestine in its entirety. As the Declaration of Independence confirmed, and as the Palestinians had argued consistently since 1917, the whole of the country, which was rightfully theirs, had been unfairly denied to them, first by the Balfour Declaration, then by the British Mandate, and then by the partition resolution.

The PNC's Political Statement called for the convening of an international conference to negotiate the Middle East conflict "on the basis of UN Security Council Resolutions 242 and 338 and the attainment of the legitimate national rights of the Palestinian people, foremost among which is the right to self determination" in accordance with the Charter of the United Nations and "the relevant UN resolutions on the question of Palestine." The settlement would have to be based on an Israeli withdrawal to the 1967 boundaries, refugee return in accordance with UN resolutions, and the formulation of security guarantees for all the states in the region by the Security Council.[21]

The Declaration of Independence and the Political Statement, issued together, should be seen and analyzed together. The two documents indicated quite clearly that the PLO had accepted partition and a two-state solution, on the basis of the 1967 boundaries. By the end of 1988, the PLO had come to the realistic conclusion that no more was feasible in the existing balance of power and in the prevailing regional and international political circumstances. Concurrently, however, this truncated Palestinian state was not accepted as a just solution. Nor did it imply a readiness for finality, that is, to end the conflict, solely on the basis of an independent state in the West Bank, Arab Jerusalem, and Gaza.

The PLO had a constant three-part formula that enshrined the national rights of the Palestinian people: their right of return, their right to self-determination, and their right to an independent state "on their national soil." It should be noted that the reference in this formula was to self-determination *and* independent statehood, and not self-determination *in an* independent state. Statehood and self-determination were not coterminous, and their juxtaposition was not intended as a form of stylistic repetition. In PLO parlance, statehood and self-determination were *two different matters*. The partition resolution and Resolution 242 ensured sovereignty and independent statehood but not self-determination, which was never linked in PLO documentation to just a part of historical Palestine, only to all of it.

The PNC resolutions, therefore, never spoke of the envisaged settlement, on the basis of the 1967 boundaries, as "just and lasting." This internationally accepted, standard, and oft-repeated terminology of Resolution 242 was omitted, no doubt intentionally. After all, Israel, according to these very same PNC resolutions, had deceived the world ever since its creation into believing that it was a democracy, when in fact, as revealed by "the crimes of the occupation and its savage, inhuman practices," it was actually "a fascist, racist, colonialist state built on the usurpation of the Palestinian land and the annihilation of the Palestinian people."[22] Peace with Israel, therefore, was pragmatically feasible, but it would hardly be just, and if circumstances allowed, it might not be lasting either.

Within the mainstream Palestinian national discourse of the 1980s, leading spokesmen of Fatah, such as Salah Khalaf, one of Arafat's closest confidants, or Khalid al-Hasan, one of the more prolific and astute political analysts of the movement, consistently explained the need to engage in the peace process and to accept the principle of land for peace. At the same time, however, as they wrestled with the rejectionists, they reaffirmed time and again that they continued to believe, as always, that Palestine from the "[Jordan] River to the [Mediterranean] Sea" was the homeland of the Palestinians, and just as the "Zionist onslaught" had occupied it "inch by inch" (shibran shibran), so the Palestinians would have to retrieve it "inch by inch." The question was not whether to do so but how.[23]

Zionism and Palestinian nationalism, according to Khalid al-Hasan, were mutually exclusive and totally irreconcilable. The "national contradiction" (al-tanaqud al-qawmi) between the two could only be resolved "by the disappearance [zawal] of one of the parties." The solution, therefore, was the "annihilation [qada ala] of Zionism" and the establishment of a democratic state on all the land of Palestine, and until then there could be no final settlement of the Palestinian question.[24]

In an article in Foreign Affairs in the late 1980s, the prominent Palestinian historian Walid Khalidi presented a considerably softer approach. He had suggested "an honorable and pragmatically [as opposed to historically or morally] just settlement" based on partition along the 1967 frontier; "an agreed limited return of 1948 Palestinian refugees to Israel proper and their unrestricted right of return to the Palestinian state"; and Arab summit and Islamic summit guarantees of this settlement "as point final."[25] Thus, "point final" would have to include an element of refugee return to Israel proper, but not Israel's annihilation.

But even this watered-down definition of Palestinian national rights went beyond the confines of the 1967 boundaries, which in practical terms meant that a Palestinian state in the West Bank and Gaza would not suffice to end the conflict with Israel. This was a definition that would continue to bedevil Israeli-Palestinian negotiations for many long years, as Israel and the Palestinians repeatedly failed to agree on what a "limited return of 1948 Palestinian refugees to Israel" really meant.

In the late 1980s and early 1990s a series of international and regional developments created unprecedented pressures on the PLO leadership to further moderate its stance on Israel and to acquiesce in a negotiated settlement, eventually leading up to the signing of the Oslo Accords in September 1993. The Soviet Union entered into a tailspin of dramatic decline unintentionally induced by *perestroika* and *glasnost*, culminating in its final collapse at the end of 1991. A new unipolar international system emerged, dominated by Israel's major ally — the United States. The collapse of the Soviet Union was accompanied by a massive wave of Jewish emigration from the former Soviet Union to Israel, boosting the country's population by almost 20 percent, that is, about one million new citizens, within the space of a decade. The impact of the Soviet immigrants on the quality and quantity of Israel's human resources was extraordinary and made a major contribution to the catapulting of the country into the twenty-first century as an ultramodern, First-World, high-tech-based economy.

As Israel appeared in many respects to be moving from strength to strength the fortunes of the PLO and the Palestinians seemed to be taking a turn for the worse. When Saddam Husayn invaded Kuwait in August 1990, the PLO and the great majority of Palestinian public opinion sided with Iraq, as they did when Saddam fought against the US forces that came to liberate Kuwait, and when he pounded Tel Aviv with Scud missiles during the Gulf War that ensued in the early months of 1991. Needless to say such positions did not endear the PLO and the Palestinians either to the United States or to the enemies of Saddam in the Arab world, especially not to the Gulf states, which in the past had been the major bankrollers of the PLO.

## Corralled from Madrid to Oslo

After the Gulf War, Arafat was isolated as he had never been before, and the PLO was virtually bankrupt. By 1991 the Intifada had lost much of its steam, and time appeared to be working against the Palestinians and their cause. Arafat was captivated by a sense of urgency to actively partake in the peace process lest the PLO be overtaken by events driven by others and left to wallow away in the diaspora. The Palestinians had little choice but to acquiesce in the Madrid Peace Conference that was convened by the United States in October 1991, despite the fact that the PLO was denied any formal representation. As Faruq Qaddumi observed, the PLO had either to join the peace process or to exit history.[26]

The Madrid formula for Palestinian representation was doubly flawed from the PLO's point of view. The Palestinian delegation to Madrid, at Israel's insistence, was based on neither the recognition of Palestinian independence nor the PLO's representative status and was therefore composed of representatives from the West Bank and Gaza who were to be part of a joint delegation with Jordan. In practice, however, the PLO was present at the Madrid conference, despite its formal exclusion. No credible Palestinian representatives from the West Bank and Gaza would have attended such a conference without the approval of the PLO. Moreover, in the substantive negotiations that followed the Madrid conference in Washington, the Palestinian delegation continued to receive instructions from the PLO and, in fact, negotiated with the United States and Israel independently of the Jordanian delegation.

While the rather fruitless exercise dragged on in Washington, elections in Israel in June 1992 returned the Labor Party to power on a platform that gave high priority to an agreement with the Palestinians.[27] An informal back channel in Oslo that began in early 1993, between Israeli and PLO interlocutors, eventually produced what were to become known as the Oslo Accords. They were in the form of a Declaration of Principles on Interim Self-Government Arrangements (DoP) and an exchange of letters between PLO chairman Yasir Arafat and Israeli prime minister Yitzhak Rabin, signed in Washington on September 13, 1993.

The accords, which may very well have saved the PLO from political oblivion, included far-reaching historical concessions to Israel in wording that the PLO had systematically avoided in the past. In response to the initial reports on the Oslo Accords, there were "immediate fulminations from the opposition" as well as protests from within the PLO Executive Committee and the Fatah Central Committee. But the Palestinian rank and file "reacted with a weary resignation" that resulted from the impact of the debilitating pressures that had mounted since 1990.[28]

The parties agreed "to put an end to decades of confrontation and conflict," to "recognize their mutual legitimate and political rights," and to achieve a "just, lasting and comprehensive peace settlement and historic reconciliation" through an agreed political process. The aim of the negotiations was to establish Palestinian self-government in the West Bank and Gaza for a transitional period that would not exceed five years, leading to a permanent settlement that was to be achieved on the basis of Security Council Resolutions 242 and 338. The permanent status negotiations would cover all the outstanding issues that went beyond the creation of the interim self-governing Palestinian Authority and that had been left in abeyance by the DoP. These included Jerusalem, refugees, settlements, security arrangements, borders, relations and cooperation with other neighbors, and other, unspecified, issues of common interest.[29]

Even more impressive, albeit less binding, were the commitments made in Arafat's letter to Rabin. The PLO recognized Israel's "right to exist in peace and security," agreed that all outstanding issues would be resolved by negotiation, renounced the use of force, and even affirmed that the articles of the Palestinian National Charter that denied Israel's right to exist and/or that were inconsistent with the commitments of Arafat's letter were "now inoperative and no longer valid."[30] The charter, however, could only be amended by the PNC. Therefore, for such a commitment to be constitutionally meaningful would require the PNC to virtually rewrite the charter. It never actually did so.

The Oslo documents had all the wording of a negotiation that was intended to put an end to the conflict by means of a two-state solution. Transforming the wording into realities on the ground, however, proved to be too tall an order, and the Oslo process ended in dismal failure. Peace treaties with Egypt and Jordan have proved not only to be attainable but also lasting. With the Palestinians, however, such a treaty has thus far remained painfully elusive.

## Palestinian-ness and the *Problématique* of Finality

The explanation lies in certain fundamental differences between the Israeli-Palestinian conflict and the inter-state conflict between Israel and the neighboring Arab states. The state order that was created in the Middle East after the First World War was an exercise in colonial map making and was, at first, fundamentally illegitimate in the eyes of most of the Arabs. Pan-Arabism, in which many Arabs believed in the first half of the twentieth century, was destined to remedy the situation by Arab unity, which would dismantle these illicit colonial creatures that formed the Arab state system. Nevertheless, with the passage of time, the state order gradually acquired legitimacy, especially in the aftermath of the decline of pan-Arabism that came in the wake of the Arab debacle in the 1967 war with Israel.

If the 1967 war was the beginning of "the end of pan-Arabism,"[31] the Gulf War of 1990–91 was the last nail in the coffin of the pan-Arab vision. In the Gulf War, numerous Arab states sided with the United States in a war against another Arab state, Iraq. Moreover, the war against Iraq was designed to restore the colonial state order, which Iraq had just challenged by occupying Kuwait and annexing it to Iraq, ostensibly in the name of Arab unity. The end of pan-Arabism paved the way for the legitimate and unapologetic pursuit of the *raison d'état*, or particular state interest (*al-khussusiyya al-qutriyya*),[32] of the individual territorial Arab state, without having to resort to verbal acrobatics or lip service to the greater Arab cause.

The Arab confrontation states had no interest in an endless war with a powerful Israel. The Palestinians were therefore left to their own devices in their continued confrontation with Israel and were compelled to fight against Israel in the Lebanon War of 1982, in the first and second Intifadas, and various campaigns in between, without being able to draw the Arabs into the fray, as they had done in 1948. Egypt and Jordan made their peace with Israel in separate peace treaties, and even the Syrians came very close to doing so themselves.

The entrenchment of the Arab territorial state since 1967 and the evolution of the Arab states' own distinctive territorial identities have reduced their respective conflicts with Israel from existential clashes in the name of Arabism to border disputes relating, in the main, to territories occupied by Israel in 1967 beyond the recognized international boundaries between these states and Israel. These borders date back to the foundation of the British and French Mandates in the Levant in the early 1920s or, in Egypt's case, to the 1906 border delineation between British-occupied Egypt and Ottoman Palestine.

Even in the most extreme cases, these disputes as they evolved after 1967 did not call the existence of pre-1967 Israel into question, and Israel's withdrawal to the international boundary was accepted as "point final." In principle, this is true of the Syrian stand as well. The problem with Syria has been the distinction between the 1967 lines and the precise delineation of the international boundary, and not Syria's readiness to accept pre-1967 Israel.

The Palestinian case, however, is fundamentally different. First, there is no internationally recognized boundary between Israel and Palestine. The lines of the 1947 partition were never accepted by the Arabs, and the armistice line of 1949, the so-called "Green Line," was never formally recognized as an international boundary either, not by the Arabs nor by anyone else. That, however, is more of a technicality than a truly substantive issue. The Palestinians, just like other Arab nations, have developed a uniquely Palestinian territorial identity. But whereas in the case of the Arab states the evolution of a territorial Egyptian, Jordanian, or Syrian identity has been conducive to peacemaking with Israel, by encouraging the reduction of the conflict with Israel to a tolerable border dispute, this is not the case with Palestine.

An unbridgeable abyss separates the Arab Palestinian and the Zionist historical narratives. Zionism, in the widely held Jewish perspective, was a heroic project of national revival, restored dignity, and self-respect. The rise of Israel as an act of defiance against the miserable predicament of the European Jewish diaspora was deeply imbedded in the Jewish collective memory and self-image. This sentiment was cultivated for decades by a scathing critique of the Jewish hopelessness and helplessness in the diaspora, which evolved into an integral part of the Jewish consciousness, as depicted for example in the poetry of the Zionist movement's poet laureate Chaim Nahman Bialik.

"In the City of Slaughter" is perhaps the most tragically moving and riveting of Bialik's poems. There he described the 1903 pogrom in Kishinev in horrifying detail, depicting Jewish men hiding in their nooks and crannies as their women were raped and murdered.[33] This pathetic manifestation of Jewish indignity and powerlessness was only the precursor to the culmination of all horror in the catastrophic destruction of the Jews in the Holocaust. Jewish national liberation, statehood, and sovereignty, as achieved in 1948, was thus the literal rising from the ashes in self-defense to finally attain political independence and historical justice for the most oppressed of all peoples.

For the Palestinians, the complete opposite was true. Zionism, in their experience, had nothing to do with self-defense or justice. It was the epitome of aggression from the start. The Palestinian Nakba, or catastrophic defeat of 1948, the loss of the homeland, exile, and refugeedom remain at the core of the Palestinian collective identity and their self-perception of victimhood. The war had ended not only in their military defeat, but in the shattering of their society and the dispersal of half of their number as refugees in other parts of Palestine and in the neighboring Arab states.

The "shared memories of the traumatic uprooting of their society and the experiences of being dispossessed, displaced, and stateless" were to "come to define 'Palestinian-ness.'"[34] The formative series of events leading up to the outbreak of war in 1948 and its tragic consequences for the Palestinians carried with them a powerful and pervasive sense of historical injustice. The Palestinian yearning, therefore, was to turn back the clock of history.

Palestinian territorial identity, therefore, related to all of historical Palestine. Indeed, Palestinian identity was formed by the struggle with the Zionist movement over the entire territory of Palestine. The Palestinian debacle in 1948, their disaster or Nakba, has become the core of Palestinian-ness, shaped in the crucible of the common destiny and historical memory of defeat and dispersal. The 1967 boundaries never determined Palestinian territorial identity, nor was their identity ever confined to the West Bank and Gaza.

Palestinian-ness was constructed by the experience and cost of Israel's creation in 1948 and not by its expansion in 1967. Palestinian-ness by definition is in conflict with Israel's very being. Israeli concessions are, therefore, at best, a partial recompense, a "relative" or "pragmatic" justice, but so long as they relate solely to the conquests of 1967 they do not address the core of the Palestinian historical grievance. A Palestinian state in the West Bank and Gaza with Arab Jerusalem as its capital is one such form of a "pragmatically just" settlement. However, while such a return of Israel to the 1967 boundaries is sufficient to end the inter-state conflict between Israel and the neighboring Arab states, it is not enough to end the conflict with the Palestinians.

Riyad al-Maliki, a Palestinian intellectual who became foreign minister in Salam Fayyad's cabinet in 2009, pointed to the fact that the Palestinians had great difficulty in producing a peace initiative of their own, since whatever they could possibly propose that had any chance of being acceptable to Israel would always fall short of what in their own minds were their just historical rights.[35] Palestinian public opinion polls reaffirmed this widely held distinction between the pragmatically acceptable and the historically just. While various polls in the West Bank and Gaza showed that the majority of the people consistently supported a two-state solution, an "even larger majority" clearly continued to "harbor irredentist claims over pre-1967 Israel as well." They envisioned the ultimate denouement of Israel in what essentially amounted to a "two-stage solution" whereby Israel would not exist as a Jewish state in the longer run. It would gradually lose its Jewish majority and eventually be incorporated into one Palestinian state that would extend from the Jordan to the Mediterranean.[36]

As opposed to Israel's other major Arab protagonists, like Egypt and Syria, which in practice only had territorial grievances that emanated from the 1967 war with Israel, the Palestinians had two files of complaint, one for 1967 and another for 1948.[37] The resolution of the so-called "1967 file" relates to the outstanding issues of borders and settlements in the West Bank (and Gaza until 2005) and to the final status of Jerusalem. As thorny as these matters may be, they do not impinge directly upon Israel's existence. The "1948 file," however, relates to two existential matters: (1) the question of refugee return to Israel proper; and (2) the issue of the national rights of the Palestinian Arab minority in Israel. Both could severely undermine Israel's viability as presently constituted, that is, as the state of the Jewish people, and it is these issues that fracture the symmetry of partition, or the two-state solution.

It is the intractable nature of questions such as these in the "1948 file" that have put an agreement on finality or "end of conflict" out of reach. For the Israelis, the ideal trade-off would have been far-reaching concessions by Israel on all aspects of the 1967 file, including Arab Jerusalem, in exchange for closure of the 1948 file. The Israeli demand for "end of conflict" on this basis or, alternatively, recognition of Israel as a "Jewish state" was an attempt to obtain from the Palestinians assurances that a two-state solution would remain the foundation for the peace process and that all outstanding questions, including the refugee issue, would be resolved in accordance with the two-state logic.

Israel was to be the homeland of the Jewish people, and Palestine would be the homeland of the Palestinian people. It followed that Jews would have the right to return to Israel and not to Palestine, and Palestinians would have the right to return to the state of Palestine and not to Israel. For the Israelis, it was to ensure that the turning back of the clock would end in 1967, with the undoing of the occupation, and not proceed further to the 1948 issues that might undo their state all together. For the Palestinians, on the other hand, closing the "1948 file" would mean the invalidation of their narrative.

The Oslo Accords provided the PLO with an entrance ticket from the wilderness of Tunis into what had become the core arena of Palestinian national political relevance in the West Bank and Gaza. But a price had to be paid for that gain, and what could be called the "Oslo dynamic" was set in motion. The institutions of the Palestinian Authority (PA) in the West Bank and Gaza, the elected presidency and the Legislative Assembly, for all intents and purposes, superseded the PLO. The PLO was steadily marginalized until it became a "hollow shell" that existed in an almost "moribund state," barely functioning in the diaspora.[38]

The Oslo Accords ushered in a new era in the annals of the PLO and the Palestinian people. The "center of national politics, primary social constituency, and statist institutions were based in one and the same location, the occupied territories."[39] The Oslo Accords thus created a new political dynamic that portended great historical significance. The new institutions were elected solely by the people of the West Bank (including Arab East Jerusalem) and Gaza and thus represented only them, as opposed to the PLO, which claimed to represent all Palestinians everywhere, including in Israel and the Palestinian diaspora. The PLO represented the claim to all of historical Palestine and was an organization that had functioned from the outset in the diaspora. The PLO, therefore, had also tended to give high priority to the diaspora constituency and its aspirations — above all, the demand for refugee return.

The PA, on the other hand, represented the West Bank and Gaza and focused on their most immediate concern, liberation from the Israeli occupation and the advance toward independent statehood alongside Israel. This meant a certain downgrading, though by no means an abandonment, of the primacy of the refugee question. The issue of Palestine, or so it seemed momentarily, was actually being reduced to the West Bank and Gaza and to the 1967 questions, at the expense of the "1948 file." Israel sought to achieve finality on that basis, that is, the Palestinians would agree to end the conflict on the basis of a grand historical bargain, whereby Israel would concede on the 1967 questions in exchange for closure of the "1948 file." But that was not to be.

Irrespective of the Palestinian leadership's intentions, the millions of refugees in the diaspora felt abandoned by the Oslo process and the creation of the PA, and came to believe that in practice the possibility of their return had become even less realistic as a result of the Oslo deal. The establishment of the PA was therefore seen as the "effective abandonment of the majority of Palestinians who live outside Palestine." The Palestinian leadership, observes Rashid Khalidi, had failed to act "on the principle that the Palestinians are a single people all of whom suffered from their collective dispossession, and that consequently the amelioration of the lot of those under occupation was only part of the resolution of the Palestine problem." Oslo had created the "unmistakable impression" that the PLO leadership was forgetting the interests of the refugees in the diaspora.[40]

To dispel such "unmistakable impressions," at the very outset of the Camp David summit, which was convened in July 2000 under the auspices of US President Clinton, the Palestinian side made it clear that there would be no trade-off between the 1967 and the 1948 "files," that is, there would be no trading of refugee rights in exchange for Israeli concessions in Jerusalem. Each Israeli concession was to be obtained on its own merits and would have no bearing on other issues.[41] The Palestinians, and first and foremost Yasir Arafat, would not agree to finality or to an "end of conflict" unless the "1948 file" and its primary issues and grievances — that is, first and foremost the refugee question — were also addressed to their satisfaction.

## The Breakdown of Mutual Trust

In addition to the huge gaps on substance, the level of trust between the parties was deeply eroded during the Oslo years. The transitional phase was supposed to have provided for confidence building to pave the way for the negotiation of the most difficult issues that had been left in abeyance for the final-status talks. In fact, quite the opposite was achieved. What was supposed to have been the "antechamber to [Palestinian] statehood, appeared to be more and more of a dead end."[42] Israel was not committed by the DoP to restrict settlement activity in the transitional phase. During the 1990s, settlement activity was increased by leaps and bounds, leading to a 75 percent increase in the settler population, from 115,700 in September 1993 to 203,000 in early 2001. Whether this was the doing of Israeli governments or of Jewish radicals who in practice had "managed to acquire veto power over the actions of the Israeli state" made no difference to the Palestinians.[43]

Settlements were antithetical to any territorial solution (exactly as the settlers intended) and thus a flagrant violation of at least the spirit of the Oslo Accords, if not its letter. By the end of the 1990s there were more settlements and less freedom of movement. Powerful Palestinian constituencies, the intellectuals, the security establishment, the media, the bureaucracy, and political activists were disillusioned by the results of the peace process and doubtful of Israel's willingness to implement signed agreements.[44]

As for the Israelis, they expected the PA to suppress violence in or emanating from the territories under their jurisdiction, with their "strong police force" that was provided for in the Oslo Accords.[45] From the very outset, it might have been too much to have expected Arafat to actively suppress what remained of the Palestinian armed struggle for Israel's sake. But the fact that he did not suppress the violence, for whatever reason — incapacity or unwillingness or any combination of the two — greatly undermined the entire logic of the peace process for the Israelis. More Israelis were killed by terrorist attacks after the signing of the Oslo Accords than before, and it did not matter to them if the lethal attacks carried out against their compatriots were masterminded by Arafat loyalists or by his adversaries.

In the words of Israel's former foreign minister Shlomo Ben Ami and one of its chief negotiators with the Palestinians, "The philosophy of interim arrangements was founded on the basis of reciprocal dishonesty—terrorism versus the continuation of settlements."[46] By the time the parties went to Camp David in the summer of 2000, the "widening gap between the vision of peace and prosperity and the grim reality of violence and suffering" allowed the oppositions on both sides to undermine public support for compromise.[47]

Equally damning of Arafat in the eyes of Israelis was his failure to abide by the undertaking he had made in his letter to Rabin to amend the PLO Charter. In April 1996 the PNC decided to amend the charter.[48] Despite the resolution, which seemed like a favorable step in the right direction, the Israelis, who were forever suspicious of Arafat's machinations, subsequently complained that nothing had actually been done. In January 1998 Arafat sent a letter to President Clinton to put the Israeli complaint to rest. He noted before the president that all sections of the charter that were incompatible with the commitments he had made in the letter to Rabin had in fact been annulled. He specifically cited twelve articles, adding that parts of sixteen other articles had been excised. In December 1998 the PNC reconvened, this time in the presence of President Clinton, and with an impressive show of hands approved the amendments to the charter.[49] But no amended text has ever been made public, and the only existing text today is still the one written in 1968, without any changes at all.[50]

After all the commotion about the charter, its amendment was virtually meaningless. For the entire exercise to have been really worthwhile, the charter should have been abolished altogether. After all, the charter was the founding document of the Palestine Liberation Organization, and as such, not surprisingly, the charter dealt only with the liberation of Palestine, its justification, and the ways and means to achieve that goal. Nearly all of the charter's thirty-three articles engaged entirely with the struggle for liberation. The remaining few related to procedural matters and to the flag and the anthem. For the charter to be congruent with partition and the idea of two states, it would have had to be rewritten from scratch.

Among the articles that were not amended were those that dealt with the seemingly innocuous issue of defining Palestine and its people. The charter describes Palestine as "the homeland of the Arab Palestinian people" and as "an integral part of the greater Arab homeland." In terms of geographical definition, Palestine "within the boundaries of the British Mandate was an indivisible territorial unit," and it was the Palestinian people who "possessed the legal right to its homeland" and who "would exercise its right to self-determination after the liberation of its homeland."[51]

One could hardly expect the Palestinians to say or believe anything else. But there was no way these articles could be reconciled with the idea of Palestine also being the homeland of another, non-Arab people or with the notion of two peoples living in two separate states on the soil of historical Palestine, in which they both exercised their respective rights to self-determination. One must therefore conclude that those in Israel who made political hay with the charter and the insistent demand for the amendment of "the parts of the charter" that called for Israel's dissolution had apparently never actually read the document. Had they bothered to do so, they would certainly have realized that their own cause required the charter's abolition rather than just its amendment.

Oddly enough, it is most likely that had the Israelis not raised the issue of the charter it would have continued to collect dust in the archives together with many other outdated documents of Israelis, Zionists, Palestinians, and others, with no recognizable consequence for the peace process. But once the question was raised, it exposed the enormous difficulty the Palestinians had in fully coming to terms with the historical legitimacy of two states, without somehow disavowing, in their own eyes, the very essence of their historical narrative and of their political patrimony. Every now and then Fatah spokespersons would even state publicly that the two-state solution was only a transitional phase and a function of the existing balance of power and the constraints of the international system. In the long run, the strategic goal was still "Palestine from the [Jordan] river to the [Mediterranean] sea."[52]

## The Failure of the Camp David–Taba Negotiations

The following discussion is not intended to be a definitive and exhaustive summary of the Camp David negotiations and their aftermath. Nor is it intended to explain what went wrong or to apportion blame for the failure. It is intended to study these negotiations solely as an illustration of the respective Palestinian and Israeli perceptions of the two-state idea and its historical meaning. The difficulties inherent in the positions of the parties on two states emerged more clearly at the Camp David–Taba negotiations held from July 2000 to January 2001. The intensive negotiations ended in predictable failure, and no agreement was reached on "end of conflict."

The first round of talks at Camp David centered on the issues of borders and Jerusalem. But already at Camp David and more so in later rounds of negotiation, it was clear that there could be no two-state solution without a more than symbolic refugee return to Israel proper.[53] In the Palestinian worldview, anything less than an independent state in the 1967 boundaries, with Arab Jerusalem as its capital and a substantial and meaningful return of refugees to Israel proper, fell short of the bare minimum that the Palestinians could possibly accept as legitimate. These, as one Israeli chief negotiator described them, were "the basic positions of a national collective," and there were no shades of difference between left or right, between generations, or between "moderates" and "extremists," and no one, from Arafat down, would deviate from this "orthodoxy."[54]

For the Palestinians, this was no more than partial recompense for their real historical loss. Arafat had no intention of negotiating for anything less, which would be a total sellout in the Palestinian scheme of things. Israeli concessions that were magnanimous in the minds of Israelis invariably fell far short of Palestinian expectations and were seen by the Palestinians as disappointing empty gestures or tactical maneuvers, which required no quid pro quo on their part. For the Israelis, however, the Palestinian predisposition looked like a constant Palestinian pocketing of Israeli concessions for nothing in return. Arafat, they concluded, expected the Israelis to roll out proposals one after the other until they reached a point that he could find acceptable, but this imaginary point was never quite clearly defined even to Arafat himself.[55]

The parties were conceptually and psychologically miles apart, locked in different historical time zones. For the Israelis, the point of departure was the territories occupied in 1967. For them, the West Bank and Gaza were 100 percent of the territories being negotiated in terms of Resolution 242. The Palestinian demand for full withdrawal to the 1967 boundaries and a substantive "right of return" was, therefore, an uncompromising "all or nothing" approach, in the Israeli view, which made an agreement impossible. The Israelis constantly complained that while they were willing to go out on a limb and even risk breaking with "sacred taboos," the Palestinians persisted in digging in to their "eternal myths."[56]

Needless to say, from the Palestinian perspective, things were seen very differently. The Palestinian point of reference was 1948 and all of British Mandatory Palestine. For them, all of the West Bank and Gaza was the meager 22 percent rump of historical Palestine, as Arafat himself repeatedly reminded President Clinton.[57] The war for all of Palestine had been lost, and Oslo itself was their great historical compromise where they had already conceded 78 percent of historical Palestine. They would concede no more. The Palestinians sought the full implementation of UN Security Council Resolutions 242 and 338 and General Assembly Resolution 194 on the refugees and would not agree to anything less. To expect them to do so was pure illusion. The notion that Israel had offered generous concessions was therefore "doubly wrong." The territory the Israelis were willing to "give up" was never theirs in the first place and was "Palestinian land occupied by military force." The Israelis were expected to implement Resolution 242 and withdraw to the 1967 boundaries, as they had agreed to do on all the fronts with the other Arab states. Moreover, most Palestinians were "more resigned to the two-state solution than were willing to embrace it; they were prepared to accept Israel's existence, but not its moral legitimacy."[58]

In the eyes of the Israelis, on the other hand, the front with Palestine was not just another Arab front. The territories in question, in Jerusalem in particular, were part of the Jewish historical patrimony of Eretz Yisrael. Some parts of the occupied territories, such as the Jewish Quarter in the Old City of Jerusalem or the Etzion Bloc, between Bethlehem and Hebron, were populated by Jews before 1948 and were overrun by Arab forces in the war. Therefore, Israeli concessions on Jerusalem, such as their agreement at Camp David, for the first time ever since 1967, to divide the city, were deemed by both Israelis and Americans to be extremely courageous, far-reaching, and generous. But they were rejected by the Palestinians as woefully insufficient.

If Israel would not concede all of what the Palestinians were convinced was rightfully theirs, including full sovereignty on the Temple Mount / al-Haram al-Sharif, the Israeli proposal was not even an approximation of what could be regarded as acceptable. The Israelis were driven to the conclusion that their magnanimity was being spurned by an Arafat who was psychologically incapable of making the grand historical compromise necessary to end the conflict. Arafat, they believed, would rather die like Abd al-Nasir "as a myth who had failed in reality" rather than accept what he feared would be seen by his own people as a sellout.[59]

The Israeli demand for an agreement on "end of conflict" only made matters worse by actually shifting the focus to the most contentious and intractable 1948 issues. In the words of Edward Said, the parties were "back to the basic, irreconcilable, the irremediably interlocked contradiction between Palestinian and Israeli nationalism."[60] In the run-up to the final-status negotiations and subsequently as the negotiations continued from Camp David, to Washington and then on to Taba, from July 2000 to January 2001, as hard a nut as Jerusalem was to crack, the refugee question was that much harder.

Palestinians in the diaspora and refugees in the occupied territories were extremely suspicious of Arafat. They feared that just as he had "capitulated" to Israel in the Oslo Accords, he might now "sign away the refugees' rights" for a statelet in the West Bank and Gaza. They were deeply concerned that they were about to be exposed to another one of those "shabby Arafatian compromises," in the caustic language of Edward Said.[61] According to Hussam Khadir, a Fatah activist from the Balata refugee camp in Nablus, speaking at the time of the Taba talks in January 2001, at no time since 1948 had the right of return been so widely asserted among the refugees themselves and the Palestinians in general.[62] It was reported that there was talk in the West Bank and Gaza of a "Refugee Intifada" if the Palestinian negotiators wavered on the right of return.[63]

Arafat, most probably, would not have conceded on the refugees anyway, but this kind of anti-Arafatist campaign could not have made matters any easier. The campaign notwithstanding, it was most unlikely that the Palestinians would acquiesce in "end of conflict" without agreement on the issue that was at the very heart of their historical grievance. Ending claims against Israel without satisfaction on refugees in the eyes of many, or even most, Palestinians would have been tantamount to treason. Sa'ib Ariqat explained to Shlomo Ben Ami in no uncertain terms, "If you want to end the conflict and to realize an end of claims, you must accept the right of return."[64]

As far as the Palestinians were concerned, Israel had to accept its "political, legal and moral responsibility for the tragedy of the refugees" and agree in principle to their "right of return,"[65] even if that was not expected to be interpreted as an actual unlimited repatriation of refugees to Israel proper. But Israel would not endorse the "right of return" under any circumstances. On this point, as opposed to all other issues, Israeli rejection was unequivocal and unanimous, across the entire spectrum of Israeli society, from the far left to the far right. Israel balked at accepting the *sole* historical responsibility for the creation of the refugee problem. That would have been tantamount to Israel's acceptance that it was born in sin. It would be understood as an admission by Israel that the refugee problem, rather than being the result of a war initiated by the Arabs and imposed on Israel, was a consequence of Israel's inherent propensity for ethnic cleansing, rooted in the predatory nature of the Zionist enterprise.[66] The Israelis could hardly be expected to do that.

Moreover, if Israel was indeed *solely* responsible for the creation of the problem, it might also follow that Israel was *solely* responsible for the solution. Israel would not accept such a demand or vision of history, nor would it accept the principle of a "right of return" that was not fully controlled by Israel. Refugee return to Israel would be acceptable only if it was capped by a specific number that Israel would determine, for admission over time, on humanitarian grounds. Such return, would not, therefore, be on the basis of an intrinsic "right of return," but in accordance with Israel's own sovereign decision.

The gap between the parties on this issue was unbridgeable. In principle, the Palestinians were reluctant to suggest a precise figure of their own for the number of refugees who ought to return to Israel proper. At Camp David, Ahmad Qurai (Abu Ala') explained that they would not present their own figures until they knew "with fair certainty the numbers of Palestinians who would ask for return or compensation."[67] During the various rounds of negotiations between Camp David and Taba, various figures were discussed. The Palestinians had spoken of between 100,000 and 300,000 as the number of refugees that ought to be admitted into Israel, and at times "much higher figures" were mentioned. At Camp David, Nabil Sha'ath suggested that the "initial figure" the Palestinians were asking for was the 250,000 refugees in Lebanon. Thereafter, a specific number should return annually. There were times when Palestinian spokesmen even argued against any limitation on the figure at all. When pressed on the matter by the Palestinians, Ben Ami proposed that Israel would admit no more than 15,000 refugees, and even this number would be spaced over a period of twenty years.[68]

Israel's approach was designed to create a mechanism of control that in Israel's calculus would not undermine the Jewish character of the state and the underlying principle of two states, one Jewish and the other Arab Palestinian. For Israel, refugee return was an irredentist encroachment into Israel proper of what ought to be resolved in the state of Palestine. Return to Israel contradicted "the very spirit of a two-state solution."[69] The Palestinians supported their case by referring to previous Israeli positions that had been more forthcoming. In 1949 during the Lausanne talks, held under the auspices of the UN-created Palestine Conciliation Commission, Israel made an offer to absorb one hundred thousand refugees, about 15 percent of the total, equivalent to well over half a million today. This Israeli proposal, strongly opposed by Israeli public opinion at the time, was made conditional upon the Arab states absorbing the rest of the refugees and signing peace treaties with Israel. The Arabs rejected these conditions, and the offer was withdrawn, never to be repeated.[70]

As the Camp David–Taba negotiations foundered, Israel and the Palestinians descended into the worst round of bloodshed they had ever experienced since 1948, with suicide bombers ravaging Israeli towns, and the Israeli military pulverizing PA installations and infrastructure and the Palestinian population in return. In late December 2000, at a meeting of the parties at the White House, President Clinton summarized the negotiating process as it had evolved until then. He presented the contours of the final settlement that he believed was attainable. These were to become known as the "Clinton Parameters" for a two-state solution.

They included the following:

Borders and territory. Israel would annex 4 to 6 percent of the West Bank, which would include the major settlement blocs and 80 percent of the settlers. A land swap would compensate the Palestinians with territory in Israel, equal to 1 to 3 percent of the West Bank.

Jerusalem. The city would be divided according to the principle of Arab-populated areas under Palestinian sovereignty and Jewish-populated areas under Israeli sovereignty. This principle would generally apply to the Old City and its holy places as well.

Security. The guiding principle was to balance between Israel's genuine security needs and Palestinian sovereignty. The Palestinian state would therefore be "non-militarized." Israel would be allowed to maintain a certain limited military presence for specified periods of time in the West Bank and would also be allowed through agreed arrangements to use Palestinian airspace for training and operational purposes.

Refugees. The basis of the settlement would be two states for the two peoples, Israel as the homeland of the Jewish people and Palestine as the homeland of the Palestinian people. The parties would recognize the right of return of the Palestinian refugees to "historic Palestine" or to their "homeland." The refugees would have five options for their final place of residence: the state of Palestine, the swap areas that would become part of the Palestinian state, resettlement in their present host countries, emigration to third countries, or admission to Israel. Israel could indicate in the agreement that it would be prepared to absorb some refugees in Israel, consistent with its sovereign decision. The implementation of such a settlement for refugees would be accepted by the parties as the implementation of UN Resolution 194.

End of conflict and end of claims. The signing of an agreement on the basis of the above principles would constitute the end of the conflict, and its implementation would put an end to all claims.[71]

The Clinton Parameters were a classic US split-the-difference compromise between the Israeli and Palestinian positions. However, bearing in mind the respective points of reference of the two parties as outlined above, in practice, this meant a position that the Israelis were bound to be more comfortable with than the Palestinians. For the Palestinians it was as if they were being asked to compromise yet again, on top of the major concession they had already made, so they argued, when they acquiesced in two states in the first place.

Both sides did not fully accept nor fully reject the Clinton Parameters. The Israelis, with certain reservations, accepted the Clinton Parameters as a basis on which to continue the negotiations. The Palestinians were more flexible on the ideas of land swaps and the ethnic basis for the partition of Jerusalem than they were on other issues, such as the sovereignty over the Temple Mount / al-Haram al-Sharif and refugee return. While Arafat did not flatly reject the Clinton Parameters, his reservations were so detailed and substantive that the Palestinian response was eventually understood by all concerned—Israelis, Americans, and Palestinians—as an essential rejection.[72]

The official Israeli response to President Clinton accepted the parameters, as they were, as the basis on which to continue the negotiations for a permanent settlement, provided the Palestinians did the same. The Israelis noted those parts of the president's ideas that conflicted with their positions (for example, their rejection of the "right of return" was far more unequivocal than that which appeared in the Clinton Parameters); they also pointed to elements that required further clarification and others that had not been addressed. These comments, however, were but an appendix to an essential "yes."[73] The Israelis could not only live with the Clinton Parameters, they were determined to commit the new incoming US Republican administration to abide by them.[74]

**Map Reflecting Actual Proposal at Camp David**

- ▓ Proposed Palestinian State
- ☐ Israeli Settlement Blocs Annexed to Israel
- ▨ Israeli Security Border

*MEDITERRANEAN SEA*

Tel Aviv

While no map was presented during the final rounds at Camp David, this map illustrates the parameters of what President Clinton proposed and Arafat rejected: Palestinian control over 91% of the West Bank in contiguous territory and an Israeli security presence along 15% of the border with Jordan. This map actually understates the final Camp David proposal because it does not depict the additional territorial swap of 1% that was offered from Israeli territory.

Jenin

Tulkarm   WEST BANK

Nablus

Qalqilya

Ramallah

Jericho

Maale Adumim

Jerusalem

ISRAEL

Bethlehem

Hebron

*Jordan River*

Dead Sea

0        10
        miles

Copyright 2004 Washington Institute for Near East Policy

*Map 3. Israel's Proposal at the Camp David Talks. Reprinted with the permission of the Washington Institute for Near East Policy*

As Dennis Ross, US Middle East envoy and chief negotiator, put it, the Israeli reservations were within the Clinton Parameters. "Barak's government had now formally accepted ideas that would effectively divide East Jerusalem, end the IDF's presence in the Jordan Valley, and produce a Palestinian state in roughly 97 percent of the West Bank and 100 percent of Gaza."[75] By this time, however, the Barak government had lost its majority in the Knesset, and its legitimacy to negotiate such matters of historical consequence had been sig-

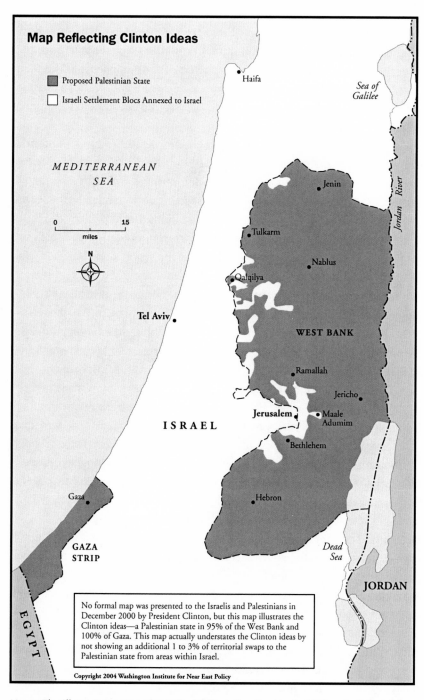

**Map Reflecting Clinton Ideas**

Proposed Palestinian State

Israeli Settlement Blocs Annexed to Israel

Haifa

*Sea of Galilee*

*MEDITERRANEAN SEA*

*Jordan River*

0        15
    miles

N

Jenin

Tulkarm

Nablus

Qalqilya

Tel Aviv

**WEST BANK**

Ramallah

Jericho

Jerusalem    Maale Adumim

**ISRAEL**

Bethlehem

Gaza

Hebron

**GAZA STRIP**

*Dead Sea*

**JORDAN**

EGYPT

No formal map was presented to the Israelis and Palestinians in December 2000 by President Clinton, but this map illustrates the Clinton ideas—a Palestinian state in 95% of the West Bank and 100% of Gaza. This map actually understates the Clinton ideas by not showing an additional 1 to 3% of territorial swaps to the Palestinian state from areas within Israel.

Copyright 2004 Washington Institute for Near East Policy

Map 4. The Clinton Parameters: the territorial dimension. Reprinted with the permission of the Washington Institute for Near East Policy

nificantly reduced. A poll conducted at the time revealed that while a decisive majority of Israeli Jews favored continued negotiations with the Palestinians, a clear majority rejected the Clinton Parameters. The respondents linked their rejection to their overall assessment that Israelis were both less confident in the Palestinians and less willing to concede after the outbreak of the second Intifada.[76]

As for the Palestinians, following his meeting with President Clinton in early January 2001, it was clear that Arafat "had effectively rejected the President's ideas." His reservations on Jerusalem, security, and refugees were all "deal killers."[77] Ross's conclusion was essentially corroborated by the Palestinians themselves. In the last round of negotiations that took place at Taba in January 2001, the Palestinians argued that they would not negotiate solely on the basis of the Clinton Parameters. In opening the negotiations, Ahmad Qurai (Abu Ala') said that the Palestinians accepted the Clinton Parameters as only one of the bases for the negotiation.[78] Elsewhere he was more forthright, stating unequivocally that the Palestinians refused to accept them.[79] In the words of another Palestinian negotiator, Yasir Abd al-Rabbu, the Clinton proposals were in the same league as the Sykes-Picot Agreement of 1916,[80] which the Arabs had always denounced as a colonialist conspiracy against them.

In the formal Palestinian response to the Clinton Parameters made in early January 2001, the Palestinian negotiating team spelled out its reservations on territory, Jerusalem, security, and refugees. The Palestinians explained that "the latest United States proposals, taken together and as presented without clarification, fail to satisfy the conditions required for a permanent peace." The measure of consideration shown for Israeli territorial and security needs was inimical to viable Palestinian statehood, to the extent that the Palestinians could not accept a proposal that secured "neither the establishment of a viable Palestinian state nor the right of Palestinian refugees to return to their homes." On the question of refugees, they contended that the issue of return to Israel proper could not depend solely on Israel's discretion. Resolution 194 specified the right of the refugees to return "to their homes" and not to their "homeland" nor to "historic Palestine." The very essence of the right of return was the freedom of choice, which the refugees should not be denied. Furthermore, without recognition of the right of return and its attendant freedom of choice, there would be no end to the conflict.[81] In the words of Mahmud Abbas, first the Israelis had to recognize the right of return, then the refugees themselves would choose whether to return or not, and then negotiations would begin on implementation.[82] In other words, it could not be just up to Israel to decide how many or which refugees would return.

In January 2001, Fatah also issued a document that listed no less than forty-four reasons for rejecting the Clinton Parameters. According to Fatah, they violated the terms of reference of the peace process on territory, Jerusalem, and refugees. On refugees, the parameters denied the Palestinians their "sacred right of return," which was the "core of the Arab-Israeli conflict." Suggesting that the refugees be absorbed in other countries was a form of "collective punishment" in that it stripped them of their freedom of choice. Rejecting the right of return meant the indefinite perpetuation of the conflict. The eventual coexistence between Palestinian Muslims and Christians and the Israelis, within the context of "historical Palestine," would thus be prevented, a choice of phrase that was reminiscent of the vintage Palestinian one-state solution.[83]

Mahmud Abbas analyzed the various options for preferred place of residence that were offered to the Palestinian refugees in the Clinton Parameters. He argued that all the options depended on the sovereign decision of other states (the Arab host countries, Israel, and third countries) except the return to the future state of Palestine. But 70 percent of the Gazans and 40 percent of the West Bankers were themselves refugees. This was "unreasonable," he concluded. When the Palestinians spoke of the right of return, they meant return to Israel. After all, it was Israel "that had expelled them" in the first place, and their abandoned property was also there. "Not a single refugee was from Gaza, Hebron or Nablus."[84]

Shlomo Ben Ami suggested to the Palestinians at Taba that hundreds of thousands of refugees could return to the swap areas, that is, to those areas of Israel proper that would become part of the Palestinian state in the final territorial arrangement. The Palestinians would be able to say that these refugees were actually returning to Israel. The idea was rejected by the Palestinians, however, because it did not allow for the refugee's free choice of where exactly to settle in Israel.[85]

Though the refugee issue was not the primary topic of negotiation in the Camp David–Taba process, usually preceded by Jerusalem and territorial matters, it was unquestionably prioritized in the Palestinian public discourse, inside the occupied territories and even more so in the diaspora. These external atmospherics could hardly be ignored, and the Palestinians were adamant from the outset at Camp David in explaining to the Americans that the "Palestinian revolution had risen from the refugee camps" of the diaspora and that there could be no agreement that "did not include a just solution for the refugee problem." In their view, the "greatest failure" of Camp David was in the refugee committee. Israel continued to "to deny its crime [of expulsion], despite all the evidence." Israel would only discuss compensation, but there was no discussion of "a timetable for the implementation of return." Israel's goal at Camp David, as seen from the Palestinian perspective, "was to obtain the Palestinian 'golden' signature on final recognition and the 'end of conflict' at a cheap price—without returning all the land, without acknowledging full sovereignty, and, most dangerous of all, without solving the refugee issue."[86]

By most accounts, Israeli and Palestinian, gaps between the parties on territorial matters were narrowed down during the Taba talks, but little or no progress was made on refugees. According to one Israeli version that was disseminated by Yossi Beilin, Israel's justice minister, who negotiated for Israel on the refugees at Taba, this was not really so. Beilin himself and Ron Pundak, one of the original architects of the Oslo Accords and a close confidant of Beilin, claimed that the negotiators at Taba "achieved a draft determining the parameters and procedures for a solution, along with a clear emphasis that its implementation would not threaten the Jewish character of the State of Israel." They had also narrowed the differences on the narrative of the evolution of the refugee problem, but there was no agreement on the number of refugees who would return to Israel.[87]

According to a summary of the Taba talks compiled by the European Union special representative for the Middle East peace process, Miguel Moratinos, on the basis of information he obtained from both parties, not much real progress was made on the refugee question. The Palestinians still demanded recognition of "the individual free choice of the refugees" between the various options offered to them, including return to Israel proper, and that the right of the refugees to return to their homes, in accordance with the Palestinian interpretation of UN Resolution 194, should not be prejudiced. The Israelis informally proposed a return of forty thousand refugees over five years, but as Beilin noted, no agreement was reached on any numbers.[88] In fact, they were "far apart" on the numbers.[89]

In the summer of 2001 Le Monde Diplomatique published what were said to be the actual documents that the Palestinians and the Israelis had presented at Taba. The Palestinians demanded that Israel recognize "its moral and legal responsibility for the forced displacement of the Palestinian civilian population during the 1948 war" and to accept that it shall consequently "bear responsibility for the resolution of the refugee problem." In accordance with UN

Resolution 194 "all refugees who wish to return to their homes in Israel and live at peace with their neighbors have the right to do so. The right of every refugee to return shall be exercised in accordance with the modalities set out in the Agreement."[90]

The Israeli position, even in the less committal form of a "private response" in a "non-paper" compiled by the most conciliatory of Israeli negotiators, Yossi Beilin, came nowhere near to bridging the gap. Israel, in this document, implied that it was one of the parties (that is, not the only party) who were "directly or indirectly responsible" for the creation of the refugee problem and, as such, would "contribute its part" to the solution of the problem together with the other responsible parties. The solution of the refugee problem "must address the needs and aspirations of the refugees, while accounting for the realities [created] since the 1948–49 war. Thus, the wish [that is, not the right] to return shall be implemented in a manner consistent with the existence of the State of Israel as the homeland for [the] Jewish people." The refugees, in order to fulfill the requirements of Resolution 194, would be able to choose between five options, one of which was return to Israel proper. But return to Israel would be "capped to an agreed limit of XX refugees" (that is, a number still to be negotiated and that, by all accounts, had never been agreed upon).[91]

Ron Pundak later argued that one of the problems in the negotiations with the Palestinians was that conciliatory positions stated privately were not repeated in public. And, as he observed, the publicly stated positions on the refugees were "excited Palestinian declarations regarding the right of return of every refugee to the State of Israel," which seriously eroded Israeli confidence in Palestinian intentions, even though the positions taken in the negotiations were far more moderate and pragmatic.[92]

However, the refugee question cannot be resolved in secret. Positions that are not made public, for whatever reason, are politically immaterial until they are brought into the open and defended in public, in a genuine effort to mobilize popular support. Nothing like that has taken place, not by any account. On the contrary, public statements by the Palestinian leadership were very consistent for years after Camp David in upholding the principle of the right of return and specifically rejecting resettlement (tawtin) in other countries.[93]

According to Palestinian negotiator Sa'ib Ariqat, it was not the Palestinian decision maker who had the right to decide on the matter. It was solely up to the refugees themselves to decide whether they wanted to return to Israel proper ("the areas of '48") or to accept some other arrangement. Moreover it was not a matter of return or compensation, as the refugees were entitled to both "return and compensation" (emphasis added).[94] Israel also had to accept its responsibility for having created the problem in the first place. After all, they did not become refugees "because of an earthquake or a natural disaster: this was a man-made disaster, an expulsion."[95]

After the Taba talks, the chief negotiators from both sides announced that "we have never been so close to attaining an agreement." As then US ambassador to Israel Martin Indyk observed, "That may have been true in relative terms, in absolute terms they were not close at all."[96] Aaron Miller, an advisor to six US secretaries of state on Middle Eastern affairs, made a similar assessment: "Anyone who believes that Israelis and Palestinians were 'this close' to an agreement at any recent negotiation, including Camp David and Taba, has spent too much time with the peace-process tooth fairy. All three issues that drive the Israeli-Palestinian conflict (borders, Jerusalem, refugees) and a fourth (security) represent a universe of unfinished business in terms of both substance and implementation."[97] The failed negotiations and the bloody struggle that ensued in the second Intifada awakened the ghosts of the past for both Israelis and Palestinians. Palestinian demands for refugee return intensified, just as their fears of expulsion were exacerbated, while Jewish fears mounted that refugee return would mean the eventual undoing of their state.[98]

It was at the Camp David talks that it also transpired that the Palestinians would not recognize Israel as "the state of the Jewish people." For the Israelis such recognition was an alternative version of finality in two states, but for the Palestinians it was tantamount to a declaration that historical Palestine was not really theirs. Shlomo Ben Ami argued before his Palestinian interlocutors that their positions on the right of return and on the holy places in Jerusalem proved that they were "unwilling to accept Israel's historical and Jewish entitlement, no matter what its borders were."[99] Indeed they were not. In their minds, it all belonged to them and not to the Jews.

The peace process had been based for decades on UN Security Council Resolution 242 passed in November 1967, as were the Oslo Accords. However, as far as the Palestinians were concerned, finality or end of conflict could only be achieved if the "1948 file" was also addressed on the basis of UN General Assembly Resolution 194 of December 1948, which related to the refugee question and which the Palestinians interpreted as an endorsement of the "right of return." For the Israelis, on the other hand, Resolution 194 had never been an acceptable supplementary basis for the process.[100]

If anything at all, Resolution 194 had to be entirely subordinated to and merged with Resolution 242, that is, as an integral part of the solution to the question of the occupied territories. But from the Palestinian point of view, it only made historical sense if Resolution 194 was appended to Resolution 242 as the basis for a settlement. Such a formula, as promoted by the Palestinians, went beyond the contours of the 1967 occupation and entered into the territory of Israel proper. The peace process was not just about statehood and the rolling back of the 1967 occupation. That could be attained in the West Bank and Gaza. It was also about the Palestinian vision of historical justice, and that included the rolling back to 1948 in some significant measure too. That could not be attained unless there were to be more than a token return of Palestinian refugees, back to where they had come from, in Israel proper.

For the Israelis, it made no sense to withdraw from territory and "then in turn exacerbate domestic demographic problems by also agreeing to absorb refugees." In the mind of many Israelis, one of the main reasons for the establishment of a Palestinian state in the first place was to provide for a fair solution to the refugee problem there and not in Israel.[101] At the heart of the refugee problem was not just a calculation of the numbers of potential returnees, but rather the heated collision between "two exclusive drives for legitimization, justice, and responsibility." The right of return was "not really about numbers as much as [it was] a competition [about] whose 'right' is symbolically more compelling: that of the Palestinians to return, or that of Israel to exist."[102]

Camp David and Taba also revealed asymmetrical perceptions of time and urgency. Shlomo Ben Ami expressed his astonishment at the fact that when it finally transpired that the last gasp at Taba had ended in failure, he discerned no sense of urgency or missed opportunity among his Palestinian interlocutors.[103] The Israelis were indeed driven by a sense of urgency and a perception that time and demography were working against them. There was, however, no logical reason for the Palestinians to share these Israeli concerns. On the contrary, if time was working against the Israelis, the Palestinians could only have surmised that time was on their side. Indeed, they were in no rush.

## The Limits of Nongovernmental Initiatives

As the second Intifada escalated, leading eventually to an Israeli reoccupation of the West Bank in the spring of 2002, unofficial negotiations by various Israelis and Palestinians continued to work to close the gaps that remained between the parties. These produced two documents agreed upon by Israelis and Palestinians, but on neither side were these ever formally adopted by the forces in power.

The first was an agreement between a former Israeli general and ex-chief of the General Security Service (GSS), Ami Ayalon, and a renowned Palestinian intellectual, Sari Nusseibeh, scion to one of Palestine's great notable families and the president of al-Quds University in Jerusalem. Ayalon and Nusseibeh succeeded where everyone else had failed, in that they covered all the critical issues, including the refugee question, fully and finally resolving them within the framework of two distinctly independent states. It was the perfectly symmetrical two-state formulation that made the Ayalon-Nusseibeh declaration, first published in July 2002, unique.

The key principles in their initiative were that "Palestine is the only state of the Palestinian people and Israel is the only state of the Jewish people"; that the permanent borders between the two states will be agreed upon "on the basis of the 4 June 1967 lines"; that "Jerusalem will be an open city, the capital of two states"; and that "Palestinian refugees will return only to the State of Palestine; Jews will return only to the State of Israel." This was the clearest formulation ever produced publicly of a perfect trade-off between the 1967 issues in exchange for closure of the 1948 file. The principles preserved Israel as the state of the Jewish people, with no refugee return to it, creating Palestine alongside as the state of the Palestinian people, in which there would be no Israeli settlers or settlements.[104]

The second unofficial agreement was the Geneva Accord, which was a very different exercise. It was formally signed in December 2003 between a group of left-wing Israelis led by Knesset member Yossi Beilin and former director general of the Foreign Ministry David Kimche, and a Palestinian representation led by senior officials of the PA, Yasir Abd al-Rabbu and Qaddura Faris. The accord was intended to prove that a fully detailed agreement, above and beyond the Ayalon-Nusseibeh general set of principles, could be reached on all issues by well-meaning people from both sides. But even these moderates from both societies could not resolve the refugee conundrum. The refugee chapter in the accord was riddled with internal inconsistency and contradiction, in an unsuccessful attempt to bridge the gap between the Palestinian freedom of choice on refugee return and the sovereign right of Israel to control admission to its territory.

The Geneva Accord, as marketed by its Israeli signatories, recognized Israel as the state of the Jewish people, did not include a "right of return" of Palestinian refugees to Israel, and designated only Israel to decide on any entry of refugees to its territory. In other words, it solved the problems of two-state finality. But a careful examination of the text of the accord reveals that none of these assertions was actually true.[105]

On the "Jewish state," the Palestinians came close but in fact stopped short of specifically recognizing Israel as such, in contrast to the Ayalon-Nusseibeh declaration, which had done so unequivocally. (Geneva recognized "the right of the Jewish people to statehood" but stopped short of recognizing Israel as the state of the Jewish people. Had the Palestinians at Geneva been willing to accept what Sari Nusseibeh had endorsed a few months earlier, they could have done so. It was not as if the right wording was unknown.)

The Palestinian signatories to the accord also denied that they had conceded on the "right of return" as their Israeli partners claimed. Indeed, the term "right of return" did not appear in the accord, but as the Palestinian negotiators explained, the entire refugee section of the accord was based on UN General Assembly Resolution 194, which was universally interpreted by the Palestinians as an endorsement of the "right of return."[106] As for the decision on whether to return to Israel proper, that was to be made by three parties: the refugees themselves, Israel, and an international commission that was to be responsible for the execution of the refugee section. It would have been an amazing coincidence if refugee free choice corresponded with Israeli state policy. In the likely event that it did not, the international commission, which included the Arab host states to the refugees, would be the arbiter between Israel and the Palestinians. This was a recipe for endless wrangling and contention rather than a formula for end of conflict.[107]

## The Reversal of the Oslo Dynamic

In the meantime it was not the well-meaning moderates on both sides who took charge of the political scene. The left in Israel disintegrated under the onslaught of the Palestinian suicide bombers, and Israeli retribution led to the steady weakening of the PA and to the general degeneration of Palestinian governance. The disintegration of the peace process and the failure of the Palestinian state-in-the-making to actually achieve sovereignty served to strengthen the hand of the Israeli right and of Hamas in Palestinian politics, and to deal "an effective blow to the whole idea of a two-state solution."[108] Hamas reached a new peak of power in January 2006, when it handsomely won the elections to the Palestinian Legislative Assembly.

Hamas had never accepted the Oslo dynamic of ostensible prioritization of the "1967 file." In the years after the failure of Camp David, Hamas made a concerted effort to reverse the Oslo dynamic and refocus the Palestinian cause on the "1948 file" and the diaspora concerns to ensure that no finality could possibly be obtained on the basis of a resolution of the 1967 issues. A perusal of Palestinian documentation, formulated with Hamas input in recent years, reveals a very deliberate inversion of the Oslo dynamic, from the narrowing down to the West Bank and Gaza, to the broadening out again to the diaspora constituency and to a concentration on the primacy of the refugee question.

In June 2006, in what became known as the "Prisoners' Document," Fatah and Hamas representatives, as well as representatives from other minor organizations, who were serving sentences in Israeli jails on a wide variety of security-related offences, signed a Document of National Reconciliation. The parties emphasized not only the need to defend the rights of the refugees but also to reorganize them and to "hold a popular representative conference" that would create organizations "that would demand the right of return and the abidance by it, urging the international community to implement Resolution 194 stipulating the right of the refugees to return and to compensation."[109]

The policy statement of the Hamas-led government of national unity, which was formed by Isma'il Haniyya in March 2007, similarly emphasized the right of return and the implementation of Resolution 194, specifically noting "the right of the Palestinian refugees to return to the lands and properties that they had left," that is, to Israel proper. The statement also specified that any agreement reached by the PLO (which formally conducted the negotiations with Israel, not the PA) would have to be approved by the Palestinians in the West Bank and Gaza *and in the diaspora.*

Any such agreement would have to be brought before a new Palestine National Council (the PLO's quasi-parliamentary body, which represented all Palestinians everywhere, and would now have to include a significant representation of Hamas itself), or alternatively "a general referendum [on the agreement] would be held by the Palestinian people inside [the occupied territories] and outside [in the diaspora]. . . ."[110]

After a hiatus of twenty years, Fatah held its Sixth General Conference in Bethlehem in August 2009. In emphasizing the centrality of the diaspora, it followed Hamas's lead, not only in supporting the refugees' "right of return to their homes [diyarihim]," but in reinforcing their ties to and representation in the movement and their association with and sense of belonging to the homeland. Furthermore, Fatah believed that it was essential to maintain the refugee camps as the living testimony to the denial of the rights of the refugees to return to their homes, until such time as their problem was resolved by their "return to their homes and country [buyutihim wabiladihim]." It was similarly essential to that end to preserve UNRWA (the United Nations Relief and Works Agency) as the refugees' international address.[111]

Even the Arab summit, in its approval of the Arab Peace Initiative as passed in March 2002 and reaffirmed in March 2007, followed suit in this regard. The Arab Peace Initiative called for comprehensive peace between the Arab states and Israel on the basis of an Israeli withdrawal to the 1967 boundaries and for an agreed solution to the refugee question based on Resolution 194 and upon "the rejection of all forms of resettlement" of refugees.[112] Israel objected to this section of the initiative more than any other, but Israeli demands for its amendment were flatly rejected on the Arab side.[113]

It was never made clear whether this rejection of resettlement referred only to states outside of Palestine or whether the return of refugees to the future state of Palestine, but not to their original homes in Israel, would also be considered a form of unacceptable resettlement. Judging by the Palestinian discourse on the matter, one can only arrive at the conclusion that any solution other than the return of the refugees to their original homes in Israel proper would be considered as a form of illegitimate "resettlement" (tawtin).

After all, the Palestinians could hardly argue that the refugees (and their descendants), who have been residents of Gaza and of the West Bank since 1948, have actually "returned." Moreover, in Israel itself, the origins of some 130,000 to 250,000 of its Arab Palestinian citizens (or their forebears) are in other parts of Israel, from which they fled or were evicted in the 1948 war. Though they live in Israel and are citizens of the state, they are still considered by themselves and by their Palestinian compatriots as refugees, who similarly have a right to return "to their original villages and towns."[114]

Since the early 1990s, this has become a central issue on the political agenda of the Palestinian minority in Israel for a number of different reasons: the increasing attention given to the Nakba narrative by the younger generation of Palestinian Arab Israelis, who are more confrontational with the state than their parents; the signing of the Oslo Accords and the related discussion of the "right of return"; and the fiftieth anniversary of the Nakba in 1998. When Jews celebrate Israel's Independence Day, these internal refugees and other members of the community commemorate *Nakba* Day as an act of defiance against the state, by making pilgrimages to the sites of abandoned and destroyed villages, demanding to return there, and declaring that "your independence day—our day of catastrophe [*yawm istiqlalikum—yawm nakbatina*]."[115]

The resolutions of the Sixth Fatah General Conference referred to Fatah's "tireless efforts to realize the right of the refugees to return, to compensation and to the retrieval of their properties," adding that this referred to all refugees irrespective of their present places of residence "including the refugees in the lands of 1948 [*aradi '48*]," that is, Israel proper. In the name of the independent Palestinian identity, the resolutions similarly rejected "compulsory resettlement or the call for an alternative homeland; there will be no resettlement in Lebanon and no alternative homeland in Jordan."[116] There could be no question that in principle *tawtin* meant any solution other than return to the original homes of the refugees.

## Annapolis and the Abbas-Olmert Talks

In November 2007 direct Israeli-Palestinian negotiations were formally relaunched at an international conference convened under the auspices of President George Bush at Annapolis, ostensibly designed to lead to an agreement based on a two-state solution as outlined in the Quartet Roadmap of April 2003. President Abbas and Prime Minister Olmert started their negotiations a few months ahead of the conference and continued until the end of 2008, when Israel's "Cast Lead" operation in Gaza and the decision to go to early elections in Israel brought the negotiations to an end.

On the basis of the available information, one has to conclude that not much evolved in the stands of the parties since they were formulated at Camp David, in relation to the Clinton Parameters, and at Taba. Despite the repeated statements to the effect that they were "closer . . . than ever" to a peace accord,[117] it was clear from pronouncements by both sides that critical differences still remained on all issues.

As Olmert observed after the opening of the Annapolis conference, the idea was to have "two nation states." One would be the Jewish state of Israel and the other the Palestinian state, which would be "the natural place" to resettle "all the [Palestinian] refugees,"[118] that is, no right of return to Israel. As far as the Palestinians were concerned, quite the opposite was true. Abbas insisted that there had to be a right of return to Israel, which would have to absorb Palestinian refugees in its territory. What remained to be determined in his view was only the number.[119]

While the Palestinians accepted that Israel would have to agree to the number of returnees, the number itself, in the Palestinian scheme of things, would have to be large enough to accommodate a true exercise by the refugees of their free choice. No precise figure was ever formally announced, but it would have to be an approximation of the number that the Palestinians assessed would actually elect to return to Israel proper. An informal Palestinian contention made to the Israelis was that the number of refugees returning would definitely not exceed the Arab population of East Jerusalem (some 250,000 to 300,000), so the demographics would not shift substantially, if at all, if and when Jerusalem would be divided into the two capitals of the two states. All the same, the notion that about 150,000 refugees would return to Israel proper, presumably to their original homes or some variation of that notion, would probably not be accepted by any Israeli government in the foreseeable future.

On territory and Jerusalem, Olmert went beyond Israel's previous offers at Taba. Even according to Abbas, Olmert was offering the equivalent of 100 percent of the West Bank, if one included the land swaps.[120] As Sa'ib Ariqat observed, the Israeli positions on territory were steadily changing for the better, from 90 percent at Camp David to 100 percent now. "Why should we rush [falimadha nasta'jil]?"[121] Abbas subsequently asserted that he and Olmert had actually finalized an agreement on security issues. According to Olmert's associates, however, it was the Israelis and the United States that had arrived at such an agreement, which the Palestinians had hitherto not accepted.[122]

But it was on refugees that Israel's position was less forthcoming than ever. An interesting evolution was taking place. On the 1967 issues the gaps were steadily narrowing, both on land swaps and on the ethnically based partition of Jerusalem. The Palestinians were willing to accept most, but not all, of the new Jewish residential areas in Jerusalem remaining in Israel,[123] but on the "1948 file" the distance between the parties was forever increasing. Israel would not budge on refugees, as the Palestinians would not on the right of return or on recognizing Israel as a Jewish state. During the talks, Olmert rejected the right of return and instead made a "humanitarian gesture," which for the Palestinians was virtually meaningless. The gaps, said Abbas, were still very wide.[124]

According to Olmert, and confirmed by Sa'ib Ariqat, Olmert had proposed

figures far lower than the Israelis had suggested in previous rounds of negotiations. He suggested the return of 1,000 refugees a year for five years—just
5,000 altogether—on humanitarian grounds, which meant on the basis of a
decision made by Israel. According to the English version of a document compiled by Sa'ib Ariqat on the negotiations with Olmert, the Palestinian counter-
proposal was 15,000 refugees per year for 10 years—150,000 altogether—on
the basis of the right of return, which meant on the basis of a decision made by
the Palestinians. Thereafter, refugees would only be permitted to settle in Israel by agreement between the parties.[125]

In Arabic, however, Ariqat's version was substantially different, widening
the divide with the Israelis even further and reaffirming Pundak's observation
on the divergence between the private and the public stances taken on this
issue. Firstly, there was no limit to the number of refugees returning, according to the right of return; and secondly, it would be the refugees themselves
(that is, not Israel) who would have the right to choose between the following
options: (1) return to Israel; (2) return to the state of Palestine; (3) remaining
where they were or emigrating to somewhere else.[126] At least on paper, this
meant that the Israelis would be obliged to accept any number of refugees who
chose to return to Israel.

In January 2011, al-Jazeera television in cooperation with the London daily
The Guardian published the contents of a trove of classified Palestinian documents on the negotiations with Israel. According to this source, the Palestinians had suggested in late 2007 the return of ten thousand refugees a year for
ten years, that is, a total of one hundred thousand refugees to Israel proper.
Though this was not substantially different from most of the figures that had
been published before, the extraordinary media hype over the so-called "Palestine Papers"[127] deeply embarrassed the Palestinian negotiators, who were re-
soundingly condemned by Hamas and by other Palestinians in the West Bank
and Gaza and in the diaspora, and no less by The Guardian and al-Jazeera as
well. They were denounced for having totally capitulated to the Israelis by conceding the inalienable "right of return" of millions of Palestinian refugees.
The Palestinian negotiators, Mahmud Abbas and Sa'ib Ariqat, immediately
backtracked and dismissed the reports as "a pack of lies," flatly denying that
they had ever made such concessions.[128]

These revelations and the reactions to them only served to highlight the
abyss that separated Israelis and Palestinians on the refugee question. The Palestinian figures suggested at different times in this negotiation (100,000–

150,000) were twenty to thirty times higher than the number Olmert had proposed (5,000). Even these figures, as unacceptable as they were to the Israelis, were widely rejected and condemned by other Palestinians as a sellout, forcing the PA negotiators into a hasty retreat. No issue was as intractable as this one, and the chances for agreement acceptable to the publics on both sides were as remote as they had ever been.[129]

The Arab Peace Initiative spoke of an "agreed" solution to the refugee question and Mahmud Abbas conceded in internal Palestinian deliberations that "it [was] illogical" to expect the Israelis to accept the return of millions of refugees, which would completely undo their state.[130] On the other hand, the consistent Palestinian position emphasized the refugees' freedom of choice on whether to return or not, rather than Israel's agreement to admit them. These positions were not necessarily contradictory, provided the number of refugees that Israel agreed to admit would be commensurate with the number of the refugees who elected to return to Israel proper. This explains the focus in the negotiations on the precise figures. But even the most conservative Palestinian estimates of the numbers of refugees who might opt for return far exceeded what Israel was willing to accept, and thus the impasse.

Oddly enough, none other than Mahmud Abbas was quoted as having told the *Washington Post* that Olmert had actually accepted the principle of right of return and the resettling of some thousands of refugees in Israel, but Abbas turned the offer down, as the gaps were too wide.[131] In all likelihood, Olmert had not done so, and he consistently claims categorically that he had not recognized the right of return. But the fact that Abbas understood that he had, and rejected the concession as insufficient, casts serious doubt on the validity of the thesis espoused by many over the years that all the Palestinians really wanted was a recognition of their "right" as a symbolic gesture, which had no practical implications.

Israeli journalists asked Abbas whether it was clear to him that on the issue of the right of return, the refugees would return only to the areas of the Palestinian state. "Not at all," he replied. "The issue is not at all clear." After all, the refugees were originally "expelled from the area of Israel, not from the West Bank and Gaza."[132] The Palestinian position on refugees was consistent and straightforward. Many in Israel and elsewhere would continue, nevertheless, to argue and believe that this was no more than diplomatic maneuvering and bargaining. The evidence is overwhelmingly to the contrary.[133]

After elections in Israel elevated Benjamin Netanyahu to the premiership in early 2009, the Palestinians sought the resumption of negotiations from where they had left off with Olmert. At least two other problems had to be overcome, above and beyond the residual issues of substance. One was that the new Israeli government was not prepared to start from Olmert's concessions, but from scratch, and on this position the Israelis also had the support of the Obama administration.[134] The other was that President Abbas would find it extremely difficult to make concessions that Hamas would not acquiesce in, at least informally.

### Hamas, the Hudna, and the Fading Two-State Option

Hamas denounced the Oslo Accords and all that stemmed from them. The organization had never failed to state unequivocally that its ultimate objective was to liberate all of Palestine "from the [Jordan] River to the [Mediterranean] Sea." All the same, in practice, it has not entirely rejected some version of the two-state idea, albeit as a temporary arrangement. When the first elections were held for the Legislative Assembly in the PA in 1996, Hamas boycotted them on the grounds that they were being held under the illegitimate auspices of the Oslo Accords. But in 2006, sensing a chance to do well, Hamas chose to participate in the elections for the very same Legislative Assembly even though, as before, it represented only the West Bank and Gaza and not all of Palestine. The rather lame Hamas pretext for this change of heart was that by then the Oslo Accords were essentially defunct.[135]

On numerous occasions Hamas spokesmen have endorsed the notion of a hudna (armistice or truce) with Israel. It is worth remembering in this context that the armistice agreements Israel signed with the Arab states in early 1949, which put an end to first Arab-Israeli war and which lasted for nearly twenty years, until 1967, were also known in Arabic as hudna. Consideration by Hamas of a hudna with Israel originated in the early 1990s shortly after the signing of the Oslo Accords. The Amman-based chairman of the Hamas Political Bureau, Musa Abu Marzuq, made a statement in that vein to the organ of the Jordanian Muslim Brethren, al-Sabil. At about the same time, Shaykh Ahmad Yasin, the founder of Hamas, then in prison in Israel, issued a similar statement suggesting a truce between Palestinians and Israelis as an interim solution to the conflict.[136]

The hudna, as opposed to the Oslo Accords, would not involve any recognition of Israel and would last for a set period of time to be agreed by the parties.

Usually they spoke of ten years.[137] The Hamas conditions for only a ten-year *hudna* were similar to and even less flexible than those offered to Israel by the PLO for a final settlement (thus, no flexibility or nuance on refugee return, no land swaps, no concessions in Jerusalem). Hamas demanded the establishment of a fully sovereign independent Palestinian state in the West Bank and Gaza, within the 1967 boundaries, with its capital in Arab Jerusalem, the dismantling of all the settlements in the West Bank (including the new Jewish residential areas in Jerusalem), and Israeli consent to the return of the refugees to their homes.[138]

In March 2007, the short-lived national unity government (which Hamas and Fatah cobbled together until the forceful takeover of Gaza by Hamas in June of that year) issued its policy statement. The government called for a "fully sovereign independent Palestinian state on all the territories occupied in 1967 with Jerusalem as its capital." The statement also stressed the government's commitment to the right of return of the Palestinian refugees to the lands and properties that they had abandoned (that is, not to somewhere in the homeland in general, but to the specific homes in Israel proper). The government, however, would only "respect" (*ihtiram*) rather than "commit" (*iltizam*) itself to the accords signed in the past by the PLO, which meant that Hamas remained faithful to its rejection of the Oslo Accords and the recognition of Israel.[139]

On June 25, 2009, in one of the more clearly articulated statements by the Hamas leadership, Khalid Mash'al, chairman of Hamas's Damascus-based Political Bureau, elaborated on the Hamas position on Palestinian statehood. First of all, Mash'al flatly rejected all of Israel's conditions on Jerusalem, the right of return, settlements, and demilitarization of the future Palestinian state. Similarly, he rejected "the so-called 'Jewishness' of Israel" and reaffirmed that "the plan, which constitutes our people's bare minimum, which we accepted in the Document of National Reconciliation as a joint political plan of all the Palestinian forces, is the establishment of a Palestinian state, with Jerusalem as its capital, with full sovereignty within the June 4, 1967 borders, after the withdrawal of the occupation forces, the removal of all the settlements, and the realization of the right of return." The right of the Palestinian refugees to return to their homes, "from which they were driven out in 1948, is both a general, national right and an individual right—the personal prerogative of over five million refugees," and "no leader or negotiator is allowed to downplay or waive this right."[140]

Though Hamas was inching toward an acceptance of two states, there was no question of whether such a two-state settlement implied finality. Hamas had no objection to the acceptance of the 1967 borders as an interim solution (*hall marhali*),[141] that is, as a way station to a one-state solution in which there was no place for Israel. All Israelis were settlers, and all of Israel was composed of settlements. Hamas made no distinction "between what was occupied in the 1940s and what was occupied in the 1960s" and refused to recognize Israel under any circumstances.[142] There was no vacillation or ambiguity and no philosophizing on "relative" or "pragmatic" justice. Israel was an abomination that Hamas rejected unequivocally.

Meanwhile in Fatah there was new thinking that actually narrowed the differences with Hamas. The failure of the Camp David–Taba process, followed by Israeli unilateralism under Prime Minister Ariel Sharon, the fruitless negotiations between Ehud Olmert and Mahmud Abbas, the more intensive international and local discourse on the one-state option during the last decade, and relentless Israeli settlement activity have all given rise in Fatah to a reassessment and to a formal revival of the one-state option.

The resolutions of the Sixth Fatah General Conference held in August 2009 referred to this option in different contexts. If the present efforts for negotiations failed to achieve desirable results, one option could be to revive "the idea of the unitary democratic state, which would reject racism, hegemony and occupation, and would develop the struggle against Israeli apartheid and racism." Another option could be "[unilaterally] declaring the establishment of the [Palestinian] state on the 1967 boundaries." In reference to the forms of struggle employed by the Palestinians against Israel, the resolutions noted that not all means were legitimate. This was particularly so if such measures ran counter to some of the movement's long-term goals, like the "future coexistence between Muslims, Christians and Jews in one democratic state."[143]

For the Palestinians, the two-state solution was never an ideal but an acceptance of an undesirable and fundamentally illegitimate reality, and was therefore never more than "relative" or "pragmatic" justice. "Pragmatic" by definition was not a fixed or permanent principle, but changed with time and circumstance. What was "pragmatic" at one stage might not be at another. Positions were therefore as fluid as the changing reality that was forever on the move, somewhere on the continuum between the status quo and "historical justice."

Whatever Israel offered, even if insufficient for an agreement, would become "a concrete basis for future negotiations, which would have to pick up" where the last round left off.[144] Each round formed a new status quo that only existed in order to be altered, as it too, like its predecessors, was no more than "relative" justice. The new status quo thus immediately became the starting point for another, different, "pragmatically" just solution that would push Israel back a little further until "historical justice" or something very close to it would finally be attained.

This was a state of mind that was always ready to change course, if and when the opportunity arose. And if the opportunity did not present itself, the new status quo would remain, and many (though clearly not all) could probably live with that too. But in principle, for the Palestinians, the two-state solution was "pragmatic" and thus open-ended, by definition. For Israel, it could not be anything but the unequivocal point final. It is here, on this point, that we encounter the underlying cause for the prolonged stalemate.

As Hussein Agha and Robert Malley have observed, the parties had never seriously contended with the core 1948 issues, aiming to fully resolve the problems that were at the root of the conflict. Essentially they restricted themselves to a process locked onto undoing the 1967 occupation, which was not the real cause of the conflict and therefore not enough to bring it to an end. The Palestinians "hoped they could achieve their goals even as they persisted in denying the Jewish people's entitlement to even part of the land; Israelis trusted that if they granted Palestinians some kind of state the whole problem would fade away. . . . Failure to deal with basic issues guaranteed their reemergence whenever the parties inched closer to a deal and recoiled from the implications of that last, fateful step. . . . Palestinians were not truly prepared to stipulate that the conflict has been terminated and all claims set aside solely in exchange for an end to the occupation, and . . . Israel was not prepared to end its occupation in exchange for less."[145]

A Palestinian leader could "not credibly proclaim that the conflict has come to a close if the solution ignores the genesis of the Palestinian plight and the historic core of its national cause. To adopt such a stand would be tantamount to conceding that the refugees . . . had waged six decades of struggle by mistake and endured six decades of suffering in vain. . . . An Israeli leader offering more to the Palestinians than what Prime Minister Olmert proposed would be accused of caving in; a Palestinian leader accepting less than what President Abbas rejected would be condemned for selling out."[146] Making the two-state idea into a reality on the ground has hitherto proved to be an impossible mission.

# 3

## ISRAEL AND THE
## TWO-STATE PARADIGM

*From Reluctant Acquiescence to Self-Interest*

The complex and convoluted acceptance by the Palestinians of the two-state idea in 1988 was eventually matched in the 1990s by Israel's somewhat less convoluted but equally reluctant acceptance of independent Palestinian statehood. For decades Israel had firmly rejected the notion, though there were occasional digressions. During the 1948 war, Israel did, albeit briefly, consider the option of an independent Palestinian state. It was clear from the pre-war deliberations between the Zionists and the Hashemites that the Zionists preferred partition to be effected by Jordanian annexation of what was left of Arab Palestine.

However, as the 1948 war ground to an end, the Israelis had momentary second thoughts. After Jordan's active participation in the war, its annexation of the West Bank was no longer regarded by the Israeli leadership as a foregone conclusion. In the summer of 1948, the Israelis seriously considered the option of an independent Palestinian state. Foreign Minister Moshe Sharett was of the opinion that Israel "ought to prefer the establishment of an independent Arab State in Western Palestine" to the option of annexation by Jordan, even if only as a negotiating tactic with King Abdallah.[1]

But beyond tactics, Ben-Gurion and Sharett shared the assessment that in the longer run Iraq might swallow Jordan, and if Jordan annexed the West Bank, in the future the Israelis would find Iraq "on our border at Qalqilya and Wadi Ara." Ben-Gurion did not think much of King Abdallah either. "It was clear, the man had no substance," he noted.[2] In any event, no realistic Palestinian option was in the offing. When the war began, there were no Palestinians of stature who would countenance compromise. By the time the war was over, the Palestinians were in such disarray that there were no Palestinians of stature who could deliver on any agreement even if there were to be one. For lack of any better choice, Israel came to terms with Jordan's annexation of what became the "West Bank," which remained part of the Hashemite Kingdom of Jordan until the union was undone by the 1967 war.

The war of 1967 was a historical watershed in Israeli domestic politics too. After the seemingly miraculous deliverance, "the secular and the pragmatic began to give way to the apocalyptic and eschatological. . . . In this way some lost sight of the original mission, which had been about saving and redeeming people and instead became about holding and redeeming land."[3]

In the wake of Israel's stunning victory, various prescriptions for the future of the "administered" or "liberated" territories were hotly but inconclusively debated in the Israeli body politic. One thing, however, was certain: the Six Day War had "undermined the Israeli majority's two-state outlook."[4] On June 19, 1967, the Israeli cabinet passed a resolution according to which Israel would return the territories occupied from Egypt and Syria in exchange for peace treaties.[5] The resolution, however, said nothing about the West Bank and Gaza. The use of terminology alone already indicated that, in the Israeli scheme of things, since these "territories" were anything but "occupied," a return to the status quo ante was not an option.

## Trapped Between the Jordanian Option and the Absorption of Arab Palestine

In the immediate aftermath of the war, Yigal Allon, one of Israel's outstanding generals of the 1948 war and deputy prime minister in Levi Eshkol's cabinet, presented a plan that envisaged the annexation of substantial swaths of West Bank territory, in the Jordan Valley and the Judean Desert, which would entail only a minimal annexation of Arab population. This, Allon argued, would enhance the country's security and defensibility on its eastern front, without undermining its Jewish character.

A corridor through Jericho would link the densely populated interior of the West Bank with Jordan to the east. Originally the Allon Plan envisaged autonomy for the Arab population, but after that was turned down by the Palestinians in the occupied territories, the plan was adapted to have the remainder of the West Bank returned to Jordan in a negotiated settlement. The Allon Plan was never formally adopted as Israeli policy, but under Labor-led governments until 1977 it did determine the location of Israeli settlements in the West Bank, especially in the Jordan Valley, while deliberately avoiding the densely populated highlands.[6]

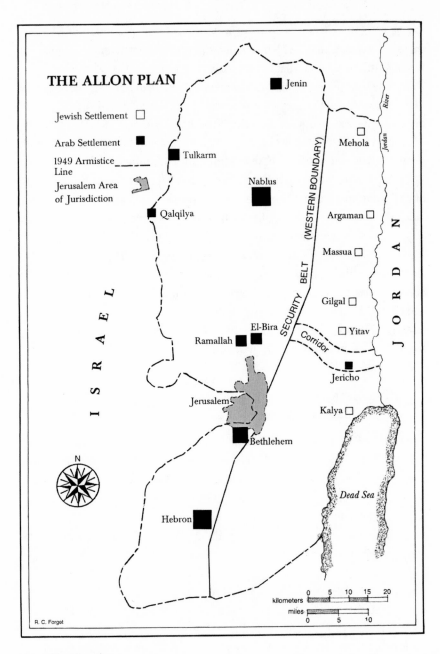

Map 5. The Allon Plan

The Allon Plan also became the basis for the so-called "Jordanian option," that is, a territorial compromise with Jordan over the West Bank. The Jordanians were quite willing to negotiate the future of the West Bank with Israel, but not on the basis of a territorial compromise. To justify their role at the expense of the Palestinians and the PLO, the Jordanians felt that they could hardly concede on large tracts of territory that the PLO and many other Palestinians argued fervently was not Jordan's to dispense with in the first place.

The Jordanians were not interested in a truncated West Bank and would settle for nothing less than all of the West Bank and Arab Jerusalem, with no more than minor, reciprocal border rectifications. Though successive Labor-led governments espoused the "Jordanian option,"[7] they never offered the territorial arrangement that might have made it possible. For Husayn, it had to be all or nothing. He told the Israelis in no uncertain terms, in September 1968, that anything else was "wholly unacceptable."[8] Allon's ideas preserved the notion of partition, albeit in substantially different territorial contours. However other ideas, which superseded partition, were not only promoted, but by the second decade of the occupation, had gained the upper hand, albeit by default rather than by deliberate decision.

In the summer of 1968, the Eshkol government put out feelers to the Palestinian leadership in the West Bank to examine the possibility of some form of Palestinian autonomy under continued Israeli control. Since the local Palestinian leadership, mostly mayors from the larger towns, had never been authorized to speak for the Palestinian people, they consulted the main external powers of the day, Jordan and the PLO. Both of these had aspirations of their own as far as the occupied territories were concerned. The local leaders were, therefore, instructed in no uncertain terms to refrain from any dealings whatsoever with Israel that went beyond the daily management of the needs of the population under occupation. The talks on autonomy, therefore, went nowhere.[9]

More significant in its lasting impact was the thinking of Moshe Dayan as it developed in the aftermath of the Six Day War. In late 1968, two dominant ministers in the Eshkol cabinet, Defense Minister Dayan and Finance Minister Pinhas Sapir, clashed head-on over policy in the occupied territories. Dayan believed in the integration of the West Bank and Gaza into the Israeli economy, to create a system in which Israelis and Palestinians lived together in one economic unit, though they would simultaneously belong to different political entities. Diplomatic stalemate after the war was a golden opportunity for

Dayan to urge the government to accept his vision of "'digesting' Judea and Samaria."[10]

This came to be known as a "functional," as opposed to territorial, solution, whereby Israel provided security and controlled the economy while the Palestinians would exercise their political rights in some form of autonomy, presumably attached to Jordan. The Palestinians would live in a sovereign Israeli framework but would be citizens of and would vote in another country. Thus Israel would control the territory but, at least in theory, would not upset the demographic balance in the country.

Sapir spurned Dayan's vision and was quite content with a Jewish state in borders not very different from the old Green Line. Sapir believed in the need to preserve Israel's Jewish character, and he argued that the incorporation of the Palestinian population of the West Bank and Gaza, together with the Palestinian Arab minority in Israel, would create an Arab minority equal to 40 percent of the total population. Considering the natural increase differential, it would not take long in such circumstances for the Arabs to become the majority in the country.[11] Sapir presciently warned all those who would listen that if Israel held on to the territories, in the end the territories would take hold of Israel. No formal decisions were adopted in the cabinet for or against Dayan or Sapir. In practice, however, in the absence of annexation or withdrawal, over time it was Dayan's integrationist scheme that was implemented, linking the economies and the infrastructures of the occupied territories and Israel. "Dayan's 'integration' plan . . . remained as a blueprint of what would happen, bit by bit,"[12] until the first Intifada upset the Israeli applecart.

The integrationist policies that were conducted by Labor-led governments, with limited Jewish settlement, mainly along the lines of the Allon Plan, never satisfied the new militant messianic right that arose in the aftermath of the 1967 victory. The Revisionist Zionist right coalesced with a revivalist religious Zionism to pressure for Jewish settlement throughout the West Bank. For them, the victory was perceived as divine deliverance. Their desire was to hasten the permanent integration of all the territory into Israel and to make eventual withdrawal impossible, and they were often successful in imposing their will on hesitant Labor governments.[13]

The rise of the Likud to power in 1977 was a strategic shift in terms of settlement policy and the entire notion of partition. The pace of settlement quickened, in line with the Likud's ideological devotion to Greater Eretz Yisrael.[14] Dayan's integrationist perceptions were welcomed by the new Likud government that Dayan was invited by Prime Minister Menachem Begin to join as foreign minister. Begin, of the Revisionist right, like Dayan of the Labor movement, albeit for more ideological and less security-driven pragmatic reasoning, did not believe in partition. Ariel Sharon, Begin's minister of agriculture, who ridiculed the demographic argument against the settlements, was the chief of operations of the accelerated settlement drive.[15]

The Camp David Accords between Begin and President Anwar Sadat of Egypt, which were signed in September 1978, did not weaken Israel's hold over the West Bank and Gaza. Israel for the very first time recognized the "legitimate rights of the Palestinian people and their just requirements." Israel even came close to acknowledging the Palestinians' right to self-determination by recognizing the right of the Palestinians to participate in the "determination of their own future."[16] Begin's critics accused him at the time of laying the groundwork for a Palestinian state. Neither Begin, however, nor his key ministers Dayan and Sharon, had any such intention.

Within the framework of the integrity of Eretz Yisrael, Begin, like Dayan, believed in some form of Palestinian self-government in the West Bank and Gaza, in association with Jordan, which would be negotiated with the participation of Egypt and Jordan and Palestinians from the West Bank and Gaza. Begin's worldview could accept "administrative self-rule," under Israeli sovereign control, but he always stopped short of accepting foreign sovereignty in any part of the country. The self-rule ideas never came to fruition. Limited self-government as pursued by Begin[17] and as proposed in the Camp David process was passionately rejected by Jordan and the Palestinians as woefully unsatisfactory. But some of the ideas that were first aired in these accords, such as transitional self-government, were later incorporated into the Oslo Accords.

In the summer of 1982 Israel invaded Lebanon with the main objective of crushing the PLO as a relevant political and military force and thus to pave the way for Israel's indefinite and unfettered absorption of the West Bank into Israel. In Sharon's grand design, the Lebanon War was intended to create a fundamentally new regional reality. The demolition of the PLO in Lebanon and the installation of a friendly Maronite-dominated government in the country were expected to create the conditions that would induce the Palestinians in Lebanon to leave for Jordan.

According to Sharon's plan, the absorption of the West Bank into Israel would similarly generate an exodus of Palestinians to Jordan. The demographic pressure of these new waves of Palestinian refugees would sweep away the Hashemite regime, and Jordan would evolve in practice into the alternative homeland of the Palestinian people, in accordance with the contention of Sharon and others on the Israeli right that "Jordan was Palestine."[18]

But the plan, as is the wont of such grand designs, went haywire. In the immediate wake of the PLO's expulsion from Lebanon, on September 1, 1982, US president Ronald Reagan published an initiative over which the United States had consulted with Jordan, but not with Israel and certainly not with the PLO. The Reagan initiative was an effort to "transform the debris" of the Lebanon War into a "resumption of the unfinished business" of Camp David.[19] It did not recognize the PLO or the idea of a Palestinian state, but it also specifically ruled out Israeli annexation of the occupied territories.[20] The United States sought to take advantage of the PLO's setback to reactivate a pivotal role for King Husayn, by suggesting the establishment of Palestinian self-government in the West Bank and Gaza, in association with Jordan.

This was very much along the lines of King Husayn's own federation plan published a decade earlier, and there could be little doubt that the Jordanians had been involved in the formulation of the US initiative. The Israelis, however, flatly rejected it. Begin and Sharon had gone to war to secure Israel's long-term control of the West Bank and Gaza, not to cede them to the Jordanians, or to anyone else for that matter.[21]

Though militarily successful, having secured the expulsion of the PLO from Lebanon, the war turned into a major political disaster for the Israeli government, both at home and abroad. The Israelis were already at loggerheads with their major ally, the United States, when further calamity struck. Israel's major Maronite partner, Bashir Jumayyil, was assassinated on September 14 by Syrian operatives, after which Maronite militiamen carried out a horrific massacre of hundreds of Palestinians in the Beirut refugee camps of Sabra and Shatila. The massacre brought on an avalanche of opprobrium on the Israeli government, from within Israel and without, for allowing such an atrocity to take place in an area that was ostensibly under IDF control.

Begin was out of his depth in the conduct of the war. He was misled and manipulated by Sharon, and he was not privy to all aspects of Sharon's "ambitious geopolitical scenario" either.[22] The Israeli public was deeply divided over the war and its conduct, and consequently large sectors of the liberal left felt that Israel's losses were an unjustifiable tragedy in this unwanted "war of choice." The Lebanon War left Begin a broken man, and his career was brought to an "unedifying close." Sharon was disgraced by the Sabra-Shatila fiasco, and his subsequent censure by an Israeli commission of inquiry banished him from the senior leadership of Israeli politics for more than a decade.[23]

In retrospect, the early 1980s, with Begin and Sharon at the helm, were the zenith of official Israeli "one-statism." These were also the years during which Gush Emunim (Bloc of the Faithful), the religious settler movement, was at the apex of its power. The war in Lebanon, however, was not only the peak of "one-stater" influence in Israeli strategic decision making, but also the beginning of its fall from grace, together with its major political protagonists. Dayan had passed away before the war, in 1981. For much of the 1980s, as of the July 1984 elections, Israel was no longer governed exclusively by the right, but by more or less evenly balanced Likud-Labor "national unity" coalitions, in which Gush Emunim's influence was reduced. During these years the establishment of new settlements in the occupied territories slowed down, but not the growth of existing ones.[24]

In these governments, the proponents of Greater Eretz Yisrael had to share power with their ideological foes who still sought a territorial compromise with Jordan. However, for the entire period from late 1983 until mid-1992, apart from a two-year hiatus (1984–86), Yitzhak Shamir, who had succeeded Begin at the head of the Likud, was Israel's prime minister. Shamir had virtually no interest in negotiations that would mean conceding any part of Greater Eretz Yisrael, and he worked hard to ensure that no proposals based on the principal of land for peace would get anywhere. In April 1987, Shimon Peres (Labor), the foreign minister in Shamir's cabinet, arrived at a secret understanding with King Husayn of Jordan, facilitated by the United States, on the procedural modalities for the convening of an international Middle East peace conference. The so-called London Agreement was scuttled by the Shamir cabinet, and the last gasp of a somewhat refined "Jordanian Option" met with dismal failure.[25]

The Intifada that erupted a few months later, in December 1987, brought home to Israelis the enormous political and moral costs of the continued occupation of millions of Palestinians and of the need to find some form of accommodation with burgeoning Palestinian nationalism. It was now obvious to an ever-growing segment of the Israeli body politic that Greater Eretz Yisrael was not only unattainable, but not even desirable.

The Intifada influenced many Israelis to reach the conclusion that the settlements had been a strategic mistake from the point of view of Israel's vital interests. The settlements locked Israel into an engagement with territories that actually undermined Israel's long-term well-being as a state with a stable Jewish majority, which was, after all, the essential raison d'etre of the entire Zionist enterprise. The majority of Israelis did not view the preservation of the settlements as a contribution to Israeli security. Nor did they equate the interests of the settlers with those of the state in general.[26]

King Husayn's announcement of Jordan's disengagement from the West Bank in July 1988 made it equally clear that the "Jordanian option" was dead and buried. The essential conclusion was that negotiations over the future of the West Bank and Gaza would have to be held with the Palestinians, which in itself meant an eventual acceptance of Palestinian statehood. Negotiating directly with Palestinians, in the long run, could hardly mean anything else.

The political right in Israel remained adamantly opposed to any territorial compromise. In the 1988 election campaign, the Likud platform contended that any withdrawal from the West Bank and Gaza would lead "ineluctably to the establishment of a Palestinian state" that would threaten the "existence of the State of Israel."[27] After the election, a new national unity government was established with Shamir as prime minister and Yitzhak Rabin of Labor as his minister of defense.

In May 1989 the cabinet approved a plan for negotiations with an elected leadership of the West Bank and Gaza for the establishment of Palestinian self-rule in these territories. The plan was denounced by the far right as a precursor to the establishment of a Palestinian state. Shamir himself was not that far from the positions of the critics from the right, but he also had to contend with the other segments of the Israeli body politic as well as the pressure from the United States and the wider international community to show moderation. Shamir's tactical approach, however, was to "formally agree to positions and then drag out any negotiations by an eternal diplomatic stonewalling."[28]

The Likud-Labor coalition fell apart in early 1990, and in the new Shamir-led purely right-wing coalition, Ariel Sharon was appointed minister of housing, strategically placed to embark on the construction of new settlements and the expansion of old ones in the occupied territories. Settlement activity increased apace, even at the price of a crisis with the US administration over loan guarantees for the financing of the absorption of the massive immigration from the Soviet Union. According to a Peace Now estimate, settlement construction in 1991 cost $1.1 billion, which was a hidden section of the budget for which government and parliamentary approval was neither sought nor given. The settlement frenzy, however, did not prevent Shamir from acceding to the US post–Gulf War initiative for an international Middle East peace conference, which eventually took place in Madrid in October 1991. Shamir went along with the proceedings of Madrid, but this was just another round of his stonewalling tactics designed to draw out negotiations indefinitely. Even so, it proved too much for the far right, and they withdrew from the coalition, leading to early elections in the summer of 1992.[29]

In the new elections, Labor, led by Yitzhak Rabin, won for the first time in fifteen years. Shamir seemed old and out of touch with the electorate, much of which, especially in the wake of the Intifada, wanted a normal life more than Greater Eretz Yisrael. In the election campaign, labor had attacked the disproportionate investment in settlements and the complications this policy had caused in the relationship with the United States. At the time, 57 percent of Israelis actually favored a settlement freeze. Interestingly, however, some of those who did not favor settlement expansion or the notion of Greater Eretz Yisrael did not vote for the left.

In fact, in Labor's election victory, a majority of Israeli Jews had voted for right-wing or for orthodox religious parties that tended to align themselves with the right. Rabin's majority therefore also rested on the Arab vote. The orthodox parties, who were not ideologically Zionist, were not averse to joining center-left coalitions, and one of them, Shas, did indeed take part in Rabin's coalition. The left wing of Rabin's coalition, the Meretz Party, pressed Rabin to negotiate with the PLO as did his foreign minister Shimon Peres and other Labor members of Knesset, supported by nearly half of the Israeli public.[30] Rabin's parliamentary majority, however, was precarious from the outset, and making far-reaching concessions to the Palestinians was bound to face strong opposition from the right, especially from its radical nationalist religious core.

## The "Lords of the Land": Israel's Radical Right

While a majority of the Israeli public was coming to terms with some variant of Palestinian statehood, the militant religious right, the heart and soul of the settler movement, did all in its power to ensure that such a state would never be established in the West Bank and Gaza.[31] The more radical proponents of the one-state Greater Eretz Yisrael solution—such as the Moledet (Homeland) Party, which espoused Arab population transfer, or the Techiya (Revival) Party, who were ardent supporters of the settler movement,[32] or their later mutations such as Habayit Hayehudi or the National Union Party—never progressed much beyond the far right-wing margins of the Israeli body politic. But irrespective of its minority status, the militant right succeeded in an extraordinary turn of events to successfully manipulate the political system and impose its own agenda on a series of either feckless or partially cooperative governments and on a largely uninvolved general public.

Israel's messianic religious right grew out of the new political landscape of the country that coalesced in the wake of the overwhelming and unexpected victory in the Six Day War. The war changed Israel's geopolitical paradigm and cultural ecology and lent credibility to messianic religious thinking. The victory was an event of mythic proportions that could be seen as a heavenly message from God.[33] Religious radicals who believed they were "fulfilling God's plan for history" played the central role in the evolution of a new radical right. They were initially buttressed by some on Israel's ideological left who were tempted by the revived possibility of Zionist control of all of Eretz Yisrael. Without intending to do so, these moderates "helped beget the religious settler movement, and then were stunned by it."[34]

For secular Jewish nationalists, Zionism was the modernist heir to religion. "Labor Zionism regarded itself as the successor to Judaism." For the post-1967 religious ultranationalists, Zionism was a radically different cause. For them, Zionism was transformed into theology. Religious redemption of the people would be attained through militant nationalism and the redemption of the land, all of it, in the name of God. The victory of 1967 was no chance turn of events but "a major step forward in the messianic process that started with the birth of modern Zionism." These were diametrically opposed worldviews that represented two totally different visions of Israel. For the believers, those on the left who argued for compromise in the name of immediate considerations of *realpolitik* had "no sense of Jewish history" and were unaware of "the full significance of the current era of redemption."[35]

For the classical Zionists, the Jewish majority state was the raison d'etre of the movement, and if partition was essential to secure that aim, in the face of Arab numbers and resistance, it was perfectly legitimate. For the post-1967 religious zealots, Jewish sovereignty over all of the land was integral to their eternal covenant with God.[36]

The settlers liked to compare themselves to the pre-state pioneers whose settlements laid the foundation for Israel's creation.[37] The comparison, however, was specious. The pre-state effort was designed to create a state for the

Jews in Eretz Yisrael / Palestine and, as of the mid-1930s, was directed, for all practical purposes, toward partition. In contrast, the post-1967 effort was not designed to secure the Jewish state in Eretz Yisrael, but to transform all of historical Palestine into the Jewish state, and in so doing to deliberately deny the Palestinians a state of their own and to make partition, or a two-state solution, impossible.[38]

In the words of Israeli author, and classical Zionist, Amos Oz, "the Zionist enterprise has no other objective justification than the right of a drowning man to grasp the only plank that can save him." That right justified only grabbing a place on the plank, not pushing others off. It gave a moral basis to partitioning the land, not for taking it all.[39] For the pre-state Zionist leadership, propaganda aside, the Arabs of the country were a national force to be reckoned with.[40] For the post-1967 national religious settlers, the Arabs were foreign interlopers whose national and civil rights could be glossed over from the perch of the highest moral ground prescribed by God Almighty. The Arabs would have to choose between submission to this divinely inspired Jewish order or emigration to any one of the many Arab states that already existed. Some in the radical right spoke in terms of recognition of the human and civil rights of the Arabs as creatures of God, equal to all, while others resorted to the extreme terms of expulsion. A lunatic fringe even considered annihilation. Generally the controversial subject of the Arabs was conveniently ignored by the radical right.[41]

From the very earliest days after the occupation in 1967, the Israeli government implemented a policy of "creating facts" on the ground, presumably as assets in a future negotiation. Just weeks after the end of the war, Jerusalem was unified as Israel's "eternal capital." Ever since, Israeli building in and around the city has continued under the official auspices of all Israeli governments without exception, leading to the settlement of some 250,000 Israelis in these new residential areas, and almost completely cutting off Arab Jerusalem from the West Bank.

In the government's haste to get things done in the immediate aftermath of the 1967 war, with a cabinet that was internally divided and with a disapproving international community, bending the rules and deception became common practice when it came to building settlements. Government officials and cabinet ministers allowed themselves to defy the laws of the country they served, in Jerusalem and elsewhere, in the name of their duty to the state. They created a paradigm that was to be perfected and enlarged upon by the religious settlers for decades thereafter, in the West Bank in particular. At times the creation of facts in the West Bank worked from the bottom up as activists pulled in sympathetic officials and officers, "intent on dragging the government after them."[42] The victory of 1967 was a triumph of the state that the secularists had built, but the process of settlement after 1967 in the occupied territories led to the gradual unraveling of that state, "blurring its borders, undercutting its authority."[43]

The settlers also eroded the state's foreign policy. For the religious right, what the "gentiles" thought about Israel was immaterial in comparison to their own inner truth. Israel's international isolation was of no concern to them; on the contrary, it was only more reason to pursue their own agenda, regardless and undeterred. In the minds of Israel's religious radicals, the secular Zionists had been wrong from the outset seeking to become a normal and accepted member of the community of nations. International isolation was God's will; otherwise the Jews would assimilate and lose their uniqueness.[44]

In the initial years of the state, Israel's first prime minister, David Ben-Gurion, spoke of the need to apply the principle of mamlakhtiyut (stateness, or state-like behavior), which meant the unqualified sovereignty and supremacy of the institutions of the secular state, the rule of law, and the state's unquestioned monopoly over the use of force. In their enthusiasm to impose their will on the state, in the name of God, the post 1967 religious settlers eroded both the rule of law and the state's monopoly over the use of force and thus undermined two of the critical pillars of the original state-building enterprise of Israel's founding fathers. "Perhaps the greatest irony of the settlements" was that they "frayed the Jewish state." Instead of continuing the consolidation of Israel, after 1967 the process was reversed. "A generation that built the state began unintentionally removing stones from its structure. The attempt to relive the bright anarchy of youth undid their accomplishments."[45]

Since the government had systematically avoided making any decisions on the future of the West Bank, "postponement became policy." The government could not answer, even for itself, the question that US president Lyndon Johnson put to Israeli prime minister Levi Eshkol: What kind of Israel do you want? The vacuum left by the lack of any guiding strategy became fertile ground for those who wished to impose their views on an indecisive leadership.[46]

In contrast to those who avoided making the necessary historical choices, the minds of the new religious Zionists were firmly made up for them by their rabbinical authorities. They were determined to ensure that no Israeli government would make any territorial concessions, even if it was democratically elected to do so. Between them and their opponents in the Israeli body politic there was a fundamental asymmetry. The radicals could establish wildcat settlements and thus create facts. Their opponents could not carry out wildcat withdrawals, or dismantle settlements.[47] That only the state itself could do, but the state had to show the resolve to take on the radicals. With few noteworthy exceptions, it failed to do so.

For the "lords of the land," settlement in all the homeland was a "supreme imperative" that took "precedence even over orders and decisions of the government." They were quick to learn, already with their initially unauthorized settlement of Hebron in 1968 "that confrontation and defiance worked wonders. For the Israeli public, it was evidence that the government was unwilling to enforce the law against those who broke it in the name of nationalism." Theirs was an ideology of illegalism.[48] For the settlers, Eretz Yisrael took precedence over the State of Israel, and the law of the land could be flouted with impunity. In their worldview, the settlement of Eretz Yisrael was the most distinguished Zionist and Jewish virtue. "Neither law nor any principle" of good governance could possibly match it. As for the state, more than deciding on settlement, "the government drifted into permitting it."[49]

After the Yom Kippur War of 1973, Labor assumed a more dovish posture, openly willing to accept territorial compromise and to engage in a peace process with the neighboring Arab states. The government was exposed ever more to the pressure tactics of the settlers, which were honed into a fine art by the Gush Emunim religious settler movement in the mid-1970s. In the view of their leaders, the government had "no right to prevent individuals and groups from living in any place on the soil of the homeland." For Gush Emunim, compromise became equivalent to blasphemy and treason. Even some in the government, like Defense Minister Peres, found it difficult to resist their "ethic of illegalism," which "valued patriotic purpose over the rule of law." Gush Emunim was thus given a helping hand by some ministers within the cabinet to coerce the government to allow them to settle near Nablus, in the heart of the densely populated West Bank. This undermined the express policy of the government, proving to the country that the government was weak, that Gush Emunim was strong, and that the old policy had been overthrown.[50]

During the first decade after 1967, until Labor lost power in May 1977, some eleven thousand Israelis (excluding East Jerusalem) settled in the occupied territories.[51] The small numbers, however, were just part of the story. It was under

Labor rule that the die was cast, the boundaries between legal and illegal were blurred, and the way was opened to increased settlement under governments of the right. In the period between the Likud rise to power in 1977 and the signing of the Oslo Accords, the number of settlers in the occupied territories increased tenfold to over one hundred thousand.

Gush Emunim developed an effective lobbying system in Israel's civil service as well as in the senior political elite, thereby building up "a pervasive system of second level support." During the 1980s they also developed an extremely effective and active lobby in the Knesset.[52] Settler determination was more than most of Israel's governments could handle. With their own means, at times even with nonsupportive governments in power, the settler movement continued to expand and the number of settlers in the West Bank increased steadily by some 5 to 6 percent annually,[53] to about three hundred thousand by 2010 (again, excluding Jerusalem). The settlers had succeeded in creating an extraordinary political reality. In effect they had forced the state into a level of integration into the West Bank that was incongruent with the policies of most of the governments of Israel for most of the time since the signing of the Oslo Accords in 1993.

In the early 1990s, for example, Yitzhak Rabin personally and Rabin's government were unsympathetic to the settlers, but the prime minister also had to manage a fragile coalition. Rabin, like Ehud Barak at the end of the decade, presumably intended to eventually evacuate many settlements. But in the meantime, they sought to avoid confrontation with the settlers and allowed settlement expansion. This was also what Israeli leaders told the Americans. Since most settlements would be evacuated in a final agreement, "it should be acceptable that during negotiations they placate their domestic opposition by allowing selective settlement to continue."[54] This was an effort not to hand over the Israeli mainstream to a belligerent right wing. It was also a futile effort to co-opt or mollify the settlers in the hope that settler resistance to the peace process would be reduced.[55]

But for many of the settlers and some of their rabbinical authorities, the Oslo Accords were an act of treason. Rabin was compared to France's Marshall Petain,[56] who had collaborated with the Nazis in World War II and was subsequently sentenced to death. "There was a tremendous gulf of bitterness between the pragmatic, secular Rabin and the settlers." Some of the settler rabbis accused Rabin of betraying the Jewish people and passed rulings that actually permitted his execution. Rabin held them in contempt and dismissed them in his characteristic brashness as "Ayatollahs." The vicious propaganda campaign of the radical religious right undoubtedly contributed to the charged atmosphere in which Rabin's assassination by a religious extremist became possible.[57]

As of the mid-1990s, successive Israeli governments adhered to a policy of not authorizing the establishment of new settlements. A legal inquiry, the results of which were published in an opinion in 2005, could not find any record of even one resolution of the government or any relevant cabinet committee, as of the early 1990s to establish a new settlement or to expand an existing one. However, the culture of illegalism among the settlers was endemic. Dozens of illegal outposts were established anyway, and existing settlements were expanded. This was achieved through systemic and systematic illegalities and misconduct by sympathetic government ministries and agencies, including parts of the legal system and officers of the IDF and the police, in collusion with the settlers. Sometimes the responsible government officials were themselves settlers. As a result of all of these factors combined, nothing was done to address or to correct the abuse of power and violations of the law.

Once the army officers understood that the politicians preferred not to clash with Jewish activists who played the patriotic card, they turned a blind eye too. Recognizing the settlers' political influence, officers were also reluctant to resort to action that they feared might damage their careers. With time, ever more officers and men of the IDF combat units came from the ranks of the national religious right, who were quite naturally very sympathetic to the settler cause. There might be a markedly higher instance of insubordination if these soldiers were ordered to remove settlers in the future.

In the late 1990s, there were hundreds of cases of illegal building or taking possession of land by settlers in the West Bank and Gaza. But no action was taken. For years the Israeli government had essentially abandoned its decision-making authority and allowed lower echelons in the bureaucracy, starting from the regional councils of the settler communities in the occupied territories, to take its place, and they were allowed to do more or less as they pleased, without formal authorization. The prolonged erosion of the rule of law continued to diminish the state's authority. The government appeared not only unwilling to enforce the law on the settlers, but also afraid to confront them.[58]

All the above notwithstanding, the settlement enterprise also had its structural weaknesses and vulnerabilities. The settlers were powerful and influential and in many ways independent. But there were serious chinks in their armor. The radical religious settlers had to pay a price for their arrogance, obtuseness, and defiance. With their "elitist ethos," the religious settlers drew on supporters from their own ranks in Israel proper to move into the occupied territories. "They became a sect, apart from the Israel they sought to lead." They had failed to "settle in the hearts" of the majority of the Israeli public.[59]

They had a dress code (modern orthodox religious, usually armed) of their own, and they were known by a Hebrew term for settlers that applied only to them (mitnahalim), different from the term that applied to settlers inside Israel proper or on the Golan Heights (mityashvim), who were part of the national consensus. Though they have made partition far more difficult, the settlers remain a small proportion of the population of the West Bank, some 10 to 12 percent, and just 5 percent of Israel's population, after forty years of effort. In half that time, under the British Mandate, the Jews had become one-third of the population of all of Palestine.

The settlement grid, the scores of smaller settlements, the bigger towns, the thousands of homes, the public buildings, the roads, the gas stations, and the industrial parks may all seem like one huge immovable object. But the entire edifice rests on the army's presence and constant protection. Without the IDF, the whole enterprise would fold like a house of cards. Clashing with the army was unacceptable to the broader public, and the settlers could not use violence against the army without a public backlash. In those instances when the state has made a stand, the settlers have invariably been defeated. They failed to prevent the withdrawal from northern Sinai in early 1982, when Israel implemented its peace treaty with Egypt.[60] They failed again to stop Sharon's unilateral withdrawal from Gaza in the summer of 2005.

Northern Sinai and Gaza were not the West Bank, biblical Judea and Samaria, and the core of ancient Israel, from which the eviction of tens of thousands of settlers would be a much taller order. The settlers, however, were not a homogeneous social group or class. There were settlements of different kinds and of various social strata. A large segment of the settler population was not composed of religious radical nationalists at all, but secular people from the lower social classes or ultra-orthodox, who were not necessarily very nationalistic either. They settled in the West Bank because of the availability of cheap subsidized housing and not because they believed that settlement was the path to divine redemption. Some settlement communities were wealthy, well kept, and relatively large, but many others looked flimsy, poor, and unkempt and were underpopulated and hanging by a thread. Some of the settlers would fight evacuation fiercely, perhaps even resorting to force. But many more would probably not offer any serious resistance.[61]

The settlers were not very popular among the Israeli public at large and would not be able to count on widespread external support. Some in the settler leadership were indeed concerned that the Israeli public had turned its back on the settlers. In certain unsympathetic circles, the settlers were even regarded as "parasites" and as "obstacles to the peace process."[62] The outbreak of the first and second Intifadas awakened Israelis to the price of occupation. The high cost of the settlements was brought home to the Israeli people and to the settlers themselves. This was a price the settlers, in all their self-assurance and belief in the total righteousness of their cause, could not afford to ignore. For decades ever since the first Intifada, a steady majority of Israelis has not supported the settlements. Public reluctance to do so was matched by a growing resentment at the funds spent on the settlements.[63]

A stable majority of the general Israeli public supported the construction of the security barrier in 2003 after the suicide bombings of the second Intifada, even though it left about one-quarter of the settler population on the "wrong" side of the fence/wall.[64] A poll conducted in early 2010 noted that of the Jewish Israeli public only 6 percent lived or had ever lived in a settlement and only about a quarter reported having relatives or friends who presently lived in one. The pollsters suggested that these figures indicated that the settler community was an isolated sector within Israeli society.

Asked whether they thought building the settlements in the first place was right or not, 47 percent of the public replied that it was right, as opposed to 40 percent who thought it was not. Interestingly enough, however, a decade earlier, in June 2001, 63 percent had believed it was right, and only 28 percent that it was not, indicating a substantial shift in public opinion against the settlements over time. Furthermore when asked whether the government should already begin to offer compensation to settlers willing to leave their settlements now and move to live inside Israel proper, the number of supporters outnumbered the opponents by 49 to 42 percent.[65] Another study found that there was "massive support" for an evacuation-compensation law.[66]

According to a poll taken in March 2010, 60 percent of the general Israeli public supported "dismantling most of the settlements in the territories as part of a peace agreement with the Palestinians," the highest level recorded since 2005. Only 33 percent were opposed, of whom 13 percent were very strongly opposed. This was the lowest level of strong opposition recorded by this pollster since 2001. As for the settlers and the extent of their resistance to such settlement evacuation, most settlers said they would either obey a government decision for a comprehensive evacuation of settlements (20 percent) or resist by legal means (52 percent), while 21 percent said they would "resist by all means," up from 15 percent in 2005.[67] These figures revealed the extreme polarization in Israeli society, with rising support for settlement evacuation, on the one hand, coupled with an increasing readiness among a militant minority of the settlers to resist evacuation, possibly even by the use of force, on the other.

In terms of basic political values, the majority of Israelis ranked the preservation of the state's Jewish majority and the achievement of peace much higher than the ideal of Greater Eretz Yisrael. An analysis of major trends in Israeli public opinion over the last twenty-five years revealed a "progressive moderation in the attitude of the Israeli public with regard to a possible political solution of the Israeli-Palestinian conflict." Israelis remained hawkish on security, and skeptical on the real possibility of attaining a lasting accommodation with the Palestinians. At the same time, however, support in principle for the establishment of a Palestinian state trebled during this period, rising from 21 percent in 1987 to 61 percent in 2006. Seventy percent endorsed a two-state solution, though in the last few years these figures have declined somewhat.[68] As the settlement enterprise continued to expand, so did the perceptual divide that set the settlers apart from the majority of the Israeli people.

This led some observers to conclude that if and when Israeli society would find the inner strength to decide to part from the occupied territories, to save itself, to return to the march of history, and to reestablish its pride of place in the community of nations, "on that day the settlements would fall one after the other."[69] Others laid the emphasis on leadership, arguing that there was "good reason to believe" that a "charismatic political leader, backed by a strong and united government and with support of the defense establishment," could make far-reaching concessions for a permanent settlement with the Palestinians that would "enjoy, albeit begrudgingly, approval of the Israeli public."[70]

These assessments may have represented no more than the wishful thinking of some Israeli moderates, but maybe not. Their assessment was no less realistic and perhaps even more so than the dire predictions of the one-stater naysayers that the settler enterprise was so impregnable that a two-state solution was no longer feasible.

## Oslo and Israel's Acquiescence in Palestinian Statehood

Settler influence notwithstanding, Labor returned to power in the summer of 1992, and in January 1993, a secret channel of talks was opened between Israel and the PLO in Oslo, culminating in the Oslo Accords of September 1993. Although the Oslo Accords stopped short of mentioning independent Palestinian statehood, Israel's recognition of the Palestinians' "legitimate and political rights" and its acceptance of the PLO as the representative of the Palestinian people came closer than ever before to acquiescence in the principle of Palestinian statehood. After all, agreeing to "view the West Bank and the Gaza Strip as a single territorial unit"[71] and withdrawing from territory that would be taken over by the PLO could not lead to anything but Palestinian statehood.

Israel's political leadership at the time did not have the courage to reveal to the public that the Oslo process was intended to result in a permanent status agreement through the creation of a Palestinian state in the majority of the occupied territories, with its capital in Arab East Jerusalem, and a "respectable solution to the refugee issue."[72] In October 1995, shortly before his assassination, Rabin told the Knesset that he envisaged a Palestinian entity that would be "less than a state" but that would "independently run the lives of the Palestinians under its authority."[73]

That, however, was no more than a temporary concealment of the fact that Israel was moving inexorably toward acceptance of Palestinian statehood. The question by now was not whether the Israeli government and a majority of Israelis accepted Palestinian statehood, but whether the Israeli state could really come to an agreement with the Palestinians on the matter and possess the political wherewithal to deliver on such a deal, if obtained. Such an agreement would require the containment and defeat of the settlers and their enterprise, which, contrary to expectations, never stopped expanding for a moment, whether the government supported it or not.

By the time the Israelis went to Camp David in July 2000 it was obvious that the negotiations were intended to result in the creation of a Palestinian state.[74] Even leaders of the Israeli right, like Benjamin Netanyahu and Ariel Sharon, understood by now that "the game had changed" and the "Palestinians had returned to history—and more specifically to Israeli history—and their presence could not be ignored." Many in the Likud accepted that most of the West Bank would eventually have to come under Palestinian sovereignty.[75]

Ehud Barak's election campaign in 1999 highlighted the imperative of disengagement from the Palestinians, and shortly before his departure for the Camp David talks, Barak declared that the creation of an "independent Palestinian entity" was the essential outcome of a settlement that would guarantee Israel's internal security and safeguard its Jewish identity.[76] Most Israelis in the meantime had developed a genuine self-interest in the two-state solution as the ultimate legitimization of Israel itself. The failure of Camp David only reinforced the widespread Israeli recognition of their own interest in a two-state solution, as attested to by the consistent public pronouncements of Israeli leaders in support of Palestinian statehood.

But the failure of Camp David, and the worst round of bloodletting between Israelis and Palestinians since 1948 that followed in its wake, had a most profound impact on Israeli thinking. While it did not reduce Israeli support for Palestinian statehood in principle, it made the Israelis all the more wary about imminent withdrawal and ever more negative on refugee return. As Israel's acceptance of Palestinian statehood became routine, the Israeli position on refugees hardened.[77] This was coupled with a more clearly articulated demand that the Palestinians formally recognize Israel as the state of the Jewish people, which, in the Israeli mind, was the ultimate antidote to refugee return. In the negotiations from Camp David to Taba there was significant movement on all issues—Jerusalem, territory and settlements, and security—but not on refugees.

On the refugee question both sides stuck to their guns, the Palestinians demanding that Israel recognize its historical responsibility for the problem and the "right of return" of the refugees, and the Israelis adamantly refusing to do either. Despite some expressions of disappointment at the time, the Israelis should not have been overly surprised by the insistent refusal of the Palestinians to recognize any inherent Jewish historical or religious attachment or right to the country or any part of it.

There was nothing new in this Palestinian point of view. It was the standard Palestinian predisposition from the very outset of the conflict. But its powerful unrelenting reiteration at Camp David was all the more reason for the Israelis to seek additional reassurances against what they suspected might be the Palestinians' long-term aspirations that went beyond statehood in the West Bank and Gaza. Thus, in accepting Palestinian statehood, Israel demanded reassurances on three key questions: that there would be no refugee return to Israel; that Israel be recognized as a Jewish state; and that security restrictions and controls, responding to Israeli desiderata, be accepted by the future state of

Palestine. While the third was partially agreeable to the Palestinians, the first two were not.

## Restrictions on Palestinian Sovereignty

Israel's acceptance of Palestinian statehood formally excluded Arab East Jerusalem, which the Palestinians regarded as the essential capital of the Palestinian state of the future. Though unaccepted internationally, in terms of Israeli law, the entire city was and remained Israel's united capital. While successive Israeli governments since Camp David had essentially acquiesced in the partition of the city, on the ground Israel continued to secure its hold on the entire city and its environs, making the future establishment of Palestinian sovereignty in the city ever more difficult.

A corollary of Israel's acceptance of Palestinian statehood was the establishment of what the Israelis believed were an essential set of restrictions on the Palestinian state, so that it would not be converted in the future from an asset contributing to Israeli security into a serious threat, especially if "end of conflict" was not attainable. However, just as refugee return was seen by the Israelis as an insufferable encroachment effectively undermining the two-state paradigm, so the Palestinians regarded some of the Israeli security requirements in the proposed Palestinian state as an intolerable intrusion, which eroded both the sovereignty and independence of their future state. Thus both sides, in their respective ways, fractured the symmetry of the two-state solution.

From the Israeli point of view, considering the country's lack of strategic depth and uniquely precarious geo-strategic circumstances, these restrictions were absolutely essential to protect the most densely populated areas of Israel from exposure to potentially devastating attack. Israel's coastal plain lay at the feet of the West Bank highlands and was easily within the range even of short-range weapons of every sort. Israeli military analysts clearly operated on the realistic assumption that an agreement between Israel and the Palestinians would not significantly alter the fundamentally conflictual relations between Palestine and Israel or that, even if it did, the new relationship might be easily overturned.

Since the signing of the Oslo Accords, Israel had demanded the demilitarization of the Palestinian state of the future. The Israelis, however, contended that demilitarization as commonly understood (limitations on war materials) was too narrowly defined and did not cover the full range of Israel's security needs. Israel, they argued, could anticipate two potential scenarios liable to unfold in the aftermath of the establishment of the Palestinian state. The first involved threats from within such a state if it were to develop into a convenient base for symmetrical or asymmetrical warfare against Israel, as happened in Gaza. The second involved threats to Israel emanating from the states to the east of Palestine, via Palestinian territory. The Israeli concept of demilitarization, therefore, included a wide variety of means needed to forestall both of these potential threats from or through the future Palestinian state.

The necessary security measures required that no Palestinian army or military capabilities, which could constitute a threat, would be established. The Palestinian state would be obliged to prevent terrorist activities, incitement and indoctrination for terrorism, and the creation of any terrorist infrastructure within its borders. Israel and Palestine would have to share a unified airspace controlled by Israel; there would need to be special security arrangements in the Jordan valley that would allow for IDF emergency deployment; Israel would control strategically vulnerable areas, such as the high ground overlooking Ben-Gurion International Airport, to prevent the disruption of civil aviation to and from Israel by missile fire from Palestinian territory; and there would have to be electromagnetic coordination for the prevention of mutual disruption or the jamming of Israeli military and civilian communications.[78]

The gaps between the parties on these issues have been very difficult to bridge. The Palestinians were willing to accept limitations on their own forces as well as the temporary stationing of international forces in their territory, as there were in Sinai or southern Lebanon, but not Israeli forces. They would not accept the broader interpretation of demilitarization as understood by the Israelis. Nor would they countenance the continued presence of Israeli forces in specified security zones in the Palestinian state after the general withdrawal, nor the continued control by Israel of Palestinian airspace. They similarly rejected Israeli supervision of the external border crossings into Palestine or the lease of territory to Israel beyond the settlement blocs, which the Palestinians thought were too intrusive anyway. All of the above, they argued, were antithetical to a fully sovereign independent Palestinian state.

As one of their interlocutors said to the Israelis at Taba in January 2001, "we want a real state that can defend itself" even though it would "not have an army that could threaten Israel." From the Palestinian point of view, the Israelis were "usurping [Palestinian] rights under the pretext of security arrangements. . . . These are issues directly linked to our sovereignty, and our national and personal dignity." Israel should solve its strategic problems in its own territory and not at the expense of the Palestinian state.[79]

The Palestinians were unwilling to accept security arrangements that not only impaired the sovereignty of their own state, but could in certain circumstances transform their territory into a potential staging ground for the conduct of war against other Arab states. The Israelis, the Palestinians complained, were having a hard time freeing themselves of their "occupation mentality [aqliyyat al-ihtilal]" and were asking for too much.[80] In a discussion with Udi Dekel, a senior advisor to Prime Minister Olmert, in July 2008, Sa'ib Ariqat dismissed the Israeli demand for a permanent Israeli military presence in certain areas of a future Palestinian state. If that was the Israeli position, he retorted, the Palestinians would prefer occupation. When there would be a Palestinian state, he continued, the only permissible Israeli presence would be civilian: "doctors, technicians . . . no soldiers."[81]

Nevertheless, Israel's reservations on the Quartet Roadmap for a settlement with the Palestinians reiterated that the envisaged Palestinian state with provisional borders would have to be "fully demilitarized with no military forces" and would only have "police and internal security forces of limited scope and armaments." It would not have the authority to undertake defense alliances or military cooperation with other countries, and Israel would have control of the entry and exit of all persons and goods and of the provisional state's airspace and electromagnetic sphere.[82]

After his election in February 2009, Prime Minister Benjamin Netanyahu made it very clear that a fundamental prerequisite for a Palestinian state was that "the territory under Palestinian control must be demilitarized with iron-clad security provisions for Israel," and he went on to reiterate the conditions as set out by Israel in the past. "If we receive this guarantee regarding demilitarization and Israel's security needs, and if the Palestinians recognize Israel as the state of the Jewish people, then we will be ready in a future peace agreement to reach a solution where a demilitarized Palestinian state exists alongside the Jewish state."[83]

The Palestinians rejected Netanyahu's proposal as "farcical." The restrictions Israel sought to place on Palestinian statehood in the name of Israeli security needs, they complained, would turn the Palestinian state of the future into an Israeli protectorate rather than an independent state. According to chief Palestinian negotiator, Sa'ib Ariqat, "not in a thousand years" would Netanyahu find "a single Palestinian who would agree" to his conditions.[84] The

Palestinian perception of a "fully sovereign and viable Palestinian state"[85] clearly did not correspond with "ironclad security provisions for Israel" as understood by the Israelis.

## Unilateralism to Break the Impasse

As they dug into their respective irreconcilable positions, Israelis and Palestinians found themselves increasingly trapped in an impasse. Much to Israel's long-term detriment, in the debate of the late 1960s between the three schools represented by Sapir, Allon, and Dayan, it was Dayan's functionally integrated single state that had emerged victorious, at least for a span of some twenty decisive years. This was partly by design and partly by the settler momentum facilitated by a combination of the determination of their supporters on the right and the irresolution of their opponents on the left.

Matters had come to a head after the failure of Camp David in 2000. There were increasing segments of the Israeli body politic who were arriving at the conclusion that if withdrawal was not possible by agreement, then Israel would have to do so unilaterally, to preserve its predominantly Jewish character. From a reluctant acceptance of Palestinian statehood, demography was transforming the Palestinian state into an urgent Israeli prerequisite.

Ironically, the new emerging Israeli majority consensus would be led by pillars of the historical right to revive the position that the dovish Pinhas Sapir had prescribed all the way back in 1968. The Israelis, however, in their very late cognition, were to find it excruciatingly difficult, if not impossible, to entirely undo what over forty years of occupation had wrought in the West Bank and Gaza, under the preponderant impact of the grit and determination of the messianic religious right.

In the late 1990s, when the Oslo process was clearly turning sour, there were some in Israeli academe who began to urge unilateral Israeli withdrawal.[86] The idea was taken up after the failure of Camp David by various nongovernmental organizations (NGOs), such the Council for Peace and Security, a body of mainly retired IDF senior officers, and in 2002 Gilad Sher, one of Barak's chief negotiators at Camp David, coauthored with Uri Saguy, a retired IDF general, an Israeli Policy Initiative for unilateral disengagement, which was published with the Van Leer Jerusalem Institute.[87]

In August 2002 Israel's National Security Council (NSC) concluded that in the light of demographic forecasts predicting an Arab majority between the

Jordan River and the Mediterranean, it had become necessary for Israel, if it wished to maintain its stable Jewish majority in a democratic state of the Jewish people, to determine its final boundaries within a relatively short time frame. If there was no Palestinian partner for an early agreement on the matter, the NSC suggested that Israel ought to do so unilaterally.[88]

These were the first years of Ariel Sharon in power as prime minister, and he was deeply influenced by this discussion. Sharon clashed head-on with the Likud Party faithful on his readiness to accept Palestinian statehood. In May 2003 he told a meeting of the Likud Knesset faction "that the occupation [hitherto an unspoken word in the Likud] could not continue forever" and that the situation in which Israel held three and a half million Palestinians "under occupation" could not be allowed to continue.[89] And it was none other than Sharon, heretofore one of the stalwarts of the Israeli right, who raised the standard of unilateral withdrawal.

It was on Sharon's watch that Israel began to build the security barrier along the border between Israel and the West Bank, which Sharon had previously staunchly opposed and dismissed as an act of extreme "silliness." The barrier was to serve the dual purpose of disengaging Israel from the West Bank and preventing the infiltration of suicide bombers, who had wrought havoc in Israeli towns since the outbreak of the second Intifada in September 2000. The barrier, supported by 84 percent of the Jewish Israeli public in early 2004,[90] was constructed partly along the old Green Line and partly protruded into the West Bank to include major Israeli settlement blocs, thereby including some 8 percent[91] of the West Bank on the Israeli side of the barrier (see map 6). The very existence of the barrier, declarations to the contrary notwithstanding, "implied recognition by the Israeli government of the continuing relevance of the 1967 border."[92]

The key spokesperson for unilateral disengagement in Sharon's cabinet was his deputy prime minister, Ehud Olmert, who blazed the trail for Sharon in a number of high-profile interviews in the Israeli press in late 2003. Olmert explained that Israel urgently had to "address the demographic issue with the utmost seriousness and resolve. . . . In the absence of a negotiated agreement . . . [Israel would] need to implement a unilateral alternative." Israel did not have unlimited time, he argued. More and more Palestinians were not interested in a two-state solution and actually sought to abandon the "Algerian paradigm" of the conflict, that is, a struggle against the occupation, in favor of a South African paradigm that would focus on "one man, one vote" in one state, rather than two states. That would not be a struggle over the fate of the West Bank and Gaza, but over Israel itself. It "would mean the end of the Jewish state."[93]

Israel, therefore, had to create a two-state reality, even if that meant a unilateral withdrawal from most of the West Bank, all of Gaza, and parts of Arab Jerusalem. The extent of the withdrawal would be determined mainly by demography, rather than by political or purely security considerations or by the dictates of national sentiment or religious tradition.[94]

On December 18, 2003, Sharon publicly declared the intention of his government, "entrusted with the duty of shaping the face of the Jewish and democratic State of Israel," to proceed to unilaterally disengage from the Palestinians if it transpired within a few months that the Palestinians were not implementing their commitments as outlined in the Quartet Roadmap, published in April that year. Israel, Sharon noted, sought direct negotiations to implement the Quartet Roadmap, and it supported the creation of a democratic Palestinian state, but it would not be held hostage by the Palestinians and would "not wait for them indefinitely."[95] In a most unexpected twist of fate, Israel had acquired a greater sense of urgency in the creation of a Palestinian state than the Palestinians themselves.

Sharon's chief advisor, Dov Weisglass, told *Haaretz* in October 2004 that the disengagement plan was designed to freeze the peace process. It was intended, so Weisglass explained, to stall the establishment of a Palestinian state and any discussion of borders, refugees, and Jerusalem. The plan made it possible to "park conveniently in an interim situation" that would distance Israel from political pressure and would force the Palestinians "to prove their seriousness."[96] Whether this was a genuine reflection of Sharon's thinking at the time or an effort to mollify the Likud, where Sharon was fighting a losing battle on his disengagement policy, is hard to know. It is clear, however, that not long after this interview was given, Sharon's mind seemed to have been finally made up, and it was not about "parking" in the West Bank.

Sharon, formerly the apple of the settlers' eye, was now shunned by all and sundry in their camp. As early as the summer of 2003, the settler leadership had come to the conclusion that Sharon was not just maneuvering. He had become a "prisoner" of the Quartet Roadmap, they concluded, and they heaped the same kind of unrestrained abuse on him as they had on Rabin. No holds were barred in their accusations: that he had declared war on God, that he was following in the footsteps of collaborators with the Nazis, that he himself was en route to committing crimes against humanity.[97] Sharon, however, was not deflected from his course. In accordance with his plan, Israel withdrew unilaterally from Gaza (and from four settlements in the northern West Bank) in August 2005. In September, Sharon told the UN that Israel had "no aspirations to rule over" the Palestinians, who like the Israelis, were "entitled to freedom and to a national, sovereign existence in a state of their own."[98]

Unable to convince his own Likud Party to go along with him on his new departure, Sharon split the party in November 2005 and founded the new centrist Kadima Party, together with a group of former Likud and Labor politicians, united almost entirely around the idea of further unilateral withdrawal from the West Bank. In January 2006, in mid-stride, Sharon was incapacitated by a massive stroke, from which he never recovered. He was succeeded at the helm by Ehud Olmert, who led Kadima to a narrow victory in new elections held in March 2006.

In speeches before the Knesset in May and June, Olmert expressed the determination of his government to carry out further unilateral withdrawals in the West Bank if negotiations with the Palestinians did not produce the desired results. "The core values" of Israel since its foundation were attached to its character as a Jewish state and a democracy. To preserve this essence of Israel, Olmert continued, "a stable and solid Jewish majority in our State" had to be maintained. The disengagement from Gaza and parts of the northern West Bank was only "an essential first step" and the "main part [was] still ahead." The Israeli settlements dispersed throughout the West Bank were not an asset but a threat to "the existence of the State of Israel as a Jewish state." Olmert spoke of removing seventy thousand settlers from the West Bank, equal more or less to the number of settlers living outside the perimeter of the Israeli security barrier. This seemed to suggest that his intention was to withdraw unilaterally to the line of the barrier. It would have been preferable to negotiate with the Palestinians over all these matters but, Olmert noted, Israel could "not wait forever." Israel could not suspend critical decisions about its future awaiting Palestinian reciprocity and efficacy and would act unilaterally if it had to. Such a withdrawal would create "a completely different reality from the one [Israel had] lived in over the last forty years."[99]

But before Olmert managed to take any steps in this direction, he was stopped dead in his tracks by what was widely seen as his poor conduct of the Second Lebanon War of summer 2006. Many of the Israeli critics of unilateral withdrawal had blamed the policy for the Hamas victory in the Palestinian elections in January 2006. Hamas had credited its own "resistance" for forcing Israel to withdraw and had in fact made this case in its election campaign. Far worse, however, for the unilateralists was the raining of thousands of rockets by Hizballah on northern Israel in the Second Lebanon War, six years after Israel's unilateral withdrawal from southern Lebanon. Rockets from Gaza on southern Israel had not stopped after the disengagement either, but it was the huge barrages of rockets fired by Hizballah on the north of the country that turned the great majority of Israelis against the idea of unilateral withdrawal from the West Bank.

The opponents of unilateralism could now argue with much conviction and credibility that experience in Gaza and Lebanon had shown quite conclusively that the policy was deeply flawed. Its implementation on the West Bank could expose the heartland of Israel in the coastal plain to similar barrages of intolerable rocketry from a Hamas-controlled Palestinian state of the future. Israel remained committed to a two-state solution, but unilateralism was shelved. As Olmert approached the end of his tenure as prime minister, in one of his last speeches to the Knesset, in November 2008, he argued that Israel would not be able to avoid the eventual decision to withdraw from the West Bank. Those who believed Israel could remain in occupation "were wrong . . . and did not see the big picture." The occupation "will not work. It is already not working." It exacted a cost from Israel that the Israelis did "not have the moral strength to bear."[100]

## The Essential Preservation of Israel's Jewish Character

The more Israel accepted the two-state paradigm, the more it tended to emphasize the essential preservation of Israel's Jewish character. After all, one of the major motivations for accepting the two-state idea in the first place was to maintain Israel's Jewishness. For the Israelis, it made little sense to accept Palestinian statehood if it eroded the nature of the Israeli state and its historical raison d'etre. The challenge to Israel on this score came at one and the same time from the two core components of the "1948 file." The first was the demand for Israel's recognition of the right of return of refugees. The second was the demand from within Israel by increasingly significant segments of the political and intellectual elite of the country's Palestinian Arab citizens to redefine Israel as "the state of all its citizens."

Though Israel was defined as the state of the Jewish people, from the very beginning it conferred citizenship and civil rights on all of its citizens, Jews and non-Jews, as clearly stated in the country's Declaration of Independence. However, Israel's Palestinian citizens did encounter various forms of discrimination and argued that the very definition of the state excluded them from participation as full equals. For Israeli Jews, on the other hand, the demand to redefine Israel as "the state of all its citizens" was a means of effacing the Jewish nationalist character of their state and an invalidation of the very heart and soul of the Zionist struggle since its inception a century and a quarter ago.

The more assertive articulation of the nationalist demands by the Palestinian Arab political elite in Israel coincided with more radical action in the field, which was especially disconcerting for the Israeli Jewish majority. Just days after the outbreak of the second Intifada, in early October 2000, Israel was rocked by massive rioting by Israeli Palestinians, the likes of which the country had not witnessed since 1948. Thirteen of the rioters were killed by Israeli police, leading to the appointment of a special commission of inquiry into the events. Relations between Jews and Arabs in Israel reached what was perhaps their lowest ebb ever.

The events of October 2000 had been brewing for decades. The Orr Commission of Enquiry,[101] which was appointed to study the causes of the riots, blamed the state for many years of discrimination, neglect, and disregard for the problems of the Arab minority. The state, the commission noted, had not shown sufficient sensitivity to the needs of the Arab population. It had not allocated state resources equally and had generally not done enough to create equality for its Arab citizens or to uproot the various vestiges of discrimination and injustice. All of the above had contributed to the ongoing ferment and the eventual outbreak of the violence. The commission therefore strongly urged the government to adopt all the necessary measures to create true equality for the country's Arab citizens and to completely remove the "stain of discrimination" from Israel's democratic structure.[102]

On the other hand, the Orr Commission impressed upon the Arab leadership in Israel the need to refrain from encouraging violence even in the pursuit of legitimate goals. The commission emphasized the incompatibility of the concept of citizenship with the representation of the state "as the enemy."[103]

The peace process with the Palestinians tended to exacerbate internal Israeli Arab-Jewish tensions rather than mitigate them, as might have been expected. The Palestinian citizens of Israel felt that the peace process had bypassed them and that in Israel itself their aspirations for equality, individual and collective, were far from being fulfilled. The general attitude of disinterest of the Jewish leadership of the state toward the Arab population remained unchanged despite the shift in the relationship with the Palestinians in the occupied territories, leaving the Palestinians in Israel with a strong sense of exclusion and alienation, which exploded in October 2000.[104]

The violent clashes evoked diametrically opposed reactions and commentaries from Arab and Jewish Israelis. From the Arab point of view, the massive demonstrations that swept Arab towns and villages were seen, on the one hand, as not only a spontaneous wave of solidarity with the Palestinians in the occupied territories, but as "the culmination of a national reawakening that had been gathering momentum for some time." On the other hand, it was an exposure of the naked brutality of the Israeli security forces, which "had the effect of legitimizing the killing of Arabs," who were seen by the Israeli police more as enemies than as fellow citizens.[105]

Israeli Palestinian intellectuals like Azmi Bishara and Nadim Rouhana argued that the October events aroused serious doubts among the Arabs in Israel as to the real value of their Israeli citizenship. The events put paid to the illusion of the integration theory, according to which peace between Israel and the Palestinians would pave the way for the full integration of Israel's Palestinian-Arab citizens into the state. The "Jewishness of the state," they claimed, was the "real obstacle to integration" and not the absence of Palestinian-Israeli peace.[106]

Among Jewish Israelis, the riots gave rise to serious misgivings about the basic loyalties of the Arab minority to the state. These concerns were exacerbated by revelations that under the surface some more ominous developments were at work. Palestinian citizens of Israel were found in some instances to be collaborating with the campaign of suicide bombings in Israel, providing various forms of logistic support, such as safe houses or transport in cars with Israeli plates, to the bombers. The first Palestinian Israeli suicide bomber carried out an attack in September 2001.[107]

The notion that in these circumstances Israel would agree to a significant increase of its Arab population through refugee return was more far-fetched than it had ever been. The doyen of Israel's defense correspondents, Ze'ev Schiff, captured the Jewish public mood when he wrote in the immediate aftermath of the riots of October 2000 that it was now clear that "it would be madness, from a security as well as a demographic point of view, to add to the Arab minority—many of whose members raised the banner of revolt against

Israel—tens of thousands of Palestinians who feel cheated and oppressed."[108] As Ehud Barak put it, Israel would "not allow even one refugee back on the basis of the 'right of return.'"[109]

Reviewing the situation some two years later, Mahmud Abbas rebuked the actions of the Palestinian minority in Israel. In their solidarity demonstrations and clashes with the Israeli police, he noted, they had hardened Israel's position on refugees, making the Israelis more reluctant than they were anyway to accept the return of Palestinian refugees to Israel proper. It would have been more helpful, according to Abbas, if the Israeli Palestinians had taken advantage of their democratic rights in Israel to help get moderate governments elected rather than disturbing the peace and adding to the anxieties of their Jewish compatriots.[110]

The events of October 2000 further encouraged thinking in Israel that not only should refugees not be admitted, but measures should actually be taken to reduce the size of the country's Arab population. This was to be achieved not by expulsion, as some on the extreme right suggested, but by border rectification, that is, by ceding territory from within Israel that was densely populated by Arabs in the expected land swap agreement with the future state of Palestine. The main area in question, known as the "Triangle," was the narrow strip of territory along the old Green Line, about sixty kilometers long and about three to five kilometers wide, that had been annexed to Israel in the 1949 armistice negotiations between Israel and Jordan. The area contained over twenty Arab towns and villages with a total population of some 250,000 people, that is, about 20 percent of the total Arab population of Israel. This area was also the scene of much of the rioting in October 2000.

This was an issue not only discussed in Israel. Hussein Agha and Robert Malley suggested that one of the options for refugee return could be for them to "live among people who share their language, religion and culture—that is, among the Arab citizens of Israel. Israel would settle the refugees in its Arab-populated territory along the 1967 boundaries. Those areas would then be included in the land swap with Palestine and end up as part of the new Palestinian state." Although the refugees would not return to their original homes, they "would get to live in a more hospitable environment—and one that would ultimately be ruled not by Israelis, but by their own people. For Israelis, meanwhile, it would improve the demographic balance, since the number of Arab Israelis would diminish as a result of the land transfer."[111]

Such a redrawing of the boundaries had never been defined as official Israeli policy. All the same, at the end of September 2010 in a speech before the very formal setting of the UN General Assembly, Israel's foreign minister Avigdor Lieberman, the firebrand leader of the ultranationalist Yisrael Beiteinu Party, proposed that an Israeli-Palestinian settlement that would be founded on "two peoples, in two nation-states, living in peace and security" ought to be obtained not through the principle of "land-for-peace" but rather on the "exchange of populated territory." Lieberman specifically clarified in his speech that he was "not speaking about moving populations, but rather about moving borders to better reflect demographic realities." He noted further that in the many cases of ethnic conflict, whether in the Balkans, the Caucasus, Africa, the Far East, or the Middle East, where effective separation between rival ethnic groups had been achieved "conflict has either been avoided, or has been dramatically reduced or resolved."[112]

Lieberman's specific clarification notwithstanding, in the media furor that ensued, he was said to have exposed "the true face of Israel." He was denounced for proposing that the Israeli Palestinians ought to be "forcibly removed from their homes and relocated," all in the service of "making Israel an 'ethnically pure' Jewish state."[113] Lieberman and his party had long waged a campaign delegitimizing the Palestinian Arab minority in Israel as basically disloyal to the state, calling for legislation that would threaten to deny their citizenship if they failed to pledge their allegiance to Israel as the state of the Jewish people. Considering his political record, Lieberman's comments at the UN were seen in a much more negative light than he may have intended. Prime Minister Netanyahu was quick to distance himself from Lieberman's statement, to deny that he had any advance knowledge of its content, and to reaffirm that these ideas did not reflect Israel's official position.[114]

Israel, needless to say, had a hard time convincing the international media that statements by the foreign minister at the UN could possibly be made without coordination with the prime minister. It was difficult to determine whether Lieberman's statement was yet another example of typical Israeli governmental dysfunctionalism or a calculated Israeli trial balloon. But the ideas that Lieberman had put forth on the redrawing of Israel's borders were not his alone, and they were indeed part of the Israeli internal political discourse and had been for some time. Moreover, as the Agha-Malley article cited above indicates, such ideas were discussed outside of Israel as well, in circles far more liberal-minded than Avigdor Lieberman.

In Israel there were unquestionably increasing concerns about the ever more apparent radicalization of the country's Palestinian minority. Ehud Barak linked the new political activism of the Palestinian minority in Israel with the refugee question. He saw them both as the irredentist Palestinian machinery for the subversion of Israel as the state of the Jewish people. In Barak's analysis, the Palestinians were actually pursuing a Palestinian state in all of Palestine. Israel was recognized for now because it could not be defeated. The Palestinian strategy therefore was to establish a state "while always leaving an opening for further 'legitimate' demands down the road." The demand of the Palestinians in Israel for the country to become "the state of all its citizens" was presented by its key protagonists as the first step toward the creation of a binational state. Refugee return, demography, and attrition would then lead eventually to a state with a Muslim majority and a Jewish minority. This "would mean the destruction of Israel as a Jewish state" and was, so Barak believed, the Palestinian vision of the future.[115]

In Barak's view, therefore, Israel's relinquishment of the occupied territories with their relatively large Palestinian population and the creation of a Palestinian state had become a "compelling imperative" for Israel. A Palestinian state was an essential precondition for the preservation of Israel's predominantly Jewish character. It logically followed that Israel's settlement activity in the occupied territories after 1967 had been "a major historical wrong turn."[116] It also followed that Israel would not accept any large-scale return of Palestinian refugees.

## Linking the Two-State Solution to Formal Recognition of Israel's Jewishness

As Israel committed itself further to the two-state paradigm, not only did it seek to maintain its Jewishness, but it demanded of the Palestinians to formally recognize it as well. The Israeli demand to recognize its Jewishness was an alternative formulation to the previous Israeli demand for "end of conflict." It was similarly designed to ensure the finality of a two-state solution, to prevent the reopening of the "1948 file," and to preempt the employment of refugee return as a means of undermining Israel within the 1967 boundaries.

In the meantime, the two-state solution acquired an unprecedented level of international legitimacy. In the wake of its endorsement in the Clinton Parameters of December 2000 and Israel's own acceptance of the idea, Resolution 1397 was adopted by the UN Security Council in mid-March 2002, "affirming a vision of a region where two States, Israel and Palestine, live side by side within secure and recognized borders."[117] The Arab League, just a few weeks later, endorsed its Peace Initiative at the end of March 2002, similarly based on a two-state solution. President Bush developed his vision of "two states living side by side, in peace and security," which was announced in June 2002 and was accepted "in principle" by Israel as a "reasonable, pragmatic and practicable" plan.[118]

This was followed in April 2003 by the more detailed "Roadmap to a Permanent Two-State Solution," released by the Quartet—the United States, the European Union (EU), Russia, and the UN. The Quartet Roadmap envisaged "a final and comprehensive settlement of the Israel-Palestinian conflict," which would "result in the emergence of an independent, democratic, and viable Palestinian state living side by side in peace and security with Israel and its other neighbors." The settlement would be arrived at in three phases: the first would be the reestablishment of security and an end to the terror and the violence; the second was a transitional phase during which efforts would be "focused on the option of creating an independent Palestinian state with provisional borders and attributes of sovereignty" as a way station to a permanent status settlement; and the third would be the attainment of the permanent status agreement and the end of the Israeli-Palestinian conflict, which would include all the outstanding issues of borders, settlements, Jerusalem, and "an agreed, just, fair, and realistic solution" to the refugee question.[119] The Roadmap was accorded further international legitimacy and stature in November 2003, when it was endorsed by the Security Council in Resolution 1515.[120]

In May 2003, the Israeli government, headed by Ariel Sharon, accepted the Quartet Roadmap but appended a list of fourteen reservations, which revealed inter alia Israeli government thinking on the meaning of a two-state solution. Most of the reservations dealt with Israeli demands of the PA on security issues and on political and other reforms within the PA. Most importantly, however, the reservations noted that any final settlement would have to include an explicit Palestinian recognition of Israel's "right to exist as a Jewish state" and their "waiver of any right of return for Palestinian refugees to the State of Israel."[121]

From this point on, statements by Israeli leaders on the country's acceptance of Palestinian statehood were invariably associated with the demand that Israel be recognized as a Jewish state. In addressing the UN General Assembly in September 2005, shortly after Israel's unilateral disengagement from Gaza, Sharon explained that Israel and the Palestinians, as neighbors, shared the Land of Israel [Eretz Yisrael / Palestine]. Israel's disengagement did not conflict with the implementation of the Quartet Roadmap, to which Israel remained committed, and the renewal of the peace process could provide for a fair compromise. But there would be "no compromise on the right of the State of Israel to exist as a Jewish state," fully secure, within defensible borders.[122] Speaking before the Knesset in June 2006, Prime Minister Ehud Olmert added to the conditions that had to be met by the Palestinians "the recognition of the State of Israel's right to exist as a Jewish state."[123]

When the peace process was renewed under the auspices of President Bush at the Annapolis Conference in November 2007, Prime Minister Olmert and Foreign Minister Tzipi Livni both made particular reference to Israel as "a Jewish state." Livni drew her inspiration from the UN Partition Resolution of 1947 to justify "the principle of two states for two peoples: one—a Jewish state, as decreed by the UN resolution, and the other—an Arab state." Therefore, Livni said,

the right thing to do is to build a shared future in two separate states: one— the State of Israel, which was established as a Jewish state, a national home for the Jewish people; and the other—Palestine—which will be established to give a full and complete solution to Palestinians wherever they may be. Those who are in Gaza and the West Bank, and those in the refugee camps in other Arab countries with temporary status, waiting for a sense of belonging to a national state—[would thus acquire] the same feeling of wholeness that the establishment of the State of Israel gave to the Jewish refugees who were forced to leave Arab countries and Europe and became partners in building Israel.[124]

It was most unlikely that her Palestinian interlocutors would accept the symmetry she drew. All the same, Livni went on to suggest to the Palestinians that they "not bemoan the establishment of the State of Israel; establish your own state, rejoice in its establishment and we will rejoice with you, since for us the establishment of the Palestinian state is not our Nakba, or disaster— provided that upon its establishment the word 'Nakba' be deleted from the Arabic lexicon in referring to Israel." Israel, she concluded, had no hidden agenda. Its withdrawal from Gaza was a risk taken on the understanding "that Gaza would not be the last step."[125] Olmert similarly called for a negotiation that would fulfill President Bush's vision of two states for the two peoples: "A peace-seeking, viable, strong, democratic and terror-free Palestinian state for the Palestinian people" and a "Jewish, democratic State of Israel, living in security and free from the threat of terror—the national home of the Jewish people."[126]

After his election in February 2009, Prime Minister Benjamin Netanyahu upped the ante by altering the language and thus the policy, making it even less likely that the Palestinians would accept what they had hitherto adamantly rejected. Israel had previously associated its acceptance of Palestinian statehood with recognition of Israel's Jewish character and a series of security arrangements. Netanyahu went beyond association and introduced a clear conditionality. Israel would only accept a Palestinian state *after* the Palestinians had accepted Israel's prerequisites on recognition and security. In a landmark speech on June 14, 2009, Netanyahu elaborated the new departure.

The root cause of the conflict, Netanyahu explained, was and remained "the refusal to recognize the right of the Jewish people to a state of their own in their historic homeland." Therefore, the first fundamental prerequisite for ending the conflict was a "public, binding and unequivocal Palestinian recognition of Israel as the nation state of the Jewish people. To vest this declaration with practical meaning, there must also be a clear understanding that the Palestinian refugee problem will be resolved outside Israel's borders. Clearly, any demand for resettling Palestinian refugees within Israel undermines Israel's continued existence as the state of the Jewish people."[127]

Netanyahu made this an issue of high principle and a "central foundation" for the resolution of the conflict with the Palestinians. In his major addresses he reiterated time and gain that there could be no end to the conflict without "Palestinian recognition of Israel as the nation state of the Jewish people." To refute the accusation that Israel as the state of the Jewish people, was by definition non-inclusive of its Arab citizens as full equals, Netanyahu declared that Israel was "both the nation state of the Jewish people and a democratic country for all its citizens, Jews and non-Jews alike, enjoying full equal rights."[128]

Though clearly a matter of high principle for Israel, Netanyahu was not averse to the temptation to degrade the recognition of Israel's Jewishness to the level of a mere tactical negotiating device to override undesirable preconditions that were being set for Israel in the peace process. When pressed by the Obama administration to extend the settlement freeze that he had previously accepted and that had expired in September 2010, Netanyahu offered to consider extending the freeze for a fixed period "if the Palestinian leadership will unequivocally say to its people that it recognizes Israel as the nation state of the Jewish people." This was not a precondition for talks, he explained. Israel would continue the negotiations in any event "without any conditions," that is, without the settlement freeze either. Needless to say, as Netanyahu must have expected, the Palestinians refused.[129]

## US Endorsement of the "Jewish State" Concept

The more adamant Israel became in its rejection of refugee return and in its concomitant demand of the Palestinians to recognize Israel's Jewish character, so it made a concerted effort to rally US backing for these positions. Already during the Camp David–Taba negotiations it transpired that the Palestinians were unwilling to formally recognize Israel's Jewishness. Even so, as already noted, the Clinton Parameters outlined a settlement for the Palestinian refugees that would have to be "consistent with the two-state approach" according to which the state of Palestine would be the "homeland of the Palestinian people" and Israel would be the "homeland of the Jewish people."[130] Shortly thereafter, in a speech in November 2001, setting out the US vision of an Israeli-Palestinian two-state solution, Secretary of State Colin Powell urged Israel to end its occupation, while he called upon the Palestinians to "eliminate any doubt, once and for all, that they accept the legitimacy of Israel as a Jewish state. They must make clear that their objective is a Palestinian state alongside Israel, not in place of Israel."[131]

A more formal direct US support for Israel as a Jewish state was expressed in an exchange of letters between Prime Minister Sharon and President Bush on April 14, 2004. Sharon outlined his plan for Israeli unilateral disengagement, which Bush welcomed as real progress toward the eventual realization of the US vision of two states—a "viable, contiguous, sovereign and independent" Palestinian state alongside Israel. Expressing US appreciation for the risk Israel was taking, Bush reassured Sharon that the US remained steadfast in its commitment to Israel's security and to its "well-being as a Jewish state." Bush noted further, again in line with Israel's position, that "an agreed, just, fair and realistic framework for a solution to the Palestinian refugee issue as part of any final-status agreement will need to be found through the establishment of a Palestinian state, and the settling of Palestinian refugees there, rather than in Israel."[132] Bush's support for Israel was most disappointing for the Palestinians, who denounced the US stand as no less than "the Second Balfour Declaration."[133]

US support for Israel as a Jewish state carried over into the Obama administration. As candidate for the presidency, Barack Obama told the annual AIPAC Policy Conference in early June 2008 that as president he would "work to help Israel achieve the goal of two states — a Jewish state of Israel and a Palestinian state living side-by-side in peace and security."[134] As president, in a speech to the UN in September 2009, Obama stated that "the goal is clear: Two states living side by side in peace and security — a Jewish state of Israel, with true security for all Israelis; and a viable, independent Palestinian state with contiguous territory that ends the occupation that began in 1967, and realizes the potential of the Palestinian people."[135]

In what evolved into the Obama administration's formal position, Secretary of State Hillary Clinton repeatedly reaffirmed the belief of the United States that "through good-faith negotiations the parties can mutually agree on an outcome which ends the conflict and reconciles the Palestinian goal of an independent and viable state based on the 1967 lines, with agreed [land] swaps, and Israel's goal of a Jewish state with secure and recognized borders that reflect subsequent developments [i.e., including certain blocs of settlements] and meet Israel's security requirements." The US commitment, she added, to the achievement of "a solution with two states living side by side in peace and security [was] unwavering."[136]

In the US National Security Strategy Survey issued by the White House in May 2010, this position was altered somewhat as follows: "The United States seeks two states living side by side in peace and security — a Jewish state of Israel, with true security, acceptance, and rights for all Israelis; and a viable, independent Palestine with contiguous territory that ends the occupation that began in 1967 and realizes the potential of the Palestinian people."[137] The new formula significantly added an emphasis on "rights for all Israelis" to assuage the concern expressed by Palestinians inside and outside of Israel that the recognition of Israel as a Jewish state might become a pretext to undermine the rights of the Arab minority as Israeli citizens.

## Palestinian Positions on Israel's Jewishness

For the Palestinians, recognition of Israel's Jewish character was tantamount to acceptance of the Israeli position on the non-return of refugees to Israel proper. Like the demand of the Palestinians to accept "end of conflict" on the basis of closure on the "1967 file," the Israeli demand of the Palestinians to recognize Israel's Jewishness was equally unacceptable to them. In the Palestinian view, both formulations required of them to essentially acquiesce in the invalidation of their narrative of 1948.

Unsurprisingly therefore, the official Palestinian response to Israel's demand to recognize its Jewishness was negative. There was but one noteworthy exception. In an interview with an Israeli paper in June 2004, Arafat was asked whether he understood that Israel had to remain a Jewish state. He replied, "Definitely . . . Definitely, I told them [the US and Israel] we had accepted [that] openly and officially in [19]88 in our PNC. . . ."[138] That, however, as already noted, was not a precise rendition of the 1988 PNC resolution. Arafat, in any event, never repeated this statement as given only in this, rather flippant, reply to the journalist question above.

As Israel became ever more insistent on the recognition of its Jewishness, so the Palestinian leadership tended to reject it. This was highlighted in the crisis between Israel and the Palestinian Authority in the run up to the Annapolis Conference between Prime Minister Ehud Olmert and President Mahmud Abbas in late November 2007 and again after Prime Minister Benjamin Netanyahu's Bar Ilan University speech in June 2009. Israel's demand that the Palestinians issue a binding statement recognizing Israel's Jewishness was rebuffed by all Palestinian spokesmen from Mahmud Abbas and Sa'ib Ariqat down.[139] An article in the semi-official Palestinian daily al-Ayyam in November 2007, on the eve of the Annapolis Conference, summed the matter up thus: "Such demands by Olmert and others from Israeli politicians . . . can only push the Palestinians with their backs to the wall . . . [which] would prompt them to redouble their efforts to regain at least the bare minimum of their legitimate rights as enshrined in the resolutions of international legitimacy [UN resolutions], which totally contradict [which they did not] Olmert's recent provocative and impossible demand."[140]

Netanyahu's June 2009 speech on the demilitarized Palestinian state and the need to recognize Israel's Jewish character was angrily dismissed by Palestinians across the board.[141] In August 2009, the resolutions of the Fatah Sixth General Conference noted the movement's "absolute and irrevocable refusal to recognize Israel as a 'Jewish state,' in order to protect the rights of the refugees and of our people across the green line [in Israel]."[142] These resolutions were reaffirmed in even more strident language by Fatah's Revolutionary Council meeting in late November 2010. The council restated Fatah's rejection, "in accordance with international law and human rights conventions, of the establishment of any racist state based on religion," thus completely deny-ing the very concept of Jewish nationhood and of Israel's right to exist as an expression of the Jewish people's right to self-determination.[143]

Moreover, in the words of a senior Fatah official, if Israel would not counte-nance refugee return, Israel should not be offered any more than a *hudna* in exchange for its complete withdrawal and closure on the issues of the "1967 file." Without the "1948 file," Israel did not deserve a peace treaty to end the conflict.[144] This was actually a position that came closer to narrowing Fatah's differences with Hamas than with Israel.

Khalid Mash'al outdid the Fatah spokesmen by dismissing the Israeli de-mand for Palestinian recognition of its Jewishness as not only blatantly racist but even reminiscent of the Nazis. Its acceptance would mean not only the "denial of the right of six million Palestinian refugees to return to their homes" but also that the Palestinians in Israel would eventually "be driven out of their cities and villages."[145]

As for nonofficial views, some were far more conciliatory. Polls suggested that about half of the general Palestinian public in the occupied territories was prepared to endorse more accommodating formulas than was the leadership. Even when Hamas won the elections in 2006, exit polls revealed that 34 per-cent of Hamas voters, 60 percent of Fatah voters, and 63 percent of voters for other parties (all in all about half of the voters) endorsed mutual recognition of Israel as a Jewish state and of Palestine as a Palestinian state in a two-state context. These findings were confirmed by further polling in late 2010.[146]

On the other hand, Ahmad Khalidi, a prominent London-based Palestinian intellectual, penned a series of excoriating rejections of the Israeli demand. There were "no conceivable circumstances," he wrote, "in which any Palestin-ian can concede their own history in favor of the Zionist narrative. It would mean that they would have to accept that for 1,400 years the Arab-Muslim presence in Palestine was transient and unlawful, and based on the false prem-ise that continuity of habitation conferred rights of ownership. Furthermore, the Palestinians would have to accept that the pulverization of Arab Palestine in 1948, and the 50 or more years of subsequent dispersal and occupation, are the rightful outcome of an illegal struggle against the real owners of the land."[147] The Palestinians could not be expected "to extend their benediction to the establishment of Israel, or internalize its legitimacy."[148]

For the Palestinians to recognize Israel as a Jewish state "implies the ac-knowledgement that *the lands they lost in 1948* [emphasis in original] are a Jewish birthright. This runs contrary to the heart of the Palestinians' historical narrative and their sense of identity and belonging." It also "invalidates the history of the Palestinians' century-old struggle and in effect demands that they should become Zionists. . . ." Israel's demand was no more than a "covert attempt to wrest Palestinian absolution for Israel's 'original sin' in taking over their homeland."[149] While the Palestinians were understandably aggrieved by the Zionist endeavor, it was precisely these absolutist Palestinian positions, totally devoid of any measure of empathy or compassion for the Jewish historical predicament, nor any recognition of Jewish historical ties to the land or of Jewish national aspirations, that made the achievement of peace such a seemingly futile exercise.

# 4 THE ALTERNATIVE

## The Promotion of the One-State Agenda

The arduous negotiations and the apparently insurmountable obstacles to an Israeli-Palestinian agreement on a two-state solution eventually gave rise to the argument that it was a useless endeavor. A far more reasonable alternative, so the argument went, was to resort to the creation of one state to be shared by Israelis and Palestinians, instead of an independent Israel with an independent Palestine alongside, over which the parties had been fighting for decades, with not much to show for their efforts. The one-state proposal, however, meant undoing Israel as presently constituted, as the state of the Jewish people, so as to pave the way for what in theory was to be a non-ethnic civic nation-state, shared by all. Calling for the undoing of Israel, unspeakable in the country's earlier years, was no longer politically unacceptable.

### Reframing the Discourse on Israel-Palestine

In the more than sixty years that have elapsed since the end of the Second World War, the discourse on Israel-Palestine has been reframed. After the war and the liberation of the death camps, the plight of the Jews imposed itself on the conscience of the international community, now reorganized in the newly formed UN. More than ever, in the wake of the Second World War and the Holocaust, the notion of Jewish statehood appeared to most fair-minded people in the West to be both timely and inherently just. Even the position of the Soviet Union, which had generally been pro-Arab on the question of Palestine, shifted in favor of the Zionists and partition. The new Soviet posture was at least partly driven by recognition of, and sympathy for, the suffering of the Jews under the Nazis and their post-war plight.[1]

Both the Anglo-American Committee of Inquiry and UNSCOP linked the rehabilitation of Holocaust survivors to the future of Palestine. Such a public discourse offered the Zionists "an unprecedented advantage in garnering world sympathy in a contest that the Palestinian Arabs simply could not win."[2] Identification with Jewish suffering had an impact on the pro-Zionist leanings of some of the members of UNSCOP. Some of them visited Jewish Displaced Persons camps in Europe and were horrified by what they saw and were equally impressed by the ardent desire of the survivors to immigrate to Palestine.

In delineating the boundaries of partition, attention was therefore also paid to the immigrant absorptive capacity of the Jewish state, a factor that undoubtedly impacted upon the decision to include the Negev within its boundaries.[3] The partition resolution as passed by the UN General Assembly urged the mandatory power to "use its best endeavors to ensure that an area situated in the territory of the Jewish State, including a seaport and hinterland adequate to provide facilities for a substantial immigration, shall be evacuated at the earliest possible date."[4]

In their lobbying efforts on behalf of partition at the UN, the underlying argument made by the Zionists focused on "the two-thousand year history of Jewish suffering and statelessness, culminating in the Holocaust, and the international community's responsibility to make amends."[5] This line of argumentation was especially effective in a UN of just fifty-seven members, the great majority of whom were European Christian nations or countries of the Western hemisphere that had come into being as the creations of European Christian emigrants, who were seriously troubled by the "pangs of Holocaust-related conscience." The countries of the Third World, who might have been more partial to the Arab cause, were for the most part yet to become members of the UN. Indeed, the approval of partition and the establishment of Israel were in many ways "Western civilization's gesture of repentance for the Holocaust . . . the repayment of a debt owed by those nations that realized that they might have done more to prevent or at least limit the scale of Jewish tragedy" during the Second World War.[6]

The Arabs of Palestine showed little compassion for the post-war plight of the Jews, nor did they realize the tremendous impact of the Holocaust on the international community. In their perception, the international community was coercing them to pay for the criminal transgressions of others. In the eyes of the Arab League, in the fall of 1944, there could be "no greater injustice and aggression than solving the problem of the Jews of Europe by another injustice," that is, by "inflicting injustice on the Arabs of Palestine."[7]

Yet, with the passage of time and the steadily receding memory of the horrors of the Holocaust, the context of the debate on Palestine has shifted dramatically in the international community. The linkage with the Holocaust has become increasingly irrelevant in the minds of many. In recent years numerous historians and commentators alike have come forth to pose the question of whether Israel's creation was really justified, in light of the protracted conflict that ensued and the suffering it has caused to the Palestinians. Avi Shlaim, one of the most renowned revisionist historians of the Arab-Israeli conflict, agreed with the assessment of Britain's third high commissioner in Palestine, Sir John Chancellor, that the Balfour Declaration had been a "colossal blunder." As Shlaim noted, it had "proved to be a catastrophe for the Palestinians" and the cause of interminable conflict.[8]

The human wreckage of the Holocaust became for many observers a closed chapter of an ever more distant past, whereas the Israeli occupation and settlement activity in the West Bank, the destitution of Gaza, and the plight of the Palestinian refugees were festering wounds very much alive in the contemporary consciousness of the international community and almost daily features on the news programs of the world.

The partition of Palestine and the establishment of Israel in 1947–48 coincided with the partition of the Indian subcontinent and the creation of India and Pakistan. Both were chapters in the end of empire and the beginning of an era of rapid decolonization that followed in the wake of the Second World War. But, as a country founded in the main by European émigrés, Israel was portrayed by the Arabs as a creature of imperialism. As the memory of the Holocaust faded, Israel was similarly portrayed by its detractors in other parts of the world as well. Israel had joined the family of nations much later than other states created by European émigrés, from most of the Western hemisphere to Australasia, which were already independent countries of long standing by the middle of the twentieth century and were also among the founding members of the United Nations.

Though not initially part of the so-called First World nor of the Soviet Bloc, Israel was never regarded as a Third World country either and was never treated as such by the liberal West. This internationalized liberal form of patronization was reserved for non-Europeans only. Thus the Palestinians and other Arabs qualified for such "Third World" compassion, but Israel never did. This was true even though at least half of Israel's Jewish population was not of European extraction, but from the Middle East, North Africa, the Caucasus, and

Central Asia. But Israel's political, intellectual, and economic elites were, indeed, predominantly European.

Israel was founded on the basis of a resolution passed by the UN when it was still dominated by the First World countries of the West. But as the Soviet Bloc coalesced and the non-aligned countries of the Third World became a bloc of their own, the international organization morphed into a body dominated by the Soviet Union and its "non-aligned" allies. From its inception, the PLO delegitimized the Zionist endeavor as a settler-colonialist enterprise that was ostensibly founded on a racist ideology. The Jews as a people had no national rights, not in Palestine / Eretz Yisrael nor anywhere else.

As support for the PLO steadily increased in the UN, backing for Israel dwindled. In 1975, in the aftermath the October 1973 war and the oil shock that accompanied it, the PLO was recognized by the UN, and concurrently the Jewish national movement, Zionism, was denounced as a form of racism in a resolution passed by the UN General Assembly.[9] The PLO's conflict with Israel was couched in terms reminiscent of the fight against racism in South Africa, and the resolutions of successive meetings of the PNC, in the 1970s and 1980s, regularly referred to the Palestinian struggle and the struggle against apartheid in South Africa as sister movements worthy of like-minded international support.

The resolution against Zionism was repealed by the UN at the end of the Cold War, in 1991. All the same, the struggle by the Palestinians and their supporters against Israel as a racist phenomenon continued unabated, as pre-1967 Israel and Israel of the occupation were conflated in the popular imagination into one image of injustice that was being inflicted on the indigenous Palestinians by their Israeli/European oppressors. Israel was increasingly portrayed by its detractors as an anachronistic colonialist creature in a postcolonial era.

Two general analytical paradigms are usually employed to explain Israeli policies and actions. Israel's supporters would tend to resort to the paradigm of conflict: Israel's policies and actions are a function of its conflict with the Palestinians and the Arabs in general, a conflict for which Israel's enemies share responsibility, for the pursuit of their objectives against Israel and its people. Israel's actions, therefore, derive from its needs of protection and self-defense in an extremely hostile neighborhood. This applies, for example, to the birth of the refugee question, born of war and not grand design;[10] to Israel's imposition of military government on the Arab minority in the early years after independence; and to the more recent construction of the security barrier, built to protect Israelis from the ravages of the suicide bombers.

Israel's opponents, on the other hand, would tend to explain Israel through a very different prism. Their paradigm is structured on what they regard as the inherent predatory nature of the Zionist enterprise, a point of departure that tends to absolve the Arabs of any responsibility for the evolution of the conflict and its consequences. According to this analysis, Zionism and the State of Israel are vilified as the two faces of a settler-colonialist expansionist design to dispossess and/or expel the Palestinians by force. The Palestinians and the other Arabs are therefore the innocent victims of Israel's inherently aggressive intent. In terms of this paradigm, the refugee problem is a creation of Israel's penchant for ethnic cleansing, just as its policies toward the Palestinian Arab minority in Israel and the construction of the security barrier are components of racism, expansionism, and land-grabbing, epitomized in the "apartheid wall," a patently racist epithet, to convey an equally obvious racist design.

Israel for the Palestinians and other critics remained an illegitimate abomination founded on a historical injustice and therefore had no inherent right to exist or to exercise self-defense. Influential Palestinian spokesmen in the diaspora condemned the Oslo Accords in no uncertain terms. The rejectionist factions of the PLO condemned "Arafat and his defeatist clique" as capitulatory and treasonous. Faruq Qaddumi, one of the founding fathers of Fatah, rejected the accords for having compromised on the basic national rights of the Palestinian people, especially on the right of return, and Edward Said scornfully dismissed the agreement as a secret deal between a very strong and a very weak partner, forcing the PLO to make embarrassing concessions in a state of "exhaustion and isolation."[11]

In contrast to the occupied territories, where the Oslo Accords were generally well received,[12] in the Palestinian diaspora they were widely understood as a blatant prioritization of the population under occupation, at the expense of the refugees and their right of return. The apparent abandonment of the refugees further delegitimized the PLO leadership and "helped to burnish the credentials of Hamas in particular."[13] Moreover, the Oslo Accords failed to achieve their goals, and by the end of the 1990s the process was in tatters.

Conversely, the 1990s, the years in which the two-state solution for Israel-Palestine failed to materialize, were the very years of the great political success in South Africa, in the peaceful transition from apartheid to democracy. After the failure of the Camp David and Taba talks and the outbreak of the second

Intifada, it became increasingly common for people to argue with greater intensity, conviction, and credibility that the two-state solution was proving to be impractical, exactly at the historical moment when South Africa demonstrated that a one-state alternative was a far more realistic proposition. The two-state paradigm began to give way to two complementary developments: the South Africanization of the discourse on Israel-Palestine, on the one hand, and an intensive campaign waged in the Palestinian diaspora on the sanctity of the right of refugee return, on the other. The one-state solution and refugee return to Israel proper were essentially two sides of the same coin. Large-scale refugee return could not lead to anything other than some variant of the one-state solution, in which the Jews became an ever-declining minority in the land between the Jordan River and the Mediterranean.

In September 2001 the UN World Conference against Racism, Racial Discrimination, Xenophobia and Related Intolerance was held in Durban, South Africa. During the World Conference, "large numbers of NGOs organized a parallel NGO Forum (sometimes confused with the conference) that, in turn, succeeded in overshadowing the formal proceedings." This was due to "the large amount of media attention the NGOs were able to generate. The NGO Forum produced what is known as the 'NGO Declaration,' which, while not an official conference document, assumed a high international profile and was signed by groups such as Amnesty International and Human Rights Watch."

The NGO declaration at the Durban conference reflected a concerted effort to undermine Israel. It denounced "Israel's brand of apartheid and ethnic cleansing methods" and called for "a policy of complete and total isolation of Israel as an apartheid state. . . ." It similarly condemned those states that were "supporting, aiding and abetting the Israeli apartheid state and its perpetration of racist crimes against humanity including ethnic cleansing [and] acts of genocide."[14]

A conference convened to commemorate the dismantling of South Africa as an apartheid state now called for the dismantling of Israel as the reincarnation of apartheid South Africa. In the words of Canadian jurist Irwin Cotler, a conference that was supposed to be dedicated to the protection and promotion of human rights increasingly spoke about Israel as being "a meta-violator of human rights and as the new anti-Christ of our time." Israel was also characterized as being, in essence, an apartheid state—not only in the occupied territories but in its very character. "The clarion call was clear: just as the struggle against racism in the twentieth century required the dismantling of South Africa as an apartheid state, so the struggle against racism in the twenty-first century requires the dismantling of Israel as an apartheid state." In Durban, Zionism was characterized "not only as racism but as a violent movement of racist supremacy."[15] In this community of NGOs, all peoples, except the Jews, had national rights. All nationalisms were legitimate; only Jewish nationalism was not.

A climate of international civil rights discourse was thus being formulated in which the singling out of Israel for selective prosecution and ultimate dissolution was not only a legitimate but even a virtuous pursuit. Paradoxically, as the two-state solution gained international legitimacy in the community of nations—as represented by UN Security Council Resolution 1397 of March 2002, the Arab Peace Initiative of March 2002, the Roadmap endorsed by the Quartet in April 2003, and Security Council Resolution 1515 of November 2003, which endorsed the Roadmap—widening circles in the nongovernmental international community waged a determined campaign to delegitimize this very same idea.

Influential works and publications by academics were reframing the debate on Israel-Palestine by questioning the validity and the legitimacy of the two-state paradigm. They promoted an alternative binational or South African style one-state solution as both a just and practical model to replace Israel.

## The Articulation of the One-State Agenda—A Critical Review

In the late 1990s and the early 2000s, the one-state discourse began to gain public prominence as the Oslo process appeared to falter and the South African model acquired the image of an enduring success. Articles in the Arab press and in scholarly and intellectual journals began to seriously address the issue of a binational state in Israel/Palestine.[16] More recently various conferences have been held in London, such as at the School of Oriental and African Studies at the University of London (November 2007), and at some North American universities, such as Harvard, MIT, and the University of Massachusetts, Boston (March 2009), and York University, Toronto (June 2009), to further the one-state idea.[17]

In late 2003 Tony Judt, the Anglo-Jewish, New York–based historian, wrote a contentious but trailblazing article in the *New York Review of Books* entitled "Israel: The Alternative." Judt lamented the failure of the Israeli-Palestinian peace process and asked, as the Israelis "grimly await the next bomber" and the Palestinians were "corralled into shrinking Bantustans," what was to be done? His answer was that Israel had arrived on the scene "too late" with a "characteristically late-nineteenth-century separatist project" into a world that had moved on, beyond the old-fashioned nation-state. The very idea of a "Jewish state" was "an anachronism." In any event, a two-state solution, which might have been possible in the past, was no longer feasible, as there were "too many settlements, too many Jewish settlers, and too many Palestinians," all living in the same space, for that to become a reality. The time had come "to think the unthinkable." Israel, Judt suggested, should be replaced by a "single binational state of Jews and Arabs."[18] As Leon Wieseltier pointed out, this was not an alternative *for* Israel, but an alternative *to* Israel.[19]

In 2005 Virginia Tilley published *The One-State Solution: A Breakthrough for Peace in the Israeli-Palestinian Deadlock*,[20] which was the first extensive academic work on the subject. Israel's settlement grid in the West Bank had become an immovable object, she argued, and as a result a two-state solution was not attainable, as attested to by the repeated failures of Israelis and Palestinians to negotiate such an agreement. The Jewish settlements had forged a reality that now confronted all the parties concerned: "only one state can viably exist in the land of historic Palestine between the Mediterranean and the Jordan River."[21] Tilley was followed by the Palestinian Ali Abunimah, who published *One Country: A Bold Proposal to End the Israeli-Palestinian Impasse* in 2006, in which he suggested that, despite everything he knew about the present state of affairs, "Israelis and Palestinians can live together in one country that they consider to be equally and simultaneously a Jewish state and a Palestinian state."[22]

In the works of activists like Tilley and Abunimah, the ostensibly immovable obstacle of the settlements was not the only justification for the one-state solution. "Israel-Palestine itself was always far too small and sensitive a region to sustain two states," Tilley opines. Hence, "the one-state solution is not an option to be argued. It is an inevitability to be faced."[23] If so, the problem is not only the settlements, but Israel itself. Indeed, their real objection is to Israel's creation in the first place, which they portray as a settler-colonial state founded on the eviction of the indigenous Palestinian population.

Tilley, at times, overstates her case. One of many examples is her representation of the "future Palestinian state," which, she contends, is suggested by the route of Israel's security barrier. Israel has "an enclave plan" for the West Bank whereby the Palestinian "Bantustan," or "walled-off Palestinian ghetto," or "gruesome apartheid system" (the intemperate language is matched only by

Map 6. Israel's security barrier. Reprinted with the permission of
Shaul Arieli

its incongruity with the reality on the ground) is hemmed into a tiny sliver of
the West Bank highlands, completely fenced in, on the west and the east, by
the Israeli barrier.[24]

In practice, however, the barrier to the west has not yet been completed,
though it has been in construction for close to a decade. But far more critically,
the eastern fence, without which there can be no "enclave," "Bantustan," or
"ghetto," does not exist at all. None of it has been built, and none of it is
planned for construction either[25] (see the Israeli barrier in map 6). Moreover,
in the Camp David–Taba negotiations between Israel and the Palestinians, well
before Tilley's book was written, Israel did not offer the Palestinians "the
twisted scrap of land remaining"[26] in the West Bank, in the "walled-off" territory of her depiction. Israel eventually offered some 95 percent of the West
Bank, which was more than twice the size of the area Tilley described.

Tilley argues repeatedly that what was on offer was a dismembered enclave
or "Bantustan" that could never have been a satisfactory basis for a state or a

stable solution.[27] However, if Israel were to annex only the major settlement blocs (the 5 to 6 percent of the West Bank that would include some 75 to 80 percent of the settlers, as proposed in the negotiations and in the Clinton Parameters), it becomes geographically impossible to dissect the West Bank into such "dismembered enclaves" (see maps 3 and 4).

Irrespective of the geographic and mathematical impossibility, Tilley insists that "the 6 percent still cut deep troughs through Palestinian territory, sustaining its partition into three enclaves . . . [a] darker fact obscured by this superficially small figure,"[28] but she does not show how that is attained. Moreover, she describes President Bush's exchange of letters with Sharon in April 2004, in which Bush implicitly acquiesced in Israel's retention of these blocs of settlement, as a "lethal endorsement" of Israel's settlement grid and of its "annexation of the West Bank."[29] Tilley's interpretation is groundless and is uniquely hers.

Tilley gives many reasons — political, economic, and religious — to explain Israel's unyielding embrace of the occupied territories. Some are valid, others less so. Tilley, however, will be proved right in the basic thrust of her argument that a one-state solution is unavoidable if, as she says, no force, within Israel or without, could muster the power to effect a meaningful withdrawal from the settlements, except for perhaps some in Gaza and a few token outposts in the West Bank.[30] What she says about Gaza has already been disproved, but the main problem is obviously on the West Bank in regard to the 80,000 to 130,000 settlers (depending on where the line is drawn) on the "wrong" side of a future boundary.[31] On that question the jury is still out.

Tilley quite correctly dismisses the ideas of some on Israel's far right for solving the Palestinian question by transforming Jordan into the future state of Palestine, thereby allowing Israel to absorb the West Bank. Arabs, she observes, "do not blend into each other readily and indiscriminately," and the belief that they do "requires willful blindness to the actual deep cultural divisions in the Arab world." She argues that Jordanians and Palestinians do not share cultural references, nationalist experience, or political culture.[32] Indeed, there are by now cohesive Jordanian and Palestinian identities both legitimately entitled to exercise their respective rights to self-determination. The idea of lumping Palestinians and Jordanians together in one state is, therefore, according to Tilley, pure fantasy, as neither Jordanians nor Palestinians will cooperate in such an endeavor and they cannot be compelled to do so either.

However, after having dwelt at some length on the irreconcilable differences between Jordanians and Palestinians, Tilley moves on to promote the notion that one state between the Jordan River and the Mediterranean, lumping Israelis and Palestinians together, would resolve the conflict between these two peoples "in one magisterial gesture." Though this one-state solution would mean creating a state with an Arab majority and "Israel would cease to be a 'Jewish State' in the sense commonly understood by most people today,"[33] this, she tells us, would be a workable solution. Thus, Tilley tries to convince her readers that what is impossible to achieve between Jordanians and Palestinians, because of their minor otherness, would somehow be attainable between Israeli Jews and Palestinians, irrespective of their major differences.

Jordanians and Palestinians are by and large Sunni Muslim coreligionists (with small Orthodox Christian minorities in both communities), who speak the same language. As Palestinian sociologist Salim Tamari[34] and many others have noted, Jordanians and Palestinians tend to think of themselves as peoples who share considerable cultural commonality.[35] In contradistinction, Israeli Jews and Palestinians have been in conflict for more than a century. One of the worst rounds of this mutual bloodletting was fought in the first decade of the twenty-first century, with the suicide bombers attacking Israel's population centers met by fierce and at times ruthless Israeli retaliation. Rockets from Gaza on Israeli civilian targets were countered by Israel's massive reprisal on Hamas in early 2009, inflicting much loss of life among combatants and civilians alike and sowing widespread destruction. Israeli Jews and Palestinians do not speak the same language, do not share the same religion, and are culturally, politically, and historically considerably much further apart than Jordanians and Palestinians.

Nevertheless, in Tilley's vision, they will peacefully coexist in this one state, after the Jews will voluntarily do what she herself tells us the Palestinians could never be expected to do, that is, to allow their national aspirations to "somehow evaporate."[36] One of the many reasons Tilley cites for Palestinian rejection of Israel's so-called "patchwork of enclaves" proposed for a Palestinian state is that defense "would be entirely impossible and would depend entirely on Israel—the historical enemy."[37] If that were really what was on offer from Israel, the Palestinians would indeed be justified in their refusal to acquiesce.

If so, however, why should the Israelis be expected to accept what is so distasteful to the Palestinians? Is it even remotely reasonable to expect them to acquiesce in some undefined form of "national home," or Jewish "Bantustan" to take a leaf out of Tilley's vocabulary, within the framework of this one state[38] and thereby place their protection in the hands of the Palestinian majority, the rest of the Arab world, and Iran? Are these not all the "historical enemies" of the Israelis? Is that not "willful blindness" of much greater measure than Tilley ascribes to those who refuse to pay heed to the comparatively minor distinctions between Jordanians and Palestinians?

Abunimah denigrates Menachem Begin for offering the Palestinians only limited "personal" autonomy, "specifically ruling out anything that smacked of territorial sovereignty or self-determination."[39] In the Camp David Accords, Begin had actually upgraded his original proposal and accepted territorial autonomy for the Palestinians. The upgrading notwithstanding, Begin's offer to the Palestinians at Camp David was insufficient and was understandably rejected. But Abunimah and the one-state advocates themselves are not offering the Israeli Jews "anything that smacked of territorial sovereignty or self-determination" either. At Camp David, Begin recognized the "legitimate rights of the *Palestinian people* and their just requirements [emphasis added],"[40] which is considerably more than the one-state supporters generally recognize for the Israelis. The "legitimate rights of the Jewish people and their just requirements" are nonexistent in their discourse.

The unitary state of Abunimah's imagination is a wish list of perfection. It would have to "rest on common values" and would be governed, among others, by the following principles: The power of government would be exercised with "rigorous impartiality" in a state that would be Jewish and Palestinian "equally, simultaneously, and without contradiction." The two peoples would enjoy linguistic and cultural autonomy. Freedom of religion would be guaranteed, and the state would actively foster "economic opportunity, social justice and a dignified life for all."[41] Other than repeatedly willing this state to become reality, issuing entreaties to the Israeli Jews and to the Palestinians to "reach out" and produce an "inclusive vision," Abunimah offers no explanation, considering everything he and everyone else knew about the past and the present, how this would in fact materialize. Such an "inclusive vision" does not even exist between Fatah and Hamas, never mind between Israelis and Palestinians.

Very few states of such perfection exist anywhere, if at all. There are none in the Middle East, and the crisis of secularism and escalating sectarianism in the Arab and wider Muslim world[42] suggest that there will not be such states in the region in the near future either. Hamas will make sure that such a state will not arise in Palestine. But Abunimah goes on to argue that there are a number

of democratic models that have successfully regulated long-standing conflicts, and he mentions Canada, Belgium, South Africa, and India, none of
which is a truly successful or applicable model. Belgium is in perennial domestic crisis, on the verge of possible dissolution; there has been a substantial
out-migration of disgruntled Anglophones from Quebec; India is a strange
example to choose, since the Indian success story was founded on partition
and a two-state solution; and South Africa was a country of racial discrimination and not ethnic nationalist conflict, where the levels of violence and consequent remnants of distrust and outright hostility were never even remotely
similar to the Arab-Israeli experience.

Indeed, marketing the one-state idea requires the systematic understate-
ment of the ferocity of conflict between Jews and Arabs, Palestinian and other.
Abunimah speaks of the "peaceful coexistence between Jews and Arabs in Palestine before the creation of Israel."[43] But as is well-known, Arab rejection of
partition in 1947 came in the wake of years of escalating conflict with the Jews
in Palestine. For the Arabs, the UN 1947 partition resolution was unacceptable, and they declared war. Tilley makes no mention at all of the first phase of
civil war that pitted the Palestinian Arabs against the Jews for six months pre-
ceding the Arab invasion, as if the Palestinian Arabs never took part in the 1948
war at all. As for the 1967 war, just out of the blue, as if a function of its innate
expansionism, "Israel seized the rest of Mandate Palestine."[44] There is no
mention of the causes that actually provoked the war.

Hajj Amin al-Husayni, the unrivaled leader of the Palestinians until the debacle of 1948, collaborated with the Nazis in the Second World War, for reasons that one could actually explain with not too much difficulty in terms of
"the enemy of my enemy." The mufti was perhaps not a Nazi, but when he
could, he did actively support the implementation of the "final solution."
Since the mufti's collaboration interferes with Tilley's portrayal of the Palestinians as being far less hostile to Jews and Zionists than they actually were,
Hajj Amin is simply dismissed as a marginal and unrepresentative figure. He
was "never a leader of more than a few reactionary Palestinian factions. His
primary accomplishment was to sideline and obscure for history those Arab
factions that sought coexistence with the Jewish-Zionist movement."[45] This is
total fabrication, as anyone, Palestinian, Israeli, or otherwise, with any knowledge of the history of Palestine would know.

Israel's security barrier, in Tilley's words, was not an act of self-defense
against the suicide bombers but a "wall of ethnic defense in the spirit of apart-

heid." Indeed, "never has the modern world seen such a breathtaking monument to ethno-racial defense."[46] Israel's "wall" (over 90 percent of which is not a wall but a fence), which would "seal the Palestinians permanently within this amputee national existence," was leading to "rising desperation and the fresh legitimization of militancy—even, for the fringe few, the capacity to see suicidal terror as a righteous act of resistance."[47] As already shown, the actual barrier is not the asphyxiating monstrosity that she has described, but in this instance she goes on to reverse cause and effect. The barrier becomes the reason for the suicide bombings rather than their consequence. As for the bombings themselves, they were "a tiny fringe phenomenon," an aberration.[48]

But this was not just the deviant behavior of a few individuals. It was a case of a people who had given themselves over "to the fury of 'the street' and the rage of suicide bombers." According to the pollsters, 60 percent of the Palestinian population, at the time, approved of suicide attacks against Israeli civilians. The bombers were a function of a "people in the throes of [a] kind of vengeance and radicalism. . . ."[49] The Jewish settlers in the West Bank are also just a fringe of Israeli society, about 5 percent (more than half of whom are children), the real fanatics among them even less. But one could not reasonably argue that their number makes their violence and other miscreant behavior toward defenseless Palestinians any less outrageous or their presence any less of an obstacle to a peace agreement. It is not their percentage that matters, but the popular and governmental support, direct or indirect, that they command. What is true in Israel is true in Palestine.

Tilley's contention that the security barrier was built "in the spirit of apartheid," that is, with an ostensibly racist motivation, ignores the many hundreds of Israelis who were killed by the suicide bombings in the buses, restaurants, and other civilian targets throughout the country. The use of the purely racist (rather than security) term "apartheid wall" completely dehumanizes the Israelis and shows no regard, concern, or compassion for their large-scale loss of life.

In South Africa, as Abunimah observes, "violence was never the main feature of the anti-apartheid struggle."[50] Constantly aware of the need to assuage white fears of black majority rule, the African National Congress (ANC) under Nelson Mandela made a concerted effort to be conciliatory. Mandela paid tribute to the Afrikaner nation and their national struggle against British imperialism. He also made a point of accepting the Afrikaners not as settlers but as indigenous Africans.[51] None of this applies to the nature of the Palestinian struggle, including that of the one-state advocates, against Israel, nor to the measure of their acceptance of the Zionist narrative.

Since the one-state advocates envisage "one secular, democratic" state, Tilley and Abunimah go to great lengths to show that the Palestinians are not only inherently moderate and tolerant in their attitude toward Israeli Jews, but also secular and democratic by nature. Tilley condemns those who do not realize the "overwhelmingly secular" nature of Palestinian nationalist politics in its first half century for being "strategically amnesiac." The Islamic tendency was only a recent and "still minority twist" in Palestinian society.[52] But this is just not so.

The Palestinian national movement never was and is not overwhelmingly secular. The two most important figures in Palestinian pre-1948 history were clerics, Hajj Amin al-Husayni, the leader of the national movement, and Shaykh Izz al-Din al-Qassam, the founding father of the Palestinian armed struggle against the British and the Zionists. In PLO documentation in Arabic, the word "secular" was never used, not in reference to the unitary democratic state of the future, nor in any other context. Polls in Palestinian universities in the mid-1990s showed that only a tiny minority of Muslim students defined themselves as secular. The victory of Hamas in the Palestinian elections in January 2006 would appear to be ample proof that the Islamic trend was not and is not an insignificant "minority twist."

In Tilley's mind, if the Israelis would only give up their state, they would have nothing to fear. The Israeli argument about security, she contends, is actually circular, insofar as the Israelis argued that Jewish statehood was essential to protect Jews from the consequences of their statehood. "For the awkward fact is that, if Palestinians came to enjoy democratic rights as citizens in one secular-democratic state, the threat of Arab attack would disappear entirely, as Arab states would have no motive to attack such a state." Moreover, even though ethnic politics would persist into the imaginable future, "competition would now be channeled into democratic mechanisms."[53]

From the outset, the Zionists sought to ensure their right to self-determination in an independent state. They were, however, violently opposed by the Palestinian Arabs in the 1920s and 1930s, long before their state came into being. The recognition of the depth of conflict convinced the Jews, already by the 1930s, that only in a sovereign state under their own control would they be able to promote Jewish immigration and indeed be secure. It was not their state that provoked the violence, but the violence that convinced the Zionists to insist on their demand for statehood and sovereign self-defense, rather than binationalism or other one-state proposals.

Zionism, or Jewish nationalism, is invariably described by Tilley with pejorative delegitimating terminology. It is hardly ever described as an exercise by the Jews of the universal right of self-determination, but almost always as an inherently aggressive and racist form of "ethnic chauvinism" or "ethnic dominion." Israel's "stated program is to reject even the suggestion of ethnic equality," she says. The "democratic inclusion of Palestinians" is rejected, as this would "wreck the Jewishness of the Jewish state,"[54] she argues, regardless of the fact that Israel's Declaration of Independence proclaims quite the opposite. "One man, one vote," the rallying cry of the anti-apartheid struggle, has been on the statute books of Israel since the day it was founded.

Tilley systematically conflates pre-1967 Israel and the occupation of the West Bank and Gaza. The Palestinians in the occupied territories are not citizens of Israel. The inclusion of Palestinians in Israel's democratic system is not the issue. Such inclusion, with all its problems and deficiencies, already exists in reference to Israel's Palestinian Arab citizens. It is the annexation of the occupied territories that would rapidly turn the Jews into a minority in an Arab-dominated state, precisely because it is automatically assumed that the Arabs would enjoy full civil rights. The alternative, that the Arabs be denied civil rights in this post-annexation state, thus creating a South African apartheid-like reality, is actually understood by most Israelis as the prime reason for this situation *to be avoided.*

Tilley is, nevertheless, indignant that "white ethno-racial domination over South African blacks was obvious, offensive, and easy to denounce. . . . Yet equally glaring juridical Jewish ethno-racial domination of Arabs somehow manifests as accidental fallout of a righteous cause." Tilley laments the fact that "European-Jewish domination of native Arabs has not triggered the visceral moral revulsion in the West" that the South African case did. She ascribes this to various causes such as "lingering orientalism" or "western gullibility" to Zionist propaganda, which permits Israel to "speciously [claim] political kinship" to the Western democracies.[55]

It could, of course, also be that the comparison was not that widely accepted because it was not "equally glaring." The analogy was perhaps not all that "obvious, offensive, and easy to denounce." Whatever one may have to say about Jewish-Arab relations in Israel, and they are not flawless, nor free of tensions and serious problems of inequality and discrimination, they are not founded on a legal infrastructure of racial discrimination. The Arabs in Israel are equal citizens of the state by law and have equal access to the political process, the courts, the education system (free and compulsory from elementary school until the end of high school, and access to the universities, based on uniform tuition for all citizens), universal health care, and social welfare. None of this applied in apartheid South Africa.

Moreover, white South Africans would hardly have rejected the characterization of their state by others as a racist apartheid state. They invented apartheid. It was also they themselves who in the end recognized that the system they had created was morally and politically bankrupt. The Afrikaners were not coerced to give up apartheid. It was not only, or even mainly, the sanctions, divestment, or external pontification that brought the system down, but the recognition by the Afrikaners themselves that apartheid could no longer be sustained, by and large, for domestic demographic, economic, moral, and political reasons.

The major problem the Afrikaners faced in the late twentieth century was the realization that the whites were being overwhelmed demographically at a rate much faster than initially predicted. Between 1910 and 1960 the white population formed 20 percent of the total population, but after 1960 it dropped steadily to 17 percent in 1976 and 12 percent in 2000. (As for the Afrikaners, the political backbone of apartheid, already by the 1970s their number had shrunk to less than 10 percent of the population.)[56]

A thriving economy could not be maintained without an ever-increasing influx of black labor into the cities, thus constantly eroding the fundamental underpinnings of apartheid. Moreover, increasing segments of the Afrikaner intellectual elite, and eventually even the Dutch Reformed Church, the moral compass of the system, would not give their blessing to its blatant immorality and to the escalating repression of the constantly growing black majority. Ultimately the Afrikaners came to the conclusion that their own survival required the undoing of apartheid.[57]

The comparison of the Afrikaner predicament with the Jews of Israel does not hold water particularly because of the diametrically opposed demographic reality whereby the Jewish Israelis are the overwhelming majority in their country, which the Afrikaners never were in theirs. The Palestinians in pre-1967 Israel constituted about 17 to 18 percent of the total population.[58] Consequently the same forms of economic interdependence were never created in Israel, nor the morally reprehensible political system designed to preserve the rule of a very small minority over a huge disenfranchised majority through the ever-increasing resort to force.

On the other hand, the nature of the ANC struggle against the apartheid regime recognized the economic interdependence with the white minority and never called for its expulsion or annihilation. Their armed struggle, as a rule, did not target white civilians, a deliberate strategy designed to reassure the white minority of the peaceful and cooperative character of black majority rule of the future. Conversely, the Palestinian armed struggle against Israel and Israelis peaked with the suicide bombings, deliberately designed to kill as many civilians as possible. As Benjamin Pogrund, the former South African newspaper editor and anti-apartheid activist, has pointed out, "There was nothing remotely like this in apartheid South Africa: Blacks did not do this and the psyche of the whites did not suffer the trauma and the memories of the Israelis."[59]

Tilley, Abunimah, and others of their persuasion would argue that the over-whelming Jewish majority in Israel was obtained by the illegitimate means of war and ethnic cleansing. The main thrust of Zionism was not the dedication to the redemption of the Jews, but to a doctrine that made "moral sense of ex-pelling ethnic others." The mission to create a Jewish state with a permanent Jewish majority "granted moral authority to 'cleansing' the land of non-Jews," or "necessitated 'cleansing' the land of its majority Arab population."[60]

Tilley cites Benny Morris, unquestionably the most authoritative Israeli "new historian" on the refugee question, to prove that Israel was indeed based on expulsion, transfer, and ethnic cleansing. All the 750,000 refugees of 1948 and the 250,000 of 1967 were the result of "deliberate campaigns" by Israeli leaderships to "cleanse" the land of the Arab presence. Morris, she notes, "was responsible for wrecking a founding myth in Israel's national narrative by documenting the Zionists' deliberate expulsion of hundreds of thousands of Palestinians from their villages in 1948."[61]

But Tilley is misrepresenting Morris. In his various works on the subject, Morris's conclusions are more nuanced and complex. He does show that while most of the refugees fled, many, indeed some hundreds of thousands, were forcefully expelled. However, Morris explicitly refutes the charge of grand de-sign. According to Morris, "the first Arab-Israeli war, of 1948, was launched by the Palestinian Arabs, who rejected the UN partition resolution and embarked on hostilities aimed at preventing the birth of Israel. That war *and not design* [emphasis added], Jewish or Arab, gave birth to the Palestinian refugee problem." Morris does say that the displacement of Arabs was "inherent in Zionist ideology" (a contention seriously contested by other Israeli historians),[62] and he notes that Zionist leaders did occasionally endorse the idea of transfer, but most importantly even he goes on to conclude that "there was no pre-war Zionist plan to expel 'the Arabs' from Palestine." The Yishuv did "not enter the war with a plan or policy of expulsion. Nor was the pre-war 'transfer' thinking ever translated, in the course of the war, into an agreed, systematic policy of expulsion."[63]

As for possibly premeditated designs of expulsion or worse, according to Morris, the story of 1948 was actually far more complex and related to both sides. The Palestinian leadership in 1948 declared that fighting would continue "until the Zionists were annihilated" in all of Palestine. Palestinian militiamen who fought alongside the Jordanian Arab Legion consistently expelled Jewish inhabitants and razed Jewish sites that were conquered. The invading Arab armies, in keeping with the "expulsionist mindset prevailing in the Arab states" did the same. In the areas of Palestine that came under Arab control during the war, that is, the West Bank, East Jerusalem, and the Gaza Strip, not a single Jew remained.[64]

Tilley explains, quite rightly, that Zionist logic has precluded the one-state solution from the outset.[65] That is indeed so, but if Zionism was really based to its very core on ethnic cleansing, it is hard to explain why the majority of Zionists and Jewish Israelis opted for partition and for two states. After all, they have had the power, as of the latter phases of the 1948 war and ever since, to expel all the Arabs of Palestine to the very last, if they so desired. Most of the Zionists for most of the time have sought and succeeded to maintain their majority by mass immigration and partition, that is, support for the conceding of territory for a two-state solution, and not by expulsion.

After the victory of 1967, Ben-Gurion was asked by an Israeli interviewer why he had not permitted the conquest of all of Palestine in the latter part of the 1948 war, when it was militarily feasible. From his explanation it was clear that he "wanted a state with a Jewish majority more than he wanted the entire homeland, and though he had no objections to Arabs fleeing, he believed that they would no longer do so unless Israel used harsher methods than he could accept."[66]

Since the 1948 war, the Palestinian Arab population in pre-1967 Israel has increased nearly tenfold. In the territories occupied since 1967, the Palestinian population has increased almost fivefold since the Six Day War. These are among the fastest-growing populations in the world, a fact hardly reconcilable with ethnic cleansing or with an expulsionist design and practice as the essential backbone of the Zionist enterprise. The Israeli-Palestinian situation is a function of conflict between two equally legitimate ethno-cultural national movements, and not a conflict born of systemic racial discrimination, disenfranchisement, exclusion, and expulsion.

Asserting that the Palestinians are democratically inclined, Tilley points for support to the fact that the Palestinian citizens of Israel have been "integrated into Israeli politics," where they have "eloquent Arab representatives to the Knesset." The Israeli Arabs were "full players in Israeli democracy and have indicated no desire to lose that status."[67] That, of course, is all true. Moreover, Tilley says, a lasting democratic ethos ran deep in Palestinian society, so much so that they "have admired Israel's democracy and hoped for something similar for the Palestinian state." Therefore if there were to be one state as she suggests, it would remain democratic thanks to this Palestinian democratic proclivity and to "Israel's ruggedly democratic institutions. Israel's sturdy democracy should be entirely capable of remaining democratic while absorbing this democratically oriented population."[68] In apartheid South Africa, needless to say, the black majority had no vote and no members of parliament, eloquent or otherwise. But elsewhere Israel is repeatedly censured as a quasi-apartheid state based on ethnic dominion and exclusion, "speciously" claiming to be a Western-style democracy. So which of her depictions of Israel is true? It is either a robust inclusive democracy or a quasi-apartheid state. It cannot be both.

Israel's Law of Return, offering Jews preferential rights of citizenship in the country, is often cited by Israel's critics as an example of its racist character.[69] But, in fact, Israel in this instance is hardly unique in the democratic world. There is no foundation in international law proscribing the sovereignty of states on immigration policy, provided the policy does not specifically exclude any particular group. If Israel is accepted as the nation-state of the Jewish people, as defined by the partition resolution of 1947, then it only stands to reason that it would also enact a law of repatriation for Jews of the diaspora, as indeed was envisaged by the same partition resolution.[70] Israeli law, as already noted, confers citizenship on non-Jews, and it does not prohibit the immigration of non-Jews. Hundreds of thousand of non-Jews have immigrated to Israel since 1948, mainly Palestinian refugees, returning under family reunification schemes, and immigrants from the former Soviet Union, usually spouses of Jews or non-Jews with Jewish ancestors.

In the European Union, the special relationship of "kin-minorities" to their "kin-states" is an accepted and recognized principle. Germany has an immigration law similar to Israel's in its preferential treatment of ethnic Germans. Preferential treatment of immigrants with national ties of kinship to the majority people is also practiced in different ways in various Western democracies such as Finland, Ireland, and Greece. A number of new Central and Eastern European democracies—Poland, Hungary, Bulgaria, Slovakia, the Czech Republic, Slovenia, and Croatia—have introduced similar laws, as have the former Soviet republics of Russia, the Ukraine, and Armenia.[71] The Scandinavian countries have immigration laws that are specifically preferential to other Scandinavians (Swedes, Danes, Fins, Icelanders, or Norwegians).[72] It would be only natural if the Palestinian state of the future would have a similar law, as indeed its draft constitution suggests it will.[73]

It is in the occupation of the West Bank that one may find relevant comparisons with South Africa of old, particularly in the fact that Israel controls a relatively large population of Palestinians, who do not enjoy equal rights with their Israeli settler neighbors. The settlers are not subject to the regime of occupation, and they enjoy all the rights of the Israeli legal system, which do not apply to the Palestinians in the West Bank. The Palestinians, as of yet, do not have a state of their own that could confer equal rights upon them too. The occupation for most Israelis, so the polls suggest, has outlived its usefulness. That is good reason for Israel to jettison the occupied territories and allow for the establishment of an independent Palestinian state. But Jewish Israelis, by and large, will not cooperate in throwing the Israel baby out with the occupation bathwater.

As much as one-state activism is about finding a "solution," the one-state agenda has for many of its advocates become a tool in the struggle against Israel. The supporters of this notion show little or no empathy for the historical plight of the Jews, their national aspirations, or their historical struggle.[74] Generally speaking, the one-state advocates discuss the Palestinian-Israeli issue almost totally divorced from its two formative contexts: the European origins of Zionism, and the Middle Eastern evolution of the Arab-Israeli conflict. Zionism, in the Jewish narrative, was not a movement of settler colonialists, but of national liberation and a consequence of the insufferable predicament of the Jews of Eastern Europe, excluded from and oppressed by the emergent nationalist movements of the late nineteenth century. The Zionists sought a national refuge in their historical homeland in Eretz Yisrael, the cradle of historical Jewish nationhood and sovereign existence. It was only here that it made any historical sense for the Jews to exercise their right to self-determination.

The Jews who immigrated to Palestine severed their ties with their countries of origin and their cultural past, as part of their ideological endeavor to create a totally new Hebrew-speaking nation and culture. That this was a colonialist exploit on behalf of the Ukrainian, Russian, Polish, or Lithuanian "mother countries" is as ridiculous as it sounds. The Zionists, as opposed to the colonialist paradigm, did not encroach on Palestine to extract its nonexistent resources and raw materials, nor to exploit its indigenous population, but to invest in the development of the country and in so doing to build their own nationhood.[75] Palestine at the end of the Ottoman era was too poor to support its indigenous population, and Jews and Arabs were emigrating at the time to America and Australia. Until 1948 the Zionists, as opposed to classical colonial movements, did not conquer the land, but bought it on the market from local as well as nonresident landowners.[76]

The Zionist enterprise was about Jewish national redemption. It was generally indifferent toward the well-being of the Arabs of Palestine and nestled for twenty crucial years, between the two world wars, under the protective umbrella of the British Mandate, without which Israel most probably would never have come into being. That, however, was a problematic relationship all along, in which most British Middle Eastern hands regarded the Zionists as far more of a nuisance and a liability to their imperial policy than an asset. The British generally believed that their interests in the region were allied with those of the Arabs and quite early on began to regard their initial pro-Zionist policy as a blunder that needed correction. Moreover, the British in the Middle East did not perceive of the Jews as white European settlers with whom they could actually identify, but rather as another category of natives who happened to be exceptionally troublesome, demanding, and pretentious.[77]

The Jews, for their part, hardly saw themselves as extensions or servants of the British Empire, to which their relationship was most ambivalent. In the first two decades of the Mandate, the British were an indispensable protector of Jewish self-determination in Palestine, but after the Second World War the Jews rose in rebellion against their own version of "Perfidious Albion," when it seemed as though the British had finally abandoned the Zionists to their fate.

The Palestinians have adopted anti-colonialist argumentation for their struggle against Israel from the very beginning. But long after most other national liberation movements have ridden themselves of their would be "colonial oppressors," the Palestinians have made far less progress in their struggle against Israel. This fact alone should be sufficient cause to reexamine the colonialist paradigm.[78] Contrary to the British in India, the French in Algeria, or the Dutch in Indonesia, the Jews of Israel (as opposed to the settlers in the West Bank who have created a variant of the French *pieds noirs* in Algeria) have no "mother country" to which they can return.

In times of stress Israelis tend to see themselves fighting with their backs to the sea. Israeli Jews for the most part were deeply motivated in the second Intifada by what was generally seen as the "war for our home," as opposed to a fight for the occupied territories, a distinction that was completely lost on the suicide bombers. By targeting Israel's cities one after the other, they provoked the widely supported construction of the security barrier and the massive Israeli retaliation that culminated in the reoccupation of the West Bank. While the great majority of Israelis supported the uprooting of the settlements from Gaza, they would not tolerate the rocketing of the adjacent Israeli towns of Sderot and Ashkelon, which again culminated in widely supported massive retaliation.

The Arabs of Palestine have violently opposed the Zionist enterprise almost from the start. They could hardly have been expected to supinely submit to a Jewish takeover of all or part of the country. But the conflict that ensued was the responsibility of both parties who consciously chose to partake in it, and both parties share in the responsibility for its consequences. The Arabs are not non-players, not just the hapless victims of a "colonialist" onslaught who are totally bereft of any responsibility for the evolution of the conflict.

Many of the measures resorted to by the Zionists and the State of Israel—from the engagement in a series of inter-state wars, to its wars against the PLO, Hamas and Hizballah, to the construction of the security barrier—are functions of this conflict and cannot be reasonably explained as if they were solely the consequence of some peculiar conspiratorial and predatory nature of the Jews and the Zionists. Such a depiction of the Israelis is fundamentally racist; it is reminiscent of the propagandistic portrayal by Israelis of their Arab enemies as inherently violent anti-Semites, as if the Arabs had no understandable and legitimate grievances against Israel. The Israeli Jews would, however, be hard-pressed to accept the view that, of the various narratives about the conflict, only theirs is entirely invalid, and that although all peoples are entitled to self-defense and self-determination, it is only they who are not.

## Nations Matter: Nation-States and the
## Ethno-Nationalism Debate

The one-state advocates are motivated at least in part by an ideological hostility to the nation-state idea in general and to ethnic nationalism in particular, of
which Israel, in their view, is an especially distasteful exemplar. But theirs is
hardly the only accepted view in the scholarly debate—on the contrary. In the
words of a renowned social scientist, Craig Calhoun:[79]

> Nationalism is not a moral mistake. Certainly it is too often implicated in
> atrocities, and in more banal but still unjust prejudices and discriminatory
> practices. It too often makes people think arbitrary boundaries are natural
> and contemporary global divisions ancient and inevitable. But it is also a
> form of social solidarity and one of the background conditions on which
> modern democracy has been based. . . .
>
> We should approach nationalism with critical attention to its limits, illu-
> sions, and potential for abuse, but we should not dismiss it. Even where we
> are deeply critical of the nationalism we see, we should recognize the con-
> tinued importance of national solidarities. Even if we wish for a more cos-
> mopolitan world order, we should be realistic enough not to act on mere
> wishes.[80]

In their argument for the one-state solution, the advocates tend to denounce Jewish ethno-nationalism while simultaneously romanticizing about
the idyllic ethnic nationalism of the rural Palestinians in the West Bank,
though, in the end, the Palestinians in the one-state scenario are also required to "abandon reactionary notions of ethno-nationalist statehood based
on Palestinian ethnic, or 'Arab,' identity."[81] Jews and Palestinians are not likely
to accept this recommendation any more than would Serbs and Croats, Czechs
and Slovaks, Romanians and Hungarians, Greeks and Turks, Kurds and Arabs,
Tamils and Sinhalese, Scots and Welshman, Flemings and Walloons, and
Quebecois and Anglo-Canadians.

Jewish (and other) ethno-nationalisms, Tilley, Judt, and others argue, are
no longer acceptable in a world where ethnic statehood has become norma-
tively obsolete and anathema. While that might still be a pervasive view in certain intellectual circles, it is not universally true in the real world. The dichotomous distinction between the implicitly illiberal and oppressive ethnic
nationalism and the liberal democratic civic nationalism is crude and far from

a reflection of the nuanced realities on the ground in different regions of the globe.

Indeed, prominent scholars of nationalism such as Craig Calhoun, Aviel Roshwald, Anthony Smith, and others have long averred that these sharp distinctions between ethnic and civic nationalism are largely artificial. The dividing line between the two is far from clear. As Smith has noted, "Even the most 'civic' and 'political' nationalisms often turn out on closer inspection to be also 'ethnic' and 'linguistic,'" such as in the French example. Moreover, Smith has argued, scholarship on nationalism suffers from the fact that even though ethnic nationalism is still the most popular form of nationalism around the world, it "continues to occupy a pariah status" in the eyes of many scholars of the subject.[82]

David Brown has therefore suggested usage of the term "ethno-cultural nationalism" instead of ethnic nationalism, in order to reflect the fact that it is not solely based on ethnic origin, with its negative connotations. Some critics have even suggested altogether discarding the term "civic nationalism" as no more than a myth invented by dominant ethnic groups to disguise the fact that they have subordinated ethnic minorities to the domination of the majority.[83]

Ethnic nationalism, tolerant of minority rights, in Slovenia for example, could be considerably more liberal than civic nationalism, which might in fact be intolerant of ethnic differences and coercive despite its rhetorical inclusiveness. This is the case in Turkish policy toward their Kurdish minority, or in French policy toward non-French-speaking minorities in the earlier years after the revolution or toward their migrant Muslim population today. Similarly the Quebecois claim to be practicing an inclusive civic nationalism in the province of Quebec, when in fact that is clearly not the policy toward the Anglophones and the use of their language in the public domain. Cases vary in their specificity; there are no universally applicable sterile decontextualized models.

At the end of twentieth and the beginning of the twenty-first century, ethnic, or (to be more charitable) ethno-cultural nationalism is as vibrant as ever, if not more so. While there are some indications in Western Europe of a certain weakening of the nation-state, due to the rising influence of the European Union, economic globalization, mass immigration from non-European countries, and the increasing legitimacy of multiculturalism, there are equally important countervailing trends.[84]

There are more nation-states in Europe today than ever before. Ethno-cultural nationalism, or the exercise by peoples of their inherent right to self-determination, is thriving, from the newly independent states of the Czech Republic and Slovakia, to the Balkans, the Baltic States, and the Ukraine, and others in the Central Asian former republics of the Soviet Union — not to mention the Basques and Catalans in Spain, the drive for independence in Southern Sudan, the Kurdish struggle for independence, the Tamils' fight for self-determination, Eritrean independence from Ethiopia, the movements for devolution in Scotland and Wales, or the seemingly endless problems Belgium has encountered in keeping Flemings and Walloons together in one country.

Tilley and others like Tony Judt and Joel Kovel may believe that the entire universe ought to accept their post-nationalist worldview. But such pontification is as condescending as it is utopian. This state of mind, ostensibly driven by universal norms of morality, also happens to ride roughshod over the universal right of peoples (that is, ethno-cultural nations for the most part) to self-determination, as enshrined by the Charter of the UN. There is no universally accepted norm that disqualifies national movements just for being national movements. The overwhelming majority of Jewish Israelis believe in their right to self-determination. They would in all likelihood refuse to accept that the dismantling of the international system of nation-states should begin with them of all people.

If ridding the world of the nation-state is the object, as Michael Walzer, the Princetonian political theorist, asks, why begin with Israel and not with France, Germany, Sweden, or Japan — nation-states that long preceded Israel? Moreover, the solution proposed by Judt would only replace one nation-state with another, as the state he proposes would rapidly transform, according to predictable demographic trends, into an ethno-national Palestinian Arab state. As for the protection of the binational order by international forces, as proposed by Judt, Walzer wonders, considering the dismal experience with such forces in places like Bosnia, Rwanda, East Timor, and Sudan, what political leader "in his right mind" would "entrust the fate of people he cared about" to such international forces?[85]

In response to the criticism, even Judt had to concede that what he really meant by binationalism was "an alternative for the future." For the present, it was "utopian." But, Judt surmised, what was utopian today could become realistic tomorrow.[86] Jewish Israelis, however, were not likely to submit to Judt's experimentation. As opposed to Judt, who, as he said, was one of those who "observe from the side," the Israelis were in the thick of it, and their lives depended on the outcome.

In the words of Tony Judt, Israel was "bad for the Jews" as they were being increasingly perceived by their gentile compatriots to be guilty by association with Israel's transgressions, and thus "non-Israeli Jews feel themselves once again exposed to criticism and vulnerable to attack for things they didn't do."[87] For some Jews in the West, like Judt and Kovel, Israel has become an embarrassing nuisance and a cause for unwelcome turbulence in their routinely placid and comfortable existence in the liberal democratic societies in which they have thrived in recent decades. Their solution for this inconvenience, however, was not only an unwarranted submission to the anti-Semites who blamed all Jews for the actions of other Jews, but it was also grossly disproportionate. Dismantling Israel and subjecting the lives of millions of Israeli Jews to the protection of some undependable international force of peacekeepers would probably be seen by most Israelis as an inexcusable disregard for their physical well-being.

## Politics as the Art of the Possible

Politics is the art of the possible. A post-nationalist, democratic world of states that would all eventually merge into one peace-loving and prosperous universe is unquestionably a better political order than the one we presently inhabit. But in a world of predominantly nation-states, we must contend with the realities as they are rather than the utopia we would prefer them to become.

The one-state advocates contend that "the two-state solution is already obsolete." Rejecting the one-state solution is therefore pointless, as there are no real alternatives to a secular democratic state.[88] But that is greatly overstating the case. Notwithstanding the "obsolete" label, there is a two-state alternative, and it is comparatively more realistic too, primarily because Israelis, Palestinians in the West Bank and Gaza, and Jordanians, all the inheritors of British Mandatory Palestine, still prefer a two-state solution to any other.

The contemporary one-state agenda builds on the foundations that were laid by the Jewish binationalists during the Mandate period. But it should be recalled that this idea never won much support among Jews and none among Arabs, and it was summarily dismissed at the time by almost all and sundry as a completely fanciful idea.

The one-state advocates also rest their prescription on the South African example. But in South Africa there never was a two-state option or a two-state reality. Indeed, except for a tiny group of hard-line Afrikaners who proposed that their people be given a small area to establish an Afrikaner homeland, the prospect of a two-state solution was never discussed nor considered during the extended negotiations over the transfer of power to African rule. Apartheid South Africa was a single state that governed a society divided by race yet integrated economically. Post-apartheid South Africa remained exactly the same single state, with precisely the same boundaries, but with a new democratic political regime and the repeal of apartheid legislation. It did not require the dissolution of an existing state. On the contrary, continuity of the institutions of state, the civil service and police, was one of the cornerstones of the new regime.[89]

It was not as if the South Africans preferred a one-state option to the two-state paradigm. There was no realistic two-state alternative to begin with. The overwhelming majority of Afrikaners supported the one-state solution, as there was no other and their survival depended on creating the new South Africa. The vast majority of Jewish Israelis are firmly convinced of quite the opposite—that a one-state "solution" would be a mortal threat to their community, and that there is another preferable and even more realistic option, which has been in existence for over sixty years, that is, the independent State of Israel, which the one-state advocates seek to dismantle. To create a two-state option in South Africa would have required the dissolution of the existing state, which was not even considered. Yet this is precisely what the one-state advocates propose for Israel, ostensibly on the basis of the South African example. Not only is the South African case dissimilar to Israel/Palestine, it is almost the complete reverse.

Advocates of binationalism like Tony Judt were assailed with a maelstrom of criticism from other equally distinguished Jewish intellectuals. Omer Bartov, an Israeli historian, criticized Judt for reading his "history backward." Poland and Serbia, based on a view of unity of nation and state, would be, in Judt's reading, anachronistic like Israel, whereas inter-war Poland with its multiethnic composition, rife with conflict, or Yugoslavia, which broke up in a sea of bloodshed, were supposed to be the enlightened examples Israel was expected to follow. The idea of a binational state was absurd, Bartov argued, not only considering recent history, but because most Israelis and Palestinians did not want it. The only truly viable solution was to create two separate states.[90]

Michael Walzer quashed the "craziness of [Judt's] proposal" for essentially arguing that since the Israeli Jews could not be persuaded to remove all of their settler brethren, "he wants to persuade them instead, all five million [now closer to six million] of them, to give up political sovereignty and remove themselves from the society of states." Judt, ignoring the fact that Israel is a state with the strongest army in the region, a flourishing economy, and the only democratic political system in the Middle East, simply "proposes to make it disappear."[91] Hussein Ibish similarly noted the "lack of logical coherence" in the argument that while Israel could not be compelled or persuaded to relinquish 22 percent of the territory of Palestine / Eretz Yisrael under its rule, it could "somehow be compelled or persuaded to relinquish or share its control of 100 percent of it." It was foolish to expect Jewish Israelis to abandon their nationalism or their national identity.[92]

Ali Abunimah claims that there "is no workable partition that is acceptable to a majority of Israelis and Palestinians."[93] But if Abunimah really seeks to secure a majority on both sides, how does he expect a majority of Israelis ever to concede not only the West Bank and Gaza but the State of Israel itself? Abunimah complains that the permanent members of the UN Security Council, the United States, and the members of the EU were not firm enough with Israel's transgressions in the occupied territories or in forcing an agreement on the parties.[94] Israelis and Palestinians had therefore failed in long years of negotiation to reach agreement on a two-state solution. Abunimah concludes that for the two sides to "reach voluntary agreement is unlikely, to say the least and there seems to be no constellation of internal or external forces that will push Israel out of the West Bank against its will."[95] If that is so what constellation was going to coerce Israelis to accept the one-state idea?

In the words of Hussein Ibish, the one-state idea was no more than a slogan or "perhaps an idea about having an idea." Moreover, most one-state advocacy remains consumed with the supposed insufficiencies of the two-state idea "rather than seriously elaborating the mechanics of a viable one-state arrangement or exploring workable strategies for its realization." It is "certainly not a program or a strategy in any meaningful sense, not least because it has no answer whatsoever about how Israel and Jewish Israelis can possibly be persuaded to willingly and voluntarily agree to any such thing, or how it could be accomplished without their agreement."[96]

The question of how to convince Israel to agree to such an outcome is nowhere addressed by partisans of the one-state approach.[97] Since for many the idea is promoted to undo the national endeavor of the Jewish Israelis, one may safely assume that its advocates do not expect the Israelis to be convinced but coerced by a combination of Arab, Palestinian, and international pressure. Palestinian advocates of the one-state idea and their supporters seek to reverse the realities on the ground that have been created in recent decades and have no interest in any meaningful compromise with Israel and Zionism. They hope to undo the consequences of the 1948 war and regain what was lost in the battlefield through the ballot box. This, however, is a position founded on intellectual abstraction and is totally divorced from the "distasteful realities of actual political conduct." Moreover, most one-state advocacy suffers from a "profound and debilitating contradiction between its ostensible goals and its actual rhetoric."[98]

While the one-state rhetoric advances the aim of an equitable, pluralistic, democratic state that would incorporate Jewish Israelis and Palestinian Arabs in a single state, without favoring either community, in practice the language of the one-state advocates is one of undisguised hostility and delegitimization toward the Israeli Jews and their national project—so much so, that for the most part they object to any negotiations with Israelis and campaign for systematic boycotts of Israelis in and out of government.[99]

Even Meron Benvenisti, one of the few Israelis who has been a consistent advocate of a binational solution, after having attended a one-state conference in Boston in March 2009, returned to Israel somewhat disillusioned. He denounced the conference proceedings as "anti-Semitic and an attack on Israel." The conference dealt with such matters as the subversion of Jewish values by Zionism, the threat of Zionism to Palestinians and to all Arabs, the need to de-Zionize Israel, and Israel's strategies of destruction and debilitation.[100]

Though Benvenisti continued to uphold his binationalist position, he subsequently wrote that "those hostile to Israel have discovered that the call for one state between the Jordan River and the Mediterranean Sea, a state based on civil and collective equality, is a powerful propaganda tool, because it is based on universal norms that enable critics to denounce Israel as an apartheid state. Israelis who seek to earnestly examine various models that could serve as the basis of a future sovereign entity at times find themselves being used as fig leaves to cover up efforts to spread anti-Israel propaganda."[101]

The "One-State Declaration" adopted in London and Madrid in late 2007, written mainly by Palestinian academics living in the United States and Britain along with a few sympathetic Israelis, reflected the most far-reaching Palestinian national concerns and included nothing intended to appeal to Jewish Israeli interests, national identity, or narratives. While calling for "just redress for the devastating effects of decades of Zionist colonization" and the unrestricted and unconditional implementation of the right of return for all Palestinian refugees, the declaration did not even attempt to provide an argument as to what Jewish Israelis could hope to gain from such a single state. Other than proposing the expulsion or disenfranchisement of the Jewish Israelis, it could have hardly been "better designed to appeal less to that constituency." The hostility of the one-state supporters to the Israeli state and to Jewish Israeli society was crystal clear.[102]

One-state advocates, as a rule, strongly object to what they perceive as undue emphasis on Israeli interests and rights. But such objections make "absolutely no sense" if their professed intention of total reconciliation, mutuality, and equality in one state is genuine. "If, however, the one-state agenda is simply a vehicle for uncompromising rejectionism and continued confrontation at every level, then these objections become readily intelligible if not sincere."[103]

Indeed, the one-state idea has become a choice vehicle of political warfare against Israel and the Zionist project. It does not seek Israeli acquiescence but collective submission to be brought about by the coercion of the international community as the natural corollary of Israel's total delegitimization. Thus the equation with apartheid South Africa and the belief, erroneous, as has been shown above, that apartheid was brought to its knees by international boycott and sanctions.

Nation-states are not about to disappear, not in Europe nor anywhere else. Moreover, "while the grievances underlying the myriad ethnic conflicts around the world have been significant," in the view of Hussein Ibish, "in most instances they cannot match the degree of antipathy, mistrust and history of violence between Israelis and Palestinians." The notion that they would "let bygones be bygones, forego their national identities and independence and join the vanguard of enlightened humanity transcending the most fundamental of modern identity categories" was, to put it mildly, "unreasonably ambitious."[104]

After all, it would be virtually impossible "to find two competing national narratives as bitterly at odds as those of the Jewish Israelis and the Palestinians." The two peoples deeply distrust each other's motivations and ambitions and perceive the other as determined to achieve total and exclusive domination and possible physical exclusion or even extermination of the other community. There is "a powerful conviction on both sides that the other party is bent on its destruction at least as an empowered national community." Existential fears, especially on the Israeli side, were further exacerbated by the pervasive ethnic and sectarian conflict throughout the contemporary Middle East. The existing regional climate, from Turkey to Iraq and Lebanon, could hardly be said to be one that favored "pluralism and equitable sectarian and ethnic power-sharing."[105]

The sectarian struggle in Iraq, between Sunnis and Shi'is, the ever-present sectarian tensions in Lebanon, the widespread insecurity of Christians in the Arab world and their constant emigration, the vicious anti-Semitic ideology of Hamas, and the incapacity of Hamas and Fatah to resolve their own disagreements peacefully are all phenomena that are hardly likely to encourage Israeli Jews to submit themselves to the mercies of eventual Muslim-Arab-Palestinian-majority rule in one state.

Zionism has achieved a Jewish-majority state, which the Israeli Jews still overwhelmingly seek to preserve. They would not willingly share sovereignty with the Arabs in one state and would fiercely resist any attempt to turn them into a minority in what they regard as their own country. Most Israeli Jews believe that this would be the end result of the establishment of any form of unitary or binational state in all of Palestine / Eretz Yisrael, given the greater Arab birth rates and the potential mass return of Palestinian refugees.[106]

As for the binational proposal put forward by Israeli advocates like Meron Benvenisti, it does not appear to be any more practical than the other one-state approaches. The prerequisite of mutual and symmetric recognition between the constituent communities is the Achilles' heel of Benvenisti's idea. As with the debate on binationalism proposed by Jews during the Mandate period, this essential reciprocity is nowhere to be found in any Palestinian formulation on the subject, and not among the one-state advocates either, Palestinian or otherwise. Theorists of consociationalism have already pointed to the need for caution when dealing "not with minor variations of the same culture, but with two quite distinct and self-differentiating cultures" where "increased contacts between the two [were] apt to increase antagonisms."[107]

Indeed, the binational model that Benvenisti sought to apply was hardly common as a model that had actually worked anywhere. Shlomo Avineri, a prominent Israeli political scientist, dismissed Benvenisti's ideas as outlandish. "Simply put," Avineri commented, "nowhere in the world has a conflict between two national movements been resolved by squeezing" the two of them "holding each other's throats, into the boiling pot of a bi-national state."[108]

Avineri pointed to the Flemish separatist party's victory at the Belgian polls in the summer of 2010 as yet another testament to "the fragility of attempts to establish and perpetuate binational states in Europe, and of binationalism as an alterative to the modern nation state." Multinationalism, he added, had received its harshest blow in the 1990s, with the domino-like collapse of the Soviet Union, Czechoslovakia, and Yugoslavia. From all these examples, he argued, a general lesson emerged for Israel. Contrary to predictions of the "death and disappearance of nationalism—commonly voiced among leftists and theorists in countries like France, England and Germany—national consciousness has not disappeared." The desire not to be subordinated to foreign rule, to find a place under the sun for one's culture, language, and history, and to "feel at home" were all major components of the human experience.[109]

It is worthy of special note in this regard that multiethnic Bosnia and Hercegovina in former Yugoslavia is proving to be largely dysfunctional as the constituent, relatively large, major ethnic groups (43.7 percent Bosnians, 31.4 percent Serbs, 17.3 percent Croats) become ever more ethnocentric and competitive with little prospect for integration and stable politics,[110] as opposed to the other more homogeneous republics that have clearly dominant ethnic majority groups, such as Slovenia, Croatia, and Serbia.

Avineri concluded that if Czechs and Slovaks, Flemings and Walloons, who had never fought each other but had different cultures and different historical memories, could not live together in one country, then one had "to be blind, ignorant, thoroughly insensitive, or all three" to think that Jews and Palestinians, who have been locked in intensive conflict for more than a century, would be able to solve their problems and maintain a democratic way of life after being forced into a single political cauldron.[111]

In early 2004, when the Cyprus problem seemed momentarily to be on the verge of a binational, consociational resolution, between the island's Greek majority and Turkish minority, Benvenisti waxed enthusiastic about the applicability of the Cypriot model to Israel/Palestine. The enlightened world and the international community were united behind UN Secretary General Kofi Annan's plan for a "bi-zonal" federation that rejected fences and ethnic separation and resolved to create a federated structure as a solution to the intercommunal conflict in Cyprus.[112]

But just weeks later the Cyprus proposal fell through after it was dealt a crushing defeat in a referendum held by the Greek Cypriots (a population of less than eight hundred thousand people), who rejected the plan as "nonfunctional and non-viable."[113] The "enlightened world" and the "international community," defied by the miniscule Greek Cypriot population, did not impose their views, and the Cyprus problem to this day remains as unresolved as it was in 2004.

More recently, at the end of 2009 and the beginning of 2010, Benvenisti restated his binationalist approach, now referring to the Irish formula of a "parity of esteem." He was met with scathing criticism from within the ranks of the Zionist center-left. Alex Yakobson argued that since this binational state would have a decisive Arab majority, after the exercise of the right of return, the chances that the Arab majority would be led by Fatah and/or Hamas to concede on the Arab nationalist nature of their state was most unlikely, to say the least. Matti Steinberg dismissed Benvenisti's concept of a "parity of esteem" as pure fantasy. Any one-state solution, he argued, would be dominated by one of the two competing communities, either by the Jews by force or by the Arabs by demographic advantage.[114]

Political scientists dealing with models of power sharing speak of the need for bargaining and reciprocity, motivation to accommodate, and a sense of shared destiny to mitigate deep-seated ethnic rivalries in divided societies. Unfortunately, in ethnically divided societies, few if any of these necessary conditions are likely to be found, especially in countries emerging from conflict, such as the Israeli-Palestinian case. When ethnic rivalries are present and the state is the prize, a zero-sum, winner-take-all outlook could be deadly to power sharing. Why would a group wish to accommodate an enemy when they could possibly have it all? If certain pertinent commitments are missing, the outcome could be violence, state erosion, and collapse. The drive for a unified democratic state must come from within the communities themselves, for it is their own common destiny that they are building, and if the necessary conditions do not exist, power sharing cannot be forced upon them, except with potentially devastating results.[115]

Establishing a binational political order requires a convergence of interests as well as a normative consensus between the elites of the two collectives. However, the cleavage between the Israeli and Palestinian leaderships is so wide that the "chances of them reaching such a level of co-operation" are "practically nil."[116]

That Israeli Jews would find the one-state notion unappealing, to say the least, is only to be expected. Perhaps even more intellectually intriguing has been the rejection of the one-state idea by many Palestinians in the West Bank. Salim Tamari, professor of sociology at Bir Zayt University, in refuting the one-state agenda as "hardly a political option," raised a number of issues. He argued that the advocates of one-state have invested no serious discussion of the ways and means and repercussions of the creation of a juridical, social, and political regime "from two antagonistic national groups in one single constitutional body," and when the binational state had no real constituency on either side. Moreover, the binationalist advocates had not addressed the formidable task of having to overcome the institutions of the Israeli state, its military establishment, and the Zionist consciousness of its people. Nor did they relate to the "cultural resistance of Palestinian nationalism to being incorporated . . . within a Europeanized and industrially superior state." And most importantly, binationalism required of the Palestinians to give up their struggle for independence for the sake of a constitutional arrangement that was bound to be met by Israeli hostility and resistance.[117]

The oft-repeated contention of the one-state advocates that the PLO itself had originally supported a binational secular democratic state was actually false. As Tamari noted, not one single Palestinian faction ever adopted binationalism as an objective. All the Islamic groups rejected it out of hand, as the Jews, as far as they were concerned, were not a nation. The idea raised by the PLO in the late 1960s and early 1970s of a secular democratic state of Jews, Christians, and Muslims "was never put forward seriously except as a slogan. It was never properly articulated within the PLO, the Palestine National council, or in any intellectual forum in that period."[118]

Polling data in Israel and Palestine consistently bore out Tamari's observations suggesting a marked preference in both societies for a two-state solution. Even when Hamas won the elections in Palestine in January 2006, exit polls revealed that a majority of 60 percent supported the peace process based on a two-state solution. Similarly in Israel, even when right-wing parties dominated the ruling coalition, the public largely supported historical compromise.[119]

A joint Israeli-Palestinian poll published in March 2010 showed that 71 percent of Israelis (73 percent in December 2009) and 57 percent of Palestinians (64 percent in December 2009) supported a two-state solution, while only 24 percent of Israelis (9 percent in December 2009) and 29 percent of Palestinians (20 percent in December 2009) supported a one-state solution. In both societies, the one-state solution was also understood to be the most difficult to implement, but at the same time there were large majorities on both sides who also believed that the chances of actually establishing a two-state solution were very low.[120] A slightly later poll, published in April 2010 by a different organization, showed that while more Palestinians still supported a two-state solution rather than a binational state (43.9 percent to 33.8 percent), the trends were possibly shifting. In June 2009 the gap had been considerably larger (55.2 percent to 20.6 percent).[121]

On both sides, in Israel and in the PA, the political elites still preferred the two-state solution. Until such time as the one-state agenda, whether unitary or binational, became a major part of the discourse in both societies, it could not seriously be considered as a plausible option. Regardless of "the wishful thinking of one-state proponents," there was no serious indication that this was about to happen on either side.[122]

The one-state advocates based their argument to a large extent on the assumption that a two-state solution was not feasible because the settler movement and its supporters were an indomitable force in Israeli politics. But this was an assertion that may very well be proved wrong "should the Israeli government and public come to believe that such a course would assure Israel peace and future prosperity."[123] Moreover, a majority of Israelis did not view the settlements as a fundamental objective of the Israeli state, nor as a contribution to security. It was therefore not unlikely that "sooner or later, some substantial withdrawal from the settlements" would take place.[124]

Overcoming the settlers would no doubt be extremely difficult for any Israeli government, but not impossible. To be categorical in assertions of the immovable nature of the settlements seemed unjustifiable, "especially from those who [were] advocating as plausible—and even inevitable—an infinitely more far-fetched scenario."[125]

## One-Statism and International Law

The one-state supporters frequently claim the moral high ground of international legality. In fact, however, their reference to international law has been manipulative and inconsistent. The UN partition resolution of 1947 partitioned Palestine into two states—one Jewish and one Arab. Israel, therefore, was founded in accordance with international law as a Jewish state, was recognized internationally as such, and was admitted to the UN as a legitimate member of the family of nations. On the other hand, the one-state idea for Israel/Palestine had no basis in international law. Countless Security Council resolutions, since the passage of Resolution 242 in 1967, have called for an end to the occupation of the West Bank and Gaza and for the recognition of Israel's right to live in peace and security. Further specificity was added in 2002 by Resolution 1397, which explicitly endorsed the two-state solution with the states of Israel and Palestine living side by side within secure and recognized borders.[126]

The international community presently accepts this two-state solution more formally than at any time in the past, and it is the official policy of the United States to endorse a Palestinian state living at peace with Israel as a Jewish state. There are no democratic principles that require of any people to relinquish their identity. There is, therefore, no democratic principle that is undermined by Israel's remaining the nation-state of the people in the name of whose right to independence the state was established.[127]

Democracy does not imply that ethnic groups must abandon their right to self-determination and, in the case of the Jews, their right to have Israel defined as their nation-state. The nation-state is in fact the state of the majority people who inhabit it, while all its citizens irrespective of ethnic group or religion are entitled to their civil rights. Defining Israel as the state of the Jewish people rests on the democratic will of its Jewish majority, and its moral underpinning is the right of the Jewish people to self-determination.[128] There is, therefore, no inherent contradiction between Israel's Jewish and democratic characteristics, provided the state ensured and respected the rights, both individual and collective, of the minority.

The "absolute and inalienable right of return [of the Palestinian refugees] to their homes and property in Israel proper" was similarly promoted by one-state advocates as the implementation of international law, as represented by UN Resolution 194 of December 1948.[129] This however was not quite so. The resolution stated that those refugees (implicitly referring also to Jewish refugees) who wished "to return to their homes and live in peace with their neighbors, *should be permitted* [emphasis added] to do so at the earliest practicable date." The language was far from unconditional and left all the key questions open. It did not specify how it would be determined nor who would determine which of the refugees would be the ones willing to live in peace with their neighbors, nor whether or when their return would be practicable.[130]

Most importantly, the resolution spoke of a permission that ought to be granted rather than an inherent right to return. In the words of Abba Eban, Israel's representative to the UN when this resolution was negotiated, the fact that "to return to territory which is now Israeli needs permission, for anyone who is not Israeli, demonstrates that it is not a question of an inherent right of any refugee, but of a sovereign act of the State of Israel."[131] The resolution also established a Conciliation Commission, which made an assessment that considering the changes that had taken place during the war and in its immediate aftermath, any plan for refugee return would have to be coordinated with Israel, and the number of returnees would have to be agreed upon and final, a position that was endorsed by the UN General Assembly.[132]

Moreover, nowhere in the resolution is it stated who bears responsibility for the creation of the problem in the first place, and the text refers only to the "governments or authorities responsible,"[133] clearly implying that all the parties, Israel and the Arabs, shared responsibility for the creation of the refugee problem. It was for all these reasons that the resolution was initially rejected by the Arabs, who in recent years have reinterpreted it to accord with their present understanding of the "right of return," rather than the initial intent of the resolution.

International law and practice on refugee return has not been entirely consistent over the years since the end of the Second World War. Initially international law opposed refugee return, in the name of stability and the reduction of ethnic conflict. Then in the 1990s, under the impact of the slaughter and the ethnic cleansing in former Yugoslavia, the international community favored Bosnian refugee repatriation. In the decade since then, there has been a reevaluation of the wisdom of this policy, considering the fact that the return has created an explosive situation that could degenerate into renewed violence at any time.

Reflecting UN second thoughts about the wisdom of implementing a right of return, the Kofi Annan plan for a settlement between Greeks and Turks in Cyprus, repeatedly updated since it was initially proposed at the end of 2002, included only limited and very convoluted possibilities for property reinstatement. It did not include any sweeping intrinsic right of return for Cypriot refugees,[134] taking into consideration the vast changes that had occurred on the ground in the last thirty or so years since the Turkish invasion of the island.[135]

In early 2010 the European Court of Human Rights ruled against Greek-Cypriots who demanded to return to their properties in the northern part of the island now under Turkish-Cypriot control. The court ruled that they were entitled to receive compensation but not to repossess their property. Considering the time that has elapsed and the changes that have occurred, the court ruled that it was necessary to ensure that the redress offered for these old injuries did not create disproportionate new wrongs.[136]

## The Palestinian Diaspora and the One-State Idea

If the one-state idea is indeed so far-fetched, who then are the Palestinian one-state supporters, and how can one explain their position? Since the one-state agenda is designed to deconstruct the State of Israel as founded in 1948 rather than the occupation of 1967, it does not focus on Israel's withdrawal from the West Bank and Gaza, as part of the peace process between the Arabs and Israel, but on securing a Middle East without Israel. The one-state agenda urges "an uncompromising confrontation with Zionism as a racist ideology and Israel as a racist state"[137] and concentrates almost entirely on the two components of the "1948 file": the refugees and the political status of the Arab minority in Israel. The one-state cause is, therefore, not surprisingly, promoted in the main by Palestinians in the diaspora and by Palestinian citizens of Israel, and less by the people of the West Bank and Gaza, who have a lot more to gain from a two-state solution than the members of the other two constituencies.

The one-state idea has been promoted most visibly by academics of Palestinian and Arab origin associated for the most part with American and British universities, such as Ali Abunimah, Saree Makdisi, Joseph Massad, and the late Edward Said in the United States, and Ghada Karmi, Ahmad Khalidi, Nur Masalha, and Karma Nabulsi in the United Kingdom, to name just a few. The one-state agenda "is a quintessentially diasporic discourse, largely reflective of the perspectives, imperatives and ambitions of those living outside of Israel and the occupied Palestinian territories." It was they, more than their brethren on the front line in Palestine, who were willing to pass up on the two-state solution "in favor of a grand experiment in almost entirely uncharted waters" that seemed to pose "significant risks and offer uncertain benefits."[138]

Indeed, for many Palestinians and other Arabs in the diaspora, the cause of Palestine has become the clarion call of their collective Arab identity, in a manner similar to the role Israel played in the identity politics of Jews in the diaspora. This was true both of Israel's ardent Jewish supporters, who endorsed virtually everything Israel did because they were Jews, and of Israel's Jewish detractors, who were deeply embarrassed, as Jews, by many of Israel's actions.

Diaspora Palestinian activists often questioned the representative credentials of the PA, which, they argued, did not speak for the majority of the Palestinian people. It was not uncommon for these activists to relate to the leaders of the PA, both Yasir Arafat and Mahmud Abbas, with a mixture of disdain and derision for their "submission" to Israel. Since a two-state solution failed to offer anything to this constituency of Palestinians, the just option in their mind was the creation of a single, democratic, secular state where Israeli Jews and Palestinians would live as equals.[139]

Edward Said, a critic of the Oslo Accords from the very outset, by the late 1990s spoke of Oslo's obvious failure, of the demographic trends toward equilibrium between Jews and Arabs in all of Palestine, and of the intertwined populations in a small territory, which made separation impossible. Said, therefore, called for a one-state solution.[140] He dismissed the Clinton Parameters as no more than an exemplar of "anti-historical bullying" and "malevolent sloppiness." They were based on the completely flawed premise that "Israel needs protection from Palestinians, not the other way round." As Palestinians, he concluded, "our first duty . . . is to close this Oslo chapter as expeditiously as possible, and return to our main task, which is to provide ourselves with a strategy of liberation that is clear in its goals and well defined in practice." Whether one liked it or not, "historical Palestine is now a bi-national reality suffering the devastation of Apartheid. That must end and an era of freedom for Arabs and Jews must soon begin."[141]

According to Ghada Karmi, the "whole question of Zionism" had to be confronted. An ideology that contended "that there must be a piece of territory that is exclusively the preserve of this one group called 'Jews' is utterly pernicious." Zionism was an ideology that had inflicted enormous suffering on the Palestinians. After having gotten rid of the native population of Palestine, to make sure that none of the original inhabitants ever came back, and "then to stuff [the state] as full as possible with Jews," was "malicious . . . antidemocratic and . . . racist." In the end there was no alternative to everyone living together in one state.[142]

Over the last decade, Ahmad Khalidi, a regular contributor to London's *Guardian* has systematically promoted the one-state agenda. He argued that the idea of a two-state solution was a "dying paradigm" being overtaken by the transformation of the "geo-political map of Palestine." Khalidi believed that a one-state solution, a unitary state or one with some form of power-sharing arrangement, had the advantage of not being contingent on developments on the ground, but on the peoples concerned changing their minds. The settlers could remain in place, both peoples could enjoy the right of return, and democracy would hold sway in one state, based on one man, one vote, South African style.[143]

Palestinian statehood in the two-state paradigm, Khalidi contended, had become "a punitive construct devised by Palestine's worst historical enemies," Israel and the United States, to constrain Palestinian aspirations territorially and to coerce them to give up on their moral rights and to renege on their history. In fact, as Khalidi pointed out very correctly, statehood was only a relatively recent addition to Palestinian aspirations. "The main Palestinian impetus after the disaster of 1948 was that of 'return'; it was more about reversing the loss of Arab land and patrimony" than a struggle for statehood. The struggle for statehood alongside Israel had only developed much later, after the 1973 war, as a result of a realistic reading of the balance of power and not out of an inherent belief in its justice. But now, as matters had evolved, this concept was "less attractive than ever."[144]

The backbone of the diaspora discourse of the one-state agenda was the "right of return" of the Palestinian refugees. The cultivation of collective memory had become "a major Palestinian national enterprise,"[145] as an integral part of the continuing struggle with Israel and of the process of nation building. The intensive cultivation of Palestinian collective memory focused ever more emphatically on the formative centrality of the Nakba to the Palestinian national being. The identification with the plight of the refugees and their "right of return" was thus to become the very core of Palestinian-ness.[146] The unsolved refugee question and "the sense of injustice at being evicted from their land pervades Palestinians' national consciousness and has defined their struggle, even more than the desire to establish an independent state."[147]

In the Palestinian national narrative, the "right of return" as a supreme national goal acquired a status of uncontested sanctity. Recent years have seen a proliferation in Palestine and in the diaspora of Palestinian memory projects, research centers, NGOs, special newspapers, political and academic conferences, and websites all devoted to the realization of the "right of return" and the rejection of resettlement.[148] The centrality of the Nakba narrative and the rekindling of the attendant "right of return" constantly energized the groundswell of support for the one-state agenda, especially among the Palestinians of the diaspora.

All generations of Palestinian refugees have sought to perpetuate the memory of the Nakba in everyday life. Palestinian poetry of return developed already in the early 1950s, followed by post-1948 Palestinian literature, which gave birth to a unique form of creativity, dominated by writers from those constituencies for whom the loss of Palestine was most acutely felt, the Palestinian diaspora and the Palestinian minority in Israel. They produced a variety of genres, from the "literature of yearning" (*adab al-ishtiqaq*) to the "literature of struggle" (*adab al-muqawama*), all representing the social and emotional roots of a dispersed people longing to be reunited by return to the homeland.[149]

The Oslo process and the Israeli-Palestinian negotiations for "end of conflict" brought the refugee question back to the very center of the Palestinian national discourse, as did the fiftieth anniversary of the 1948 war and the Nakba in 1998. The Oslo process provoked an internal Palestinian debate on national priorities between the goal of return and the goal of statehood. There was considerable concern among refugees in the diaspora and in the occupied territories that Arafat might compromise on their "right of return" for the sake of statehood. Pressure was brought to bear on the leadership not to do so, and the sweeping response to this debate in the general Palestinian public was to reject any concessions on the "right of return."[150]

The failure of the Camp David–Taba negotiations, due in considerable measure to the emergence of the refugee conundrum as the ultimate deal breaker, resulted in the second Intifada, which all Palestinian factions presented as stemming from the Palestinian refusal to concede on refugee return.[151] The collapse of the Oslo process further justified the linkage between the Palestinian refugee "right of return" and the promotion of the one-state alternative to the failed two-state paradigm. For the Palestinian supporters of the one-state agenda, refugee return was the essential prerequisite for the reconstruction of pre-1948 Palestine as one unitary state with a decisive Arab majority.

One could expect the Israelis to admit to their share of historical responsibility for the creation of the refugee problem and to accept their commensurate moral obligation to participate in the resolution of the issue. Israel could also be expected to acquiesce in the payment of compensation and to agree to at least some symbolic measure of return. It would, however, be most unrealistic to expect Israel to accept sole responsibility for the problem and to open its borders to large numbers of Palestinian refugees.

Those Palestinians and their supporters who advocated the one-state idea and insisted on the full realization of the "right of return," for all refugees who wished to exercise it, knew that they were rendering an agreement impossible, with all the suffering that the continuation of the conflict would entail for the peoples concerned. This would be true especially for the Palestinians who would remain under occupation and for the refugees who would continue to "languish in camps, in the pursuit of an unrealizable goal," instead of returning to an independent state of Palestine, for example.[152]

## The Palestinian Arab Minority in Israel as
## Proponents of a One-State Solution

The Palestinian Arab minority in Israel was the second major Palestinian constituency among whom support for the one-state idea was significant. This was particularly true of their intellectual elite, more so than of the general public. Like the diaspora constituency, the Palestinians in Israel did not remain part of Arab Palestine even though they remained on their land. The 1947 UN partition resolution, cognizant of the fact that national minorities would remain in both the Jewish and the Arab states, called upon the parties not to allow any discrimination on the grounds of race, religion, language, or sex in their respective states. The minorities were to be allowed unfettered use of their language, and each state was required to "ensure adequate primary and secondary education for the Arab and Jewish minority, respectively, in its own language and its cultural traditions."[153] Israel's record in all of the above was far from perfect, yet in most respects it did actually meet these requirements.

But in the Jewish majoritarian State of Israel, the relatively small Palestinian Arab minority felt that they had been denied their homeland almost as much as did the refugees. In the early years of the state, after the 1948 war, the Arab minority was seen by the state as a potential fifth column that might be used by the Arab states in another war against Israel. A policy of control was imposed on the Arabs mainly in the form of the military government that remained in force until 1966. Though the Arabs enjoyed equal political rights from the start, living in a state that defined and conducted itself as the nation-state of the Jews, the Arabs were never quite fully integrated as equals in Israeli society and its body politic.

While the Jewish majority tended to suspect the loyalty of the Arabs, the Arabs resented the State of Israel for having transformed them into a minority in their own country. The 1967 war was a watershed in the relationship between the Palestinian Arab minority and the state. With the abolition of the military government shortly before the war, rapid educational and economic development, and the post-war exposure to their Palestinian brethren in the newly occupied territories, the Palestinians in Israel went through an intensive process of politicization chiefly expressed in an increased identification with the wider Palestinian nationalist movement.[154]

Grievances against the state steadily mounted. By the late 1960s, "the explosion of Palestinian national consciousness" engulfed the Arab minority in

Israel, which began to identify itself as an integral part of the Palestinian people, as represented by the PLO, to whom they felt a sense of belonging far more
than to the State of Israel.[155] By the 1970s the term "Israeli Arabs" was frowned
upon, still used only by Jews, as the Arabs in Israel increasingly defined themselves as Palestinians or as Palestinians who were Israeli citizens.[156] Their
Israeli-ness was their residence, not their collective identity.

The 1990s were the beginning of another new era in Jewish-Arab relations
in Israel. A by-product of the peace negotiations between Israel and the PLO
was gradual disintegration of the old patterns of minority-majority relations in
Israel and the consolidation of "particularist national Palestinian patterns" of
political behavior in Israel itself. These were manifest in the critical examination of Israel as a Jewish democratic state, the perception of the Arab minority as
a national Palestinian minority with collective rights, and the reopening of the
domestic "1948 file" relating to issues of land ownership and the "right of return" of internal refugees (that is, Palestinians in Israel who were Israeli citizens
but who had been displaced in 1948 from other parts of what became Israel).[157]

The Arab intelligentsia in Israel increasingly considered the Arab population as an "indigenous minority" that viewed the "ethnic state that was founded
on its homeland as a forcible dictate"[158] and, as such, a fundamentally illegitimate enterprise. As they argued, if Israel defined itself as the state of the Jewish
people, it automatically excluded its non-Jewish minority as full equals.[159]

As the state of the Jewish people, they argued, Israel gave its Jewish citizens
a sense of primacy and thus engendered "discrimination against the Arab citizens of Israel" on a daily basis. The Arabs had no entity that was officially defined as their state, and they could not identify with the symbols of the Israeli
state, such as the flag and the anthem, since they were rooted entirely in the
ideological heritage of the Jewish majority.[160] Moreover, as a minority, the influence of the Arabs in Israel on the affairs of state at all levels was seriously
limited. The Israeli political system was not conducive to political organization on a binational countrywide basis that would campaign for the "conversion of Israel into the state of both Jews and Arabs."[161]

The rallying cry of the Palestinian minority's intellectual leadership was,
therefore, the conversion of Israel from the "state of the Jewish people" to the
"state of all its citizens,"[162] a demand that became ever more strident in the wake
of the Oslo Accords. For the Palestinians in Israel, much like their brethren in
the diaspora, the Oslo Accords, with their focus on the future of the West Bank
and Gaza, offered very little, if anything at all, to address their grievances.

In reality, however, their struggle was not for Israel to become an Israeli state of all its citizens. After all, Palestinians in Israel of this persuasion did not call for the formation of an Israeli identity that would supersede both the Jewish and Arab Palestinian national identities in the name of a unitary civic "Israeli-ness." On the contrary, they were very emphatic about the Palestinian Arab nationalist character of the minority in Israel. The "state of all its citizens" was therefore, in practice, a means for the elimination of Israel's Jewish character. As espoused by its Palestinian Israeli advocates, it was a forerunner to the creation of one unitary Palestinian state in which the Palestinians in Israel would, at long last, overcome their minority status in a country that would regain its Arab majority and thereafter revert to its primarily Arab national—rather than any novel binational—character.[163]

A leading figure in the Israeli Palestinian intellectual elite, campaigning as of the mid-1980s and early 1990s, to convert Israel into the "state of all its citizens" was the former member of the Knesset Azmi Bishara. In addition to Israel shedding its Jewish character, Bishara called for the establishment of a Palestinian state in the West Bank and Gaza and for the exercise of the "right of return" by the Palestinian refugees. In practice, this would be a process that could not culminate in anything other than the eventual formation of one unitary Arab state from the Jordan River to the Mediterranean Sea.[164] Indeed, as Bishara himself observed, the organization of the Arab community in Israel by its collective national identity could sow the seeds of the one-state solution.[165]

The clashes of October 2000 deepened the divisions between Arabs and Jews in Israel. Intercommunal tensions were clearly on the rise in Israel, with increasing manifestations of mutual intolerance and collective hostility. The events "perhaps caused irreparable damage to the fabric of a relationship that was already frayed." Nadim Rouhana observed that it was "becoming increasingly obvious that the problem of the Palestinians in Israel is an integral part of the larger Palestinian problem."[166] There was a resurgence of previously rather amorphous demands for the establishment of independent national institutions for the Palestinian Arab citizens of Israel and for the formal recognition of their rights not only as individuals but "as a cohesive national group."[167]

The issues of the Palestinians in Israel and the rest of the Palestinian people were interlinked, as were the potential visions for a solution. The two-state solution as a slogan of consensus was losing its appeal. Israeli Palestinians were arriving at the conclusion that "a two-state solution might perpetuate their inferior status in an ethnic Jewish state rather than ameliorate their predicament." A one-state solution, binational or otherwise, was no longer seen as an unrealistic goal, and it was, therefore, "no surprise that some of the most vocal supporters of a one-state solution are Palestinian Israelis."[168]

In late 2006, leading Palestinian Arab intellectuals, political leaders, and activists in Israel compiled a detailed forty-page document entitled *The Future Vision of the Palestinian Arabs in Israel*. The document, the first major collective articulation of the Arab minority's stance toward the state, rejected the designation of Israel as a Jewish state, which they argued was exclusionary and denied them full equality.[169]

Israel, they argued, was an unquestionably illegitimate and unacceptable reality. In *The Future Vision* document, the Palestinian Arab leadership in Israel referred to the State of Israel as the culmination of a "colonialist process" (*amaliyyat istitan*), initiated by a "Zionist-Jewish elite in Europe and the West," and imposed on "the indigenous population" with the assistance of "classical Imperialist countries." Israel, "seeing itself as an extension of the West in the Middle East," continued to "implement internal Imperialist policies [*siyasat isti'mariyya dakhiliyya*] against its Palestinian Arab citizens."[170] Israel is thus set up in the full colonialist regalia, in opposition to the inherently morally superior indigenous Palestinian population, who define themselves in contradistinction to the Jewish "settler" state. They are dismissive in their nonrecognition of the Jewish national movement, the background to its emergence, and its sacrifice and struggle of over a century.

*The Future Vision* refuses to accept that the great majority of Jewish Israelis regard the establishment of the State of Israel as the fulfillment of the Jewish people's inalienable right to self-determination. By denigrating Israel as a colonialist enterprise of a European elite, it recognizes no place in the Jewish national revival for the masses of the European Jewish underclass or their dispossessed Middle Eastern Jewish brethren. The Zionist enterprise is thus entirely reframed as anything but a multifaceted movement of national liberation, as the Jews would tend to see it.

For the great majority of Jewish Israelis, the establishment of the State of Israel was the ultimate attainment, against all the odds, of a normal national existence, as deserved by all peoples, and the guarantee of their collective survival in dignity, instead of their horrific history of suffering, intolerance, and physical annihilation. An integral and essential facet of this attainment of sovereignty and independent statehood was the cultural revival of the Jews as a Hebrew-speaking nation, not only living in their own state but also creating in their own language. Of all Israel's achievements, one may argue that this Hebrew cultural revival, in the form of Israel's world-class literature, theater, press, and institutions of academic excellence, is by far its most impressive. To have all of this reduced in *The Future Vision* document to nothing more than the equivalence of the coffee-growing settlers in Kenya or their tobacco-cultivating brethren in Rhodesia is, in the eyes of Israeli Jews, groundless, disrespectful, and demeaning.

The UN partition resolution of 1947 was based on the essential symmetry inherent in the idea of independent statehood for two equally legitimate national causes. Not so in *The Future Vision*. Israel is not only a colonial construct, it is not a democracy either. Israel is an "ethnocracy" in which one dominant ethnic group imposes "extreme structural discrimination and national oppression" on another.[171] For this to be corrected, according to *The Future Vision*, and for the Arab minority to enjoy full equality with the Jewish majority, the Palestinians in Israel must be recognized as a national minority.

Actually, this is an entirely reasonable demand in and of itself. The Jewish majority in Israel could and should seriously engage with the Palestinian Arab minority to work out as amicable an understanding as possible of what national minority rights mean exactly and how to go about making such an understanding a viable and mutually acceptable reality. As Yakobson and Rubinstein have already pointed out, a country that specifically defined itself in its own basic laws as a Jewish state should also explicitly recognize its Palestinian Arab minority in its basic laws and future constitution as a national minority.

The problems begin, however, when the fulfillment of this demand for full equality is coupled with the contention of Israel's Palestinian minority that the Jewish majority must simultaneously recognize its own fundamental illegitimacy and also concede its right to self-determination. For such full equality to be achieved, *The Future Vision* argues, Israel cannot define itself as the state of the Jewish people. That Palestinians do not accept the Zionist narrative is understandable. However, it is less reasonable for them to require its invalidation by the Jewish majority in Israel as a basis for negotiation. It would be equally unreasonable for the Jewish majority to expect the Palestinians to relinquish their own narrative and to accept that of the Zionists. Expecting the Palestinians to formally recognize Israel as a Jewish state (rather than just acquiescing in it) or to declare "end of conflict" solely on the basis of a resolution of the 1967 issues are typical examples of similarly unrealistic Israeli expectations.

All the same, it is incumbent on the Jewish majority to recognize Palestinian rights to self-determination and independent statehood and also to recognize the rights of Israel's Palestinian Arab citizens as a national minority. But this could only be part of a reciprocal equation, wherein the minority in Israel would have to accept, rather than delegitimize, the rights of the majority. Minority rights could hardly be interpreted to mean the denial of the majority's rights.

The Orr Commission formed in Israel after the October 2000 clashes, stressed that coexistence would require both sides to show empathy and understanding for the sensitivities of the other. This means, on the one hand, that the Arab citizens of Israel would have to recognize and accept that Israel represented the yearnings of the Jewish people for a state of their own and that the Jewishness of the state was its very essence for the Jewish citizens of the state. The Jewish majority, on the other hand, would have to bear in mind that the state was not only Jewish but also democratic. This would mean that there could be no compromise over the full equality of the Arab citizens, and their identity, culture, and language had to be respected.[172]

Some in Israel's Palestinian Arab intelligentsia have argued that to acquiesce in Israel's Jewish character would require of Israel to be Jewish as Sweden or England is Christian. This contention refuses to accept that Judaism is not only a religion but an ethno-cultural national identity. For most Israelis, Israel is Jewish as Greece is Greek or Denmark is Danish. The denial of Jewish nationhood follows in the footsteps of the PLO and Hamas charters, which similarly denied Jewish national rights in order to dismiss the State of Israel as no more than a colonialist exploit.

The Future Vision Document purports to speak in favor of consociational democracy, that is, the symmetrical mutual recognition within one state of the national identities and rights of its constituent peoples, such as in Belgium between the Flemish and Walloon communities, or the Anglophone and Francophone Canadians. Indeed there is a lot to be said for the consociational model as a potential framework for Arab-Jewish relations in Israel. But the application of the model in The Future Vision falls seriously short.

First, it is not based on mutuality. The minority's national rights are to be recognized by the majority, but the minority in this particular case refuses to recognize the national rights of the majority. Second, the classical model of consociationalism speaks of proportionality. Yet The Future Vision accords the Arab indigenous minority superior rights, with no obligations, in comparison to those of the Jews, immigrant or indigenous. The Arab Palestinian minority in Israel is about 17 to 18 percent of the total population,[173] which *The Future Vision* seems to believe should override the rights of the majority, even though the latter comprises about 80 percent of the population.

If it really were consociational symmetry, fairly based on reciprocity and proportionality, there would be no insurmountable difficulty to find an equitable formula for mutual recognition of majority and minority national rights and to accord the minority various forms of autonomy—municipal, fiscal, and cultural. One could even imagine a discussion on the minority having a flag and anthem of its own. The problem with *The Future Vision* document is not what it demands *for* the Palestinian Arab minority, but what it wishes to *take from and deny* the Jewish majority. *The Future Vision*, therefore, is not really framed in a consociational context of mutual recognition, but rather in a context of conflict-inducing denial.

In 1948, the newly declared State of Israel undertook to "foster the development of the country for the benefit of all its inhabitants" and to "ensure complete equality of social and political rights to all its inhabitants irrespective of religion, race or sex."[174] Israel, unfortunately, has not lived up to the lofty principles enshrined in its own Declaration of Independence. No one could reasonably contend that Israel's democracy is without blemish. Many Jews believe that, as the state of the Jewish people, Israel is under a moral and political imperative to do everything possible to correct the failings and injustices in its relationship with its Palestinian Arab minority. But, Israelis would argue, this obligation does not extend to the unacceptable proposition that Israel should dismantle itself in the process.

A certain measure of terminological confusion clouds the discussion of the one-state idea. For many, "binational" and "one-state" are used interchangeably as if they mean one and the same thing. But in fact they do not. A binational state suggests a form of recognized national identity for both Jews and Palestinians within a single state, based on some agreed formula of consociational power sharing between the two peoples. For some advocates of the one-state solution, however, binationalism is not an essential or permanent component. For them, one unitary state means a Palestinian Arab state, with a Jewish minority, considering the clear Arab majority that would rapidly be created by the foreseeable demographic trends and substantial, as opposed to symbolic, refugee return.

There is, therefore, a possible link between binationalism and a unitary Palestinian Arab state in the sense that what might begin as some form of binational entity would in all likelihood be no more than a temporary way station that would soon morph into a unitary Arab state, with an ever-declining Jewish minority, for the demographic reasons stated above. It should be recalled that the traditional Palestinian idea of a unitary state, if one was to go by the positions taken during the British Mandate and subsequently in the National Charter of the PLO, was of an ethnic Arab nation-state, "the homeland of the Arab Palestinian people," which would be part of the "greater Arab homeland."[175]

As'ad Ghanem, one of the key authors of *The Future Vision*, already made this very clear in his writings in the late 1990s. The anomaly of the Palestinian citizens of Israel, whereby they neither belonged to the state of Palestine nor fully associated or identified with the state of their citizenship, Israel, could only be resolved "in a liberal or egalitarian binational state."[176] This binational state, however, could not be contained in pre-1967 Israel, as the Jewish majority would continue to maintain its dominance, and the Arabs would therefore "continue to suffer distress and crisis." The state would therefore have to encompass all of British Mandatory Palestine, where the Jewish and Arab populations would be more or less equal in number, and the Arabs "could obtain significant numerical reinforcement" that would allow them to resolve the issue of "their distressed identity."[177]

Eventually refugee repatriation would be realized in this binational state, where the new "Palestinian-Israeli balance" would open the borders to their return.[178] The refugees would then tip the balance irrevocably in the Arabs' favor. As Ghanem is fully aware, the Israeli Jews would oppose this attempt to annul their right to self-determination.[179] But, in Ghanem's scheme of things, the Jews would gradually be coerced to acquiesce in this process.

In his scenario, the situation would evolve as it had done in South Africa. The Jews in this binational state would face Palestinian resistance to what would still initially be continued Jewish domination. The consequent repression would result in mounting international pressure on the Jews to acquiesce in power sharing and joint institutions, including military and security organizations representing both peoples. Thus the Arabs of Israel would be able to "escape their distress and enjoy normal development."[180] Where that would place the Jews of Israel is a question that Ghanem does not explore.

Though *The Future Vision* document resorts to the binational rhetoric of the consociational model, it is, in practice, replete with a South Africanized subtext. This is an obvious deduction from the attempt to portray Zionism as an inherently illegitimate racist, European, colonial-settler enterprise in conflict with the indigenous people. In the South African case, only the interim constitution for the initial transitional phase was based on the consociational power-sharing model. It soon gave way to uninhibited ANC majoritarian single-party dominance in a unitary democratic state.[181]

Some key observations on *The Future Vision* could be summed up as follows:

- The Palestinian Arab intelligentsia in Israel has assumed a position that rested on the traditional Palestinian national narrative that had always delegitimized Zionism and the State of Israel. That is hardly extraordinary nor entirely unexpected. It is nevertheless highly problematic for such a position to be taken by citizens of Israel. They employ the narrative that has been used by Israel's mortal enemies to justify the state's dissolution as the basis on which they seek to discuss their place within the State of Israel. It would be virtually impossible for the Jewish majority to negotiate on such a foundation.

- Full citizenship of the Palestinian Arab minority, according to *The Future Vision*, could only be achieved if the Jews abandoned their national identity and its respective symbols. This demand would seem to most Israeli Jews to be so excessive as to arouse the suspicion that it is not even addressed to them, but to the international community[182] in what appears to be an effort to mobilize it against Israel. This, in turn, could only fuel the Jewish perception of the Arab minority as hostile, and even potentially subversive, and further impede the chances of *The Future Vision* document becoming a sound basis for Jewish-Arab coexistence.

- These positions are firmly rooted in the historical Palestinian rejection of the symmetry of partition. In essence, *The Future Vision* does not accept the two-state formula of one Arab state and one Jewish state, but rather one Arab state and one other nondescript faceless entity, which would eventually merge with an Arab Palestine. Coupled with the right of return of the Palestinian refugees to Israel proper, the Arab defeat of 1948 would be completely reversed, while the concept of two states would be nullified forever more. In the early 1980s, the Palestinian Arab minority in Israel forged a consensus urging the government of Israel to recognize the PLO and agree to the establishment of a Palestinian state in the West Bank and Gaza, with Arab Jerusalem as its capital.[183] "Two states for the two peoples" (*dawlatayn lil-shaʿbayn*) was the slogan. However, after Israel shifted its positions toward the acceptance of these principles, the authors of *The Future Vision* document have now moved the goalposts to what are in fact variants of the one-state solution.

## The One-State Agenda in the Occupied Territories

The third but relatively weakest Palestinian constituency of one-state advo-cates is in the West Bank and Gaza, where one-state rhetoric has also begun to surface somewhat more intensively in recent years. However, as opposed to the discussion in the diaspora and among the Palestinian minority in Israel, it has usually been employed by senior Palestinian political spokesmen as an im-plicit threat against Israel, in effect warning the Israelis that if progress is not made toward the creation of a two-state solution, the Palestinians would de-mand Israeli citizenship in one state, or the foundation of a binational state.[184]

The first prominent PA official to warn that time for a two-state accommo-dation was running out was the then PA minister of finance and now prime minister Salam Fayyad. In a memorandum submitted to the Bush administra-tion in October 2002, he warned that Israeli settlement expansion was under-mining a future two-state agreement.[185] In early January 2004, then Palestinian prime minister Ahmad Qurai (Abu Ala') caused quite a stir when he expressed his "private opinion" that if Israel continued building the security fence, ex-panding settlements, and confining the Palestinians in cantons, the Palestin-ians would opt for a binational one-state solution.[186] This came at a time of vigorous debate in the occupied territories when more and more Palestinian intellectuals were voicing the same sentiment while also raising the question of whether the Palestinian Authority should be maintained or dismantled.

For the Palestinians, the PA, as it was established through the Oslo Ac-cords, was the nucleus of the independent Palestinian state in the making in the West Bank and Gaza, including East Jerusalem. As the peace process ap-peared to be going nowhere, with Israel seemingly incapable of making the necessary concessions for the creation of a viable Palestinian state, a growing number of Palestinians were suggesting that the PA was turning into a sort of "middleman" for the Israeli occupation in the territories.

They were suggesting either that this authority be ensured the prospect of developing into an actual state or that it be disbanded to force Israel to bear the full burden of occupation without the facade of a Palestinian partner. Such a step, it was thought, would also force Israel to face the consequences of the shrinking dream of Palestinian statehood, an outcome that would certainly harm Palestinians, but would also inflict great damage on Israel, which would miss a historical opportunity to secure its long-term existence.[187] The threat did not materialize, but serious doubt was being cast on the feasibility of a two-state solution in the occupied territories, for the first time since Oslo, from within the ranks of the supporters of the peace process.

The Fatah Congress of August 2009 specifically noted the option of reverting to the historical demand of a unitary democratic state, in all of Palestine, if no progress was made toward a two-state agreement with Israel. In November 2009, chief Palestinian negotiator Sa'ib Ariqat went so far as to proclaim that successive Israeli governments had "destroyed any chance of reaching a two-state solution." The Palestinians should perhaps "refocus their attention on the one-state solution, where Muslims, Christians and Jews live as equals."[188]

In a paper released by Ariqat in December 2009, he suggested that the Palestinians "develop credible alternatives to the traditional two-state solution," such as a one-state or a binational state solution, or even possibly declaring the Oslo Accords partially or completely null and void, a move that would seriously undermine any form of cooperation with Israel on security or other matters. It is worthy of note, however, that these recommendations came in two very brief paragraphs at the end of a twenty-two-page document. They seemed more like an afterthought than a really developed option in a paper whose main thrust was devoted to the effort to reach a two-state solution. In the document's Arabic version, the one-state alternative merited no more than an implicit reference in half of one sentence, as follows: The PA would "remain committed to the option of two states along the 4 June 1967 boundaries, but warned that the continuation of Israeli settlement activities, imposing of facts on the ground and diktats, would wreck the two-state option."[189]

The above would seem to reinforce the assessment that the talk of one state coming from the leaders of the PA was much more of a threat for foreign consumption than a genuine policy option. Indeed, Ariqat told *Haaretz* that the binational option was not the PA's preferred course of action, but simply the default option based on Israel's continued refusal to resume the negotiations from the point they left off during the previous US administration.[190]

Palestinian intellectuals in the West Bank, such as Bir Zayt professor Ali Jarbawi (by far the most prolific and outspoken on the subject), al-Quds University president Sari Nusseibeh, human rights activist Jonathan Kuttab, and others, have all similarly expressed the view that Israeli actions on the ground were making a two-state solution impossible to realize. Jarbawi urged the Palestinians to reject the "rump state" they were being offered and to dismantle the PA so as to force Israel to resume the occupation. Israel would thus be driven into a corner from where it would "not be able to halt the march toward a binational state." Or, alternatively, just the threat would give the Israelis cause to think twice before rejecting Palestinian positions on a two-state solution. After all, with the passage of time, the binational state would become a state with a Palestinian majority.[191] As Jarbawi put it, if the Israelis were afraid of the political effects of demography, the Palestinians ought to use demography against them. Threatening the Israelis with the one-state solution was "the medium for gaining the two-state solution."[192]

Nusseibeh said that he continued to prefer the two-state option, but the fact was that it was faltering, and with it Fatah was faltering too. It was "time maybe to rethink, to bring Fatah around to . . . the old-new idea, of one state."[193] Kuttab proposed a binational state that included strong institutional and constitutional mechanisms that would protect the rights of both peoples. These would include a bicameral parliament that would have a lower house elected by proportional representation and an upper house based on parity, a rotating presidency, and constitutional provisions to protect minority rights.[194]

Hamas, which did not recognize the Jews as a people, naturally rejected the binational idea and consistently opted in principle for a democratic single-state solution. A binational state, Khalid Mash'al argued, was not a practical solution. It would put the Palestinians at a disadvantage, competing with the Jews and begging for their rights. As the experience of the Arabs of 1948 has shown, the Palestinians would end up becoming no more than an "appendage to a state of occupation" (mulhaqan bidawlat ihtilal).[195]

It was becoming clear to many observers and analysts, Palestinians and others, that if what was attainable at the Camp David–Taba talks in 2000 was missed again, "the essence of the Palestinian-Israeli conflict will change over the coming decade, from a struggle over the terms of partition of historical mandate Palestine into two separate states, to one over the identity and political nature of a single modern-day Israel."[196] Generally, polls still consistently showed that a majority of the people in the West Bank and Gaza preferred a two-state solution, but the idea was clearly losing traction, commensurate with people's declining faith in its feasibility.

## Israeli Opponents of the Two-State Paradigm

As a rule, among Jewish Israelis, ideas of binationalism or a single unitary state were treated with the utmost distrust and suspicion. Binationalism, which had originally emerged during the British Mandate as a conciliatory

Jewish idea to accept less than statehood, was now transformed into an Arab idea to deny the Jews the statehood they had successfully achieved. There are, however, Jewish exceptions to this rule. Some Israelis, anti-Zionists in their political persuasion, and few in number, have supported the one-state approach as advanced by its Palestinian advocates and their supporters.

Another exception is, of course, the Jewish settlers of the radical right, who believe in one state dominated by Jews in the name of their God-given right. Their dominance would be ensured by force, irrespective of whether the Jews were the majority in such a state or not, and in which the Arabs who remained would presumably be disenfranchised second-class citizens.

Then there were those like Moshe Arens, an exemplar of the old-style liberal Revisionist right, who supported the one-state idea, including equality for all the Palestinian citizens of the state that would encompass Israel and the West Bank. Arens, however, very conveniently for his argument, deflated the number of Palestinians in the West Bank to 1.5 million (instead of the widely accepted population figure of 2.5 million). He also left the Gaza Strip entirely out of the equation (thereby halving the Palestinian population in the area between the Jordan and the Mediterranean),[197] as if there was anyone anywhere, Palestinian or otherwise, who would accept Gaza as the fulfillment of Palestinian rights to statehood. Moreover, those on the settler right who supported Arens's ideas were less forthcoming on Palestinian rights. Citizenship for the Palestinians would be "gradual," in what would become not a binational state but a greater Israel. As Shlomo Avineri pointed out, a careful perusal of their comments on the subject revealed that they were not actually proposing automatic citizenship and genuine equality, but rather a process of naturalization that could take generations. In the meantime, that would leave most of these new "Israelis" essentially disenfranchised in a state that would really begin to look more like old South Africa, which appeared to be the dream of these old-new one-staters of the Israeli far right.[198]

A very different kind of exception to the Israeli rule, from within the ranks of the Israeli Zionist establishment, was the former deputy mayor of Jerusalem Meron Benvenisti. For well over a decade he has been the leading Jewish Israeli advocate of a binational solution. Benvenisti's point of departure was, however, very different from that of the usual cadre of one-state supporters. Though he adamantly opposed the Israeli occupation of the West Bank and Gaza, Benvenisti identified with the original Zionist enterprise.[199] Benvenisti therefore tended to argue that binationalism was not a stepping stone to a uni-

tary state, as most one-state supporters believed, but actually an essential, realistic means to maintain the Zionist ideal and its moral rectitude. Binationalism, in his mind, was the only practical alternative to a two-state solution or a
unitary state, both of which, he argued, were completely unrealistic. For Benvenisti, therefore, it was not a question of whether to form a binational state,
but which model of binationalism to choose.

He envisaged a consociational democracy in which collective ethnic-national
rights would be recognized in a power-sharing agreement between the communities that would include defined political rights for the minority, as well as possible territorial cantonal divisions. Power sharing and federated cantons would
allow for "soft borders" that would ease dealing with controversial issues such
as Jerusalem, refugees, and settlers. Everything, however, depended on the recognition between the communities being mutual and symmetric.[200]

A newly formulated questioning or rethinking of the two-state idea has also
been articulated by members of the Zionist center or center-right. Giora Eiland, a retired IDF general, and Efraim Inbar, a political science professor at
Bar Ilan University, both argued that the two-state paradigm was out of date.
Their argument, however, did not suggest replacing two states with one, but
rather to opt for "a regional approach" and draw in Jordan and Egypt as partners for the partition of historical Palestine instead of the PA and the Palestinians, to provide "security control and civil administration."[201]

In their view, the Israelis and the Palestinians are presently incapable of
reaching a historical compromise. Israel's persistent settlement activity has
undermined Palestinian faith in Israel's good intentions, and Israelis have little faith in the Palestinian desire to end the conflict or to fulfill their commitments. The Palestinians, so Inbar argues, are inept and "not able to build a
state." Therefore, "the inevitable conclusion" is that the two-state option is
"no longer relevant."[202] According to Eiland, a two-state solution is untenable.
Israel cannot give up all of the West Bank, support an unviable Arab state, and
also bear the consequences of the ensuing instability.[203] The revival of the idea
of a Jordanian-Palestinian federation or confederation therefore makes sense,
particularly since the rise of Hamas, which gives Jordanians and Palestinians
good reason to support such an outcome.[204]

Inbar suggested "redirecting Gaza toward Egypt and re-linking the West
Bank to Jordan." This would be a "more effective way to deal with Palestinian
nationalism than granting it statehood. . . . Their involvement could be legiti-
mized by claiming they will play an interim role until the Palestinians are ready

for self-governance."[205] Benny Morris also suggested a renewed Jordanian involvement in the form of a Jordanian-Palestinian federative or confederative connection, to contend with the problems engendered by the potentially limited viability of a Palestinian state restricted to the West Bank and Gaza and by its limited capacity to absorb refugees. Such a fusion of Jordan and Palestine would provide the expanses of Jordan for Palestinian refugee resettlement and also allow for Jordan's highly regarded and powerful army to play a role in effectively "reining in the militants."[206]

However, looking at these proposals from the Jordanian point of view, they would most probably be rejected as ill-intended plans to have the kingdom sucked into policing the Palestinians on the West Bank for Israel's sake. At the same time, the East Bank would be swamped with Palestinian refugees, turning the original Jordanians into an ever-declining minority in their own country.

As an alternative, Eiland also suggested a regional agreement to make a two-state solution more appealing and palatable to the parties. He proposed that Egypt and Jordan cede territories in northern Sinai and in the Jordan Valley, respectively, to the Palestinian state. The added territory would allow for the expansion of the overpopulated area of the Gaza Strip and would also allow Israel to annex some 13 percent of the West Bank instead of 4 to 5 percent. Such an annexation would reduce the number of settlers that would have to be evicted by Israel from some hundred thousand to about thirty thousand.[207]

The problem with this kind of Israeli thinking was that it rested on the false assumption that the neighboring Arab states could somehow be persuaded to operate against what they firmly believed to be their own vital interests, in order to serve the greater purpose of what were actually Israel's security concerns. Egypt was extremely reluctant to contemplate such a role, and its construction of a barrier along the border between Egypt and the Gaza Strip was indicative of a conscious Egyptian effort to prevent the Israelis from "throw[ing] Gaza" in their face.[208]

Jordan's reluctance to follow this Israeli line of thinking was even greater and was a product of the profound change that has taken place in Jordan's historical perception of its role in Palestine. Some in Israel have yet to recognize the depth of this Jordanian change of heart and mind. Eiland points out that the idea of a Jordanian-Palestinian federation would be attractive to the Israeli right, who believe that Palestinian national aspirations "should be fulfilled in Jordan."[209] Needless to say, that would be no consolation for the Jordanians. For them, this idea would be no less than the realization of their worst nightmares.

# 5 THE EVOLUTION OF THE JORDANIAN ROLE

Israeli ideas for recruiting the Jordanians to pull the chestnuts out of the fire were unrealistic. The Jordanians did not have the slightest intention of doing so and could not be forced into this role either. Jordan, which had once been so deeply involved in the Palestinian question, has been more decisive and successful than the Israelis in disengaging, albeit never quite completely. Jordan's disengagement notwithstanding, the difficulties encountered in the negotiations between Israel and the Palestinians, the problems inherent in creating a Palestinian state in the relatively small territory of the West Bank and Gaza, and the demographic reality in which there were probably more Palestinians in Jordan than in the West Bank frequently gave rise to the question of whether, or at what cost, Jordan could be enticed to reengage in Palestine.

## The Era of Jordanian Dominance in Palestine

Jordan's disengagement was a long, arduous, and very hesitant process and came to fruition only after the Jordanians had invested every effort to control the fate of Arab Palestine. The change of course was therefore all the more significant. Since the late 1930s, when the partition of Palestine had first been formally proposed, Jordan actively sought the annexation of the Arab part of Palestine to the Hashemite realm. Throughout the years of the Second World War, Jordan's King Abdallah I had tirelessly continued to cultivate his relationship with the Jewish Agency and to enhance his influence with the mufti's rivals among the Palestinian Arabs—the Nashashibis and their allies. With Jews and Arabs, and with the British, of course, he probed relentlessly for common ground on variations of the notion of union between Palestine and Transjordan under his crown.

Abdallah's true ambition was to have all of Palestine attached to his kingdom, with some form of autonomy for the Jews. This would have enabled him to have his cake and to eat it too, that is, to subdue the mufti and the Palestinian national movement, and to spare himself the embarrassment of having to acquiesce in partition as part of an understanding with the Zionists. But Abdallah was astute enough to know that his preference was unattainable and that, in the real world, partition and annexation of the Arab part to Jordan were the only game in town. It was this that he told the British, the Americans, and the Jews.[1]

After the Second World War, it did not take long for the Zionists and Abdallah, who as of May 1946 was the newly crowned king of the independent Hashemite Kingdom of Jordan, to resume in earnest their efforts to arrive at a common understanding on the future of Palestine. The fact that the Palestinian national movement was still led by King Abdallah's implacable rival Hajj Amin al-Husayni was all the more reason for Jordan's unshakable conviction that its supreme interest lay in playing a decisive role in Arab Palestine.

For the Hashemites the choice was stark. It was they who had to determine the fate of Arab Palestine, lest Arab Palestine decide theirs. As for the Zionists, they too for the most part preferred partition and annexation by Jordan, to have the relatively friendly Hashemites on their eastern border, rather than an independent Palestinian state, headed by their mortal enemy Hajj Amin.

As Abdallah imparted to his Jewish interlocutors in November 1947 shortly before the passage of the partition resolution in the UN, he wanted the Arab part of Palestine incorporated into his realm. He had no interest in the formation of another Arab state that would allow the mufti to return to Palestine to interfere with his designs and have Hajj Amin and the other Arabs ride him ragged. "I want to be the rider, not to be ridden," Abdallah explained.[2]

Hajj Amin, still in exile and ostracized internationally after having thrown in his lot with the Germans during the Second World War, was at an enormous disadvantage in his competition with Abdallah. The king had uninhibited access to each of the other key players, with whom the mufti had no truck at all—the Zionists and the British. Not to mention Abdallah's inroads to Hajj Amin's rivals among the Arabs of Palestine.

The passage of the UN partition resolution meant war, and when the war ended, a series of armistice agreements were signed between the State of Israel and its Arab neighbors, who had invaded Palestine the day after the Israelis had declared their independence in May 1948. The agreements were signed in 1949 with Egypt (in February), Lebanon (in March), Jordan (in April), and Syria (in July). The Iraqis, though they had participated very significantly in the war, had no common boundary with Israel. They could thus afford to keep

their Arab nationalism untainted, without having to sully themselves by signing an armistice with the Jews.

The Palestinians were notably absent from all of these negotiations. The
rump of Arab Palestine that became known as the West Bank had been captured in the war by the Jordanians, with the help of the Iraqis. It was formally
annexed, with Israeli acquiescence, to the Hashemite Kingdom in 1950, as Israel and Jordan sought to contain and constrain the remnants of Palestinian
nationalism between them. Though Abdallah had an array of advantages over
the mufti in the struggle for dominance in Arab Palestine, he had one major
deficiency—his lack of legitimacy, in the eyes of the Palestinians and of the
other Arabs, to represent Palestine. This was always true and remained so in
later years when the protagonists changed from Abdallah to Husayn and from
Hajj Amin to Arafat and the PLO.

When Hajj Amin declared the independence of Palestine and set up the All-
Palestine Government in Gaza, in October 1948, the declaration was well received by the populace in the West Bank. But as opposed to Hajj Amin, the
Jordanians were actually in full control of all that remained of Arab Palestine
(except for the Gaza Strip), and that made all the difference in the world. According to the official Jordanian narrative, their brave soldiers had saved
(inqadh) the West Bank from the Zionists. They had a point, but it never really
helped them in the legitimacy battle.

The Jordanians would subsequently contend that the first parliamentary
elections held in the united kingdom on both banks of the Jordan River in
April 1950 were in fact an act of Palestinian self-determination. The parliament that was elected then, representing the people on both the East and the
West Bank, voted to formalize the unification of the two banks on April 24,
1950. Many would argue that the Palestinians had no real alternative. Thus,
despite their efforts, the Jordanians were tarnished as usurpers by many Palestinians and other Arabs, a blemish they never managed to shed entirely.

In practice Jordan became the inheritor of Palestine, and the Jordanians had
every intention of keeping it that way. The West Bank, politically, administra-
tively, and economically subordinate to the East Bank, was tightly integrated
into the Jordanian kingdom. Since the capital was in Amman, the entire state
bureaucracy was centered there. All the heavy industry and then the first university were also situated on the East Bank, partly for security reasons, stemming from the fear that Israel might occupy the West Bank, and partly just to
make sure that the West Bank never acquired the wherewithal to form an inde-

pendent power base to challenge the regime in Amman. As a result of these policies, there was a steady outflow of Palestinian migrants from the West Bank to the East Bank, in search of jobs and higher education.

This was all part of a grand design to Jordanize the Palestinians through integration into the Jordanian state. The constant migration between 1948 and 1967 from the West Bank to the East Bank, in addition to the Palestinian refugees who had settled on the East Bank in 1948, steadily increased the Palestinian population of the East Bank. Initially this process may have appeared to the Jordanians to further their project of de-Palestinization or Jordanization by integration, the conferring of citizenship, and, on the quiet, refugee resettlement. But the project met with only limited success.

Some Palestinians became Jordanians in the fullest sense, truly loyal citizens who identified with their new adoptive state, and who just happened to be "Jordanians of Palestinian origin." But with many others this was not so. With the revival of the Palestinian national movement from the late 1950s onward, most Palestinians in Jordan tended to identify themselves first and foremost as Palestinians. With the passage of time, their distinct national consciousness and their demographic weight began to be seen by the original Jordanians as a potential threat to East Banker hegemony over the very core of their political patrimony. The effort to Jordanize the Palestinians was a double-edged sword. Its failure, the East Bankers feared, might possibly lay the groundwork for the potential Palestinization of Jordan.

From the outset, the relationship between the East and West Banks was not one of equals. As long as the kingdom spanned both banks of the river, the Palestinians were the decisive majority in the country, but they were underrepresented in all walks of political life. Jordan's domination of Palestinian affairs lasted until the West Bank was lost to Israel in 1967. From then onward, Jordanian fears of having the tables turned on them constantly grew, and it was now the Jordanians who were concerned that the Palestinians might one day take over their kingdom.

## Jordan's Loss of the West Bank: The End of an Era

The defeat in 1967 severely reduced Jordan's capacity to manipulate Palestinian affairs and arrested the process of Jordanization of the West Bank that had been in the making since 1948. The crushing defeat of pan-Arabism in the Six Day War and the consequent entrenchment and legitimization of territorial nationalism in the Arab world likewise contributed to the accelerated reemergence of an autonomous Palestinian national movement. Palestinian-ness was now fueled not only by the collective memory of the disaster of 1948, but also by the reality, the myth, and the imagery of the armed struggle waged by the constituent factions of the PLO, from Jordanian territory. In his hour of weakness after the 1967 defeat, Husayn had allowed the fighting forces of the PLO, the fida'iyyun, to wage their "popular liberation war" against Israel from bases on the East Bank.

Fida'i popularity in the late 1960s was at its peak, to the extent that even Husayn himself had no choice but to treat them with respect. The Jordanian state was in retreat before the fida'iyyun, even though the heroic "war of liberation" was in fact a dismal failure. The Israelis improved their defenses and kept the fida'iyyun out for the most part. They retaliated to Palestinian cross-border attacks with artillery shelling and aerial bombardment that forced the fida'iyyun out of the Jordan Valley and away from the border zone. Israeli retaliation also triggered the exodus of some hundred thousand of the valley's inhabitants, as the area was turned into a virtual war zone.[3]

The damage to the Jordanian economy was staggering. The evacuees from the valley became internal refugees, as the valley itself, one of Jordan's most intensely cultivated and modernized agricultural regions, was turned into a wasteland. While the war for the liberation of Palestine was not working, the fida'iyyun were gradually taking over Jordan. The fida'iyyun who had left the frontline were now assuming control over the country's Palestinian refugee camps, including those in the heart of the capital Amman. These were being transformed into extraterritorial Palestinian bases that were out of bounds to the Jordanian authorities, including the king himself. The fida'iyyun not only had their own military, but their own hospitals, judicial system, prisons, schools, and taxation, just about all the accoutrements of a state in the making.

Their gun-toting men swaggered through the city streets in their uniforms, insulting the womenfolk, often fleecing and otherwise molesting the public, or driving their unlicensed vehicles. They were a law unto themselves, as they seized control of the public space, "behaving as if they owned the place."[4] The state continued steadily to contract, greeted by the fida'iyyun with disrespectful scorn. Not for the first time in the kingdom's history, many from within the country, and more from without, began to treat the monarchy as if its days were numbered. The regime began to resemble an empty shell that had lost its will to survive.

Husayn hesitated to take action. His indecision, however, had sound reasoning. He was loath to engage in a head-on collision. He fully realized that a war with the PLO, which was what a collision meant, could spell the loss of the last vestige of legitimacy for Jordan's historical role in the Palestine question. For Husayn this was not just a matter of dynastic ambition or prestige, but the long-term security of the Hashemite Kingdom, which would always be deeply affected by whatever happened across the Jordan River, in Palestine.

The problem now, however, was more immediate. It was not about what might happen across the river in the future, but about what was already happening in Amman. Concessions to the fida'iyyun by Husayn were deflating Jordanian sovereignty and crippling the political establishment of the East Bank. The very existence of the political order in Jordan seemed to be in the balance. The East Bank establishment and all its key personalities supported the institution of the monarchy and the personality of the king, to the hilt. He embodied their political patrimony, in which they, and not the Palestinians, were the ruling elite. They constantly appealed to the king, explaining in no uncertain terms that they thought he had gone too far to avoid confrontation and that he was endangering the existence of the regime. More concessions to the fida'iyyun to avoid conflict would leave the monarchy without a leg to stand on. The choice was clear. The fida'iyyun had to be brought to heel. The state within a state, or as the fida'iyyun tended to call it, the "dual power" structure (izdiwajiyyat al-sulta),[5] had become intolerable.

On the other side of the divide, there was a similar division between Arafat and most of the Fatah leadership, and the more radical left-wing factions, the Popular Front for the Liberation of Palestine (PFLP) and the Democratic Front for the Liberation of Palestine (DFLP), who were champing at the bit and pressing for a showdown with the monarchy. The Marxists believed that the Hashemite regime was in the long run a mortal enemy of the Palestinian national movement and could never be a trusted ally. The Hashemites had to be overthrown so that Amman could become "the Hanoi" of the Palestinian struggle, from whence would come the liberation of Palestine.[6] There could be no liberation of Palestine as long as the Hashemites ruled over the East Bank. Fatah did not disagree in principle as to the fundamental divide between the basic interests of Jordan and the Palestinians.[7] But taking on the Jordanians prematurely, Arafat feared, might risk the continued existence of the PLO's vitally important Jordanian haven.

Though correct, Arafat's reasoning did not prevail. Matters came to a head in the summer of 1970. In mid-September King Husayn declared martial law. Burgeoning Palestinian nationalism under the banner of the PLO clashed with the Jordanian state in a bloody civil war that erupted on September 17 and dragged on until July 1971, when the last remnants of the PLO's fighting forces were finally banished from the kingdom. The civil war drove home to the Jordanians three crucial historical lessons: Jordan had to recognize that a coherent Palestinian identity had come to fruition and could no longer be ignored or "Jordanized"; that the new reality required a restructuring of the historical relationship with the West Bank; and that the new Palestinian national vitality and collective energy might, in certain circumstances, be directed against the very existence of the kingdom on the East Bank, threatening, so the Jordanians feared, to transform their country into an "alternative homeland" (al-watan al-badil) for the Palestinians.

The exhausting and bloody struggle against the PLO forces steadily drove the Jordanians to the conviction that there were Palestinian and other forces in the Arab world that were bent on the destruction of Jordan in order to set up an "alternative homeland" for the Palestinians in its place. In Israel too, there were those on the political right who believed in such a solution to the Palestinian problem, adding further to Jordan's anxieties, which were slowly but surely developing into an obsession.

The Jordanians, in their victory on the battlefield, had saved their country. But they were simultaneously coerced to come to terms with the evolution of Jordan's association with Palestine. The first formal shift came in March 1972 when King Husayn proposed the reconstruction of the East Bank–West Bank union on a more balanced federative foundation rather than the straightforward assimilation of the Palestinians into the Hashemite Kingdom.

In the immediate aftermath of the war, the PLO was at an all-time trough of its political evolution. The initial wave of extreme censure of Jordan among West Bankers subsided, and local leaders there still spoke of the West Bank as an integral part of Jordan.[8] Husayn, who was in desperate need of a new formula for Jordanian-Palestinian relations, sought to exploit the PLO's hour of weakness to ensure continued Jordanian centrality in the determination of the political fate of the Palestinians.

The "United Arab Kingdom" envisaged a federative union between two autonomous, ostensibly equal, "regions" of Palestine and Jordan. In practice, the fine print of the federation proposal clearly preserved East Bank supremacy. Husayn's plan for the formation of a federative union between the East and

West Banks was to be based on an autonomous region of Jordan on the East Bank (qutr al-Urdunn), with Amman as its capital, and an autonomous region of Palestine (qutr Filastin) on the West Bank and any other Palestinian territory that "would be liberated" (yatimm tahririha), with Arab Jerusalem as its capital.[9]

This was an idea that had been in the making for some time. Shortly after the loss of the West Bank in the Six Day War, in late 1968 and early 1969, Husayn had publicly suggested that once the West Bank would be restored to Jordan, the people there would enjoy the right to self-determination, and a greater measure of decentralization would be offered to the Palestinians. The idea was not pursued any further, as the crisis-prone relations with the fida'iyyun consumed all the monarchy's energies and attention. But it was clear to Husayn that the conclusion of the war against the fida'iyyun called for a new historical departure.

Husayn realized that Jordan had no choice but to finally recognize Palestinian rights to self-determination in a political entity of their own. As he explained to the royal committee that drew up the federation plan, the time had come to recognize the Palestinian identity. It was unrealistic in the new circumstances to contemplate an unmodified return to the pre-1967 formula of unity.[10] This was a historical watershed. Jordan under King Husayn was shifting its historical role in Palestine from inheritor to partner, albeit senior partner, of Palestine. In later years that would evolve further, to become a partnership of equals between Jordan and the PLO, and eventually Jordan's role was reduced to no more than that of an interested outsider.

In 1972, however, the federation Husayn had in mind was to be obtained in accordance with Jordanian state interests, which were then still understood to require the preservation of East Bank supremacy and control in the relationship. The federation plan recognized the Palestinian right to autonomous government, with a parliament and a judiciary of their own in the Palestinian region. Yet it simultaneously ensured East Bank constitutional, political, and symbolic supremacy. The king would remain the head of state and chief executive authority of the United Kingdom, which would have one military, subordinate directly to the king, who would remain the commander in chief. Defense and foreign affairs and all matters pertaining to the kingdom as a unified international personality would be in the hands of the federal government that would unite both autonomous regions, and Amman would be the capital of the united kingdom.

The federation was an attempt to reclaim Jordan's representative role in Palestinian affairs, and thus, over the heads of the PLO, Husayn appealed to all Palestinians wherever they may be, all of whom belonged to "this Arab country [balad]" provided they were true Palestinians in their sense of "loyalty and belonging" and not associated with "deficiency and deviation," in other words the PLO.[11]

Above all, however, Husayn's appeal was addressed to the Palestinians in the West Bank in the hope that they would be sufficiently receptive for him to pry the people away from the PLO, offering them not only autonomy, but also a possible way out of the Israeli occupation. This was to be a constant refrain in Jordanian policy for many years thereafter: it was the people of the West Bank themselves (and by implication Palestinians elsewhere too) who had the inalienable right to determine their own fate, not the PLO. Husayn consistently distinguished between the organization and "the people." The PLO was fundamentally illegitimate, not elected by anyone, imposing itself by force and intimidation, whereas the people, of course, were the democratic source of authority and should therefore be allowed to make their own choices freely.

All West Bankers, virtually without exception, had kith and kin on the other side of the river. Many traded with the East Bank or had business interests there. West Bankers were, therefore, genuinely interested in a close relationship with Jordan. That did not mean they were necessarily supportive of the Hashemite regime, which they generally were not. But Jordan was playing on Palestinian sentiments in favor of the close bond, by offering the federation, which the PLO clearly feared might appeal to West Bankers, as a more realistically available option than "popular liberation war."

The response from the West Bankers was mixed, hardly an enthusiastic endorsement but not universal rejection either. Support among the older generation of pro-Jordanian notables represented a shrinking constituency.[12] More ardent Palestinian nationalists and the younger generation, whose support for the PLO was constantly on the rise, greeted the federation plan with skepticism. The process of Jordanization, arrested in 1967, was being supplanted by a rejuvenated Palestinian nationalism that was gaining momentum through the occupied territories, gradually marginalizing Jordan and its supporters. When Husayn tried to organize a conference of Palestinians in Amman in support of his plan, he found no takers and he had to drop the idea.[13]

The PLO could not possibly have matched the Jordanian offer at that juncture. Reeling from the devastating blows it had sustained in Jordan, the PLO had lost much of its regional stature and heroic aura, at a time when its foot-hold in the West Bank was still rather limited. Moreover, it hadn't the slightest intention of coming to terms with Israel then, and Israel was equally disin-clined to negotiate with the organization.

Husayn's proposal was made shortly before municipal elections that the Israelis were organizing in the occupied West Bank. In the PLO analysis, there-fore, the federation was a product of Jordanian-Israeli collusion designed to produce an alternative leadership in the West Bank that would help to tempt or coerce the West Bankers into accepting the federation with Jordan as a wel-come alternative to the Israeli occupation. Thus, despite the generally mixed reception to the federation in the West Bank, the PLO leadership panicked. After all, a Jordanian-Israeli deal, sanctioned by the people of the West Bank, could have consigned the PLO to the trash heap of history.

A Popular Palestinian Conference was hastily convened by the PLO in Cairo in early April 1972 to denounce Husayn and his plan and to pressure Palestin-ians not to lend any credibility to the Jordanian venture. As much as Husayn sought to reestablish the Hashemite mantle of representation of the Palestin-ian cause, so the PLO endeavored to destroy it without trace. The PLO could not accept the parceling of the Palestinian people into subsections, one under occupation and the other in the diaspora. The people were one, and all were represented by the PLO, their "sole legitimate representative."

As a "popular conference" it was intended to convey the message that this was not just another meeting of the PLO and its quasi-parliamentary body, the Palestine National Council (PNC), but a conference that fully represented the Palestinian people wherever they were, beyond the organic structure of the PLO. Needless to say, Jordan and Israel made sure that Palestinians from their territories did not participate.

The tone of the conference was viciously anti-Jordanian, condemning the federation plan as a conspiracy in cahoots with Israel. In recognition of the wide support in the West Bank for strong links to the East Bank, the PLO pro-posed a union of both banks of the Jordan River, uniting the Jordanian and Palestinian peoples in a joint struggle against both Israel and the Hashemite regime. Fatah, like its left-wing partners, as of "Black September" 1970 fully subscribed to the unrelenting struggle to overthrow the Jordanian monarchy. Thus, in their minds, the two banks of the river were indeed naturally linked to each other, but any political union between them would have to be attained not in cooperation with the Hashemites, but by their ouster.

The PLO offered the Palestinians more fire and brimstone, while Husayn was offering an agreement with Israel and a way out of the occupation by negotiation. That, needless to say, required the cooperation of Israel. There could be no doubt that the federation plan, though addressed to the Palestinians in the West Bank, was similarly directed to the government of Israel, without Husayn explicitly saying so. But Israel was not interested, and Husayn was unceremoniously rejected. In a speech to the Knesset, Prime Minister Golda Meir dismissed Husayn's federation proposal as "presumptuous and unilateral." Meir scolded the king for seeking to determine the future of territories that were not his to determine in the first place, without any explicit suggestion of negotiation or peace with Israel.[14] Federation was doomed from the start.

Israel was not prepared to negotiate a withdrawal to the 1967 boundaries (with minor reciprocal modifications) and the redivision of Jerusalem, which were Husayn's constant territorial desiderata.[15] In the PLO, they sighed in relief. In later years, Arafat surmised, with more than a touch of exaggeration, that had Israel accepted Husayn's proposal, the king would have shown up in Jerusalem on the morrow to sign a peace treaty. That, indeed, would have spelled the end of the PLO. As Arafat told one of his biographers, the organization would "have been finished. Absolutely finished. Sometimes I think we are lucky to have the Israelis for our enemies. They have saved us many times!"[16] After the October War in 1973 and the recognition by the Arab League of the PLO as the "sole legitimate representative" of the Palestinians in October 1974, the chances of an Israeli-Jordanian agreement over the West Bank gradually disappeared.

For years the Jordanians were convinced that the Israelis had intentionally scuttled any chance of an agreement with Jordan in order to pave the way for the eventual recognition of the PLO as the spokesman for the Palestinians in Jordan's stead. This, so this line of thinking went, was to enable Israel to then contend "that it had no one to talk to" and thereby to hold on to the occupied territories indefinitely. It is often the case that Arab analyses of Israel's actions ascribe to the Jews in general, and to the Israelis in particular, an exaggerated measure of sophistication, prescience, and common sense. They leave very little room for the shortsightedness and misplaced self-assurance of Israeli decision makers that so profoundly characterized their collective folly after 1967.

For a decade after "Black September," relations between Jordan and the PLO were overtly hostile. This, however, changed in the aftermath of Israel's invasion of Lebanon in the summer of 1982. Israel's expulsion of the PLO from its last effective autonomous base of operations created a new situation. These were days of further decline and disarray for the PLO, and Husayn sought to make the most of the Palestinian predicament, by pressuring Arafat to cooperate with Jordan in the peace process. Husayn realized that he could not advance without the PLO, but he did not want to see the PLO going off on a tangent of its own either or falling into the grasp of the Syrians.

The new circumstances were seen from Washington as conducive to a new departure on the Palestinian question. It was then that US president Ronald Reagan published his Middle East peace initiative. It was crafted no doubt with Jordanian input and proposed Palestinian self-rule in the West Bank and Gaza in close association with Jordan, as the best possible opportunity for lasting peace.

Husayn welcomed the Reagan initiative as the most courageous American stand ever taken since 1956, when President Dwight Eisenhower excoriated Israel for its attack on Egypt in the Sinai Campaign.[17] However, Husayn's efforts to come to an understanding with Yasir Arafat on Jordanian-PLO coordination on the Reagan initiative came to naught. Moreover, the Israeli governments of the time, Menachem Begin's cabinet and that of Yitzhak Shamir, who succeeded Begin, were staunchly opposed to the idea of foreign sovereignty in any part of historical Eretz Yisrael. They spurned the initiative, and the Reagan Plan went nowhere.

But Husayn did not give up. In January 1984, he revived the Jordanian parliament that represented both banks of the kingdom. Parliament had been indefinitely dissolved in late 1974, in ostensible compliance with the Arab League resolutions, which had recognized the PLO as the "sole legitimate representative" of the Palestinians. The Jordanians, in ostensibly accepting the resolutions, could hardly continue the operation of a parliament that also represented the people of the West Bank. It followed, therefore, that the revival of the parliament ten years later, for which other domestic political explanations were officially given, was undoubtedly intended to undermine the PLO's representative status. In September 1984, Jordan became the first Arab state that had severed ties with Egypt after the signing of its peace accords with Israel, to restore diplomatic relations with Cairo. "The message from the palace was clear: by making peace with Israel, Egypt had done the right thing, a course that the king wished to emulate."[18] This would require bringing the PLO into the Jordanian fold.

From the PLO's point of view, these were ominous Jordanian maneuvers.

Hani al-Hasan, one of Arafat's closest confidants, noted at the time that "no Palestinian strategist can afford to remove his eyes from Jordan for even a minute. The only Arab state able to replace us [as a party to a political settlement] is Jordan." Moreover, "no Palestinian strategist can ignore the geographical fact that the Palestinian state-to-be will have two entrances: one from the East Bank" and the other from Egypt into Gaza. The PLO would not be able to ensure free access to the West Bank except by "having cooperative ties with Jordan."[19]

Thus, despite all the suspicion of Jordan, in November 1984, the PLO convened the seventeenth session of the Palestine National Council (PNC) in Amman of all places, hardly the natural habitat of the PLO after September 1970. Forced out of Lebanon, and just having barely survived a Syrian-inspired internal rebellion in the spring of 1983, Arafat had little room for maneuver. Desperately seeking to escape Syrian tutelage, Amman was not the worst of options. In defiance of Syria, the PNC was held under the slogan of "no to containment, no to custodianship, and no to subordination" and in the name of "legitimacy, freedom, and independent decision."[20] Though defiant of the Syrians, these were the brave words of an organization in distress. The price to pay was an increasing PLO dependence on the Arab states most committed to the peace process with Israel — Jordan and Egypt.

Husayn made no secret of his objective — to induce the PLO to enter into a partnership with Jordan. Shortly after the PNC in Amman, Husayn told the Egyptian parliament in early December 1984 that "Jordan would not be a substitute for the Palestinians in any negotiations, but it was prepared to be a partner with the [PLO] in a peace initiative or peace endeavor to solve the Palestinian question."[21] After some two years of haggling, in February 1985, Husayn and Arafat finally arrived at an agreement on political coordination. Jordan had moved a step closer toward a partnership of equals with the Palestinians when Husayn and Arafat agreed to form a confederative union between the two states of Jordan and Palestine. They quibbled for months thereafter whether this meant two independent states or not, and by February 1986 they fell apart again in another of their acrimonious altercations.

## The Intifada and the Decision to Disengage

The Palestinian uprising against the Israeli occupation in December 1987, the first Intifada, was the end of the road for the Jordanians and their maneuvers on Palestine. The Jordanians had been fighting a rearguard battle against the national revival of the Palestinians for thirty years. The certain anti-Jordanian thrust of the Intifada was not missed in Amman, and it was as clear an indication as any that Jordan's cause had finally been lost. The argument that the Jordanians had made since the adoption of the Arab summit resolutions in 1974, which had recognized the PLO as "the sole legitimate representative" of the Palestinian people, that the PLO had in effect been imposed on the people of the occupied territories by an Arab League decision, had clearly been disproved by the Intifada. Husayn now admitted that the Palestinian people had "elected the PLO." Jordan, therefore, could "not carry any more burdens."[22]

More immediately, the Intifada had the ingredients of the Jordanians' ultimate nightmare scenario—an effort by Israel to convert Jordan by force into Palestine, "the alternative homeland conspiracy" (mu'amarat al-watan al-badil), as the Jordanians called it. Since the rise of the Likud to power for the first time in Israel in 1977, Jordan dreaded this possibility with ever-increasing intensity. Some Likud leaders, such as Yitzhak Shamir and Ariel Sharon, were outspoken advocates of the Israeli right-wing contention that "Jordan is Palestine" and that all of Palestine west of the Jordan River ought to be Greater Israel. In June 1982, in the midst of Israel's war against the PLO in Lebanon, King Husayn sent a letter to US president Ronald Reagan expressing his fear that Sharon's ambition was to drive the Palestinians from Lebanon into Jordan, where they would be joined by others driven from the West Bank and Gaza. These expulsions would pave the way for an eventual Israeli occupation of Jordan, whereby a docile Palestinian government would be installed in Jordan at the expense of the Hashemite Kingdom.[23]

As seen from Amman in December 1987, the Israelis had no intention of withdrawing from the West Bank and Gaza, the Palestinians had risen in rebellion against the occupation, and the Intifada was simultaneously cementing the ties of solidarity between the Palestinians in the occupied territories and the Palestinian citizens of Israel. As one of Jordan's main dailies pointed out at the time, the rising national consciousness of the Palestinians in Israel would serve "the long-term objective of driving an Arab demographic wedge into the heart of the Zionist entity," which was already showing signs of "old age . . . and disintegration."[24]

Rather than sharing such triumphalism, Husayn expressed the fear that the coalescence of the Palestinians in the West Bank and Gaza with their brethren in Israel was giving rise to a trend of "greater extremism" in Israel.[25] The Jordanians now feared that the "demographic aggression" about which they had been concerned for so long might just come to pass if the Israelis were to become sufficiently desperate.

There were two ways of confronting the threat. Jordan could seek Arab endorsement for its continued role in the peace process on the Palestinian track to try and avert disaster, or Jordan could disengage into the recluse of its own protective shell. At the Arab summit in Algiers in early June 1988, Husayn made a gallant last effort to obtain all-Arab recognition for Jordan's special status in Palestinian affairs that at least in theory would not conflict with or undermine the PLO's representative status. The king waxed historical as he surveyed Jordan's role in Palestine since the Arab Revolt led by the Hashemites in the First World War. The period of unity between the East and West Banks prior to 1967 was "a living model" of the greater Arab union to which all Arabs aspired at the time, when identity with the territorial state (qutriyya) was far less acceptable. If the Palestinians now preferred secession (infisal), that was their free choice, which Jordan would respect and accept.

In the heyday of pan-Arabism in the 1950s and 1960s, infisali (secessionist) was almost synonymous with "treason" in the patriotic discourse of the time. If Husayn had thought for a moment that the use of this language would evoke a negative impression of the PLO by his listeners, it fell flat. Husayn's argument that Jordan's distinctive association with Palestine was a function of "geographic proximity, the intermix of population (al-tamazuj al-sukkani), cultural integration, economic integration, and a common historical experience" similarly fell on deaf ears.[26] Husayn's plea before the summit was shunned, and for him it was the last straw.

For Husayn, this was a humiliating personal defeat.[27] He was sorely disappointed, angry, and resentful. Since the outbreak of the Intifada, Jordan's Palestinian policy had been undergoing a reassessment. The time had now come for Jordan to seriously rethink where it stood on Palestine. The procrastination was over. After the Algiers summit, Husayn finally and fully internalized the understanding that his effort to circumvent the PLO in an alliance with the people of the West Bank and Gaza, which the rest of the Arabs would somehow be convinced to acquiesce in, was no more than an exercise in futility. But if Jordan was to have no major role in the West Bank, it had to take the necessary precautions to protect the integrity of the kingdom on the East Bank. Jordan had to ensure that the Intifada would not spill over into Jordan, possibly by an Israeli act of massive Palestinian expulsion.

Both threatened and exasperated by the Palestinians, King Husayn finally declared Jordan's disengagement from the West Bank, coupled with the king-dom's unequivocal acceptance of independent Palestinian statehood. In the main, this was a move to protect Jordan from the vagaries and vicissitudes of Palestine. For the long-term, Husayn still remained interested in some form of special link between Jordan and a future state of Palestine. But it was the short-term considerations that prevailed, including no small measure of pique.

On July 31, 1988, in a speech to the nation, Husayn announced Jordan's legal and administrative disengagement from the West Bank.[28] All Jordanian civil servants in the West Bank were retired except for the some thirty-five hun-dred employees of the Ministry for Endowments (awqaf) and Religious Affairs. They cared for the mosques and the religious courts throughout the West Bank and especially in Jerusalem, with its Muslim holy places on the Temple Mount / al-Haram al-Sharif, for which the Jordanians remained responsible, to safeguard the "Islamic cultural presence in the occupied Palestinian terri-tory."[29] The most significant step of all, however, was the decision to deny the rights of citizenship of the entire West Bank population. All Jordanian citizens residing in the West Bank prior to July 31, 1988, were henceforth to be consid-ered Palestinians and not Jordanian nationals.

The people of the West Bank would still be allowed to obtain "temporary" passports, valid for two years instead of the regular five, but these would serve solely as travel documents and would not entitle their bearers to any rights, nor require of them the fulfillment of any obligations of citizenship. This placed West Bankers on a par with residents of the Gaza Strip, who had previ-ously acquired such "temporary" passports without becoming Jordanian citi-zens. The disenfranchisement was designed above all to prevent West Bankers from taking up residence on the East Bank in the future, which as Jordanian citizens they would have been fully entitled to do.

The decision to disengage was not solely a function of Jordan's loss of con-trol of the West Bank in 1967 and the re-Palestinization of the Arab-Israeli con-flict that ensued. It was also a direct consequence of Jordan's obsessive preoc-cupation with the "alternative homeland conspiracy." Jordan's anxieties in this regard had clearly been exacerbated by the Intifada. At the time of the disen-gagement, various Jordanian spokesmen linked the decision to the "alterna-tive homeland" issue. Crown Prince Hasan explained that Jordan was "not the alternative repository for the Palestinian people." It was "not waste land."[30] Foreign Minister Tahir al-Masri, himself of Palestinian origin, observed how important it had become in these circumstances for Jordan to take "daring steps" that would "emphasize the Palestinian identity in Palestine,"[31] that is, not in Jordan.

Jordan thus became a most ardent supporter of the two-state solution, not because of any particular devotion to the Palestinian cause but purely through self-interest. A Palestinian state, distinct from Jordan, the Jordanians believed, "would bury, once and for all" the "Jordan is Palestine" theory.[32] While finally accepting the Palestinian national identity of the West Bank, and pressuring Israel to do the same, it was vitally important for Husayn to declare to all and sundry that Jordan was not Palestine. Jordan was Jordan, and only Palestine was Palestine. The Chamber of Deputies representing both banks of the Jordan River was replaced, after new elections in November 1989, by a parliament that represented only the East Bank.

The disengagement process was also accompanied by a deliberate and conscious effort to cultivate a particular Jordanian identity. The monarchy and the East Banker elite sought to create and disseminate a shared Jordanian historical heritage and searched energetically for content from which to produce, if not to fabricate, a "usable Past."[33] In this Jordan was no different from other nations that similarly went about constructing what Benedict Anderson has referred to as an "imagined community,"[34] bolstering the legitimacy of the territorial state by providing it with historical content to "transform it into a 'community of memory,' namely a nation-state."[35]

According to the new Jordanian National Charter, ratified in 1991, Jordan had been a fountainhead of civilization, development, and prosperity since time immemorial, and the country came into being in the modern era as an expression of the self-determination of the already extant Jordanian people, rather than as a consequence of colonial mapmaking. This was the fulfillment of the distinct Transjordanian identity (hawiyya sharq urdunniyya munfasila), which harked back to the days of the Ottoman Empire.

Jordanian stateness also meant that the kingdom unapologetically followed its own raison d'état, in making peace with Israel, for example. The naked pursuit of state interest (al-khussusiyya al-qutriyya) without paying even as much as lip service to pan-Arabism was raised to the level of a guiding principle by King Abdallah II. He coined the slogan "Jordan First" (al-Urdunn awalan) in the very early years of his reign, as of the end of 2002.[36]

The dramatic act of disengagement from the West Bank and the promotion of Jordanianism did not mean that Jordan was disengaging from the Palestinian question. It did mean that Jordan no longer had any intention of restoring the pre-1967 status quo ante, that is, to independently re-incorporate the West Bank into Jordan, but Jordan still had a vital interest in the future resolution of the Palestinian question. Geography and demography would not allow the Jordanians to simply walk away from Palestine. Disengagement did not mean disinterest.[37]

Just a year after Israel and the PLO signed the Oslo Accords, Jordan and Israel concluded a peace treaty on October 26, 1994.[38] For Jordan, the peace treaty was more than a bilateral agreement with Israel. It was also a platform of mutual understanding with Israel whence to secure a foothold in the Palestinian-Israeli final-status negotiations. All the final-status issues—borders, settlements, Jerusalem, and refugees—interested the Jordanians and all impinged in one way or another upon their own national security.[39]

The great and possibly insurmountable difficulty remained just how, in practice, the Jordanians could achieve that calibrated measure of influence, after having disengaged from Palestine and having declared that the Palestinians themselves were entirely responsible for their own affairs. How could Jordan retain the impact it desired without reclaiming the role it no longer wanted in the negotiations on the Palestinian track? The Jordanians have never quite managed to come up with a good answer to that question.

## Post-Disengagement: Jordan, the Palestinians, and the West Bank

Time and again in recent years the Jordanians have declared that they do not have any intention of reclaiming the role they once had in Palestine. King Abdallah II believed in the most urgent need to reach a two-state solution that would allow the Palestinians to establish their independent state on their national soil. The Jordanians saw themselves at the epicenter of a region in turmoil. The Iranian nuclear program and the threat of war between Iran and Israel, the war in Afghanistan, continued instability in Iraq, Lebanon constantly tottering on the verge of disaster, upheaval in Egypt, and the Israel-Palestine conundrum on Jordan's doorstep all gave the Jordanians cause for perpetual strategic anxiety.

In Abdallah's view, an Israeli-Palestinian accord was crucial to prevent the region from "sliding into darkness" and to provide the essential peace and stability for Israel and the Palestinians. It would also ensure Jordan's own long-term security and finally put the fantasy of the "alternative homeland" to rest. The notion of delegating control of the West Bank to Jordan was categorically rejected by Abdallah. Not only was the idea unacceptable but it was, in his mind, part of a nefarious scheme to transfer the Palestinians from the West Bank to Jordan.[40]

The king was emphatic: "Jordan absolutely does not want to have anything to do with the West Bank. All we would be doing is replacing Israeli military with Jordanian military." Jordan was not interested in becoming an alternative occupier. The Palestinians did not want that either, and nothing short of a truly independent Palestinian state would suffice. The establishment of a Palestinian state was not only a Palestinian right, but a Jordanian strategic interest and a condition for regional stability. Jordan's only role was to assist the Palestinians in achieving their rights and building their institutions.[41]

Abdallah was not playing tactics. He meant every word. The Hashemites did not harbor any secret ambition to take over the West Bank, which, they feared, could only undermine the Jordanian entity on the East Bank. Conversely, a viable Palestinian state would underscore the uniqueness of the Jordanian identity on the other side of the Jordan River, which was the genuine supreme interest of the monarchy and of the political establishment in Jordan.

Any developments that seemed to the Jordanians to impede the realization of a viable two-state solution were understood as strategic threats to the kingdom's long-term well-being. One such instance was the exchange of letters between President Bush and Prime Minister Sharon in April 2004. The Jordanians were extremely disturbed by the American support for Israel's position on the possible annexation of the main settlement blocs in the West Bank and on the non-return of refugees to Israel proper. For the Jordanians, this meant an American retreat from their formerly unequivocal support for a viable two-state solution and therefore assuming a position that the Jordanians feared seriously undermined their long-term security.

The Jordanians spared no effort to obtain a counter letter from President Bush to King Abdallah. The letter, made public during a visit to the White House by the king in May 2004, reaffirmed the president's continued support for his vision of two states as well as the US commitment not to prejudice the outcome of final-status negotiations. Mindful of Jordan's concerns about Israel's plans for unilateral disengagement and the erection of Israel's security barrier (which the Jordanians managed to convince themselves would be so harmful to the local population as to "drive them out of the West Bank"), President Bush reassured the king that the United States "views Jordan's security, prosperity, and territorial integrity as vital," and it would "oppose any developments in the region that might endanger [Jordan's] interests."[42]

Jordan's extraordinary interest in Palestine was a reflection of the fact that Palestine and the Palestinians were woven into the very inner fabric of Jordanian politics and society. With about half, maybe slightly more, of the country's population of Palestinian descent, Palestine was not primarily an issue of foreign policy, but a facet of the kingdom's most sensitive domestic affairs. Protecting Jordan's interests via the United States was one thing; playing a more interventionist role in the West Bank was quite another. A more activist Jordanian role in the West Bank would have immediate ramifications for the kingdom's domestic equilibrium. Jordanian-Palestinian relations on the East Bank touched upon every dimension of Jordanian society, in all walks of life, from the football league, to the workings of the economy and the most sophisticated intricacies of the political system and, of course, the future relationship with Palestine.

Both King Husayn and King Abdallah II firmly believed that "Jordan is Jordan, and Palestine is Palestine." They actively promoted Jordanian-ness and sought to buttress a particular Jordanian identity in the face of the Palestinian challenge. Nevertheless, both father and son simultaneously sought the inclusion and integration of Jordan's Palestinian citizens into the kingdom as loyal Jordanians, rather than having them become an embittered, marginalized, and potentially irredentist opposition. Husayn and Abdallah both resorted to expressly inclusive language when talking about the sense of belonging to the Jordanian people. Husayn referred to all Jordanians "from every origin and of any descent" (min shata al-manabit wal-usul), and Abdallah likewise referred to his people as "Jordanians of their various origins" (al-Urdunniyyun min mukhtalif manabitihim).[43] But a systematic policy of inclusion and integration while promoting distinctive Jordanian-ness at the same time called for especially deft political tightrope walking.

Palestinians in Jordan were generally more willing to become an integral part of the kingdom than their East Banker compatriots were inclined to accept them. The East Bankers dominated the political order and have historically been the backbone of the Hashemite monarchy. They were jealous of their preeminence and privilege and of their control of what they firmly believed to be their political patrimony. They had no intention of sharing their dominance with anyone. Israelis or others with expectations that the Jordanians would take upon themselves new responsibilities in the West Bank should be cognizant of the sensitivities that surround the Palestinian question for Jordan as a major *domestic* political concern.

The East Banker elite tended to see the Palestinians as politically threatening because of their demographic weight and the perceived economic power and influence that they wielded through their long-standing preponderance in the private sector of the Jordanian economy. Tensions between Jordanians and Palestinians were palpable and pervasive and surfaced regularly in a variety of different contexts. East Banker Jordanians routinely referred disparagingly to their Palestinian compatriots as "Belgians," as if to suggest that they were total foreigners who did not belong. Jordan's two leading football clubs, Faysali (Jordanian) and Wahdat (Palestinian), were bitter rivals, and it was commonplace for their fans, naturally Jordanians and Palestinians respectively, to exchange obscenities and national insults and to generally provoke and fight each other.

Off the playing field, East Bankers took exception to what appeared to them to be excessive Palestinian influence. A most instructive example of this phenomenon was the predominantly East Banker conservative opposition to King Abdallah's reform program known as the National Agenda, launched in early 2005.[44] If reform in Jordan meant the incorporation of Palestinians into the upper echelons of the ruling elite and the privatization of the economy from which the Palestinian-dominated private sector might mostly benefit, the East Banker establishment was liable to resist.

The National Agenda drew a lot of fire from the East Banker elite in parliament, in the media, and among the intellectuals for being far too integrationist toward the Palestinians. The opposition contended that the efforts to confer a sense of belonging on Jordan's Palestinian citizens threatened to "dismantle [tafkik] the structure of the Jordanian state, while altering its national identity." Moreover, they accused the reformers of also seeking to finally resettle (tawtin) the Palestinian refugees in Jordan, thereby relinquishing the right of return and creating a permanent Palestinian controlling majority in the kingdom.[45]

A conservative bloc in parliament led the charge. Parliament tended to be a bastion of conservatism and an obstacle to political reform. This was due to the fact that the electoral system favored rural and tribal conservative East Bankers, at the expense of the more politicized and Palestinian urban constituencies. The conservative bloc threatened to vote no confidence in the government for two reasons: one was because southerners griped over the fact that there were too many northerners in the cabinet, but the other, more serious grievance was the appointment of the reform-minded Palestinian Basim Awadallah as minister of finance. He was a Western-educated economist and one of the rising stars in King Abdallah's inner circle, and a prime mover in the reform project. The conservatives would not yield unless he was fired.

In an extraordinary act of submission to this "loyal opposition," King Abdallah and his prime minister, Adnan Badran, accepted Awadallah's resignation.[46] This was a most impressive show of force by the conservative East Banker elite that was plain for all to see, and it was the beginning of a major rollback of the entire reform project. The conservatives assailed the reformists as "neo-liberals," who, they charged, were "implementing an American agenda against the Jordanian state."[47]

In the conservatives' mind, a merit-based system, which might offer openings to talented Palestinians, was a direct assault on their time-honored privileges and those of their families. Since they would not attack the king directly, they attacked the reformers instead. No countervailing force existed to match the influence of the traditional elite, and their fierce opposition led to the demise of the National Agenda before it had a chance to make any headway.[48] The king subsequently appointed Awadallah to the even more important post of chief of the royal court in April 2006, only to be pressured by the all-powerful East Banker elite to remove him once again two years later, in September 2008.[49]

More recently, in the summer of 2009, the king felt compelled, not for the first time, to orchestrate an intensive media campaign to refute rumors making the rounds in Amman's political salons, by those with "suspicious agendas," that Jordan was giving up on the "right of return" of Palestinian refugees. Jordan, so the rumors also suggested, was even facing US and Israeli pressure to agree to massive refugee resettlement in Jordan, to facilitate the evolution of Jordan into the "alternative homeland" for the Palestinians. East Banker sensitivities were heightened further by the Israeli demand of the Palestinians that they recognize Israel's Jewishness. The Israeli position was immediately interpreted in Jordan as the logical extension of Israel's rejection of any "right of return" for Palestinian refugees or, even worse, the justification for the expulsion of Palestinians from pre-1967 Israel.

Needless to say, all these rumors were all emphatically denied by King Abdallah, who reiterated Jordan's unwavering support for the "right of return" and for compensation, that is, in line with the Palestinian position—not return or compensation, but both.[50]

These kinds of rumors were symptomatic of the extreme sensitivity and ap-prehension among Jordanians on the refugee question. They originated in two sources, the ultranationalist East Bank elite and the Islamist opposition, who were both strongly supportive of refugee return and firmly opposed to resettle-ment in Jordan. The nationalists wanted to keep Jordan for the Jordanians, and for the Islamists, this was as good an opportunity as any to criticize the regime and to undermine Israel.

King Abdallah, denials notwithstanding, did have a credibility problem on the refugee question. Abdallah staunchly supported the two-state solution, for which he saw no realistic alternative. It was clear to the Jordanians, to the gov-ernment, and to much of the general public that in a two-state solution Israel would refuse to accept anything more than symbolic Palestinian refugee re-turn to Israel proper. Moreover, in the Jordanian-Israeli peace treaty, UN Reso-lution 194 dealing with refugee return was not even mentioned. Jordan and Israel had agreed that the refugee problem would be resolved, inter alia, through the "implementation of agreed United Nations programs and other agreed international economic programs . . . including assistance to their set-tlement" ("settlement" in the Arabic version was rendered as tawtin, which in the Arabic political discourse was the antithesis of "return," awda).[51]

The ultimate resolution of the refugee question would probably mean that a significant number of Palestinians (certainly not all the refugees) would relo-cate from Jordan to the Palestinian state and possibly some to Israel. Among Jordanian nationalists there was an oft expressed opinion that Palestinians who chose not to return and to remain in Jordan should be disenfranchised and become citizens of Palestine anyway and, as Palestinians, should exercise their political rights in Palestine and not in Jordan. Jordanian nationalists re-ferred to this notion as "political return" (al-awda al-siyasiyya),[52] meaning that these Palestinians could remain in Jordan and keep their property, their jobs, and their businesses, but their political rights would "return to Palestine."

In the meantime, nearly three thousand Palestinians from the West Bank who did not posses Israeli residency permits for the West Bank were stripped of their Jordanian citizenship in recent years. This was ostensibly a means of blocking Israeli schemes to transfer Palestinians to Jordan, but was actually intended to reduce the number of Palestinians in the kingdom, succumbing to pressure coming from East Bankers.[53]

For decades Jordan and Israel sought simultaneously, and at times in part-nership, to contain the Palestinian national movement. They had a lot in common in their fear of being overwhelmed by Palestinian demography and political hostility. More recently Israel's unwavering position against refugee return has been stridently condemned by the Jordanians, who again see the looming specter of final refugee resettlement in Jordan as the forerunner to the "alternative homeland" scenario. Not only is the Israeli position an obstacle to an agreement with the Palestinians, they believe, but it threatens to permanently saddle Jordan with a huge Palestinian population. Thus, the positions of Jordan and Israel do not only diverge, they are diametrically opposed on an issue that both sides regard as truly existential, touching on the raw nerves of their collective being.

As in the more distant past, Jordan and Israel are driven by similar interests. But as opposed to the past when these interests converged, leading the two countries into a covert strategic understanding, presently their common fear of being overwhelmed by Palestinian demography is driving Jordan and Israel apart. In light of the monarchy's onerous, endless, and thankless task of cautiously calibrating the domestic political sensitivities between the Jordanian and Palestinian citizens of the kingdom, and its dependence on the staunchly nationalist East Banker elite, it would be extremely unlikely for the king to accede to the suggestion that Jordan immerse itself in the running of the West Bank, bringing 2.5 million more Palestinians under its control. To do so would mean provoking a head-on collision with the East Banker elite and inviting the proverbial bull into the china shop of East Bank politics. Though history and politics are all about the unforeseen and the unintended, that the Jordanians would choose to go down this tortuous path presently appears to be a nonstarter.

Historically, Israel and Jordan failed in their endeavor to jointly absorb Palestine and contain Palestinian nationalism. But Palestinian nationalism in its more secular form, as reconstructed, articulated, and represented by the PLO, had lost its monopoly over Palestinian politics by the first decade of the twenty-first century. Hamas came to the fore, driving the more secular Palestinian nationalists onto the defensive before the forces of political Islam. These pose new challenges to Israel and to Jordan.

The Jordanians would unquestionably prefer a Palestinian nationalist state in the West Bank that would stand in contradistinction to the Jordanian East Bank, as opposed to an Islamized Palestine that might make no distinction between itself and the Muslim state of Jordan. The Jordanian Muslim Brethren were deeply divided between "hawks" (mainly Palestinians) and "doves" (mainly Jordanians), with the "hawks" pressing for a more confrontational posture toward the regime and a closer association with Hamas.[54] The Jordanian authorities were extremely sensitive to the web of connections between Hamas and the Jordanian Muslim Brethren (some Jordanians of Palestinian origin were members of both organizations), and they strongly disapproved of what they feared were the potentially subversive links between the two.

In an effort to placate the Jordanians, the chairman of Hamas's Political Bureau, Khalid Mash'al, took the trouble, in the summer of 2009, of reassuring them that Hamas had no interest in meddling in Jordan's internal affairs.[55] Mash'al's declarations, however, actually had a negative affect. By suggesting that Hamas would not engage in subversion in Jordan, Mash'al was also intimating that Hamas could do otherwise if it so desired. The Jordanian objection to any connections between Hamas and the Jordanian Muslim Brethren only became all the more extreme. King Abdallah made it very clear that Hamas was not a Jordanian party and that Jordanian policy did not allow any non-Jordanian movement to operate in Jordan.[56] Would the shared concerns and fears about Hamas lead the Jordanians and the Israelis to revert to patterns from the past? Was that at all in the realm of the possible? Presently it would appear not to be so.

For the meantime, the Jordanians had other, more urgent concerns. In their acute sense of strategic anxiety, they were genuinely apprehensive about Palestine and the continued stalemate in the peace process with Israel, which in their assessment harbored only serious dangers for Jordan and the region as a whole. No matter how fervently supporters of the Israeli right pressed the issue, Jordan showed no interest in resuming control of the West Bank (the same could be said of Egypt and Gaza) to become alternative occupiers or, worse still, co-occupiers with the Israelis. Israeli right-wing ambitions in this regard were, therefore, "simply an empty fantasy."[57] Jordanian desperation with the Israeli-Palestinian impasse was having a very different effect. There were some in the Jordanian establishment who were beginning to argue that perhaps Jordan should diversify its options and lend its support to the one-state idea, even though they knew Israel would not be forthcoming. Such a tactic, they surmised, might pressure the Israelis to rethink their policies.[58]

## A Confederation for the Future

Jordan's present-day reluctance to get directly involved in the West Bank does not rule out the possibility of a closer relationship in the more distant future with an independent state of Palestine. The Jordanians and the Palestinians have had their bouts of conflict, but these pale in comparison to the virtually incessant bloodletting of Israelis and Palestinians. It is difficult to imagine Israeli Jews and Palestinians, after decades of horrific conflict and profound mutual distrust, sharing a confederation or any other form of binational state. Confederation between Jordan and Palestine, however, would seem to be a more realistic proposition.

First of all, it is an idea that has been part of the Jordanian and Palestinian political discourse since the early 1970s, and it has enjoyed considerable support by many, if not a majority, of Jordanians and Palestinians. As the Palestinian sociologist Salim Tamari has pointed out, since most West Bankers and even some Gazans were Jordanian citizens until not that long ago, and since about half of Jordan's population was of Palestinian origin, it was potentially a lot more meaningful for Palestine to be linked in a binational relationship with Jordan rather than with Israel, "particularly when one takes into account cultural factors."[59]

Indeed, despite the very real cleavages between Jordanians and Palestinians, they also had a lot in common. Historically, the secular nationalist rift between Jordanians and Palestinians was a late-twentieth-century phenomenon and a product of modern nationalism, and therefore considerably more shallow than the ancient divisions between Sunnis and Shi'is or between Muslims and Christians that hark back to the seventh century.

Though Palestinian-ness and Jordanian-ness were authentic nationalist sentiments, they coexisted with other historical, cultural, religious, and linguistic identities that actually united the two peoples, more than they set them apart. Most Jordanians and Palestinians were inclined to believe that the historical ties between their two peoples were unique and that in the longer run their two countries would indeed share a special relationship, in some sort of union or confederation.[60] There would, however, certainly be those in the Jordanian political elite and in certain parts of the intelligentsia for whom the idea would remain an anathema.

In the summer of 2007, after a long hibernation, the idea of a Jordanian-Palestinian confederation resurfaced in the Israeli and the Arab press after a visit paid by former Jordanian prime minister Abd al-Salam al-Majali to Israel to discuss the issue with Israeli officials and opinion makers.[61] The timing, one may safely assume, was connected to the stalemate between Israel and the Palestinians in the wake of the Hamas victory in the Palestinian elections in

January 2006 and the formation in March 2007 of the Palestinian unity government headed by Isma'il Haniyya of Hamas. Majali, no doubt, had King Abdallah's blessing, yet at the very same time the king himself publicly dismissed
the idea of confederation as premature. The king explained that it was a matter
to be discussed only after the establishment of an independent Palestinian
state and would be concluded solely on the basis of the free choice of the Jordanian and Palestinian peoples.[62]

The apparent contradiction stemmed from the fact that the Jordanians were
desperately looking for ways to break out of the impasse. By suggesting the
possible agreement in advance on a confederation as the ultimate solution,
they hoped to coax the Israelis into moving ahead with the Arab Peace Initiative that had just been reaffirmed at the Riyad summit in March 2007. The object was to get the Israelis to agree to negotiations on a Palestinian state that
would be linked in an eventual confederation with Jordan. But the Jordanians
had no intention of negotiating for the Palestinians or of assuming any administrative function in the West Bank, as the Israelis may have wanted to believe.
Moreover, in Jordan the idea was given a very cool, if not hostile, reception. For
the most part, it was rejected as another Israeli maneuver to drag the Jordanians, willy-nilly, into the infamous "alternative homeland" scenario.[63]

Even those in Jordan and Palestine who favored a confederation also agreed
that an independent Palestinian state had to be established first. Palestinians
sought to guarantee their independent statehood, and Jordanians preferred
not to get involved in Palestine prematurely. Jordanians did not want to under-
cut Palestinian independence and leave Jordan vulnerable to an overly intimate
relationship with Palestine, which might eventually erode the Jordanian-ness
of their own political patrimony on the East Bank.

If and when Israel disengages from the West Bank, that territory, land-
locked between Israel and Jordan, will become more dependent on Jordan and
the Arab world beyond. Israel would be creating a strategic reality more reminiscent of the situation that had prevailed between 1948 and 1967. At some
point, Jordanians and Palestinians would have to sit down and work out the
terms of their relationship.

Aside from the influential Jordanian nationalists who instinctively rejected
any close association with Palestine, there were others, equally nationalist,
like Abd al-Salam al-Majali and more of his most influential East Banker clan,
who saw in a confederation an opportunity to create a political order with legislative assemblies in Jordan and Palestine that would enable Palestinians in

Jordan to exercise their political rights in Palestine rather than in Jordan, even though they would most probably continue to be residents of Jordan.[64]

The confederation could provide new formulas for citizenship and civil rights that would allow the Jordanians to feel more secure by excluding the Palestinians on the East Bank from the Jordanian political system and having them exercise their rights of participation in the politics of Palestine instead. In the meantime, for post-disengagement Jordan, any role in the West Bank was predicated on the establishment of a Palestinian state. Jordan was not interested in intervening to forestall a Palestinian state. On the contrary, its supreme interest was to see one created. As one well-placed Jordanian put it, "The two-state solution must not be allowed to die."[65]

# 6 THE REVIVAL OF THE TWO-STATE IMPERATIVE

It was abundantly clear that a one-state solution was not about to be implemented, nor would it be in the foreseeable future. But a two-state solution, resolving all issues in abeyance, was not in the offing either. At the same time, the Palestinians across the board, at least in principle, did not accept an interim or provisional agreement. Thus, they rejected the notion of a Palestinian state in provisional boundaries without closure on the final status issues of refugees and Jerusalem. As Ahmad Khalidi pointed out some years ago, no Palestinian leadership could accept such a state that deferred these two most emotive issues. They would be denounced and possibly even violently opposed by both the Islamist and the nationalist opposition in Palestine itself, and by the refugee and diaspora constituencies as well.[1] In practice, however, recent developments in the West Bank seem to suggest a measure of Palestinian flexibility on this matter, in tandem with the coming to fruition of some critical structural transformations in the Palestinian body politic.

The process whereby the center of gravity of Palestinian politics has shifted inexorably into the occupied territories has been consummated. This was the culmination of a long process of enormous historical consequence that had begun in the early 1980s, after the PLO's expulsion from Lebanon. Since then, the role of the diaspora has been steadily sidelined. While the constituencies of Palestinian politics in the diaspora and in Israel were important in their own right, they could not successfully override the essential core of the Palestinian nationalist endeavor in the occupied territories.

The West Bank and Gaza were unquestionably the heartland of Palestine, and it was here that there appeared to be a growing sense of urgency, which was not apparent in the Arafat era, to break out of the impasse, to erode the status quo and thereby preserve the practicality of the two-state option. If there were those in the diaspora who challenged the representative credentials of the PA, there were just as many or more in the West Bank who would argue

with equal force and conviction that the diaspora and the Palestinian Arab minority in Israel were secondary and only auxiliary components to the national
core in the homeland, in Palestine.[2] And it was the people of the occupied territories who had the upper hand.

By the summer of 2009, the PLO, the PA, and Fatah, after its Sixth Conference in August 2009, were all in the grip of Mahmud Abbas and the Fatah political elite of the West Bank. Not only were the Fatah Central Committee and
Revolutionary Council firmly in the hands of West Bankers, but so was the
Executive Committee of the PLO, after Abbas hastily added replacements from
the West Bank for members who had passed away.

In conjunction with this institutional development, there was an identifi-
able and coherent school of thought in the West Bank that believed that the
self-interest of the West Bankers had to be secured first, and that meant ridding themselves of the occupation and creating two states. The West Bank
came first, and "the culture of the [refugee] camp and exile" (thaqafat al-
muhayyam wal-manfa) would continue to retreat "in favor of the culture . . . of
the homeland"[3] and its daily struggle against the occupation. In line with this
thinking, the PA focused on a desperate effort to resuscitate the fading two-
state option. For the PA, this was an unquestionably preferable path to follow,
rather than declaring statehood on less than a solid foundation or giving up on
the two-state solution altogether and opting for one state instead.

The diaspora and the Israeli Arab intelligentsia, with their utopian one-
state ideas, could wait, as could the refugees. "Palestine was the homeland of
the Palestinians, and the people of the [West] Bank, Jerusalem and the [Gaza]
Strip (four million) are the main center of gravity of the Palestinian people, and
it was they who are the bearers of sovereignty and the decision makers." After
all, it was they who bore the brunt of the confrontation with the occupation
and of the building of the institutions of the Palestinian state.[4] They were not
conceding on the refugee issue but setting priorities, and the most urgent
cause was to save the two-state paradigm. Far too many West Bankers understood that the alternative to two states was not one state in wonderland, but
some variant of recurrent violence and bloodshed.

## Palestinian Unilateralism and the Fayyad Plan

It was in this state of mind that in late August 2009 Palestinian prime minister
Salam Fayyad unveiled a government program, "Palestine: Ending the Occu-

pation, Establishing the State." The program, which came to be known as the "Fayyad Plan," was to build the institutions of a Palestinian state within two years, regardless of progress in the stalled peace negotiations with Israel. The "establishment of an independent, sovereign, and viable Palestinian state" was essential for "peace, security and stability" to thrive in the region. The Palestinians were determined to continue to preserve and advance the two-state option, as the window of opportunity for a viable two-state solution was being "mortally threatened by Israel's settlement policy." The continuation of this expansion would "undermine the remaining opportunity of building an independent Palestinian State on the Palestinian territory occupied in 1967." The plan therefore set out national goals and priorities and operational instructions for ministries and official bodies that were all meant to hasten the end of the Israeli occupation and pave the way for independent statehood, which "can and must happen within the next two years."[5]

The idea was to build a de facto Palestinian state by mid-2011, with functioning government, judicial and municipal institutions, police forces and public services, and so on, while also "liberating the Palestinian national economy from external hegemony and control, and reversing its dependence" on Israel. Fayyad's plan was geared toward the ultimate aspiration of establishing an internationally recognized independent state in the Palestinian territories occupied in 1967, with East Jerusalem as its capital, and he urged Israel to cease forthwith all settlement activities in Jerusalem and its environs to save the two-state solution from being "terminally undermined." Israel had to begin immediately to dismantle the obstacles to a two-state solution. It was required, therefore, to undo the infrastructure of occupation and create the space for international efforts to reach a just and lasting peace. As for the refugee question, it would be addressed later, in the final-status negotiations, on the basis of UN Resolution 194, but the Fayyad Plan reaffirmed that "no political settlement" could be "accepted by Palestinians without a just and agreed solution to this fundamental issue."[6]

Simultaneously with the state-building process, the PA envisaged an approach to the UN Security Council to pass a resolution that would endorse "the establishment of a Palestinian State, with East Jerusalem as its capital, on the 4 June 1967 border." The Security Council had already endorsed the idea of a Palestinian state, but the PA was now seeking a specific delimitation by the council of the state's frontiers along the 1967 boundaries. Moreover, the PA sought the inclusion of a "call for a just resolution to the Palestinian refugee issue in accordance with UN General Assembly Resolution 194," in such a forthcoming Security Council resolution. This, the Palestinians explained, was not a unilateral declaration of independence, but a means to preserve the two-state option and the corresponding pursuit of an "international imposition of [the] final status solution" on the parties "based on international law." If and when such a Security Council resolution was passed, the Palestinians would seek recognition of Palestine as a member state of the United Nations.[7] In practice, this was an effort to force Israel into a final negotiation on borders, with the international community in support of the Palestinian territorial desiderata, or alternatively to obtain international recognition for Palestinian rights to statehood and sovereignty without having to obtain Israeli consent.[8]

With all the trappings of statehood in place, Fayyad intended to invite Israel to recognize the hopefully well-functioning Palestinian state and to withdraw from territories it still occupied, or to be forced to do so by the pressure of international opinion. "The program we have embarked upon," he said, "was not supposed to be in lieu of a political process. It was supposed to reinforce it."[9] In practice, the Fayyad Plan would be very similar to a Palestinian state with provisional boundaries, except that it would presumably have international recognition of, but not actual control over, the 1967 boundaries, on the basis of which Israel would be required to negotiate.

In the words of one of the key moving forces behind the plan, the minister of planning and administrative development in Fayyad's cabinet, Ali Jarbawi, who was in the past one of the more outspoken advocates of the one-state alternative, the ongoing implementation of the plan represented for the first time in years visible and tangible progress toward making the two-state solution a reality.[10]

The results on the ground were impressive. US- and Jordanian-trained Palestinian security forces established unprecedented law and order in West Bank cities. (Law and order also meant jailing Hamas operatives by the hundreds. For Hamas, the law and order was no more than a joint PA-US-Israeli effort to subdue the Islamists in the West Bank. The measures taken included the vigorous repression of pro-Hamas preachers in the mosques of the West Bank, all designed to weaken Hamas in the area ruled by the PA.)[11] The new levels of security enabled Israel to remove dozens of roadblocks and checkpoints. The aim from the outset was to secure a major principle of modern statehood: a single armed force, subordinate to the government, with no rival militias roaming the streets. For all intents and purposes, this was already the case in the West Bank. The law and order and the opening up of the West Bank to free movement of people and goods led to a dramatic improvement in the economic climate, which also augured well for Fayyad's state-building project.

A minority alternative to breaking the impasse with Israel was the proposal to dissolve the PA in an attempt to force Israel to assume full responsibility for a renewed occupation and then to wage a "campaign of civil resistance against Israeli apartheid" for a one-state solution in Israel/Palestine.[12] But that was not an easy choice either. Israel would probably not rush to resume the occupation, and that would leave a void in Palestinian cities, which threatened the people with the dreaded specter of revived anarchy and lawlessness. The chaos that might ensue could possibly even pave the way for a Hamas takeover of the West Bank too, hardly a desirable option for the Fatah-dominated elite currently in office.

Moreover, hundreds of thousands of Palestinians were dependent for their livelihoods on the salaries of the 145,000 employees of the PA. The rather grim reality that might result from the dissolution of the PA could also be accompanied by an escalation of conflict with Israel long before it produced any so-called "solutions." These ideas fell on deaf ears in the West Bank. They were discarded by various Arab commentators almost the moment they were offered, as "empty threats."[13]

Though the Fayyad Plan seemed to have started off well, Fayyad himself was politically vulnerable. Despite his internationally acclaimed success, he had no domestic political base, and his plan, therefore, rested on frail political foundations. He was the ultimate outsider, educated and admired in the West, but one who had never been a member of Fatah and had never taken an active part in the national struggle. When he ran in the 2006 elections, the Third Way party he founded, dedicated to fighting corruption, won only two seats.[14] (Fayyad ran together with another "outsider," Hanan Ashrawi, a Western-educated Christian woman, on the margins of a society that had voted Hamas into office.)

Fayyad could be removed at a moment's notice if the "men of the fist" in Fatah so desired, if a reconciliation with Hamas so required, or if elections were held. Some in Fatah were not happy with Fayyad's style of governance, which they feared might undo the system of patronage that they thrived on. The strongmen of Fatah might, however, be reluctant to depose Fayyad, realizing that his ouster could jeopardize the international aid that was handsomely provided by the donor countries with few questions asked, because of their confidence in Fayyad's integrity. Fayyad's foreign credentials were at one and the same time the source of his strength and his weakness.

Both Mahmud Abbas and Salam Fayyad had legitimacy problems. Abbas's term as president expired in January 2009 and was extended with dubious legality. Fayyad was never elected. He was appointed after the dissolution of the government of national unity headed by Ismai'l Haniyya of Hamas, following the Hamas coup in Gaza in the summer of 2007. The Fatah conference held in Bethlehem in August 2009 was a symbolic injection of new vitality. The very fact that the conference convened at all, after a twenty-year hiatus, was seen as an achievement in itself, but the somewhat euphoric initial appraisals of Fatah's resurrection soon gave way to more sober assessments that continued to highlight Fatah's dysfunctional flaws.

The organization still suffered from internal intrigue and dissension, including direct challenges to the authority of Mahmud Abbas. There also seemed to be a lack of clear ideological orientation, characterized by constant waffling between peace with Israel and talk of continuation of the struggle. In the eyes of many Palestinians and others, by wedding the PA and Fatah to the peace process, Abbas had turned them into a weak combination resting "on the bayonets of the occupation" and depending on Israel and the United States for their survival. No one with the required legitimacy or history was waiting in the wings to replace Abbas. Even the much-heralded Marwan Barghuti, jailed in Israel for security offences, was less widely popular than regularly suggested in the foreign media. As matters stood, the Palestinian national movement after Abbas might very well "tear itself apart."[15]

Gone were the days when Fatah was the organizational incarnation of the Palestinian national struggle. The battle with Hamas was far from over, and genuine reconciliation remained elusive. Hamas was opposed to the Fayyad Plan, also because it was unquestionably directed against them too, and they could not be ignored. Hamas was deeply entrenched in Gaza, and it was "merely in hibernation in the West Bank." It was not going to wither away, and there was "no easy way to use fleeting opinion polls to toss Hamas out of power."[16] Its control of Gaza looked "set to endure." Hamas had "demonstrated its ability not merely to survive" but also to keep itself "at the heart of Palestinian national politics and decision-making."[17] Hamas was buoyant and self-assured, after having weathered the years of sanctions and other Israeli punishment imposed on their independent redoubt in Gaza, no matter how many times the PA tried to denigrate their regime as the "emirate of darkness [al-imara al-zalamiyya]."[18]

Hamas had an Arab media and political presence that outstripped that of

Fatah by far. The most popular TV channel in the Arab world, al-Jazeera (which was watched in the West Bank and in Gaza far more than any other channel and only a fraction less than all the rest combined), was a veritable propaganda arm of Hamas. The influential branches of the Muslim Brethren and like-minded organizations throughout the Arab and Muslim world were natural bastions of support for Hamas. The ruling elites in both Iran and Turkey were instinctively sympathetic to Hamas. Even pro-Fatah Arab regimes were reluctant to openly side with Fatah so as not to unnecessarily antagonize their influential Islamist oppositions.[19] The upheaval in Egypt in early 2011 and the overthrow of President Husni Mubarak, a key ally of the PA, further emboldened Hamas, who hoped and expected to profit from the changes in Cairo.

For Fatah to gain any ground, there would have to be meaningful and tangible progress in the peace process with Israel, but the divergence between Fatah and Hamas was itself a major obstacle to such progress. It would be extremely difficult if not impossible for the PA leadership to make critical historical decisions without at least the acquiescence of Hamas, which in all likelihood would not be forthcoming for any agreement with Israel. In the present balance of power, the PA could not impose its authority over the Gaza Strip, thereby raising the specter of an illegitimate three-state reality west of the Jordan, seriously undermining the very idea of a stable two-state solution.

Moreover, if no progress was to be made and the Palestinians chose to return to violence, Hamas would probably be a more a credible candidate for the mission, in the eyes of a broad segment of the Palestinian public, and the scales could be tipped even further against Fatah and the option of a negotiated settlement. The Fayyad Plan with its focus on statehood pushed the "1948 file" onto the back burner, much to the displeasure of the diaspora constituency. If the insider voices did not make the expected political gains, the diaspora voices would probably become far more audible. The exhaustion of the national movement in Palestine would leave very little hope for what remained of the peace process.

In October 2009, the PA decision to accede to US and Israeli pressure to defer the ratification at the UN Human Rights Council in Geneva of the Goldstone Report, which accused Israel of war crimes in Gaza, earned Mahmud Abbas and Fatah the opprobrium and contempt of many ordinary Palestinians. The "scandalous PA misstep" rapidly turned into a public relations and political disaster, further instilling the negative image of the PA as a pliable tool in the hands of the United States and Israel. The PA leadership was overwhelmed by the "avalanche of vitriolic condemnations" ranging from accusations of treason to incompetence and powerlessness.[20] The disclosures made by The Guardian and al-Jazeera in January 2011 on the negotiations with Israel, and the tendentious interpretation given to them by these two sources were a similarly insufferable embarrassment to the PA leadership.

The tarnished posture of the PA and the political fiascos that shaped it were naturally exploited to the hilt by Hamas and its superior media presence to enhance their credentials as the genuine and upright Palestinian patriots. Fatah often tried to shore up its credibility by highlighting its formative, historical role in the struggle against Israel. The trouble with that message was that it virtually conceded that resistance at present was, in fact, the preserve of Hamas, who spared no effort to ridicule those for whom negotiating with Israel was everything, even if they had nothing to show for it.

The advent of the right-wing Netanyahu government in Israel in March 2009 was cause for profound and pervasive despair in the PA. The "track of 'negotiations as [a way of] life' had arrived at the terminus."[21] It was becoming ever more widely accepted that the Oslo process had exhausted itself. The peace process was at an impasse, the efforts for reconciliation with Hamas had met with failure, and Abbas wasn't getting any younger either. These were all representations of what increasingly began to look like the end of an era. The Fayyad Plan was itself already an integral part of the thinking of this new era that appeared to put more faith in unilateral actions directed to acquiring international endorsement of Palestinian statehood rather than pursuing a fruitless negotiation with the incumbent Israeli government.[22]

For the political center and left in Israel, who saw the two-state solution as the key to a secure Jewish-majority state at peace with its neighbors, Fayyad was a breath of fresh air.[23] Between Fayyad and the Labor Party component of the Netanyahu government there was a common thread. Both Defense Minister Ehud Barak and Fayyad fully recognized the urgency of establishing a two-state reality. Sharing a podium with Fayyad at the Herzliya Conference in early February 2010, Barak warned that Israel risked becoming "an apartheid state par excellence" if it did not negotiate the terms of Palestinian statehood soon, and Fayyad spoke of the need to see that the occupation was "indeed on its way to being rolled back."[24]

Even from the predominantly right-wing government in power, Israel's objections to Palestinian unilateralism were comparatively muffled and half-hearted. Fayyad was said to be receiving support, on the quiet, also from Israel.[25] Fayyad suggested that Israel could help further augment his state-building project by handing over more West Bank territory to Palestinian security control. That did not seem immediately likely, and Netanyahu's refusal to maintain a freeze on Jewish settlement activity could not make matters any easier.

There was a considerable measure of skepticism about the room for maneuver the Israeli government would allow Fayyad. At some point down the road Fayyad's unilateralism might meet with Israeli resistance. It could not, therefore, be a really sustained policy unless there was some form of negotiating process or at least coordination between the parties. In the meantime, Fayyad accumulated international support. In December 2009, the Foreign Affairs Council of the European Union issued a statement reiterating "its support for negotiations leading to Palestinian statehood . . . and its readiness, when appropriate, to recognize a Palestinian state." The EU fully supported the "implementation of the Palestinian Authority's Government Plan 'Palestine: Ending the Occupation, Establishing the State' [the Fayyad Plan] as an important contribution to this end and will work for enhanced international support for this plan."[26]

In March 2010, the representatives of the Quartet (US, EU, Russia, and the UN), meeting in Moscow, expressed their unequivocal support for the "Palestinian Authority's plan of August 2009 for building the Palestinian state within 24 months," and they urged "all states in the region and in the wider international community to match the Palestinian commitment to state-building by contributing immediate, concrete, and sustained support for the Palestinian Authority."[27] In late 2010 and early 2011, more than ten Latin American countries led the way in granting formal recognition to the independent Palestinian state in the making.

## The Resurfacing of Variants of Israeli Unilateralism

Simultaneous with the Fayyad phenomenon, in the Israeli political and intellectual center, a revived unilateralism was creeping back into the discourse after years in which the idea had been discredited, following the withdrawal from Gaza and the war in Lebanon. Since the war with Hizballah in 2006, quiet was sustained on the Lebanese front, and relative calm was similarly maintained on the border with Gaza since the "Cast Lead" campaign that ended in January 2009. What looked like Israel's successful deterrence was giving rise to a more positive reassessment of unilateral withdrawal, in which deterrence figured as a possibly effective alternative to occupation.

In November 2009, one of the leaders of the Kadima Party, Shaul Mofaz, proposed that Israel withdraw unilaterally from some 60 percent of the West Bank, to allow for the establishment of a Palestinian state in provisional boundaries, to be followed at a later stage by further withdrawals through negotiation.[28] Leading columnists and writers, such as Ari Shavit, argued that Palestinians of all shades were not "willing to pay the price the Palestinians must pay in order to implement the two-state solution." But at the same time the "occupation is destroying Israel. It is undermining Israel's ethical, democratic and diplomatic foundations. But both Hamas and Fatah are making it very difficult to end the occupation. With Hamas . . . arming itself to the teeth and enjoying the support of about one-third of the Palestinians," it could veto any diplomatic progress. Fatah, however, was "unwilling to recognize the Jewish nation-state" and objected to a demilitarized Palestinian state. There was, therefore, no chance for a peace treaty. The alternative to the unattainable final-status agreement was "not a continuation of the status quo," but an Israeli initiative. Israel had to deal with the existential threat of the occupation by itself. Time was running out, and the "writing [was] on the wall."[29]

According to Gadi Taub, a writer and professor of communications and public policy at the Hebrew University, Israel had proved that it could handle the Qassam rocket threat effectively and it did not need the settlements to do so. Representing the views of many Israelis, he argued that the settlements had become a major foreign policy liability and contributed nothing to Israeli security. On the contrary, a majority of the public realized that Israel could only have a stable Jewish majority inside the borders of the old Green Line. If the Kadima Party wished to seize the mantle of the Israeli political center, it had to admit publicly that there would be no real peace soon, because the Palestinians do not intend to concede on the "right of return." Israel, nevertheless, would have to acquiesce in partition, even without an agreement. And, above all, Kadima had to unequivocally position itself against the settlements and tell the Israeli people the truth: that the settlements were the "greatest existential threat to the Zionist enterprise in our time."[30]

Writing in late 2010, Shlomo Avineri urged Israel to adopt a unilateralist alternative plan for implementation if and when talks with the Palestinians were to end in failure. The difficulties encountered by President Barack Obama in just trying to get the Israelis and Palestinians to the negotiating table showed how hard it would be to achieve a peace agreement even if talks did resume. Avineri suggested that if the talks failed, Israel should seize the initiative and implement an Israeli unilateral plan to protect its vital interests. The plan would include the following: Israel would lift the siege on the Gaza Strip, which had not fulfilled its purpose of toppling Hamas; it would announce its willingness to hand over the great majority of the West Bank to the Palestinians; Israel would evacuate illegal West Bank settlement outposts; it would offer a generous evacuation-compensation program to be set up for West Bank settlers who wish to return to Israel proper; and construction in Jewish settlements that were situated beyond the security fence would be halted. The plan, Avineri noted, would be acceptable to a broad consensus of Israelis from left to right, and, he concluded, the time had come to understand that "we [the Israelis] have to try to shape our destiny ourselves rather than waiting for Godot."[31]

There were even those on the moderate right who espoused unilateral withdrawal of settlements, arguing that if it was so clearly understood that Israel needed to dismantle the great majority of the settlements in the West Bank, for its own sake, why not go ahead and do it unilaterally and deploy in the West Bank only those IDF units that were required strictly for Israel's self-defense.[32]

Ehud Barak, in a speech in Washington in February 2010, argued that a successful peace process with the Palestinians was "a compelling imperative for the State of Israel . . . [and] the uppermost responsibility of any Israeli government." The reasoning was "painful but simple." One sovereign entity between the Jordan River and the Mediterranean Sea would inevitably become either non-Jewish or non-democratic. The only way to avoid these undesirable outcomes would be to "delineate a borderline" with the West Bank and to secure an Israel with a "solid Jewish majority for generations to come" on one side of the boundary and a viable Palestinian state on the other.[33]

Barak was not advocating unilateralism. He spoke highly of Fayyad's efforts and expressed his confidence in the Israeli "silent majority" supporting the necessary painful concessions, provided that there was readiness on the other side, and that it was clear that Israel was not dancing "this tango alone."[34] Nevertheless, considering the existential urgency and the well-known obstacles to an agreement, logically at least, unilateralism remained an option that could not be excluded, barring the unlikely event that Barak was willing to leave Israel's fate in the hands of a Hamas or Fatah veto.

Some Arab observers even expressed the concern that the Fayyad Plan might evolve into a series of moves that had the potential of becoming part of a larger duet of parallel or coordinated unilateralism involving actions by both parties. Israel might be urged into renewed unilateralism of its own if it feared the dissolution of the PA and/or pressure toward a unitary state. Such actions might result in the creation of a Palestinian state in provisional boundaries and the annexation of the major settlement blocs by Israel, leaving Jerusalem and refugees for later. The Palestinians would not formally have to acquiesce in such an interim arrangement, to which they were actually opposed, at least in principle. There were those who suspected that the PA leadership may even prefer such an informal arrangement, as they would be absolved from the need to make some difficult historical concessions.[35] Fayyad, however, made it abundantly clear that he aimed for an independent and sovereign state. The Palestinians, he said, were "not looking for a state of leftovers—a Mickey Mouse state."[36]

It had become the conventional wisdom that a conflict-ending agreement on all the issues, including Jerusalem and refugees, was not presently feasible.[37] Some suggested front-loading the border question and thus bypassing the current obstacle of settlements.[38] After all, an agreement defining the territorial extent of a Palestinian state would resolve the settlements issue as well. Once there was a border, it would at last be clear what was Israel and what was not.

Another option was for Israel and Palestine to sign an armistice agreement, similar to the ones Israel signed with the Arab states in 1949.[39] Still others were speaking of various unilateral options, coordinated or otherwise. These were all variations on the same theme: in the absence of an "end of conflict" agreement, it was imperative to establish at least some form of interim arrangement that would temporarily defer Jerusalem and refugees, but would create a two-state reality, and thereby maintain the viability of the two-state option. Fayyad and the PA, on the one hand, and various Israeli sources, on the other, shared considerably more common ground than perhaps immediately met the eye, driven by their extreme fear of the dangers inherent in an extended impasse, gravitating by default into a one-state reality.

All of the above tended to demonstrate that while a one-state reality might be an eventual end result, the majority of Palestinians in the occupied territories and most Israelis did not see such an outcome as a desirable solution. The Palestinians, who in theory should have been more inclined to the one-state scenario, were actually engaged in a desperate effort to preserve the viability of the two-state option. In Israel, formerly outmoded ideas of interim solutions or of Israeli unilateralism were back in vogue in the public domain, precisely because of the extreme undesirability of the one-state "solution" to the overwhelming majority of Jewish Israelis.

As Ehud Yaari, the doyen of Israeli Arab affairs commentators, put it, "Israel must offer Palestinian statehood for less than peace before the Palestinians and their leaders abandon the two-state model altogether." According to Yaari, some key Israeli officials, including Defense Minister Barak, were advocating the pursuit of interim arrangements, a path that Netanyahu also seemed to be considering. Yaari proposed that an interim agreement or armistice should determine the provisional boundary between Israel and a Palestinian state. Final-status issues like refugees, Jerusalem, and outstanding border/settlement questions would be deferred to a separate track of negotiations that would convene following the armistice agreement. The armistice would however include certain partial and preliminary solutions for some of the final-status issues.[40]

It would naturally require a major international and Arab diplomatic effort to convince the PA to overturn its position against interim solutions. This might be assisted by the promise of early and tangible results and guarantees to keep moving toward a final-status agreement. In Yaari's estimation, the signing of such an armistice would be the greatest breakthrough in Arab-Israeli peacemaking since Israel's treaty with Jordan. "Instead of allowing such issues as the refugees and the status of Jerusalem to delay the establishment of a Palestinian state, [the armistice] would constitute a major step toward ending the occupation, fundamentally reconfigure the conflict, and make prospects for a final-status agreement far brighter than ever before."[41]

In the meanwhile, despite the domestic criticism they faced, Abbas, Fayyad, and Fatah were holding their own in the West Bank, albeit with Israeli and US cooperation, and according to polls conducted from late 2009 to late 2010, they still enjoyed a large measure of public support, with approval ratings ranging between 45 and 60 percent, much higher than for Hamas.[42] Even so, the outcome of an Israeli withdrawal from the West Bank was anyone's guess, and a Hamas takeover was not an unlikely possibility. It was the fear of such an eventuality that fueled the thinking among some Israelis of coaxing Jordan to reengage, also for its own self-interest, to protect the kingdom from a West Bank "Hamas-stan." Jordan, however, as noted above, had no intention of preempting Palestine, and Jordan was, therefore, not a candidate for creating obstacles to the two-state pursuit.

From the point of view of all three protagonists in historical Palestine, on both sides of the Jordan River, the overriding consensus and the most realistic of options was still two states for the two peoples west of the river. It will remain for the Jordanians and the Palestinians (and not the Israelis) to decide what, if any, special relationship they may choose to have between them in the future. Moreover, in the long run, Israel will have to allow for Palestinian control of the border crossings between Palestine, Jordan, and Egypt. If Israel genuinely seeks to disengage and to enable two independent states to coexist, it cannot disengage from Palestine with one hand and lock the Palestinians in with the other.

# CONCLUSION

With the failure of the peace process and after seventeen long years since the signing of the Oslo Accords, the two-state solution lost much of its appeal, legitimacy, and practicality in the eyes of all concerned. The entrenchment of the Israeli settlements and the fecklessness of successive Israeli governments (with the surprising exception of Ariel Sharon) in contending with the challenge of the settler movement have been major obstacles to the attainment of a two-state solution. The political disarray in Palestine—with the PA and Hamas at loggerheads ever since the Hamas electoral victory in 2006 and the takeover of Gaza in 2007, the dispirited condition of the PA, and the concomitant ideological fatigue and organizational stagnation of Fatah—also made the successful negotiation of a two-state agreement an unrealistic prospect.

With memories of the rocketry from Gaza and southern Lebanon still fresh in their minds and the unprecedented turmoil that swept through the entire Middle East in early 2011, there was widespread uncertainty among Israelis, even among supporters of the two-state solution, about the wisdom of imminent withdrawal from the West Bank, at a time when the PA might not be able or willing to guarantee security. There was therefore, an equally widespread tendency to support the continuation of the status quo, even among those who would in principle prefer to rid Israel of the occupation. In such complicated political circumstances, those who continued to endorse the two-state solution also had to "acknowledge how much of the framework supporting it [had] collapsed."[1]

However, the conclusion that some drew from this grim assessment, that a one-state "solution" was the viable alternative to the faltering two-state paradigm, was offering a remedy that would in all likelihood be infinitely worse than the existing malady. The self-proclaimed moralists who assessed reality not on the grounds of what it was but on the basis of what they believed it ought to be, in a world ostensibly founded on ethics, justice, and legal rectitude, and on the constantly disproved assumption about the rationality of political actors, had little connection with the real world. In the real world, the highly combustible mixture of power, emotion, collective identity, political culture, and ideology, which were all of no consequence in the moralists' worldview, actually dominated the political order.

As Nathan Brown has put it, the advocates of a binational state, or what he has so aptly dubbed as the "one-state non-solution," generally "fall into the trap of holding out an admirable utopian solution without analyzing what such a state would be like in practice or how entrenched adversaries could ever construct such a state. In a sense, the one-state solution resembles communism — a utopian idea many found preferable to the grim realities but that led to horrifying results in practice."[2]

One should have no illusions, Hussein Ibish observes, "that the final abandonment of a two-state agenda" will simply "give way to a campaign of nonviolent resistance, boycotts and sanctions that will somehow succeed in bringing Israel to its knees." For boycott, divestment, and sanctions (BDS) to be effective would require a radical shift in the intimate linkages between the US government, institutions, and corporations and general American society with Israel. On the other hand, Israeli institutions, organizations, corporations, military, intelligence, industry, research and development, and scientific research were all interwoven very intricately with US counterparts,[3] and less intensively with many other countries, from the EU to India, China, and Japan. BDS in the globalized world of today was a very different form of operation than in the pre-globalized era of the struggle against South Africa. Moreover, even in South Africa, BDS was not the major factor that induced the historical policy shift.

Abba Eban once commented that "not for a single minute in a day do the . . . Palestinians and the Israelis share a common memory, sentiment, experience or aspiration."[4] The real alternative to the two-state agenda was not Israel's imminent collapse into a one-state "solution" but escalating "conflict, violence and occupation that [would be] increasingly dominated by religious fanatics on both sides." The alternative to the two-state paradigm was not the utopian paradise of one state, but catastrophe.[5] The evolution of a one-state reality might very well be the outcome of the final demise of the two-state idea, but that was very likely to be a horrendous situation of escalating conflict, not only in the occupied territories but across the Green Line, in Israel proper, too. The clashes of October 2000 in Israel were just the foretaste of what the impasse might eventually produce.

The one-state idea was proposed outside of history. It was as if there were no past or present to inform our thoughts about the future. The proponents of the one-state idea spoke of an ideal order entirely imagined and divorced from just about everything we know about the past and the present in Israel/ Palestine and beyond. Either the supporters of the idea were naïve in the extreme, or alternatively, and as was more likely, they knew only too well that this was a recipe for further conflict. But it would be further conflict in which, if the one-state advocates had their way—as As'ad Ghanem, for one, has had the intellectual honesty to make very clear—it would be the final and decisive round in the struggle against the Zionists.

The Arab one-state advocates and their supporters sought to remove the conflict from the arena of military confrontation, where the Israelis were far too strong, to the arena of universal human rights. In this arena and in the international forums where these issues were presently adjudicated, the Israelis were outnumbered in a disfigured process whereby international law was politically manipulated and selectively implemented in what was now commonly referred to as "lawfare." Palestinian human rights were routinely upheld without question, while those of the Israelis were systematically ignored or overruled. In these forums, the Israelis were repeatedly pushed onto the defensive in a system that in practice singled Israel out for selective prosecution, making a mockery of the principle of equality before the law.

In the scheme of the one-state advocates, the Israeli Jews, after having had their state undone, would become a defenseless minority that would finally be beaten into submission. After all, it was the power of the Israeli state that had heretofore proved to be the insurmountable obstacle. Once the Israelis no longer possessed their majoritarian state, as a defenseless minority they would not stand a chance. That was a road that would not be taken voluntarily by Jewish Israelis of any stripe.

Uri Avnery, the leader of Israel's ultra-left Peace Bloc, scoffed at the idea of one state: "It takes quite a stretch of the imagination to believe that Israelis and Palestinians will come together, serve in the same army, enact the same laws and pay the same taxes. One wonders how such a state would function."[6] Yossi Klein Halevi, a centrist Israeli writer, ridiculed the "notion that Palestinians and Jews, who can't even negotiate a two-state solution, could coexist in one happy state." The proposition was "so ludicrous that only the naïve or the malicious would fall for it."[7] Thus far even Fatah and Hamas were incapable of agreeing between themselves on maintaining one Palestinian Authority. And these two, together with the Jews of Israel were expected by the one-staters to coexist in one such "happy state." Indeed, it could only boggle the mind.

Benjamin Pogrund, the former South African anti-apartheid journalist and activist, concluded that, in contradistinction to South Africa, "the prospect of one state [in Israel/Palestine] is so impossible that it is surprising that anyone even goes on talking about it. Perhaps those who do so actually have a hidden agenda: Their aim is not so much to end the plight of refugees and bring Israelis and Palestinians together but rather to eliminate Israel."[8]

There was a tendency in the academic, diplomatic, and more popular discourse on international relations to focus on what local players should be doing or could be coaxed or coached into doing, rather than on what it is that the local players really wanted or intended to do, and/or were actually capable of doing. This was true of Iraq, Afghanistan, Cyprus, the Balkans, and a host of other countries in the Middle East, as well as on both sides of Israel/Palestine.

There was an exaggeration of the capacity of external players to engineer the behavior of local players. Simultaneously, there was an underestimation of the capacity of local players, with their own desires, political culture, traditions, shortcomings, and constraints, to demonstrate sheer grit and to persevere to obtain what they believed were their historical rights and/or their existential interests. The external powers, as great as they may be, simply did not have such existential interests in these local conflicts and were invariably unwilling to invest the energies required to actually coerce the locals to do what they had no intention of doing.

Some of the most experienced former US hands in Middle East peacemaking have drawn insightful lessons from their protracted personal involvement. Great powers have limitations, "Gulliver's troubles," as Aaron Miller aptly described them. Miller contends that "an outside power can play a positive role, but it is at a distinct disadvantage. In conflicts where memory, identity, and history figure prominently, a great power—especially a great power from far away—has far less stake in a particular outcome than does a small power in the heart of the contested region.

Smaller nations will do just about anything to survive and are not inclined to listen to or even trust advice offered by a distant power whose political and physical survival is not at stake." Great powers "aren't always so great when they get mixed up in the affairs of small tribes," and the Middle East is "littered with broken illusions of great powers who believed they could impose their will on smaller ones," from the French in Algeria to the Soviets and the United

States in Afghanistan, and the British and the Italians in many places in between.[9]

The parties would do well to distinguish between the attainable and the unachievable. Camp David might not have failed, says Martin Indyk (formerly the National Security Council's senior Middle East expert, assistant secretary of state for Near East affairs, and twice US ambassador to Israel), if the United States had "admitted the improbability of resolving all the issues in one summit." Then the Americans "could perhaps have conditioned both sides to the concept of a partial agreement" that would have solved the territorial issues first, established a Palestinian state, and "set a framework and timetable for agreeing on the other issues."[10] That may have been true then and was probably true now.

Generally speaking, it would, therefore, seem advisable for external powers to make a genuine effort to start off by seeking to determine what it was that the locals really wanted, or were capable of living with, at least temporarily. Temporary, of course, was not as secure as permanent, but temporary was better than nothing at all. Moreover, temporary had an implicit advantage over permanent in that it enabled the parties to concede without appearing to posterity to have sold out. The armistice agreements between Israel and the Arabs after the 1948 war lasted for nearly twenty years. Had the negotiations at Rhodes in 1949 focused on "end of conflict," they probably would have achieved nothing at all and the parties might very well have been back at each other's throats for a "second round" in no time.

The Palestinians in the West Bank accepted Jordanian annexation and citizenship, which allowed them a much better life than that of many if not most other Palestinians. It was legitimate mainly because it was portrayed as a temporary arrangement and therefore not construed as an abandonment of the homeland or of the "right of return." This "temporary" arrangement for Palestinian Jordanians has lasted for over sixty years, and most of the people involved would probably shudder at the thought of suddenly being denied the very tangible privileges of Jordanian citizenship, in the name of a more permanent "end of conflict" or any other elusive concept.

Unilateral had a lot in common with the temporary. It did not entail "concessions on vital rights or points of principle." Both sides in theory could engage in "parallel unilateralism" whereby Israelis might withdraw unilaterally from certain areas, without concessions on other issues of principle like refugees, for example, and the Palestinians would develop their institutions of self-rule and statehood, without the shackles of Israeli preconditions. This could be the "only temporary, if as yet fuzzy, way out,"[11] an idea proffered by Ahmad Khalidi in 2005.

Going beyond the temporary or the provisional to achieve "end of conflict" has failed repeatedly. In successive rounds of negotiations, the gaps were narrowed very significantly on all matters relating to borders and settlements and even on Jerusalem and security arrangements, that is, on all the components of the "1967 file" that pertain to the future of the West Bank and Gaza. At the same time, however, little if any real progress was made in resolving the 1948 question of refugee return. In fact the abyss between the parties has actually widened, as both sides have felt compelled to dig in further in defense of their historical positions.

The question of the "right of return" was at the very core of the Nakba narrative, and it created seemingly insurmountable constraints on Palestinian decision makers. The Nakba narrative assumed mythic proportions in the last few decades. It completely dominated the Palestinian perception of their collective memory, their national identity, and their corporate psyche. It was the major source of inspiration for Palestinian cultural creativity in all its forms, the fine arts and academic endeavor in just about every discipline, from the social sciences, to the humanities and law.

The Nakba narrative was the heart and soul of the Palestinian collective being. Palestinian leaders have, as a result, repeatedly recoiled from any irreversible concession or commitment that might suggest acquiescence in finality short of Israel's acceptance of refugee return and all that it entailed in terms of refugee freedom of choice and the option of return to Israel proper.

For Israel, this was a nonstarter. As a sovereign state whose historical raison d'être was to be the state of the Jewish people, it could not possibly allow Palestinian refugees to be the only ones to decide whether they would return to Israel proper or not. Ultimately it would be up to Israel to determine how many refugees it would be willing to admit, if any at all. For the Palestinians, this was totally unacceptable, and they continued to demand an Israeli acquiescence in some form of the "right of return," the scope of which would have to be negotiated and agreed upon. No matter how long the negotiations continued, the Palestinians would not back down in this issue.

In response, the Israeli official discourse shifted in emphasis from the unattained "end of conflict" to the demand that Israel be recognized as the nation-state of the Jewish people. The shift represented an Israeli recognition of the supreme priority of preventing an opening of the "1948 file" and pre-empting the potential challenge of the 1948 questions to Israel's core identity and raison d'être as the state of the Jewish people. But expecting the Palestinians to accept either one of these formulations in exchange for a solution of only the 1967 questions was to expect them to invalidate their narrative of Palestinian history and of 1948 in particular. No amount of pressure or cajoling would convince the Palestinians to concede that Palestine, or any part of it, was "Jewish," nor would they "end the conflict" without rolling back 1948, at least in part.

Equally unreasonable was the parallel Palestinian demand that the Israelis concede their right to self-determination and to define their state as the state of the Jewish people. The Jews did not wage a struggle for over a century to create a state of their own, against all the odds, in extremely trying circumstances, and with huge sacrifice, only to be told to give up its heart and soul in exchange for a grudging acceptance by the neighborhood.

Such narrative-invalidating demands made by both sides were pointless exercises that peace negotiations could well do without. Nations could not be expected to negotiate their histories. That was better left to the historians and the classrooms rather than to the so-called "peace process," where such fanciful intellectual acrobatics only added impediments to the virtually insurmountable political obstacles that already existed. First the parties had to obtain a mutually tolerable agreement on the ground. Rewriting the peoples' core narratives could wait for later.

On another level, Israel's new emphasis on the "Jewish state" was not only a demand from the Palestinians but also a subconscious reordering of national priorities. For the Israelis, the preservation of their state as the state of the Jewish people was paramount, even if it meant sacrificing "the end of conflict." That is, if ending the conflict required of Israel to undermine or abandon its character as the nation-state of the Jewish people, this was not a price the great majority of Israelis were willing to pay. Essentially this was the same conclusion Ben-Gurion had drawn in the 1930s when he posited that partition and increased Jewish immigration, which meant continued conflict with the Arabs, were preferable to peace if peace meant forfeiting the historical objective of creating a nation-state for the Jewish people.

For both Israelis and Palestinians, a two-state solution was not an ideal, but the lesser evil. The positions of both sides fractured the perfect symmetry of the two-state paradigm. Due to the centrality of the refugee cause for the Pal-

estinians, two states, without at least some significant element of refugee return to Israel, could never really be accepted as point final, and even that was
doubtful. For the Israelis, on the other hand, it was imperative for the two
states to bring an end to active conflict, at least in the sense that the Palestinian
state alongside Israel would not become the staging ground for continued
warfare of any kind. Consequently, the Palestinian state that the Israelis were
willing to endorse was never a fully sovereign and independent member of the
family of nations, but an emasculated, demilitarized, and supervised entity,
with Israeli control of its airspace and possibly of its borders too, and some
element of Israeli and/or foreign military presence, as well.

Land for peace, so it transpired, was an inappropriate formula for the
Israel-Palestine conundrum. Land for peace was a concept that related to the
inter-state border disputes. It was born in November 1967 in UN Security
Council Resolution 242, designed to resolve the territorial issues that arose
from Israel's conquests in the Six Day War. It was formulated when Israel was
expected to exchange land with Egypt, Syria, and Jordan (not Palestine) for
peace.

The crux of the Israel-Palestine issue was not about an exchange of land,
between Israel and the Palestinians for peace. The Israel-Palestine conflict
could not be reduced to an inter-state border quarrel over the West Bank and
Gaza. The questions on the table related not just to Israel's borders and the
"1967 file," but to the "1948 file" and to Israel's very being. Reducing the problem to its 1967 dimensions and essentially closing the "1948 file" was the way
Israel understood the inherent logic of the two-state solution. That required
of the Palestinians to concede on refugees, but they would not do so and declare "end of conflict" in the same breath. If the Palestinians would have to
concede on refugees, Israel, in return, would have to rescind its demand for
full peace and "end of conflict."

Thus, the realistic Israeli-Palestinian equation was not land for peace. The
more attainable equation was land, and no more than land (that is, no refugee
return beyond a symbolic gesture), in exchange for a two-state arrangement
that would not be peace in the full sense and would not formally end the conflict either. In essence it would be more akin to a hudna, an armistice, that
would last for as long as the parties had an interest in its preservation. In the
real world, this would be equally true of a full-blown peace treaty, even if the
Palestinians and the Israelis signed the most extensive, ostensibly ironclad
commitments to end the conflict for all time. Neither one of them would

strictly abide by any agreement the moment they assessed it was working against their existential interests. For the cynics in Israel, this is commonly known as "signing on the ice." The commitments melt away, and in the heat of the Middle East this can happen very quickly.

Perhaps counterintuitively, the *advantage* of such an armistice *and not its deficiency* would be in its provisional and temporary nature. As we have already seen, when the parties inch closer to a deal, they tend to recoil from the implications of that last, fateful step, as the weight of their historical narratives and/or the potential condemnation for abandoning the cause prevent leaders from actually making the momentous decisions. It is actually this *lack of finality* that would allow the parties to concede on their great historical principles, without actually appearing to have done so, precisely because the concession would be neither final nor theoretically irreversible.

This required precarious maneuvering, but it might be the only realistic avenue to pursue. Such ideas have recently been gaining currency. The discussion above of Ehud Yaari's armistice idea was one example. Similar ideas were presented by Nathan Brown, who suggested an Israeli-Palestinian cease-fire, including Hamas, that could develop into a five- or ten-year armistice.[12] Another is an article by Walter Russel Mead suggesting that Israel might have to "pay virtually the full price of peace—withdrawal from settlements, some kind of solution in Jerusalem and other concessions—without getting full peace."[13] Indeed, that might be so. From the outset, such maneuvers would not be intended to deliver peace. But, as Nathan Brown put it, they would be "likely to allow Israelis and Palestinians to live together for a time, during which—with significant international effort—the conflict can be led to evolve into more tractable forms."[14]

The Palestinian-Zionist conflict originated in the project of the Jewish national movement to create an independent nation-state in Eretz Yisrael / Palestine, as an expression of their right to self-determination and as a project of national salvation and redemption from centuries of persecution. The Palestinian Arabs, however, never had any particular compassion for the Jewish problem nor did they ever accept that the Jewish problem should be resolved at their expense, in whole or in part, and they resisted the Zionist project with all their might. The wars fought against Israel had disastrous consequences for the Palestinians, but their fight against Israel has not been abandoned.

For some, there was a realization that compromise was unavoidable and that the two nations should be able to achieve a limited form of their respective national ambitions in two separate independent states. For others, like Hamas, the conflict had to continue, including by means of armed resistance to the Zionist enterprise. For many of the one-state advocates, the struggle had taken on a new form of political "lawfare," ostensibly founded on international legality, whereby Israel was to be dismantled in the name of a certain, rather lopsided, reading of international law and justice, which trumped any and all of the rights that the Jews might claim for themselves. For the one-state advocates, all nations had collective rights, except the Jews.

This, in essence, was the one-state agenda. It was not a solution based on compromise or recognition of any residual national rights of the Zionists. It was the reincarnation of the original position adopted by the Arabs of Palestine since the very onset of the conflict: that Palestine was the legitimate homeland of the Palestinian people, which should rightfully become a unitary Arab state that might accept within its midst a Jewish minority, but not a Jewish state.

Expecting either one of the parties to capitulate to the historical visions of justice of the other side would be unrealistic. Thus, proposing agendas such as the one-state idea, which entirely ignored the interests and national aspirations of the Israeli Jews, was in effect a prescription for eternal strife. Similarly, ideas of Palestinizing Jordan, or eternal occupation by Israel of the West Bank and Gaza, or other means of skirting the explicit recognition by Israel of the national rights of the Palestinian people were not blueprints for conflict resolution either. They were recipes for the prolongation or even the escalation of the Israeli-Palestinian conflict and the attendant blood, sweat, and tears.

There were three sets of domestic negotiations that would have to take place to set the stage for an acceptable arrangement. The Israeli left, moderate right, and center would have to arrive at some form of consensus that would allow for the withdrawals Israel had to make for any kind of settlement, interim or final, to hold water. It would be similarly imperative for Hamas and Fatah to come to a political understanding that would enable the Palestinians not only to negotiate, but also to unite Gaza and the West Bank into one territorial unit. (Israel, in the meantime, would have to guarantee safe passage between the two for that to become a reality.) In Jordan, original Jordanians and Jordanians of Palestinian descent would have to negotiate their own relations, as well as the ties between the Hashemite Kingdom of Jordan and the emergent state of Palestine. All of these meant a long haul.

When it comes to the receding option of two states, both Israelis and Palestinians have made their negative contributions. History, after all, is not only "about what others do to you; it is also about what you do to shape history."[15] The Palestinians faced an insurmountable ideological barrier in incorporating the Nakba narrative into the political framework of a two-state solution. The Israelis implemented a settlement policy after 1967 that was based on the obfuscation of partition and a two-state solution. For Israel, this was a disastrous miscalculation. Historically, partition served the Zionist cause more than it served the Arabs, who had always opposed it, for good reason from their point of view. Eroding the two-state idea was, therefore, an insufferable strategic disservice to Israel and to the cause of self-determination for the Jewish people.

Irrespective of the rights and wrongs of the implementation of the British Mandate over Palestine, it gave birth to three distinct political entities, Israel, Jordan, and Palestine, with particular collective identities of their own. Israel is Israel, Jordan is Jordan, and Palestine is Palestine, each deserving of its inherent right to self-determination and independence. Any attempt to deny any one of the three its rightful place among the family of nations will prolong the conflict and perpetuate the bloodshed.

This was fully understood by a majority of Israelis, Palestinians in the occupied territories, and Jordanians, not as a utopian ideal but as the most promising, or the least damaging, road to be taken toward possible peaceful coexistence. The silent majorities, who supported the two-state agenda, unfortunately did not control the narratives on either side, nor did they shape the actual policies of their respective leaderships.

But if the leaderships in Israel and Palestine mustered the courage to do what was required to achieve a two-state solution, they would have the majorities of their respective publics behind them. A partition into two states still held out the greatest hope for a peaceful accommodation of the political differences between Jewish Israelis and Palestinians and for the exercise of their respective rights to ethno-cultural self-determination. The failure of the parties to produce a two-state solution would lead by default to the creation of a one-state reality. But, as opposed to the convictions of the one-state advocates, the actual prospects for such a reality to produce peace were extremely remote or even nonexistent.

In their Myths, Illusions, and Peace, Dennis Ross and David Makovsky have criticized American neoconservatives and some self-styled realists for being "guided far more by their sweeping belief systems about what ought to be than by looking at what actually exists." The same would apply to the one-state advocates (in the same league as the so-called realists), whose prescriptions, precisely like those of the neoconservatives and the self-described realists, "are not just doomed to fail, but bound to make things worse."[16]

The one-state agenda in its various manifestations had virtually no chance of convincing the great majority of Israelis to go along with it. Nevertheless, it had unquestionably eroded the legitimacy of both Israel and the two-state solution. It played an instrumental role in Israel's gradual isolation, similar in some ways to the pariah status once reserved for apartheid South Africa. Israelis complained that they were being treated unfairly by bigotry and bias. And they certainly were. But if they choose to ignore the corrosive effect of the one-state campaign and the escalating delegitimization of Israel in the academia, intelligentsia, and political elites of the West—exacerbated in part by Israel's own actions, settlements in particular—they will do so at their peril.

The unprecedented domestic political turmoil that swept through the Middle East in the early months of 2011 did not alter this assessment. On the contrary, it gave increased urgency to the need for Israelis and Palestinians to make the historical decisions required of them to turn the two-state imperative into a reality. From Tunisia, Egypt, and Libya to Bahrain and Yemen, with Syria and Jordan in between, the countries that make up Israel's strategic environment were shaken to the core and appeared to be considerably less stable than they had been for decades.

However successful the current uprisings may be in upsetting the political order, it would take a long time before the underlying socioeconomic causes of the recent upheavals could be satisfactorily addressed. The new regimes that might emerge from the current convulsions—and there is no certainty whether they will be markedly different from their predecessors or more of the same—could very well be facing new outbursts of popular disaffection when the presently high hopes for rapid, if not miraculous, change are dashed, as is all too likely to be the case.

Regional destabilization notwithstanding, the Palestinians, at an impasse in negotiations with Israel, continued to forge ahead in their effort to achieve further international recognition for an independent state in the West Bank, the Gaza Strip, and Arab Jerusalem. They were hoping to obtain a favorable resolution by the UN General Assembly as well, which would endorse the 1967 lines as the future boundary of the Palestinian state and thereby coerce Israel to contend with Palestinian territorial desiderata that would have the explicit support of much of the international community. Against this backdrop of in-

creasing regional uncertainty, a growing sense of Israeli isolation, and potential Palestinian diplomatic advances at Israel's expense, the debate in Israel on
the two-state solution was revived with an ever more acute sense of impending
crisis.

For the political right in Israel, this was hardly the time for magnanimous
concessions to the Palestinians, when the regional environment seemed so
unsettled. However, many of those in the political center and center-left made
the opposite case. Israeli Defense Minister Ehud Barak warned in March 2011
that Israel would face an unprecedented "diplomatic tsunami" of international
delegitimization if it did not launch a political initiative of its own to advance
peace with the Palestinians.[17] In early April a group of former senior officers in
the IDF, officials in the Israeli defense establishment, and some scholars and
businessmen urged the Israeli government to adopt a political initiative for the
implementation of a two-state solution more or less along the lines of the
Clinton parameters.[18]

The ultimate outcome of the turmoil in the Middle East was pure guess-
work. There were, however, various indications that the Arab world around
Israel was becoming more overtly hostile. It was a world in truly dire straits
from which Israel had to disengage. Despite the regional convulsions, and
even because of them, Israel was required to find the ways and means of ending its occupation of the West Bank, with or without an agreement with the
Palestinians, preserving only the absolute minimum of territory for national
security in the new circumstances.

The realities of the Arab world finally put paid to any residual illusions of a
"new Middle East" with which Israel ought to integrate. They also forced many
outside the region to recognize at long last that, despite widespread hostility
to Israel in the Arab world, it had always been "gold-plated nonsense" to argue
that the Israel-Palestine conflict was the "core issue" of the entire Middle East.
"Now the world can see that the peoples of Egypt, Tunisia, Libya, Yemen, Syria
and Bahrain have troubles aplenty that have nothing to do with Israel. There
could be peace between Israelis and Palestinians tomorrow, but it wouldn't
relieve [the peoples of those countries] from the yoke of tyranny. For them,
Israel is not 'the heart of the matter,' as the cliche always insisted it was." The
heart of the matter was the collective grievance of these peoples against their
regimes "who have oppressed them day in, day out, for 40 years or more."[19]

As a number of Israeli analysts have pointed out, precisely because Israel
was not the core issue, it was not in Israel's interest to inject itself into the af-

fairs of the Arab world. Generally speaking, the Israelis would be wise to leave the Arabs to engage in their own problems and to refrain from gratuitously provoking a reorientation of Arab attention to the conflict with Israel.[20] Moreover, Israel's own longevity and survivability dictated a resolution or at least a reasonable *modus vivendi* or interim arrangement with the Palestinians. For Israel and for the Palestinians in the West Bank and Gaza, their conflict was indeed the "heart of the matter," and Israel had no interest in allowing the problems of occupation to fester until they also exploded in some massive popular manifestation of Palestinian resentment.

Unfortunately, the problems that have plagued Israeli-Palestinian negotiations have not been ameliorated by the uprisings of the Arab street.

- Throughout the Middle East the prevailing conventional wisdom in the capitals of the region and among the Palestinians, Fatah and Hamas alike, invariably assumed that a post-Mubarak Egypt would be a polity in which the Muslim Brotherhood and other, even more radical Islamists, would be major power brokers. This might be true of new political orders, if there are to be any, in other countries, and would presumably not facilitate peacemaking between Israel and the Palestinians.

- As the Palestinians sought international recognition of their state-in-the-making, efforts toward reconciliation between Fatah and Hamas were revived in the early months of 2011.[21] Such a rapprochement, by no means a foregone conclusion, was essential for the promotion of one internationally recognizable Palestinian government. At the same time, it was a necessary precondition for an agreement with Israel, and an obstacle that could make peacemaking with the Israelis that much more difficult.

- The upheavals in the Arab world did not bypass Israel's neighbor across the river, Jordan, which Israelis had always regarded as a crucial buffer for more hostile neighbors farther to the east. Though the Jordanians appeared to have matters under control, the somewhat higher probability of instability on Israel's eastern front would make the Israelis even more reluctant than they had been hitherto to part with the Jordan Valley.[22] This factor could only complicate further the more profound impediments, like Jerusalem and refugees, to a negotiated peace accord with the Palestinians.

The already existing obstacles to a two-state solution, therefore, appeared to be mounting, but in both camps there was an increased awareness of the critical need for a breakthrough. As the Palestinians forged ahead with their statehood project, pressure increased in Israel for a corresponding Israeli initiative. Such an initiative was unlikely to lead to an overall agreement between the parties, but it could lead to some form of Israeli complement, unilateral or otherwise, to the essentially unilateralist Palestinian pursuit of recognition. Together they could actually contribute to the establishment of a two-state reality.

In the real "new Middle East," Israel would be well advised, whether with an agreement with the Palestinians or without one, to reduce unnecessary friction and to protect itself as best it could from the negative fallout of a region in deep socioeconomic and political malaise. Israel was incapable of solving the problems of the Middle East. It could only do its level best to keep its distance and disengage. There was no single more important component of this disengagement than the creation of a two-state reality between Israel and Palestine that would put an end to Israel's occupation of most of the West Bank and provide the foundation for a state in the West Bank and Gaza. Such a state, though fraught with inherent uncertainties, could also provide the basis for a future agreement between the parties that would ultimately lead to the resolution of most, if not all, of the remaining outstanding issues.

# NOTES

## Introduction

1. Aviel Roshwald, *The Endurance of Nationalism: Ancient Roots and Modern Dilemmas* (Cambridge University Press, 2006), pp. 254–256.
2. Aviel Roshwald, *The Endurance of Nationalism*, pp. 254–256.
3. Craig Calhoun, *Nations Matter: Culture, History, and the Cosmopolitan Dream* (London and New York: Routledge, 2007), p. 117.
4. Aviel Roshwald, *The Endurance of Nationalism*, pp. 256–275.
5. Aviel Roshwald, *The Endurance of Nationalism*, pp. 266, 274–276. It was precisely the ostensible lack of such loyalty that Walt and Mearsheimer ascribed to AIPAC, in their attack on the Israel lobby; see John Mearsheimer and Stephen Walt, *The Israel Lobby and US Foreign Policy* (New York: Farrar, Straus and Giroux, 2007).
6. Arend Lijphart, "Introduction: Developments in Power Sharing Theory," in Arend Lijphart, *Thinking about Democracy: Power Sharing and Majority Rule in Theory and Practice* (London and New York: Routledge, 2008), p. 7; Arend Lijphart, "The Puzzle of Indian Democracy: A Consociational Interpretation," in *Thinking about Democracy*, pp. 28–30, 42.
7. Timothy Sisk, quoted in Marisa Traniello, "Power-Sharing: Lessons from South Africa and Rwanda," *International Public Policy Review*, vol. 3, no. 2 (March 2008), p. 31.
8. Eugene Rogan, *Frontiers of the State in the Late Ottoman Empire: Transjordan, 1850–1921* (Cambridge University Press, 2002), p. 98.
9. Peter Gubser, *Politics and Change in al-Karak, Jordan* (Oxford University Press, 1973), pp. 15, 26
10. Kamal Salibi, *The Modern History of Jordan* (London: I. B. Tauris, 1993), pp. 38, 45.
11. W. Deeds (Jerusalem) to John Tilley (Foreign Office), 18 October 1920, in *Palestine Boundaries, 1833–1947*, vol. 3 (Archive Editions, 1989), p. 675. Extract from conference on Middle East affairs on the position of Transjordan in relation to Palestine Mandate, 26 February 1921. CO 732/3 in *Records of Jordan (R of J), 1919–1965*, vol. 1: 1919–1922 (Archive Editions, 1996), p. 292.
12. Joseph Nevo, *King Abdallah and Palestine: A Territorial Ambition* (London: Macmillan Press, 1996), p. xiii.
13. Mary Wilson, *King Abdullah, Britain and the Making of Jordan* (Cambridge University Press, 1987), p. 53.
14. Kamal Salibi, *The Modern History of Jordan*, p. 94.
15. Daniel Pipes, *Greater Syria: The History of an Ambition* (Oxford University Press, 1990), p. 72.

16. Kamal Salibi, *The Modern History of Jordan*, p. 95.
17. Benny Morris, *Righteous Victims: A History of the Zionist-Arab Conflict, 1881–1999* (New York: Alfred A. Knopf, 1999), p. 129.
18. Benny Morris, *Righteous Victims*, pp. 135–38.
19. Charles Geddes (ed.), *A Documentary History of the Arab-Israeli Conflict* (New York: Praeger, 1991), pp. 38, 154.
20. Charles Geddes, *A Documentary History*, pp. 157–158.
21. Mary Wilson, *King Abdullah*, p. 158; Daniel Pipes, *Greater Syria*, pp. 71–81; Yoav Gelber, *Jewish-Transjordanian Relations, 1921–1948* (London: Frank Cass, 1997), pp. 167, 222, 231.
22. Joseph Nevo, *King Abdallah and Palestine*, p. 9.
23. Mary Wilson, *King Abdullah*, p. 120.

## Chapter 1. Between Binationalism and Partition

1. Benny Morris, *Righteous Victims*, pp. 80, 107.
2. Itzhak Galnoor, *The Partition of Palestine: Decision Crossroads in the Zionist Movement* (Albany: SUNY Press, 1995), p. 131.
3. Colin Shindler, *A History of Modern Israel* (Cambridge University Press, 2008), p. 134.
4. Shabtai Teveth, *Ben Gurion and the Palestinian Arabs* (Oxford University Press, 1985), pp. 132–134.
5. Anita Shapira, *Land and Power: The Zionist Resort to Force, 1881–1948* (Stanford University Press, 1992), p. 164.
6. Yosef Gorny, *Zionism and the Arabs 1882–1948: A Study of Ideology* (Oxford: Clarendon Press, 1987), pp. 119–123.
7. Benny Morris, *One State, Two States: Resolving the Israel/Palestine Conflict* (New Haven: Yale University Press, 2009), pp. 44–47.
8. Anita Shapira, *Land and Power*, pp. 188–192.
9. Benny Morris, *One State, Two States*, p. 48.
10. Yosef Gorny, *Zionism and the Arabs*, pp. 281–286.
11. Craig Calhoun, *Nations Matter*, p. 125.
12. Benny Morris, *One State, Two States*, p. 48.
13. Anita Shapira, *Land and Power*, p. 168.
14. Itzhak Galnoor, *The Partition of Palestine*, pp. 127–131.
15. Benny Morris, *One State, Two States*, pp. 48–52; Tamar Hermann, "The Bi-national Idea in Israel/Palestine: Past and Present," *Nations and Nationalism*, vol. 11, no. 3 (2005), p. 385.
16. Yosef Gorny, *Zionism and the Arabs*, pp. 295–298.
17. Summary of Peel Commission Report, in Laura Zittrain Eisenberg and Neil Caplan, *Negotiating Arab-Israeli Peace: Patterns, Problems, Possibilities*, Second Edition (Indianapolis: Indiana University Press, 2010), Appendix B; documents online http://naip-documents.blogspot.com/2009/09/document-7.html.

18. Ihud Proposals to UNSCOP, 23 July 1947, in Itamar Rabinovich and Jehuda Reinharz (eds.), *Israel in the Middle East: Documents and Readings on Society, Politics, and Foreign Relations, Pre-1948 to the Present*, Second Edition (Waltham, MA: Brandeis University Press, 2008), pp. 60–61.

19. Itzhak Galnoor, *The Partition of Palestine*, p. 285.

20. Anita Shapira, *Land and Power*, p. 206.

21. Bernard Wasserstein, *Israelis and Palestinians: Why Do They Fight? Can They Stop?* (New Haven: Yale University Press, 2003), pp. 106–107, 114.

22. Neil Caplan, *The Israel-Palestine Conflict: Contested Histories* (Malden, MA; Oxford: Wiley-Blackwell, 2010), p. 25.

23. Summary of Peel Commission Report, in Laura Zittrain Eisenberg and Neil Caplan, *Negotiating Arab-Israeli Peace: Patterns, Problems, Possibilities*, Second Edition (Indianapolis: Indiana University Press, 2010), Appendix B; documents online http://naip-documents.blogspot.com/2009/09/document-7.html; Morris, *Righteous Victims*, pp. 138–139.

24. Shabtai Teveth, *Ben-Gurion: The Burning Ground, 1886–1948* (Boston: Houghton Mifflin, 1987), pp. 587–590, 606.

25. Shabtai Teveth, *Ben-Gurion: The Burning Ground*, pp. 609–613.

26. Benny Morris, *Righteous Victims*, pp. 142–144.

27. This was an Anglo-American Committee of Inquiry that was established in November 1945 to study the question of the Jewish refugees in Europe and their possible immigration to Palestine.

28. "The Arab Case for Palestine: Evidence Submitted by the Arab Office, Jerusalem, to the Anglo-American Committee of Inquiry, March 1946," in Walter Laqueur and Barry Rubin (eds.), *The Israel-Arab Reader: A Documentary History of the Middle East Conflict*, Fifth Revised and Updated Edition (New York: Penguin, 1995), p. 80.

29. "The Arab Case for Palestine," pp. 81–87.

30. "The Arab Case for Palestine," pp. 86–88.

31. Arab Higher Committee response, in Ruth Lapidot and Moshe Hirsch (eds.), *The Arab-Israeli Conflict and Its Resolution: Selected Documents* (Dordrecht: Nijhoff, 1992), pp. 33–58.

## Chapter 2. The Palestinians and the Two-State Idea

1. Mahdi Abdul Hadi (ed.), *Documents on Palestine*, vol. 1 (Jerusalem: PASSIA, 1997), pp. 189–190.

2. Avi Shlaim, "The Rise and Fall of the All-Palestine Government in Gaza," *Journal of Palestine Studies*, vol. 20, no. 1 (Autumn 1990), p. 40.

3. Avi Shlaim, "The Rise and Fall of the All-Palestine Government in Gaza," p. 50.

4. Charter of the PLO 1968, clauses 1, 2, 15, 19, 20, 22, www.fatehmedia.net/ar/m-t-f.

5. Charter of the PLO 1964, clause 7; Charter of the PLO 1968, clause 6.

6. Ernest Main, *Palestine at the Crossroads* (London: George Allen & Unwin, 1937), pp. 287–309.

7. The Arab Case for Palestine, in Walter Laqueur and Barry Rubin (eds), *The Israel-Arab Reader*, p. 80.

8. Ruth Lapidot and Moshe Hirsch (eds.), *The Arab-Israeli Conflict and Its Resolution*, p. 57.

9. Avraham Sela, "The Palestinian Arabs in the War of 1948," in Moshe Maoz and Benjamin Z. Kedar (eds.) *The Palestinian National Movement: From Confrontation to Reconciliation?* (Tel Aviv: Ma'arakhot, 1997), pp. 132–133 (Hebrew).

10. Charter of the PLO 1968, clause 9.

11. *Middle East Record (MER)*, vol. 4 (1968) (Jerusalem: Israel Universities Press, Shiloah Center for Middle Eastern and African Studies, Tel Aviv University, 1973), pp. 448–450; MER, vol. 5 (1969–70), pp. 375–378, 387–394.

12. Yezid Sayigh, *Armed Struggle and the Search for State: The Palestinian National Movement, 1949–1993* (Oxford: Clarendon Press, 1997), p. 280.

13. Yezid Sayigh, *Armed Struggle and the Search for State*, pp. 335–336.

14. *Al-barnamij al-siyasi al-marhali li-munazzamat al-tahrir al-Filastiniyya* [The Phased Political Program of the PLO], approved by the PNC on 8 June 1974, www. fate hmedia.net/ar/m-t-f.

15. Matti Steinberg, "Nationalism and Marxism in the Approach of the PFLP," in Matti Steinberg, *Facing Their Fate: Palestinian National Consciousness, 1967–2007* (Tel Aviv: Yediot Aharonot, 2008), pp. 97–101 (Hebrew).

16. Yezid Sayigh, *Armed Struggle and the Search for State*, p. 545.

17. See, e.g., Salah Khalaf to *al-Yawn al-Sabi*, 7 November 1988.

18. George Habash in *al-Hadaf*, 15 May 1988.

19. *Wathiqat i'lan al-istiqlal* [Declaration of Independence], 15 November 1988, www .fatehmedia.net/ar/m-t-f. English translation available at http://naip-documents .blogspot.com/2009/09/document-53.html.

20. Rashid Khalidi, *The Iron Cage: The Story of the Palestinian Struggle for Statehood* (Boston: Beacon Press, 2006), p. 195.

21. *Mashru' al-bayan al-siyasi sadara an al-majlis al-watani al-Filastini* [Political Statement of the 19th PNC, 12–15 November 1988], in *Filastin al-Thawra*, 20 November 1988, pp. 6–9. English translation available at http://naip-documents.blogspot. com/2009/09/document-54.html.

22. Political Statement of the 19th PNC, 12–15 November 1988.

23. Speech by Salah Khalaf at the 17th PNC, 22–29 November 1984, full text in *Shu'un Filastiniyya*, November–December 1984, pp. 174–184.

24. Khalid al-Hasan, *Al-ittifaq al-Urdunni-al-Filastini lil-taharruk mushtarak "Amman—11 February 1985"* [The Jordanian-Palestinian Agreement for Joint Action "Amman—11 February 1985"] (Amman: Dar al-jalil lil-nashr, 1985), pp. 10, 79–81.

25. Walid Khalidi, "Toward Peace in the Holy Land," *Foreign Affairs*, vol. 66, no. 4 (Spring 1988), p. 788.

26. Yezid Sayigh, *Armed Struggle and the Search for State*, p. 643.

27. Avi Shlaim, "The Oslo Accord," *Journal of Palestinian Studies*, vol. 23, no. 3 (Spring 1994), p. 28.

28. Yezid Sayigh, *Armed Struggle and the Search for State*, p. 653.
29. Walter Laqueur and Barry Rubin (eds.), *The Israel-Arab Reader*, pp. 599–601.
30. Walter Laqueur and Barry Rubin (eds.), *The Israel-Arab Reader*, p. 611.
31. See Fouad Ajami, "The End of Pan-Arabism," *Foreign Affairs*, vol. 57, no. 2 (Winter 1978–79), pp. 355–373.
32. These were the words, for example, of Jawad al-Anani, the Jordanian foreign minister, explaining his country's separate negotiations with Israel on a peace treaty in 1994 (*al-Watan al-Arabi*, 22 July 1994).
33. Anita Shapira, *Land and Power*, p. 37.
34. Beshara Doumani, "Palestine Versus the Palestinians? The Iron Laws and the Ironies of a People Denied," *Journal of Palestine Studies*, vol. 36, no. 4 (Summer 2007), p. 52.
35. Riyad al-Maliki, "Nahwa mubadarat salam Filastiniyya" [Towards a Palestinian Peace Initiative], *al-Ayyam*, 13 May 2004.
36. David Pollock, "Palestinian Public Opinion: Tactically Flexible, Strategically Ambitious," *Washington Institute for Near East Policy, Policy Watch*, no. 1731, 9 December 2010.
37. Both Lebanon and Jordan have serious problems with Palestinian refugees from 1948, whom they would like to see leaving their countries. But as long they leave Lebanon and Jordan, it is not a matter of principle for either of these countries if these refugees return to Israel proper or to some other country.
38. Rashid Khalidi, *The Iron Cage*, p. 151.
39. Yezid Sayigh, *Armed Struggle and the Search for State*, p. 663.
40. Rashid Khalidi, *The Iron Cage*, pp. 171, 180–181.
41. Shlomo Ben Ami, *A Front without a Rearguard: A Voyage to the Boundaries of the Peace Process* (Tel Aviv: Yediot Aharonot, 2004), p. 134 (Hebrew).
42. Rashid Khalidi, *The Iron Cage*, p. 158.
43. Oren Barak, "The Failure of the Israeli-Palestinian Peace Process," *Journal of Peace Research*, vol. 42, no. 6 (November 2005), pp. 723, 731.
44. Hussein Agha and Robert Malley, "Camp David: The Tragedy of Errors," *New York Review of Books*, vol. 48, no. 13 (9 August 2001).
45. See Article VIII of the DoP, in Walter Laqueur and Barry Rubin (eds.), *The Israel- Arab Reader*, p. 602.
46. Shlomo Ben Ami, *A Front without a Rearguard*, p. 358.
47. Oren Barak, "The Failure of the Israeli-Palestinian Peace Process," pp. 728–729.
48. *Middle East Contemporary Survey* (MECS), vol. 20 (1996), pp. 152–153.
49. MECS, vol. 22 (1998), pp. 490–491.
50. See section on the PLO on the official Arabic website of Fatah, www.fatehmedia .net/ar/m-t-f. This website refers to the Oslo Accords as an agreement signed with "the Zionist enemy."
51. *Palestinian National Charter 1968*, Articles 1–3, in www. fatehmedia.net/ar/m-t-f.
52. See, e.g., Abu Ali Shahin, interview in *al-Quds*, 15 November 2000, and Faysal al-Husayni, interviews in *al-Safir*, 21 March 2001, and *al-Arabi*, 24 June, 2001.

53. Ahmed Qurie, *Beyond Oslo, the Struggle for Palestine: Inside the Middle East Peace Process from Rabin's Death to Camp David* (London: I. B. Tauris, 2008), pp. 178–181; Martin Indyk, *Innocent Abroad: An Intimate Account of American Peace Diplomacy in the Middle East* (New York: Simon and Schuster, 2009), pp. 333–334.

54. Shlomo Ben Ami, *A Front without a Rearguard*, p. 153.

55. Shlomo Ben Ami, *A Front without a Rearguard*, p. 229.

56. Shlomo Ben Ami, *A Front without a Rearguard*, pp. 171, 194, 200.

57. Akram Hanieh, "The Camp David Papers," *Journal of Palestine Studies*, vol. 30, no. 2 (Winter 2001), pp. 86, 89, 95.

58. Mahmud Abbas (Abu Mazin), interview in *al-Ayyam*, 28–29 July 2001; Hussein Agha and Robert Malley, "Camp David: The Tragedy of Errors"; Akram Hanieh, "The Camp David Papers," p. 80.

59. Shlomo Ben Ami, *A Front without a Rearguard*, pp. 140, 150, 163, 188, 190–193, 228–230.

60. Edward Said, "Introduction: The Right of Return at Last," in Naseer Aruri (ed.), *Palestinian Refugees: The Right of Return* (London: Pluto Press, 2001), p. 5.

61. Elaine Hagopian, "Preface," and Edward Said, "Introduction: The Right of Return at Last," pp. ix, 4–5.

62. Khaled Amayreh, "No Waiving the Right of Return," *al-Ahram Weekly*, 25–31 January 2001.

63. Richard Murphy and Muhammad Muslih, "The Right of Return for Palestinians Has to Be Taken Seriously," *International Herald Tribune*, 4 January 2001.

64. Shlomo Ben Ami, *A Front without a Rearguard*, p. 371.

65. Ahmad Qurai (Abu Ala'), interview in *al-Ayyam*, 29 January 2001; similarly, Mahmud Abbas (Abu Mazin), interview in *al-Ayyam*, 28–29 July 2001.

66. Shlomo Ben Ami, *A Front without a Rearguard*, pp. 223–224, 359–360, 378.

67. Ahmed Qurie, *Beyond Oslo*, p. 237.

68. See, e.g., Mahmud Abbas (Abu Mazin) to *al-Ayyam*, 30 July 2000; Shlomo Ben Ami, *A Front without a Rearguard*, pp. 142–143, 372, 440; Ahmed Qurie, *Beyond Oslo*, p. 239.

69. Yossi Alpher, "A Blow for the Chances of Peace," *Bitterlemons: Palestinian-Israeli Crossfire*, 29 June 2009, www.bitterlemons.org.

70. Benny Morris, *The Birth of the Palestinian Refugee Problem Revisited* (Cambridge University Press, 2004), pp. 572–580; see also Neil Caplan, *The Lausanne Conference, 1949: A Case Study in Middle East Peacemaking* (Tel Aviv University: Moshe Dayan Center for Middle Eastern and African Studies, Occasional Paper 113, 1993), chapter 9.

71. William Jefferson Clinton, "Proposal for Israeli-Palestinian Peace, 23 December 2000," in Itamar Rabinovich and Jehuda Reinharz (eds.), *Israel in the Middle East: Documents and Readings*, pp. 518–521. Text of Clinton Parameters also available at http://naip-documents.blogspot.com/2009/10/document-97.html.

72. Gilead Sher, *Just Beyond Reach: The Israeli-Palestinian Peace Negotiations 1999–2001* (Tel Aviv: Yediot Aharonot, 2001), pp. 381–382 (Hebrew); Shlomo Ben Ami, *A Front without a Rearguard*, pp. 404–405.

73. Gilead Sher, *Just Beyond Reach*, pp. 372–374; Shlomo Ben Ami, *A Front without a Rearguard*, p. 388.

74. Gilead Sher, *Just Beyond Reach*, pp. 388–389, 392–395, 398, 406; Shlomo Ben Ami, *A Front without a Rearguard*, p. 432.

75. Dennis Ross, *The Missing Peace: The Inside Story of the Fight for Middle East Peace* (New York: Farrar, Straus and Giroux, 2004), pp.755–756.

76. Ephraim Ya'ar and Tamar Hermann, "Peace Index for December 2000," *Haaretz*, 4 January 2000.

77. Dennis Ross, *The Missing Peace*, pp. 755–756.

78. Ahmed Qurie, *Beyond Oslo*, p. 301.

79. Ahmad Qurai (Abu Ala'), interview in *al-Ayyam*, 29 January 2001.

80. Quoted in Colin Shindler, *A History of Modern Israel*, p. 287.

81. *Mulahazat wa-as'ila Filastiniyya hawla al-afkar al-Amrikiyya* [Palestinian Remarks and Questions on the American Ideas], text as in *Al-Ayyam*, 2 January 2001; see also "Remarks and Questions from the Palestinian Negotiating Team Regarding the United States Proposal," 1 January 2001, Document 98, http://naip-documents.blogspot.com/, and Ahmed Qurie, *Beyond Oslo*, pp. 289–291.

82. Mahmud Abbas in speech in November 2002 in Gaza, as reproduced in *al-Hayat*, 26 November 2002.

83. "The 44 Reasons Why Fatah Movement Rejects the Proposals Made by US President Clinton," January 2001, Jerusalem Media and Communications Centre, www.jmcc.org/documents.aspx.

84. Mahmud Abbas (Abu Mazin), interview in *al-Hayat*, 23–24 November 2000; Mahmud Abbas (Abu Mazin), interview in *al-Ayyam*, 28–29 July 2001.

85. Shlomo Ben Ami, *A Front without a Rearguard*, p. 447.

86. Akram Hanieh, "The Camp David Papers," pp. 76–77, 82, 92.

87. Yossi Beilin, "An Israeli View: Solving the Refugee Problem," *Bitterlemons: Palestinian-Israeli Crossfire*, 31 December 2001, www.bitterlemons.org; Ron Pundak, "From Oslo to Taba: What Went Wrong?" *Survival*, vol. 43, no. 3 (Autumn 2001), pp. 43–44.

88. Text of the Moratinos "Non-Paper," available at http://naip-documents.blogspot.com/2009/10/document-101.html; the Moratinos Document was also published in *Haaretz*, 14 February 2002.

89. Martin Indyk, *Innocent Abroad*, p. 372.

90. "Palestinian Paper on Refugees," Taba, 22 January 2001, in *Le Monde Diplomatique*, English Edition, http://mondediplo.com/focus/mideast/palestinianrefugees200101.

91. "Israeli Private Response on Palestinian Refugees," Taba, 23 January 2001, in *Le Monde Diplomatique*, English Edition, http://mondediplo.com/focus/mideast/israeliresponserefugees200101.

92. Ron Pundak, "From Oslo to Taba: What Went Wrong?" pp. 43–44.

93. See, e.g., Nakba Day Speeches by Yasir Arafat as in *al-Hayat al-Jadida*, 16 May 2003, and *al-Hayat* and *al-Ayyam*, 16 May 2004; speech by Mahmud Abbas in Palestinian Legislative Assembly, in *al-Ayyam*, 24 November 2004.

94. Sa'ib Ariqat, interview in *al-Dustur*, Amman, 25 June 2009.

95. Sa'ib Ariqat, "The Question of Refugees Is the Essence of the Palestinian Question," interview in *Palestine-Israel Journal*, vol. 15, no. 4 (2008) and vol. 16, no. 1 (2009), pp. 115–116.

96. Martin Indyk, *Innocent Abroad*, p. 372.

97. Aaron David Miller, *The Much Too Promised Land: America's Elusive Search for Arab-Israeli Peace* (New York: Bantam Books, 2008), p. 369.

98. Michael Milshtein, "The Memory That Never Dies: The Nakba Memory and the Palestinian National Movement," in Meir Litvak (ed.), *Palestinian Collective Memory and National Identity* (New York: Palgrave Macmillan, 2009), p. 64.

99. Shlomo Ben Ami, *A Front without a Rearguard*, pp. 167, 220.

100. Abu Mazin, interview in *al-Ayyam*, 28–29 July 2001; Shlomo Ben Ami, *A Front without a Rearguard*, p. 372.

101. Giora Eiland, *Rethinking the Two-State Solution*, Washington Institute for Near East Policy, Policy Focus, No. 88 (September 2008), p. 21.

102. Laura Zittrain Eisenberg and Neil Caplan, *Negotiating Arab-Israeli Peace*, p. 239.

103. Shlomo Ben Ami, *A Front without a Rearguard*, p. 447; Colin Shindler, *A History of Modern Israel*, p. 288.

104. Ayalon-Nusseibeh Declaration in *Journal of Palestine Studies*, vol. 33, no. 2 (Winter 2004), p. 158.

105. For the full text of the Geneva Accord, see www.geneva-accord.org/mainmenu/english.

106. See, e.g., Qaddura Faris quoted in *al-Hayat*, 14 October 2003, and Jamal Zaqut, "Wathiqat jinif adah lil-kifah al-siyasi" [The Geneva Document Is an Instrument for the Political Struggle], in *al-Hayat al-Jadida*, 30 November 2003.

107. Asher Susser, "The Refugee Section: A Shaky Foundation," *Haaretz*, 11 December 2003.

108. Salim Tamari, "No Obvious Destination," *al-Ahram Weekly*, 18–24 September 2003.

109. Paragraph 9, *Wathiqat al-wifaq al-watani*, 28 June 2006 (Moshe Dayan Center Arabic Press Archives).

110. *Barnamij hukumat ra'is al-wuzara al-mukallaf Isma'il Haniyya*, al-Jazeera [Program of the Government of Prime Minister Elect, Isma'il Haniyya], 17 March 2007, www.al-jazeera.net/News.

111. *Al-barnamij al-siyasi liharakat al-tahrir al-watani al-Filastini*, "Fath" [The Political Program of the Palestinian National Liberation Movement, "Fath"], Sixth General Conference, pp. 15, 26, www.fatehconf.ps.

112. Riyad summit resolutions as published in *al-Sharq al-Awsat*, 31 March 2007.

113. Saudi Foreign Minister Sa'ud al-Faysal was rather adamant, noting in March 2007 that there would be "no amendment to the Arab peace initiative. We have said this 20 times before . . . and this is the last. . . ." See Joshua Teitelbaum, *The Arab Peace Initiative: A Primer and Future Prospects* (Jerusalem Center for Public Affairs, 2009), p. 21.

114. Nur Masalha (ed.), *Catastrophe Remembered: Palestine, Israel and the Internal Refugees* (London: Zed Books, 2005); *Al-tasawwur al-mustaqbali lil-Arab al-Filastiniyyin fi Isra'il 2006* [The Future Vision of the Palestinian Arabs in Israel 2006], The

National Committee for the Heads of the Arab Local Authorities in Israel, p. 15, www.arab-lac.org.

115. Elie Rekhess, "The Arabs of Israel after Oslo: Localization of the National Struggle," *Israel Studies*, vol. 7, no. 3 (Fall 2002), pp. 26–32.

116. *Al-barnamij al-siyasi liharakat al-tahrir al-watani al-Filastini*, "Fath," Sixth General Conference, pp. 8, 15, www.fatehconf.ps.

117. E.g., *Haaretz*, 6 September 2008.

118. Olmert interview with PBS *NewsHour* on 27 November 2007, "Israeli PM: Tough Choices Ahead in Mideast Peace Process," http://www.pbs.org/newshour/bb/middle_east/july-dec07/olmert_11-27.html.

119. Mahmud Abbas, interview in *Haaretz*, 14 September 2008.

120. Mahmud Abbas, interview in *al-Sharq al-Awsat*, 20 December 2009.

121. Sa'ib Ariqat, interview in *al-Dustur*, Amman, 25 June 2009.

122. Gil Hoffman, "Abbas: We Reached Deal with Olmert on Security," *Jerusalem Post*, 19 December 2010.

123. "The Palestine Papers," in *The Guardian*, 23 January 2011.

124. Kevin Peraino, "Olmert's Lament," *Newsweek*, 22 June 2009; Mahmud Abbas, interview in *Haaretz*, 14 September 2008.

125. Shaul Arieli, "Bridging the Gap," *Haaretz*, 10 April 2009; Ehud Olmert, interview in *The Australian*, 28 November 2009; Sa'ib Ariqat, *The Political Situation in Light of the Developments with the US Administration and Israeli Government and Hamas Continued Coup d'Etat: Recommendations and Options* (Jerusalem: The Center for Democracy and Community Development, December 2009), p. 4.

126. Sa'ib Ariqat, *The Political Situation in Light of the Developments*, Arabic version, p. 3.

127. *The Guardian*, 23–24 January 2011.

128. *The Telegraph*, 25 January 2011.

129. *The Guardian* also published documents that according to the newspaper's own interpretation meant that the Palestinians had offered to limit refugee return to Israel to a purely symbolic overall total of just 10,000. This was based on a statement made by Sa'ib Ariqat in an internal Palestinian discussion in June 2009 during which he observed that Olmert had accepted the return of "1,000 refugees annually for the next 10 years" — a total of 10,000. (Olmert, as we have seen, had actually suggested only 5,000.) The "Palestine Papers" did not include any subsequent offer, but Ariqat had told US Middle East envoy George Mitchell four months earlier, in February 2009, that "on refugees, the deal is there." Piecing these two statements together, made to different people within the space of four months, *The Guardian* draws the conclusion that Ariqat had actually accepted the 10,000 figure, a proposal he had in fact not made to anyone, Israeli or otherwise. *The Guardian* backs up its conclusion with a story that Ariqat had offered another incredibly low figure in a document circulated to EU diplomats in early 2010 in which the PA had ostensibly agreed to accept an Israeli proposal to allow in 15,000 refugees. But no such offer was ever made to the Israelis, and in the document referred to by *The Guardian* Ariqat actually speaks of a Palestinian (not Israeli)

proposal for the return of 15,000 refugees *a year for ten years*, that is, 150,000 and not 15,000 (see Ariqat document cited above in note 125). Moreover, in the 2007 document where the Palestinians themselves mention the figure of 10,000 as their own, they similarly refer to 10,000 *a year for ten years*, that is, 100,000 and not 10,000 (see *The Guardian*, 24 January 2011). Even condemnations of the PA negotiators on al-Jazeera and most other sources referred only to the 100,000 figure. They too, apparently, did not accept *The Guardian's* dubious methodology on the "10,000." The notion that Ariqat could have possibly thought that such ridiculously low figures of 10,000–15,000 would be even remotely acceptable to his own people is unbelievable. One of the complaints of the Palestinian negotiators was that in the "Palestine Papers" Israeli positions were on occasion presented as Palestinian ideas (*The Telegraph*, 25 January 2011). This would appear to be one of the more blatant of such examples.

130. Meeting Minutes, President Abbas meeting with the Negotiations Support Unit, 24 March 2009, http://www.ajtransparency.com/files/4507.pdf.

131. Jackson Diehl, "Abbas's Waiting Game," *Washington Post*, 29 May 2009.

132. Mahmud Abbas, interview in *Haaretz*, 14 September 2008.

133. Reaffirmed most recently in an article published by Sa'ib Ariqat, "The Returning Issue of Palestine's Refugees," *The Guardian*, 10 December 2010.

134. Sa'ib Ariqat, *The Political Situation in Light of the Developments*, English version, p. 9.

135. Mahmud al-Zahar, on www.elaph.com, 1 October 2005, as in MEMRI, Special Dispatch 1028, 18 November 2005.

136. Azzam Tamimi, *Hamas: A History from Within* (Northampton, MA: Olive Branch Press, 2007), p. 158.

137. Tamimi, *Hamas*, p. 159.

138. See, e.g., Ahmad Yasin, on al-Arabiyya TV, 9 January 2004, in *World News Connection*; Mahmud al-Ramhi, quoted in *al-Hayat al-Jadida*, 19 January, and Isma'il Haniyya, in *al-Ayyam*, 22 January 2006; Khalid Mash'al, in *New York Times*, 5 May 2009; Usama Hamdan, in *Kull al-Arab*, Nazareth, 18 December, 2009.

139. *Barnamij hukumat ra'is al-wuzara' al-mukallaf Isma'il Haniyya* [Program of the Government of Prime Minister Elect, Isma'il Haniyya], 17 March 2007, www.al-jazeera.net/News.

140. Khalid Mash'al, address on Al-Aqsa TV, 25 June 2009 as in MEMRI, Special Dispatch 2423, 29 June 2009.

141. Khalid Mash'al, in *al-Ahram*, 30 March 2005.

142. Mahmud al-Zahar, interview in *al-Sharq al-Awsat*, 18 August 2005, http//aawsat .com/english, as in MEMRI, Special Dispatch No. 964, 19 August 2005; Shaykh Nazzar Rayan to al-Jazeera TV, 16 September 2005, as in MEMRI, Special Dispatch No. 991, 21 September 2005; Khalid Mash'al on al-Jazeera TV, 29 January 2006, as in MEMRI, Special Dispatch 1081, 31 January 2006.

143. *Al-barnamij al-siyasi liharakat al-tahrir al-watani al-Filastini*, "Fath," Sixth General Conference, pp. 8, 16, www.fatehconf.ps. Note the absence of the word "secular" in the reference to the democratic state. This was not new and had consistently

been so in Arabic texts of the PLO and Fatah. "Secular" was for the most part reserved for foreign consumption.

144. This is how Akram Hanieh described the Camp David summit; see Akram Hanieh, "The Camp David Papers," p. 92.

145. Hussein Agha and Robert Malley, "Israel and Palestine: Can They Start Over?" *New York Review of Books*, vol. 56, no. 19, 3 December 2009.

146. Hussein Agha and Robert Malley, "Israel and Palestine: Can They Start Over?"

## Chapter 3. Israel and the Two-State Paradigm

1. Yoav Gelber, *Independence Versus Nakba* (Tel Aviv: Kinneret, Zmora-Bitan, Dvir, 2004), pp. 436–438 (Hebrew).

2. Yoav Gelber, *Independence Versus Nakba*, pp. 444–446, 476–477.

3. Rich Cohen, *Israel Is Real* (New York: Farrar, Straus and Giroux, 2009), p. 271.

4. Benny Morris, *One State, Two States*, p. 81.

5. Government of Israel, "The Land for Peace Principle, 19 June 1967," in Itamar Rabinovich and Jehuda Reinharz (eds.), *Israel in the Middle East: Documents and Readings*, pp. 238–239.

6. Benny Morris, *One State, Two States*, pp. 84–87; Bernard Wasserstein, *Israelis and Palestinians: Why Do They Fight? Can They Stop?*, pp. 123–125.

7. The "Jordanian option" has come to mean different things, and the use of the term consequently causes no small measure of confusion. It is also commonly, but erroneously, used to denote the idea of the Israeli right to transform Jordan into Palestine (see, e.g., Curtis Ryan, *Inter-Arab Alliances: Regime Security and Jordanian Foreign Policy* [Gainesville: University Press of Florida, 2009], p. 148). At times this leads to the mistaken association of the Israeli Labor Party with the "Jordan is Palestine" idea (see, e.g., Yezid Sayigh, "The Palestinian Strategic Impasse," p. 17), which was actually opposed to what they actually had in mind, in restoring part of the West Bank to the Hashemites. The Labor Party sought a deal with the Hashemites, not their demise.

8. Avi Shlaim, *Lion of Jordan: The Life of King Hussein in War and Peace* (London: Allen Lane, 2007), pp. 288–292.

9. Shlomo Gazit, *The Carrot and the Stick: Israel's Policy in Judea and Samaria, 1967–1968* (Washington, DC: Bnai Brith Books, 1995), pp. 144–151.

10. Shlomo Gazit, *The Carrot and the Stick*, p. 172.

11. Shabtai Teveth, "The Conflict between Moshe Dayan and Pinhas Sapir: 1968 Analysis," in Itamar Rabinovich and Jehuda Reinharz (eds.), *Israel in the Middle East: Documents and Readings*, pp. 225–226.

12. Dan Schueftan, *The Disengagement Imperative: Israel and the Palestinian Entity* (Haifa University Press/Zmora-Bitan, 1999), pp. 43–45 (Hebrew); Gershom Gorenberg, *The Accidental Empire: Israel and the Birth of the Settlements, 1967–1977* (New York: Times Books, 2006), pp. 174–175, 320.

13. Colin Shindler, *A History of Modern Israel*, pp. 142–143.

14. Bernard Wasserstein, *Israelis and Palestinians: Why Do They Fight? Can They Stop?*, pp. 125–126.

15. Colin Shindler, *A History of Modern Israel*, p. 169.

16. Text of the accords in Itamar Rabinovich and Jehuda Reinharz (eds.), *Israel in the Middle East: Documents and Readings*, pp. 376–378.

17. For Begin's December 1977 "plan for self-rule," see http://naip-documents .blogspot.com/2009/09/document-35.html.

18. Colin Shindler, *A History of Modern Israel*, p. 173; Avi Shlaim, *Lion of Jordan*, pp. 416–417.

19. Neil Caplan, *The Israel-Palestine Conflict*, p. 195.

20. For the text, see http://naip-documents.blogspot.com/2009/09/document-42 .html.

21. Avi Shlaim, *Lion of Jordan*, pp. 418–419.

22. Avi Shlaim, *Lion of Jordan*, p. 416.

23. Colin Shindler, *A History of Modern Israel*, pp. 180–181.

24. Ehud Sprinzak, *The Ascendance of Israel's Radical Right* (New York, Oxford: Oxford University Press, 1991), p. 146; Gershom Gorenberg, *The Accidental Empire*, p. 369.

25. Laura Zittrain Eisenberg and Neil Caplan, *Negotiating Arab-Israeli Peace*, chapter 3. Text of the agreement available at http://naip-documents.blogspot.com/2009/09/ document-48.html; Colin Shindler, *A History of Modern Israel*, pp. 202–203.

26. Neil Caplan, *The Israel-Palestine Conflict*, p. 200; Bernard Wasserstein, *Israelis and Palestinians: Why Do They Fight? Can They Stop?*, p. 156.

27. Colin Shindler, *A History of Modern Israel*, p. 211.

28. Colin Shindler, *A History of Modern Israel*, pp. 214–215.

29. Colin Shindler, *A History of Modern Israel*, pp. 218–226.

30. Colin Shindler, *A History of Modern Israel*, pp. 228–232.

31. This heading comes from the title of Akiva Eldar and Idith Zertal, *Lords of the Land: The Settlers and the State of Israel, 1967–2004* (Tel Aviv: Kinneret, Zmora-Bitan, Dvir, 2004) (Hebrew).

32. Colin Shindler, *A History of Modern Israel*, p. 211.

33. Ehud Sprinzak, *The Ascendance of Israel's Radical Right*, p. 300.

34. Gershom Gorenberg, *The Accidental Empire*, pp. 4–5.

35. Ehud Sprinzak, *The Ascendance of Israel's Radical Right*, pp. 110–112; Gershom Gorenberg, *The Accidental Empire*, pp. 21, 25, 66, 161.

36. Gershom Gorenberg, *The Accidental Empire*, pp. 267.

37. Akiva Eldar and Idith Zertal, *Lords of the Land*, pp. 246–247.

38. Asher Susser, "The Settlements of Forgery and Deception," *Haaretz*, 30 July 2009.

39. Gershom Gorenberg, *The Accidental Empire*, p. 135.

40. Benny Morris, *Righteous Victims*, p.136.

41. Ehud Sprinzak, *The Ascendance of Israel's Radical Right*, pp. 121–124; Akiva Eldar and Idith Zertal, *Lords of the Land*, pp. 284–286.

42. Gershom Gorenberg, *The Accidental Empire*, pp. 45, 71.

43. Gershom Gorenberg, *The Accidental Empire*, p. 5.

44. Akiva Eldar and Idith Zertal, *Lords of the Land*, pp. 281–283.

45. Gershom Gorenberg, *The Accidental Empire*, pp. 360–361.

46. Gershom Gorenberg, *The Accidental Empire*, pp. 83, 130–132.

47. Gershom Gorenberg, *The Accidental Empire*, pp. 93, 136.

48. Akiva Eldar and Idith Zertal, *Lords of the Land*, p.246.

49. Ehud Sprinzak, *The Ascendance of Israel's Radical Right*, pp. 119–120; Gershom Gorenberg, *The Accidental Empire*, pp. 158–160.

50. Gershom Gorenberg, *The Accidental Empire*, pp. 293–294, 339, 352.

51. Gershom Gorenberg, *The Accidental Empire*, p. 358.

52. Ehud Sprinzak, *The Ascendance of Israel's Radical Right*, pp. 142, 146–147.

53. Colin Shindler, *A History of Modern Israel*, pp. 334–335.

54. Martin Indyk, *Innocent Abroad*, p. 411.

55. Akiva Eldar and Idith Zertal, *Lords of the Land*, pp. 170, 176, 183–188, 204–205, 294–295; Colin Shindler, *A History of Modern Israel*, p. 278.

56. Akiva Eldar and Idith Zertal, *Lords of the Land*, pp. 188–189, 208–211.

57. Colin Shindler, *A History of Modern Israel*, pp. 260–265.

58. Daniel Kurtzer, "Behind the Settlements," *The American Interest* (March/April 2010), pp. 5–6, 9, 13; Akiva Eldar and Idith Zertal, *Lords of the Land*, pp. 196, 220–223, 228–231, 235–239, 376, 384, 406–407, 410, 416, 424–426; "Summary of the Opinion Concerning Unauthorized Outposts," 10 March 2005, compiled by former prosecutor Talya Sason, www.mfa.gov.il/MFA/Government/Law/Legal; Eyal Press, "Israel's Holy Warriors," *New York Review of Books*, vol. 57, no. 7 (29 April 2010).

59. Ehud Sprinzak, *The Ascendance of Israel's Radical Right*, p. 108; Gershom Gorenberg, *The Accidental Empire*, p. 352; Akiva Eldar and Idith Zertal, *Lords of the Land*, p. 235.

60. Ehud Sprinzak, *The Ascendance of Israel's Radical Right*, pp. 151–152, 159–161.

61. Akiva Eldar and Idith Zertal, *Lords of the Land*, pp. iii–viii.

62. Akiva Eldar and Idith Zertal, *Lords of the Land*, pp. ix, 235.

63. Colin Shindler, *A History of Modern Israel*, p. 324.

64. Colin Shindler, *A History of Modern Israel*, pp. 329–330.

65. Ephraim Yuchtman-Ya'ar and Tamar Hermann, *War and Peace Index*, March 2010 (Tel Aviv University, The Evens Program in Mediation and Conflict Resolution and The Israel Democracy Institute).

66. Yehuda Ben-Meir and Olena Bagno-Moldavsky, *Vox Populi: Trends in Israeli Public Opinion on National Security, 2004–2009*, Institute for National Security Studies, Memorandum 106, November 2010, p. 12.

67. *Settlers Opinion Poll*, March 2010, by Truman Institute for the Advancement of Peace, Hebrew University, Jerusalem, www.truman.huji.ac.il/poll-view. asp?id=327; analysis by Alvin Richman, "Israeli Public's Support for Dismantling Most Settlements Has Risen to a Five-Year High," *World Public Opinion Org*, 15 April 2010, www.worldpublicopinion.org/pipa/articles/brmiddleeastnafricara/ 659.php.

68. Yehuda Ben-Meir and Olena Bagno-Moldavsky, *Vox Populi*, pp. 12, 99–104.

69. Akiva Eldar and Idith Zertal, *Lords of the Land*, pp. iii–viii.

70. Yehuda Ben-Meir and Olena Bagno-Moldavsky, *Vox Populi*, p. 104.

71. Text of DoP in Walter Laqueur and Barry Rubin (eds.), *The Israel-Arab Reader*, p. 601.

72. Ron Pundak, "From Oslo to Taba: What Went Wrong?," p. 36.

73. Colin Shindler, *A History of Modern Israel*, p. 327.

74. Shlomo Ben Ami, *A Front without a Rearguard*, pp. 147, 179.

75. Colin Shindler, *A History of Modern Israel*, pp. 269, 273.

76. David Makovsky, *A Defensible Fence: Fighting Terror and Enabling a Two-State Solution*, Washington Institute for Near East Policy, April 2004, p. 6.

77. Yezid Sayigh, "Arafat and the Anatomy of a Revolt," *Survival*, vol. 43, no. 3 (Autumn 2001), pp. 53–54.

78. Maj. Gen. (res.) Aharon Ze'evi Farkash, "Key Principles of a Demilitarized Palestinian State," in *Israel's Critical Security Needs for a Viable Peace* (Jerusalem Center for Public Affairs, 2010), pp. 52–67.

79. Gilead Sher, *Just Beyond Reach*, pp. 399, 403, 408; see also Shlomo Ben Ami, *A Front without a Rearguard*, p. 215.

80. *Al-Hayat*, 27 January 2001; Mahmud Abbas, interview in *al-Ayyam*, 28–29 July 2001; Shlomo Ben Ami, *A Front without a Rearguard*, pp. 432–433, 438.

81. See conversation between Ariqat and Dekel, 2 July 2008, in Palestine Papers, http://english.aljazeera.net/palestinepapers/2011/01/201112512170239319.html.

82. *Haaretz*, 27 May 2003.

83. "PM's Speech at the Begin-Sadat Center at Bar-Ilan University," 14 June 2009, www.pmo.gov.il.

84. Khaled Abu Toameh, "PA: Netanyahu has Buried Peace Process," in *Jerusalem Post*, 15 June 2009; Sa'ib Ariqat, quoted in *al-Hayat al-Jadida*, 15 June 2009; Ghassan Khatib, "A Farcical Position on Statehood," *Bitterlemons: Palestinian-Israeli Crossfire*, 15 June 2009, www.bitterlemons.org.

85. See Sa'ib Ariqat, *The Political Situation in Light of the Developments with the US Administration and Israeli Government and Hamas Continued Coup d'Etat: Recommendations and Options* (Jerusalem: The Center for Democracy and Community Development, December, 2009).

86. Prominent among these was Dan Schueftan of Haifa University, who published *The Disengagement Imperative: Israel and the Palestinian Entity* (Haifa University Press/ Zmora-Bitan, 1999) (Hebrew).

87. See www.vanleer.org.il/Data/UploadedFiles/Publications/55_PDF.pdf.

88. Bernard Wasserstein, *Israelis and Palestinians: Why Do They Fight? Can They Stop?*, p. 139.

89. Colin Shindler, *A History of Modern Israel*, p. 296; Akiva Eldar and Idith Zertal, *Lords of the Land*, p. 561.

90. David Makovsky, *A Defensible Fence*, pp. 1, 7.

91. Giora Eiland, *Regional Alternatives to the Two-State Solution*, BESA Memorandum No. 4 (The Begin-Sadat Center for Strategic Studies, Bar-Ilan University, January 2010), p. 33.

92. Bernard Wasserstein, *Israelis and Palestinians: Why Do They Fight? Can They Stop?*, p. 149.

93. Ehud Olmert, interview with David Landau, in *Haaretz*, 15 November 2003.

94. Ehud Olmert, interview with Nahum Barnea, in *Yediot Aharonot, Weekend Magazine*, 5 December 2003.

95. "Address by PM Ariel Sharon at the Fourth Herzliya Conference," 18 December 2003, in www.mfa.gov.il.

96. Colin Shindler, *A History of Modern Israel*, p. 316.

97. Akiva Eldar and Idith Zertal, *Lords of the Land*, pp. 563–564.

98. "PM Sharon Addresses the UN General Assembly," 15 September 2005, www .mfa.gov.il.

99. Ehud Olmert, interview with Karby Leggett, in *The Wall Street Journal*, 12 April 2006; "Address by Interim PM Olmert on Presenting the New Government to the Knesset," 4 May 2006, www.pmo.gov.il, and "Address by PM Ehud Olmert at the Special Knesset Session on the Condition of the Gush Katif Evacuees," 27 June 2006, www.mfa.gov.il.

100. "Rabin Memorial: Address by PM Ehud Olmert at Special Knesset Session," 10 November 2008, www.mfa.gov.il.

101. The commission was headed by Supreme Court Justice Theodore Orr.

102. The Official Summation of the Orr Commission Report, as printed in *Haaretz* Online English Language Edition, 2 September 2003, paragraphs 3, 24, and 25. http://www. jewishvirtuallibrary.org/jsource/Society_&_Culture/OrCommissionReport.html.

103. Orr Commission Report, paragraphs 30–32.

104. Elie Rekhess, "The Arabs of Israel after Oslo," pp. 8, 33–35.

105. Azmi Bishara, "Reflections on October 2000: A Landmark in Jewish-Arab Relations in Israel," *Journal of Palestine Studies*, vol. 30, no. 3 (Spring 2001), pp. 56–58; Nadim Rouhana, "Shaking the Foundations of Citizenship," *al-Ahram Weekly*, 27 September–3 October 2001.

106. Azmi Bishara, "Reflections on October 2000," p. 58.

107. Elie Rekhess, "The Arabs of Israel after Oslo," p. 34; Colin Shindler, *A History of Modern Israel*, p. 293.

108. Ze'ev Schiff, "Many Useful Lessons to Be Drawn" in *Haaretz*, 10 October 2000.

109. Benny Morris, "Camp David and After: An Exchange (1. An Interview with Ehud Barak)," *New York Review of Books*, vol. 49, no. 10 (13 June 2002).

110. Speech by Mahmud Abbas in Gaza in November 2002, as reproduced in *al-Hayat*, 26 November 2002.

111. Hussein Agha and Robert Malley, "A Solution Is Possible Now," *The Guardian*, 29 March 2002.

112. General Debate of the 65th General Assembly on 28 September 2010, Speech by Deputy Prime Minister and Foreign Minister, Avigdor Lieberman, http://www .israel-un.org/statements-at-the-united-nations/general-assembly/315-ga65gd2 8092010.

113. E.g., Alex Kane, "Avigdor Lieberman's Speech Shows the True Face of Israel," http://mondoweiss.net/2010/09/avigdor-liebermans-un-speech-shows-the-true-face-of-israel; and Abdel Bari Atwan, "Peace Has Been Failed Again Fading Hope," *Gulf News*, 16 October 2010.

114. *BBC News: Middle East*, 28 September 2010, www.bbc.co.uk/news/world-middle-east-11429959?print=true.

115. Benny Morris, "Camp David and After: An Exchange."

116. Benny Morris, "Camp David and After: An Exchange."

117. UN Security Council Resolution 1397, 12 March 2002, www.un.org/Docs.

118. "George W. Bush, Remarks on the Middle East, 24 June 2002," as in Itamar Rabinovich and Jehuda Reinharz (eds.), *Israel in the Middle East: Documents and Readings*, pp. 533–535; "Speech by Prime Minister Ariel Sharon at Herzliya Conference," 4 December 2002, www.mfa.gov.il.

119. Document text as in Itamar Rabinovich and Jehuda Reinharz (eds.), *Israel in the Middle East: Documents and Readings*, pp. 536–540.

120. UN Security Council Resolution 1515, 19 November 2003, available online at http://www.un.org/Docs/sc/unsc_resolutions03.html.

121. *Haaretz*, 27 May 2003.

122. "PM Sharon Addresses the UN General Assembly," 15 September 2005, www.mfa.gov.il.

123. "Address by PM Ehud Olmert at the Special Knesset Session on the Condition of the Gush Katif Evacuees," 27 June 2006, www.mfa.gov.il.

124. "Address by Vice Prime Minister and Minister of Foreign Affairs Tzipi Livni at the Annapolis Conference," 27 November 2007, www.mfa.gov.il.

125. "Address by Vice Prime Minister and Minister of Foreign Affairs Tzipi Livni at the Annapolis Conference," 27 November 2007, www.mfa.gov.il.

126. "Address by Prime Minister Ehud Olmert at the Annapolis Conference," 27 November, 2007, www.mfa.gov.il.

127. "PM's Speech at the Begin-Sadat Center at Bar-Ilan University," 14 June 2009, www.pmo.gov.il.

128. See "Prime Minister Netanyahu's Speech at the Opening of the Knesset Winter Session," 11 October 2010; "Prime Minister Netanyahu addresses the General Assembly of the Jewish Federations of North America," 8 November 2010; and "Excerpts from Prime Minister Netanyahu's Statement to the Knesset," 1 December 2010, www.mfa.gov.il.

129. "Prime Minister Netanyahu's Speech at the Opening of the Knesset Winter Session," 11 October 2010.

130. Rabinovich and Reinharz, *Israel in the Middle East*, p. 520.

131. Speech by Colin Powell at the University of Louisville, 19 November 2001, full text in *The Guardian*, 20 November 2001.

132. Letter from US President George W. Bush to Prime Minister Ariel Sharon, 14 April 2004, www.mfa.gov.il.

133. Headline in *al-Ayyam*, 15 April 2004.

134. Speech by Barack Obama at AIPAC Policy Conference, 4 June 2008, www.aipac.org/Publications.

135. "Text of President Obama's Speech to the UN General Assembly," *New York Times*, 23 September 2009.

136. Statement by Secretary of State Hillary Clinton, on 25 November 2009, www
.state.gov/secretary (see the same wording in Secretary Clinton's statement in
January 2010 as reported in *The Washington Post*, 9 January 2010); speech by Secretary
of State Hillary Clinton before AIPAC Policy Conference, 22 March 2010, in
which Clinton referred no less than three times to US identification with Israel's
aspiration to remain a "democratic Jewish state," www.state.gov/secretary.

137. US National Security Strategy Survey, http://www.whitehouse.gov/sites/default/
files/rss_viewer/national_security_strategy.pdf.

138. Yasir Arafat, interview in *Haaretz*, 18 June 2004.

139. E.g., "Report: Abbas Reiterates Refusal to Recognize Israel as Jewish State,"
*Haaretz*, 1 December 2007.

140. Ali Jaradat, "Matlab ta'jizi wa tafjiri" [A Paralyzing and Explosive Demand],
*al-Ayyam*, 19 November 2007. In a discussion with Israeli foreign minister Tzipi
Livni in November 2007, Sa'ib Ariqat angrily retorted that she could "call [Israel]
what you want" (*The Guardian*, 24 January 2011). The interpretation by the
al-Jazeera–*Guardian* combination of this caustic riposte as a willingness to
recognize Israel's Jewish character was a tendentious absurdity designed to
discredit the Palestinian negotiators as craven collaborators. It was hardly a
commitment by the Palestinians to do anything of the kind. In actual fact they
consistently stood their ground on this issue and flatly rejected the Israeli position, as Ariqat was obviously doing in this conversation as well. In internal Palestinian deliberations in June 2009, it is clear from the context that Ariqat's contention
that this was a "non-issue" (see "Ariqat Meeting with Negotiation Support Unit
and Heads of Committees," 16 June 2009, http://www.ajtransparency.com/en/
document/4660) was intended not to imply acquiescence, but rather to indicate
that the PA had no intention of seriously broaching the matter.

141. Khaled Abu Toameh, "PA: Netanyahu Has Buried Peace Process," *Jerusalem Post*,
15 June 2009; Sa'ib Ariqat, quoted in *al-Hayat al-Jadida*, 15 June 2009; Ghassan
Khatib, "A Farcical Position on Statehood," *Bitterlemons: Palestinian-Israeli Crossfire*,
15 June 2009, www.bitterlemons.org.

142. *Al-barnamij al-siyasi liharakat al-tahrir al-watani al-Filastini*, "Fath," Sixth General
Conference, p. 17, www.fatehconf.ps.

143. Khaled Amayreh, "Fatah Tells Abbas to Play It Tough," *al-Ahram Weekly*, 2–8
December 2010.

144. Bilal al-Hasan, "Isra'il wa-khittat al-khud'a al-jadida" [Israel and (Its) New Plan
of Deception], *al-Quds*, 15 June 2009.

145. Khalid Mash'al, on al-Aqsa TV, 25 June 2009, as in MEMRI, Special Dispatch,
No. 2423, 29 June 2009.

146. Jacob Shamir and Khalil Shikaki, *Palestinian and Israeli Public Opinion: The Public
Imperative in the Second Intifada* (Bloomington: Indiana University Press, 2010),
pp. 146–147; David Pollock, "Palestinian Public Opinion: Tactically Flexible,
Strategically Ambitious," *Washington Institute for Near East Policy, Policy Watch*,
no. 1731, 9 December 2010.

147. Ahmad Khalidi, "A One-State Solution," *The Guardian*, 29 September 2003.
148. "Israel's Celebration Remains a Palestinian Catastrophe," *The Guardian*, 12 May 2008.
149. Ahmad Khalidi, "A Recipe for Resentment," *The Guardian*, 26 May 2009.

## Chapter 4. The Alternative: The Promotion of the One-State Agenda

1. Benny Morris, *1948: The First Arab-Israeli War* (New Haven: Yale University Press, 2008), pp. 40–41.
2. Neil Caplan, *The Israel-Palestine Conflict: Contested Histories*, pp. 106–107.
3. Benny Morris, *1948*, pp. 47; Neil Caplan, *The Israel-Palestine Conflict*, p. 108.
4. Ruth Lapidot and Moshe Hirsch (eds.), *The Arab-Israeli Conflict and Its Resolution*, p. 35; http://naip-documents.blogspot.com/2009/09/document-9.html.
5. Benny Morris, *1948*, pp. 53.
6. Benny Morris, quoting Michael Cohen, *Palestine and the Great Powers* (p. 292), in *1948*, pp. 57–65.
7. Neil Caplan, *The Israel-Palestine Conflict*, p. 105.
8. Avi Shlaim, *Israel and Palestine: Reappraisals, Revisions, Refutations* (London: Verso, 2009), p. 24.
9. Negotiating Arab-Israeli Peace, Appendix B: Documents Online, http://naip-documents.blogspot.com/2010/02/document-31.html.
10. Benny Morris, *The Birth of the Palestinian Refugee Problem, 1947–1949* (Cambridge University Press, 1988), p. 286.
11. Meir Litvak, "The Palestine Liberation Organization," MECS, vol. 17 (1993), p. 173; Avi Shlaim, "The Oslo Accord," p. 35.
12. Elie Rekhess, "The West Bank and the Gaza Strip," MECS, vol. 17 (1993), pp. 219–220.
13. Rashid Khalidi, *The Iron Cage*, p. 181.
14. NGO Forum at Durban Conference 2001, www.ngo-monitor.org/article/ngo_forum_at_durban_conference_.
15. Irwin Cotler, "Beyond Durban: The Conference against Racism That Became a Racist Conference against Jews," Global Jewish Agenda (December 2001), www.jafi.org.il/agenda/2001/english/wk3–22/6.asp; Irwin Cotler, "Durban's Troubling Legacy One Year Later: Twisting the Cause of International Human Rights Against the Jewish People," *Jerusalem Issue Brief*, vol. 2, no. 5 (Jerusalem Center for Public Affairs, August 2002).
16. E.g., Samir Qatami, "Netanyahu's Obstruction and the Buried Peace," *al-Ra'y*, 15 March 1997; Jenab Tutunji and Kamal Khaldi, "A Binational State in Palestine: The Rational Choice for Palestinians and the Moral Choice for Israelis," *International Affairs*, vol. 73, no. 1 (January 1997), pp. 31–58; the December 2001–January 2002 issue of the *Boston Review* was devoted to a debate on the binational idea in Israel/Palestine.
17. Ziad Hafez, "The Palestine One-State Solution: Report on the Conference Held in Boston, Massachusetts, March 2009," *Contemporary Arab Affairs*, vol. 2, no. 4 (October–December 2009), p. 528; Hussein Ibish, *What's Wrong with the One-State Agenda?* (Washington, DC: American Task Force on Palestine, 2009), p. 27.

18. Tony Judt, "Israel: The Alternative," *New York Review of Books*, vol. 50, no. 16 (23 October 2003).

19. Leon Wieseltier, "Israel, Palestine, and the Return of the Bi-national Fantasy: What Is Not to be Done," *The New Republic*, 27 October 2003.

20. Virginia Tilley, *The One-State Solution: A Breakthrough for Peace in the Israeli-Palestinian Deadlock* (Ann Arbor: University of Michigan Press, 2008).

21. Tilley, *The One-State Solution*, p. 1.

22. Ali Abunimah, *One Country: A Bold Proposal to End the Israeli-Palestinian Impasse* (New York: Metropolitan Books, 2006), p. 16.

23. Tilley, *The One-State Solution*, pp. 86–87; similarly Abunimah, *One Country*, pp. 27–28, 34–36.

24. Tilley, *The One-State Solution*, pp. 2, 73, 75.

25. See the route of the barrier, built and planned, in map 6.

26. Tilley, *The One-State Solution*, p. 3.

27. Tilley, *The One-State Solution*, pp. 4–6

28. Tilley, *The One-State Solution*, p. 84.

29. Tilley, *The One-State Solution*, pp. 128, 208.

30. Tilley, *The One-State Solution*, p. 3

31. For a variety of options, see *Getting to the Territorial Endgame of an Israeli-Palestinian Peace Settlement: A Special Report by the Israeli-Palestinian Workshop of the Baker Institute's Conflict Resolution Forum* (Houston: Rice University, James A. Baker III Institute for Public Policy, 2010).

32. Tilley, *The One-State Solution*, pp. 8–9.

33. Tilley, *The One-State Solution*, p. 9.

34. Salim Tamari, "The Binationalist Lure," *Boston Review*, December 2001–January 2002.

35. Tilley's suggestion that the special ties between Jordan and Palestine and between Jordanians and Palestinians are a "Zionist fiction" (*The One-State Solution*, p. 8) is an unfortunate combination of bias and sheer ignorance. One need only read what Jordanians and Palestinians say and write about themselves, rather than having foreigners explaining to them who they "really" are.

36. Tilley, *The One-State Solution*, p. 9.

37. Tilley, *The One-State Solution*, pp. 67–68.

38. Tilley, *The One-State Solution*, p. 13.

39. Abunimah, *One Country*, p. 61.

40. Camp David Frameworks for Peace (September 17, 1978) as in Laqueur and Rubin, *Documentary History*, p. 406.

41. Abunimah, *One Country*, pp. 109–111.

42. See Asher Susser, *The Rise of Hamas in Palestine and the Crisis of Secularism in the Arab World*, Brandeis University, Crown Center for Middle East Studies, Essay Series, February 2010.

43. Abunimah, *One Country*, p. 16.

44. Tilley, *The One-State Solution*, p. 79.

45. Tilley, *The One-State Solution*, p. 165.

46. Tilley, *The One-State Solution*, pp. 17, 86.

47. Tilley, *The One-State Solution*, p. 45

48. Tilley, *The One-State Solution*, p. 163.

49. Fouad Ajami, "Palestine's Deliverance," *Wall Street Journal*, 27 June 2002.

50. Abunimah, *One Country*, p. 153.

51. Abunimah, *One Country*, p. 149.

52. Tilley, *The One-State Solution*, p. 203.

53. Tilley, *The One-State Solution*, pp. 168, 223.

54. Tilley, *The One-State Solution*, p. 143.

55. Tilley, *The One-State Solution*, pp. 141–142.

56. Hermann Giliomee, *The Afrikaners: Biography of a People* (Charlottesville: University of Virginia Press, 2003), pp. 598, 601.

57. Hermann Giliomee, *The Afrikaners*, pp. 587–600, 620–625, 631.

58. This excludes the Arabs of Jerusalem who were not part of pre-1967 Israel and are not likely to remain part of Israel in any future settlement.

59. Benjamin Pogrund, "Different Histories, Different Futures," *Palestine-Israel Journal*, vol. 15, no. 4 (2008) and vol. 16, no. 1 (2009), p. 91.

60. Tilley, *The One-State Solution*, pp. 132, 137, 173–174.

61. Tilley, *The One-State Solution*, pp. 72, 185, 200. Tilley refers to the expulsion of 400,000 refugees [the figure usually quoted is 250,000] in 1967. Morris does not deal with this issue in his works on 1948, but by most credible accounts, including Morris in his book surveying the history of the Arab-Israeli conflict, this was by and large not a case of expulsion, but genuine flight. Some fled during the fighting, and others left afterwards. As they crossed into Jordan, they were even required by the Israeli authorities to sign a document stating that they were leaving of their own free will (Benny Morris, *Righteous Victims*, p. 328).

62. See, e.g., Joseph Heller, *The Birth of Israel, 1945–1949: Ben-Gurion and His Critics* (Gainesville: University Press of Florida, 2003), pp. 295–299.

63. Benny Morris, *The Birth of the Palestinian Refugee Problem Revisited* (Cambridge University Press, 2004), p. 588.

64. Benny Morris, *1948*, pp. 408–411.

65. Tilley, *The One-State Solution*, p. 194.

66. Ben-Gurion interview with Haim Gouri, quoted in Gershom Gorenberg, *The Accidental Empire*, p. 17.

67. Tilley, *The One-State Solution*, pp. 198, 202.

68. Tilley, *The One-State Solution*, pp. 203–204.

69. See, e.g., Joel Kovel, *Overcoming Zionism: Creating a Single Democratic State in Israel/Palestine* (Toronto: Pluto Press, 2007), p. 97; Abunimah, *One Country*, pp. 118–119.

70. Alexander Yakobson and Amnon Rubinstein, *Israel and the Family of Nations: The Jewish Nation State and Human Rights* (Tel Aviv: Schocken, 2003), pp. 237–238 (Hebrew).

71. Yakobson and Rubinstein, *Israel and the Family of Nations*, pp. 224–233.

72. See, e.g., Act on Swedish Citizenship, which gives such preference to immigrants and adopted children from these countries, at www.regeringen.se/content/1/c6/02/91/91/dcdd4a24.pdf.

73. Yakobson and Rubinstein, *Israel and the Family of Nations*, p. 238.

74. Tilley, *The One-State Solution*, pp. 177, 181.

75. Avi Bareli, "Forgetting Europe: Points of Departure in the Debate on Zionism and Colonialism," in Tuvia Friling (ed.), *An Answer to a Post-Zionist Colleague* (Tel Aviv: Yediot Aharonot, 2003), pp. 305–307 (Hebrew).

76. Yoav Gelber, "The History of Zionist Historiography: From Apologetics to Denial," in Benny Morris (ed.), *Making Israel* (Ann Arbor: University of Michigan Press, 2007), p. 68.

77. Anita Shapira, *Land and Power*, p. 159.

78. Yoav Gelber, "The History of Zionist Historiography," p. 69.

79. Craig Calhoun, one of the leading social scientists of our time is University Professor of the Social Sciences at New York University and president of the US Social Science Research Council.

80. Craig Calhoun, *Nations Matter*, p. 1.

81. Tilley, *The One-State Solution*, pp. 32–33, 142.

82. Anthony Smith, *Nationalism and Modernism* (London: Routledge, 1998), pp. 126, 212–213.

83. See David Brown, *Contemporary Nationalism: Civic, Ethnocultural and Multicultural Politics* (London: Routledge, 2000), p. 52; and Bernard Yack, "The Myth of the Civic Nation," in Ronald Beiner (ed.), *Theorizing Nationalism* (Albany: SUNY Press, 1999), as quoted in Yakobson and Rubinstein, *Israel and the Family of Nations*, p. 407.

84. Yakobson and Rubinstein, *Israel and the Family of Nations*, p. 282.

85. "An Alternative Future: An Exchange," *New York Review of Books*, vol. 50, no. 19 (4 December 2003).

86. "An Alternative Future: An Exchange," *New York Review of Books*, vol. 50, no. 19 (4 December 2003).

87. Tony Judt, "Israel: The Alternative."

88. Tilley, *The One-State Solution*, p. 14.

89. I am very grateful to Professor Joel Barkan (of the Center for Strategic and International Studies in Washington, D.C.), Dr. Greg Mills (of the Brenthurst Foundation in Johannesburg, South Africa), and Dr. Gary Sussman (of Tel Aviv University) for helping me to get this factually correct.

90. "An Alternative Future: An Exchange," *New York Review of Books*, vol. 50, no. 19 (4 December 2003).

91. "An Alternative Future: An Exchange," *New York Review of Books*, vol. 50, no. 19 (4 December 2003).

92. Hussein Ibish, *What's Wrong with the One-State Agenda?*, pp. 29, 54.

93. Abunimah, *One Country*, pp. 20, 51–54.

94. Abunimah, *One Country*, p. 36.

95. Abunimah, *One Country*, p. 54.
96. Hussein Ibish, *What's Wrong with the One-State Agenda?*, pp. 37, 77.
97. Rashid Khalidi, *The Iron Cage*, p. 209.
98. Hussein Ibish, *What's Wrong with the One-State Agenda?*, pp. 88–90.
99. Hussein Ibish, *What's Wrong with the One-State Agenda?*, pp. 90–91.
100. Ziad Hafez, "The Palestine One-State Solution," p. 529.
101. Meron Benvenisti, "The Binationalism Vogue," *Haaretz*, 30 April 2009.
102. Hussein Ibish, *What's Wrong with the One-State Agenda?*, pp. 92–93.
103. Hussein Ibish, *What's Wrong with the One-State Agenda?*, pp. 112–113.
104. Hussein Ibish, *What's Wrong with the One-State Agenda?*, pp. 57–59.
105. Hussein Ibish, *What's Wrong with the One-State Agenda?*, pp. 60–62.
106. Benny Morris, *One State, Two States*, p. 188.
107. Arend Lijphart, "Consociational Democracy," in Arend Lijphart, *Thinking About Democracy*, p. 35.
108. Quoted in Tamar Hermann, "The Bi-national Idea in Israel/Palestine," p. 389.
109. Shlomo Avineri, "Bye to the Binational Model," *Haaretz*, 2 July 2010.
110. Caroline Hornstein Tomic, "State-Building and Ethnicity in the Western Balkan Region" (discussion paper presented at Brenthurst Foundation "Fault Lines" Conference, Jerusalem, February 2010).
111. Shlomo Avineri, "Bye to the Binational Model," *Haaretz*, 2 July 2010.
112. Meron Benvenisti, "The Key Word is Bi-zonal," *Haaretz*, 26 February 2004.
113. "Embassy News," Embassy of Cyprus, Washington DC, 22 January 2010, www .cyprusembassy.net/home.
114. Meron Benvenisti, "Thus Israel Became a Bi-national State," *Haaretz*, 22 January; Alexander Yakobson, "A Binational State? Here?," *Haaretz*, 29 January; Matti Steinberg, "Day Dreaming," *Haaretz*, 4 February 2010.
115. Marisa Traniello, "Power-Sharing: Lessons from South Africa and Rwanda," *International Public Policy Review*, vol. 3, no. 2 (March 2008), pp. 29, 40–42.
116. Tamar Hermann, "The Bi-national Idea in Israel/Palestine," pp. 398–399.
117. Salim Tamari, "The Binationalist Lure," *Boston Review*, December 2001–January 2002.
118. Salim Tamari, "The Binationalist Lure."
119. Jacob Shamir and Khalil Shikaki, *Palestinian and Israeli Public Opinion*, pp. 146–147.
120. "PSR—Survey Research Unit: Joint Palestinian-Israeli Press Release," 22 December 2009 and 20 March 2010, www.pcpsr.org/survey/polls. A different Israeli poll, also conducted in March 2010, produced similar results. Among Israeli Jews, 66 percent supported the two-state solution, as opposed to 14 percent who supported a binational state; see Ephraim Yuchtman-Yaar and Tamar Hermann, *War and Peace Index*, March 2010.
121. "Poll No. 70, April 2010—on Governance and US Policy," Jerusalem Media and Communications Center, www.jmcc.org/documents.
122. Hussein Ibish, *What's Wrong with the One-State Agenda?*, pp. 83–85.
123. Benny Morris, *One State, Two States*, p. 194.
124. Bernard Wasserstein, *Israelis and Palestinians*, pp. 158–159.

125. Hussein Ibish, *What's Wrong with the One-State Agenda?*, p. 41.

126. Hussein Ibish, *What's Wrong with the One-State Agenda?*, pp. 22, 86–87.

127. Yakobson and Rubinstein, *Israel and the Family of Nations*, p. 218.

128. Ruth Gavison, *Haaretz*, 19 November 2007; Yakobson and Rubinstein, *Israel and the Family of Nations*, p. 242.

129. See Elaine Hagopian, "Preface," in Naseer Aruri (ed.), *Palestinian Refugees: The Right of Return* (London: Pluto Press, 2001), p. vii; similarly, Susan Akram, "Re-interpreting Palestinian Refugee Rights under International Law," and Salman Abu-Sitta, "The Right of Return: Sacred, Legal and Possible," in Naseer Aruri (ed.), *Palestinian Refugees*, pp. 165–207.

130. Eyal Benvenisti, "International Law and the Right of Return," *Palestine-Israel Journal*, vol. 15, no. 4 (2008) and vol. 16, no. 1 (2009), pp. 44–45.

131. Abba Eban, quoted in Maurice Stroun, "Permission to Return or Right of Return," *Bitterlemons-api: Discussing the Arab Peace Initiative*, Edition 4, 15 December 2010, www.bitterlemons-api.org.

132. Eyal Benvenisti, "International Law and the Right of Return," pp. 45–46.

133. UNGA Resolution 194, 11 December 1948, in Itamar Rabinovich and Jehuda Reinharz (eds.), *Israel in the Middle East: Documents and Readings*, pp. 89–92.

134. See "Annex VII: Treatment of Property Affected by Events Since 1963," *Annan Plan for Cyprus*, www.hri.org/docs/annan/.

135. Eyal Benvenisti, "International Law and the Right of Return," p. 46.

136. Akiva Eldar, "The Ladder to Climb Down from the Tree," *Haaretz*, 11 March 2010.

137. Hussein Ibish, *What's Wrong with the One-State Agenda?*, p. 15.

138. Hussein Ibish, *What's Wrong with the One-State Agenda?*, pp. 17–18.

139. Saree Makdisi, "Good Riddance, Abbas," *Foreign Policy*, 6 November 2009; Ziad Hafez, "The Palestine One-State Solution: Report on the Conference Held in Boston, Massachusetts, March 2009," *Contemporary Arab Affairs*, vol. 2, no. 4 (October-December 2009), p. 530.

140. Edward Said, "The One-State Solution," *New York Times Weekend Magazine*, 10 January 1999; Edward Said, "The One-State Solution," in *Culture and Resistance: Conversations with Edward Said*, interviews by David Barsamian (Cambridge, MA: South End Press, 2003), pp. 5–7.

141. Edward Said, "Trying Again and Again," *al-Ahram Weekly*, 11–17 January 2001.

142. "Call It a Cucumber," interview with Ghada Karmi, in *Bitterlemons: Palestinian-Israeli Crossfire*, 19 January 2004, www.bitterlemons.org.

143. Ahmad Khalidi, "The End of the Two-State Solution?" *The Guardian*, 18 July 2003; "A One-State Solution," *The Guardian*, 29 September 2003; "Israel's Celebration Remains a Palestinian Catastrophe," *The Guardian*, 12 May 2008.

144. Ahmad Khalidi, "Thanks, But No Thanks,"*The Guardian*, 13 December 2007.

145. Meir Litvak, "Introduction: Collective Memory and the Palestinian Experience," in Meir Litvak (ed.), *Palestinian Collective Memory and National Identity* (New York: Palgrave Macmillan, 2009), p. 14.

146. Michael Milshtein, "The Memory That Never Dies," p. 49.

147. Hussein Agha and Robert Malley, "A Solution Is Possible Now," *The Guardian*, 29 March 2002.

148. See, e.g., on the conference held in Damascus in November 2008 as reported in "Mu'tamar haqq al-awda" [The Right of Return Conference], *al-Thawra*, 24 November 2008.

149. Michael Milshtein, "Memory 'from Below,' Palestinian Society and the Nakba Memory," in Meir Litvak (ed.), *Palestinian Collective Memory and National Identity* (New York: Palgrave Macmillan, 2009), pp. 72, 79–80.

150. Preface by Elaine Hagopian, in Naseer Aruri (ed.), *Palestinian Refugees: The Right of Return* (London: Pluto Press, 2001), p. vii; Michael Milshtein, "Memory 'from Below,'" p. 76.

151. Michael Milshtein, "The Memory That Never Dies," pp. 59–60.

152. Hussein Ibish, *What's Wrong with the One-State Agenda?*, pp. 48–49.

153. "Text of UN General Assembly Resolution 181," in Ruth Lapidot and Moshe Hirsch (eds.), *The Arab-Israeli Conflict and Its Resolution: Selected Documents*, p. 39.

154. Itamar Rabinovich, "From 'Israeli Arabs' to 'Israel's Palestinian Citizens', 1948–1996: Analysis," in Itamar Rabinovich and Jehuda Reinharz (eds.), *Israel in the Middle East: Documents and Readings*, pp.183–187

155. Nadim Rouhana, "The Political Transformation of the Palestinians in Israel: From Acquiescence to Challenge," *Journal of Palestine Studies*, vol. 18, no. 3 (Spring 1989), pp. 45, 49.

156. Itamar Rabinovich, "From 'Israeli Arabs' to 'Israel's Palestinian Citizens,'" p. 184.

157. Elie Rekhess, "The Arabs of Israel after Oslo," pp. 1–2.

158. Nadim Rouhana, Nabil Saleh, and Nimer Sultany, "Voting without a Voice: About the Vote of the Palestinian Minority in the 16th Knesset Elections," in Asher Arian and Michal Shamir (eds.), *The Elections in Israel, 2003* (New Brunswick: Transaction, 2005), quoted in Shindler, *A History of Modern Israel*, p. 284.

159. Nadim Rouhana, "The Political Transformation," p. 55.

160. As'ad Ghanem, *The Palestinian-Arab Minority in Israel, 1948–2000: A Political Study* (Albany, NY: SUNY Press, 2001), pp. 158, 161.

161. As'ad Ghanem, *The Palestinian-Arab Minority in Israel, 1948–2000*, p. 170.

162. Nadim Rouhana, "The Political Transformation," p. 46.

163. Yakobson and Rubinstein, *Israel and the Family of Nations*, pp. 278, 372.

164. Yakobson and Rubinstein, *Israel and the Family of Nations*, pp. 246–257.

165. Azmi Bishara, "The Essential Agenda," *al-Ahram Weekly*, 4–10 March 2004.

166. Nadim Rouhana, "Shaking the Foundations of Citizenship," *al-Ahram Weekly*, 27 September–3 October 2001.

167. Elie Rekhess, "The Arabs of Israel after Oslo," pp. 15, 21, 23.

168. Nadim Rouhana, "Shaking the Foundations of Citizenship."

169. *Al-tasawwur al-mustaqbali lil-Arab al-Filastiniyyin fi Isra'il 2006* [The Future Vision of the Palestinian Arabs in Israel 2006], The National Committee for the Heads of the Arab Local Authorities in Israel, p. 5, www.arab-lac.org.

170. *The Future Vision*, Arabic text, pp. 5, 9.

171. *The Future Vision*, Arabic text, pp. 5, 9.

172. Orr Commission Report, paragraph 55.

173. Not counting the some 250,000 to 300,000 Arabs of Jerusalem who are not Israeli citizens.

174. "The Declaration of the Establishment of the State of Israel," 14 May 1948, www.mfa.gov.il.

175. PLO Charter 1968, paragraph 1, as in www.fatehmedia.net/ar/m-t-f.

176. As'ad Ghanem, *The Palestinian-Arab Minority in Israel, 1948–2000*, p. 180.

177. As'ad Ghanem, *The Palestinian-Arab Minority in Israel, 1948–2000*, pp. 182–184.

178. As'ad Ghanem, *The Palestinian-Arab Minority in Israel, 1948–2000*, p. 195.

179. Elie Rekhess, "The Arabs of Israel after Oslo," p. 19.

180. As'ad Ghanem, *The Palestinian-Arab Minority in Israel, 1948–2000*, pp. 196–200.

181. Marisa Traniello, "Power-Sharing: Lessons from South Africa and Rwanda," *International Public Policy Review*, vol. 3, no. 2 (March 2008), pp. 28, 35; Matthijs Bogaard, "Power Sharing in South Africa: The African National Congress as a Consociational Party," in Sid Noel (ed.), *From Power Sharing to Democracy: Post-Conflict Institutions in Ethnically Divided Societies* (Quebec City: McGill-Queens University Press, 2005), pp. 164–183.

182. There are repeated references in the document to the international community as a player in the issues at hand, and one even speaks of international protection (himaya) for the Arab minority (*The Future Vision*, Arabic text, pp. 6, 11, 18).

183. Nadim Rouhana, "The Political Transformation," p. 47.

184. Hussein Ibish, *What's Wrong with the One-State Agenda?*, pp. 105–107.

185. Gary Sussman, "The Challenges to the Two-State Solution," *Middle East Report*, no. 231 (Summer 2004), p. 11.

186. As reported in *al-Ayyam*, 9 January 2004.

187. Ghassan Khatib, "A Ton of Regret," and Yossi Alpher, "Green Line and Red Line," *Bitterlemons: Palestinian-Israeli Crossfire*, 19 January 2004, www.bitterlemons.org; Muhammad Yunis, "Fariq istratiji yutalib bi-waqf al-mufawadat wainha' khiyar al-dawlatayn wa-i'adat tashkil al-sulta" [Strategic Group Demands Cessation of Negotiations, End of Two-State Option and Reconstruction of the PA], *al-Hayat*, 30 August 2008.

188. Khaled Abu Toameh and Tovah Lazaroff, "Erekat: PA May Ditch Two-State Solution," *Jerusalem Post*, 5 November 2009; John Whitbeck, "Two States or One: The Moment of Truth," *al-Ahram Weekly*, 12–18 November 2009.

189. Sa'ib Ariqat, *The Political Situation in Light of the Developments with the US Administration and Israeli Government and Hamas Continued Coup d'Etat: Recommendations and Options* (Jerusalem: The Center for Democracy and Community Development, December, 2009), passim. Arabic version: *Taqrir hass, al-mawqif al-siyasi ala du' al-tatawwurat ma' al-idara al-Amrikiyya wal-hukuma al-isra'iliyya wa-istimrar inqilab Hamas: al-tawsiyat wal-khiyarat*, p. 13.

190. Akiva Eldar, "Palestinians Threaten to Adopt One-State Solution," *Haaretz*, 26 February 2010.

191. Ali Jarbawi, "Hawla 'al-wathiqa al-Swisriyya': likai la nastamirr fi tahn al-hawa'" [On the "Swiss (Geneva) Document": So That We Do Not Continue to Tread Water (Grind Air)], al-Hayat, 21 October 2003; "The Remaining Palestinian Options," The Arab World Geographer / Le Geographe du monde arabe, vol. 8, no. 3 (2005), p. 120; "Hawla al-ajinda al-kharijiyya lil-'islah': al-hala al-Filastiniyya" [On a Foreign Affairs Agenda for "Reform": The Palestinian Situation], al-Mus-taqbal al-Arabi, no. 335, January 2007, pp. 87–88.

192. Ali Jarbawi, "We Will Give You More of Us," Bitterlemons: Palestinian-Israeli Crossfire, 22 December 2003, www.bitterlemons.org.

193. Sari Nusayba, interview with Akiva Eldar in Haaretz, 18 August 2008.

194. Jonathan Kuttab, "Steps to Create an Israel-Palestine," Los Angeles Times, 20 December 2009.

195. Khalid Mash'al, in al-Ahram, 30 March 2005.

196. Yezid Sayigh, "The Palestinian Strategic Impasse," Survival, vol. 44, no. 4 (Winter 2002–3), pp. 15, 19.

197. Moshe Arens, "Israeli Citizenship for the Palestinians," Haaretz, 2 June 2010.

198. Jonathan Freedland, "The Israeli Right Has a New Vision—Jews and Arabs Sharing One Country," The Guardian, 27 July 2010; Shlomo Avineri, "The Untruth behind the Truth of the Right," Haaretz, 4 August 2010.

199. See, e.g., his exchange with Edward Said in 2000, as quoted in Hussein Ibish, What's Wrong with the One-State Agenda?, p. 24.

200. Meron Benvenisti, "Which Kind of Bi-National State?," Haaretz, 20 November 2003.

201. Giora Eiland, Rethinking the Two-State Solution; Efraim Inbar, The Rise and Demise of the Two-State Paradigm (Bar Ilan University, Begin-Sadat Center for Strategic Studies, Mideast Security and Policy Studies, No. 79, April 2009).

202. Giora Eiland, Rethinking the Two-State Solution, pp. 3–4; Efraim Inbar, The Rise and Demise of the Two-State Paradigm, pp. 1–2, 20–21.

203. Giora Eiland, Regional Alternatives, pp. 18–19.

204. Giora Eiland, Rethinking the Two-State Solution, p, 30.

205. Efraim Inbar, The Rise and Demise of the Two-State Paradigm, p. 19.

206. Benny Morris, One State, Two States, p. 200.

207. Giora Eiland, Rethinking the Two-State Solution, p. 34

208. Dina Ezzat, "Beyond the Wall," al-Ahram Weekly, 24–30 December 2009.

209. Giora Eiland, Regional Alternatives, p. 35.

## Chapter 5. The Evolution of the Jordanian Role

1. Yoav Gelber, Jewish-Transjordanian Relations, pp. 207, 211; Joseph Nevo, King Abdallah and Palestine, pp. 56–59.

2. Joseph Nevo, King Abdallah and Palestine, p. 72.

3. Yezid Sayigh, Armed Struggle and the Search for State, p. 243.

4. James Lunt, Hussein of Jordan: Searching for a Just and Lasting Peace (New York: William Morrow, 1987), p. 121.

5. Yezid Sayigh, *Armed Struggle and the Search for State*, p. 251.
6. Yezid Sayigh, *Armed Struggle and the Search for State*, pp. 244, 248.
7. Moshe Shemesh, *The Palestinian Entity, 1959–1974: Arab Politics and the PLO*, Second Revised Edition (London: Frank Cass, 1996), p. 132.
8. *Middle East Record (MER)*, vol. 5, 1969–70 (Tel Aviv University, Shiloah Center for Middle Eastern and African Studies, 1977), p. 391.
9. Full Arabic text of the speech in *al-Ra'y*, 16 March 1972.
10. Adnan Abu-Odeh, *Jordanians, Palestinians and the Hashemite Kingdom in the Middle East Peace Process* (Washington DC: US Institute of Peace, 1999), pp. 174, 206.
11. *Al-Ra'y*, 16 March 1972.
12. Emile Sahliyeh, *In Search of Leadership: West Bank Politics Since 1967* (Washington DC: The Brookings Institution, 1988), p. 36
13. Moshe Shemesh, *The Palestinian Entity*, pp. 167–181, 225, 258.
14. *Divrei Haknesset*, Third Session of the Seventh Knesset, Meeting 284, 16 March 1972, pp. 1842–1843.
15. Dan Schueftan, *Jordanian Option: Israel, Jordan and the Palestinians* (Tel Aviv: Yad Tabenkin, 1986), pp. 331–332 (Hebrew); Moshe Zak, *Husayn Makes Peace: Thirty Years and One More on the Road to Peace* (Bar Ilan University, BESA Center, 1994), pp. 46, 161–163, 179–180, 192 (Hebrew).
16. Alan Hart, *Arafat: A Political Biography*, Revised Edition (London: Sidgwick and Jackson, 1994), p. 320.
17. *Middle East Contemporary Survey (MECS)*, vol. 6(1981–82), pp. 682–683; MECS, vol. 7 (1982–83), pp. 631–632.
18. Philip Robins, *A History of Jordan* (Cambridge University Press, 2004), p. 160.
19. Hani al-Hasan, in *Filastin al-Thawra*, 21 April 1984, quoted in Shaul Mishal and Reuben Aharoni, *Speaking Stones: Communiques from the Intifada Underground* (Syracuse University Press, 1994), p. 7.
20. MECS, vol. 9 (1984–85), pp. 187–188.
21. Speech by King Husayn to the Egyptian Parliament on 3 December 1984, in *Ashara a'wam min al-kifah wal-bina* [Ten Years of Struggle and Building]: A Collection of Speeches by King Husayn from 1977–1987, collected and edited by Ali Mahafza (Amman: Markaz al-kutub al-Urdunni, 1988), pp. 603–609.
22. *Radio Amman*, 3 May 1988; *Jordan News Agency*, 10 May 1988.
23. Nigel Ashton, *King Hussein of Jordan: A Political Life* (New Haven: Yale University Press, 2008), p. 234.
24. *Al-Dustur*, Amman, 28 January 1988.
25. *Time*, 2 May 1988.
26. "Official Arabic Text of Husayn's speech at Algiers Summit, 7 June 1988" (Moshe Dayan Center Archives).
27. Avi Shlaim, *Lion of Jordan*, p. 461.
28. Full Arabic text in *al-Ra'y*, 1 August 1988.
29. *Radio Amman*, 4 August 1988; *Jordan Times*, 6 August 1988.
30. *Jordan Times*, 28 June 1988.

31. Tahir al-Masri, quoted in al-Dustur, Amman, 13 July 1988.

32. Marwan Muasher, The Arab Center: The Promise of Moderation (New Haven: Yale University Press, 2008), p. 26.

33. Emmanuel Sivan, "The Arab Nation-State: In Search of a Usable Past," Middle East Review, vol. 19, no. 3 (Spring 1987), pp. 21–30.

34. Benedict Anderson, Imagined Communities: Reflections on the Origin and Spread of Nationalism, Revised Edition (London and New York: Verso, 1991).

35. Emmanuel Sivan, citing Eric Hobsbawm in "The Arab Nation-State," p. 28.

36. Asher Susser, "Jordan — In the Maze of Tribalism, Jordanianism, Palestinianism, and Islam," in Asher Susser (ed.), Challenges to the Cohesion of the Arab State (Tel Aviv University: Moshe Dayan Center, 2008), pp. 106–107.

37. Marwan Muasher, The Arab Center, p. 30.

38. Text available as Document 76 at http://naip-documents.blogspot.com/.

39. Asher Susser, The Jordanian–Israeli Peace Negotiations: The Geopolitical Rationale of a Bilateral Relationship (The Leonard Davis Institute of the Hebrew University of Jerusalem, 1999), pp. 22–25.

40. See, e.g., King Abdallah's interviews with Randa Habib, AFP, 16 May 2009, and with La Republica, 19 October 2009, Press Room, www.kingabdullah.jo.

41. King Abdallah's interviews with Ghassan Charbel, al-Hayat, Part II, 10 November 2009, and with Fareed Zakaria on CNN, 29 January 2010, Press Room, www.kingabdullah.jo.

42. Marwan Muasher, The Arab Center, pp. 212–214, 217.

43. See statements by Husayn as reported in al-Dustur, 24 August 1993 and 13 October 1993, and by Abdallah as reported in al-Ra'y, 29 June 2002.

44. National Agenda, 2006–2015: The Jordan We Strive For, http://www.nationalagenda.jo.

45. "Al-sahafa wal-islah — niqash al-hawiyya wal-musharaka al-Filastiniyya" [The Press and Reform — A Debate on Identity and Palestinian Participation], 21 May 2005, www.ammannet.net; Ghayth Tarawina, "His Majesty Meets with Senators," al-Ra'y, 3 June 2005; Marc Lynch, "In Jordan, the Knives Are Out for the National Agenda," The Daily Star, 16 November 2005.

46. Letter from King Abdallah to Prime Minister Adnan Badran, 16 June 2005, in Royal Speeches and Letters, www.kingabdullah.jo.

47. Marwan Muasher, "Jordan's Future Agenda," Jordan Business (March 2009), p. 48.

48. Marwan Muasher, "Jordan's Future Agenda," pp. 48–49.

49. A few months later Abdallah dismissed the chief of domestic intelligence, Muhammad Dhahabi, a stalwart of the East Banker elite, as a way of settling scores and preserving his authority.

50. All the Jordanian dailies for a few days in early August carried numerous reports and analyses of the king's remarks made at the army headquarters on 4 August 2009, see, e.g., al-Ra'y, al-Dustur, al-Arab al-Yawm, 5, 8 August 2009, and Jordan Times, 6, 7 August 2009.

51. "Article 8, Treaty of Peace between the Hashemite Kingdom of Jordan and the State of Israel, 26 October 1994," www.kinghussein.gov.jo/peacetreaty.html.

52. See Tariq al-Tall, "Al-Ustura wa-siwa al-fahm fi al-alaqat al-Urduniyya-al-Filastiniyya" [Myth and Misunderstanding in Jordanian-Palestinian Relations], al-Siyasa al-Filastiniyya, vol. 3, no. 12 (Fall 1996), pp. 154–159.

53. Michael Slackman, "Some Palestinian Jordanians Lose Citizenship," New York Times, 13 March 2010.

54. Hassan Barari, "Mishal in Amman," Jordan Times, 1 September 2009.

55. Hassan Barari, "Jordan: An Arena for Hamas?" Jordan Times, 15 September 2009.

56. King Abdallah's interview with Ghassan Charbel in al-Hayat, Part II, 10 November 2009, Press Room, www.kingabdullah.jo.

57. Hussein Ibish, What's Wrong with the One-State Agenda?, pp. 121–122.

58. Hassan Barari, "Does Jordan Have an Option," Jordan Times, 1 December 2009.

59. Salim Tamari, "The Bi-nationalist Lure."

60. Mustafa Hamarneh, Rosemary Hollis, and Khalil Shikaki, Jordanian-Palestinian Relations: Where To? Four Scenarios for the Future (London: The Royal Institute of International Affairs, 1997), pp. 108–111.

61. Ben Kaspit, "The King's Initiative: A Hashemite-Palestinian Kingdom," Maariv, 18 May 2007.

62. King Abdallah, interview in al-Ahram, as reproduced in translation in Jordan Times, 10 May 2007, and Editorial in al-Ra'y, 12 June 2007.

63. See, e.g., Musa Kaylani, "Some People Never Learn," Jordan Times, 27 May 2007.

64. Ian Bremmer, "A Difficult Plan Whose Time Has Come," New York Times, 15 June 2007.

65. Marwan Muasher, The Arab Center, p. 229.

## Chapter 6. The Revival of the Two-State Imperative

1. Ahmad Khalidi, "Palestinians Can Play the Israeli Game," The Guardian, 24 August 2005.

2. Some thought this was positive, others found it disturbing, but the trend itself was undeniable. See in this regard two brilliant analyses: Bilal al-Hasan, "Khiyaran yutasari'an: dawlat al-daffa al-gharbiyya am wahdat al-qadiyya al-Filastiniyya" [Two Choices Wrestle One Another: The State of the West Bank or the Unity of the Palestinian Cause], al-Sharq al-Awsat, 30 August 2009; and Hamada Fara'ana, "Hutwatan lil-imam wusulan lil-thalitha" [Two Steps Forward Leading to a Third], al-Ayyam, 2 September 2009.

3. Hamada Fara'ana, "Two Steps Forward Leading to a Third."

4. Hamada Fara'ana, "Two Steps Forward Leading to a Third."

5. "Program of the 13th PNA Government (The 'Fayyad Plan')," Maan News Agency, 22 November 2009, www.maannews.net/eng/Print.aspx?ID=238206; Isabel Kershner, "Palestinian Leader Maps Plan for Separate State," New York Times, 25 August 2009.

6. "Program of the 13th PNA Government (The 'Fayyad Plan')."

7. Sa'ib Ariqat, The Political Situation in Light of the Developments with the US Administration and Israeli Government and Hamas Continued Coup d'Etat: Recommendations and Options (Jerusalem: The Center for Democracy and Community Development, December,

2009). Arabic version: *Taqrir hass, al-mawqif al-siyasi ala du' al-tatawwurat ma' al-idara al-Amrikiyya wal-hukuma al-isra'iliyya wa-istimrar inqilab Hamas: al-tawsiyat wal-khiyarat.*

8. Ghassan Khatib, "Two Alternatives: Backward or Forward," *Bitterlemons: Palestinian-Israeli Crossfire,* 23 November 2009, www.bitterlemons.org.

9. Leslie Susser, "Salam Fayyad: The Palestinian with a Plan for Statehood," www .jta.org/news/article/2010/03/08.

10. Ali Jarbawi, "What Is Israel Afraid Of?," *Bitterlemons: Palestinian-Israeli Crossfire,* 15 March 2010, www.bitterlemons.org.

11. See speech by Khalid Mash'al on 11 October 2009 on TV-Middle East, as in Mideastwire, 14 October 2009; Janine Zacharia, "Palestinian Authority Cracks Down on Mosques to Promote Moderate Islam," *Washington Post,* 15 December 2010.

12. Ghada Karmi, "Where Next for Palestinians?" *Bitterlemons: Palestinian-Israeli Crossfire,* 23 November 2009, www.bitterlemons.org.

13. Hani al-Masri, "Waqf al-mufawadat bidun badil aswa min isti'nafiha" [Stopping Negotiations without an Alternative Is Worse Than Resuming Them], *al-Ayyam,* 8 December 2009; Azmi Bishara, "An Honorable Exit," *al-Ahram Weekly,* 10–16 December 2009.

14. Leslie Susser, "Salam Fayyad."

15. Editorial in *al-Quds al-Arabi,* 5 August 2009; Urayb al-Rantawi, "His Excellency 'The Chief of Negotiators'" [Fahamat "kabir al-mufawidin"], www.alqudscenter. com, 9 December 2009; Salah al-Naami, "Fatah Riven with Fights," *al-Ahram Weekly,* 9–15 December 2010; Hussein Agha and Robert Malley, "Nothing Left to Talk About," *New York Times,* 14 December 2010.

16. Nathan Brown, *After Abu Mazin? Letting the Scales Fall from Our Eyes,* Carnegie Endowment for International Peace, Web Commentary, 10 November 2009, www .carnegieendowment.org/publications/index.cfm?fa=view&id=24131.

17. Yezid Sayigh, "Hamas Rule in Gaza: Three Years On," *Middle East Brief,* no. 41, Brandeis University, Crown Center for Middle East Studies, March 2010, pp. 1, 6.

18. See, e.g., Speech by Mahmud Abbas, 11 October 2009, as in *al-Ayyam,* 12 October 2009.

19. Hamada Fara'ana, "Al-sira' al-Fathawi al-Hamasawi" [The Fatah-Hamas Conflict], *al-Ayyam,* 28 October 2009.

20. Khaled Amayreh, "Embarrassed and Denounced," *al-Ahram Weekly,* 8–14 October 2009.

21. "Negotiations as [a way of] life" was a slogan used by Sa'ib Ariqat for which he became the target of endless ridicule, mainly, but not only, by Fatah's critics.

22. Hani al-Masri, "Awdat al-wa'i" [The Return of Consciousness], *al-Ayyam,* 10 November 2009.

23. Yossi Alpher, "The Best Option," *Bitterlemons: Palestinian-Israeli Crossfire,* 15 March 2010, www.bitterlemons.org.

24. Howard Schneider, "Palestinian Premier Speaks at Israeli Conference," *Washington Post,* 3 February 2010.

25. Ehud Yaari, "Armistice Now: An Interim Agreement for Israel and Palestine," *Foreign Affairs,* March/April 2010, p. 57.

26. Text of Statement by the Foreign Affairs Council of the European Union, 8 December 2009, www.consilium.europa.eu/ueDocs/cms_Data/docs/pressdata/EN/foraff/111829.pdf

27. Text of Quartet Statement on Israel/Palestine, 19 March 2010, www.themajlis.org/2010/03/19/transcript.

28. Mazal Mualem, "Kadima Warms to Mofaz Plan for Hamas Talks, Despite Livni Opposition," *Haaretz*, 10 November 2009.

29. Ari Shavit, "Hamas Still Wants to Liberate 'All of Palestine,'" *Haaretz*, 17 December 2009.

30. Gadi Taub, "Kadima [which in Hebrew means 'Forward'] Is Walking Backward," *Yediot Aharonot*, 23 March 2010.

31. Shlomo Avineri, "Israel Needs a Plan B if Mideast Talks Fail," *Haaretz*, 30 November 2010.

32. Stuart Cohen, *Flaws in General Eiland's Alternatives*, BESA Center Perspectives Papers, No. 99 (Bar Ilan University, The Begin-Sadat Center for Strategic Studies, 7 February 2010).

33. Ehud Barak, "Israel 2010: Strategic Threats, Strategic Opportunities," lecture at the Washington Institute for Near East Policy, 26 February 2010, www.washingtoninstitute.org/templateC07.php?CID=515.

34. Ehud Barak, "Israel 2010: Strategic Threats, Strategic Opportunities."

35. Urayb Rantawi, "Mitchell khasara jawla . . . fama huwa masir al-harb idhan?" [Mitchell Lost a Round . . . But What Then Is the Fate of the Fight?], al-Dustur, 20 September; Saleh al-Naami, "Band Aid Proposal," al-Ahram Weekly, 19–25 November 2009; Hani al-Masri, "Min al-mubakkir na'i al-mufawadat" [From the Start We Have Understood the Negotiations], al-Ayyam, 24 November 2009; Hani al-Masri, "Stopping Negotiations without an Alternative Is Worse Than Resuming Them," al-Ayyam, 8 December 2009.

36. Akiva Eldar, "Palestinian PM to *Haaretz*: We Will Have a State Next Year," *Haaretz*, 2 April 2010.

37. Aaron Miller, "US, Israel Get Back into the Ring," *Politico*, 4 April 2010.

38. *Washington Post*, 9 January 2010.

39. Ehud Yaari, "Armistice Now," pp. 50–62.

40. Ehud Yaari, "Armistice Now," pp. 52–53, 60.

41. Ehud Yaari, "Armistice Now," pp. 61–62.

42. Palestinian Center for Public Opinion, Poll no. 168, 4 November 2009; PSR, Palestinian Public Opinion Poll No. 35, 23 March 2010; David Pollock, "Palestinian Public Opinion: Tactically Flexible, Strategically Ambitious," *Washington Institute for Near East Policy, Policy Watch*, no. 1731, 9 December 2010.

## Conclusion

1. Nathan Brown, *Sunset for the Two-State Solution*, Carnegie Endowment for International Peace, May 2008; *After Abu Mazin? Letting the Scales Fall from Our Eyes*,

Web Commentary, Carnegie Endowment for International Peace, 10 November 2009.

2. Nathan Brown, *Sunset for the Two-State Solution*.

3. Hussein Ibish, interview with Jeffrey Goldberg in *The Atlantic*, 3 November 2009.

4. Abba Eban, "Peace: The Only Alternative Left" and "Israel Has No Alternative to Rabin's Realism," *New Perspectives Quarterly*, vol. 10, no. 1 (Fall 1993) and vol. 13, no.1 (Winter 1996), as quoted in Jenab Tutunji and Kamal Khaldi, "A Binational State in Palestine," pp. 35, 55.

5. Hussein Ibish, "Against a One-State Solution," Informed Comment in www .juancole.com/2009/11/ibish-against-one-state-solution.html,

6. Quoted in Benjamin Pogrund, "Different Histories, Different Futures," p. 95.

7. Quoted in Tamar Hermann, "The Bi-national Idea in Israel/Palestine," p. 394.

8. Benjamin Pogrund, "Different Histories, Different Futures," p. 95.

9. Aaron David Miller, *The Much Too Promised Land*, pp. 31, 37, 44–45. "Gulliver's troubles" was adapted by Miller from Stanley Hoffman's *Gulliver's Troubles, or the Setting of American Foreign Policy* (New York: McGraw Hill, 1968).

10. Martin Indyk, *Innocent Abroad*, pp. 306, 339.

11. Ahmad Khalidi, "Palestinians Can Play the Israeli Game," *The Guardian*, 24 August 2005.

12. Nathan Brown, *Palestine and Israel: Time for Plan B*, Carnegie Endowment for International Peace, February 2009.

13. Walter Russell Mead, "Israel's Strategic Failure," *American Interest Online*, 3 June 2010.

14. Nathan Brown, *Palestine and Israel: Time for Plan B*.

15. Kenneth Stein, "Caplan's *Contested Histories* Considered," Review Essay in *Middle East Journal*, vol. 64, no. 2 (Spring 2010), pp. 299–300.

16. Dennis Ross and David Makovsky, *Myths, Illusions, and Peace: Finding a New Direction for America in the Middle East* (New York: Viking, 2009), pp. 314–315.

17. *Haaretz*, 13 March 2011.

18. Ethan Bronner, "Prominent Israelis Will Propose a Peace Plan," *New York Times*, 4 April 2011.

19. Jonathan Freedland, "Where's the Goldstone Report into Sri Lanka, Congo, Darfur — or Britain?" *The Guardian*, 6 April 2011.

20. See, for example, Maj. Gen. (Ret.) Amos Yadlin, "Winds of Change in the Middle East: An Israeli Perspective," Speech at the Washington Institute for Near East Policy, 30 March 2011.

21. *Jerusalem Post*, 29 March 2011; available online at www.maannews.net/eng, 7 April 2011.

22. Dore Gold, "Israel's Requirements for Defensible Borders in a Rapidly Changing Middle East," Prepared Statement before the Foreign Affairs Committee of the US House of Representatives, Washington, DC, 5 April 2011.

# BIBLIOGRAPHY

## Primary Sources

ISRAEL

"The Declaration of the Establishment of the State of Israel," 14 May 1948, www.mfa
.gov.il.

*Divrei Haknesset*, Third Session of the Seventh Knesset, Meeting 284, 16 March 1972,
pp. 1842–1843.

"Israeli Private Response on Palestinian Refugees," Taba, 23 January 2001, in *Le Monde
Diplomatique*, English Edition, http://mondediplo.com/focus/mideast/israeli
responserefugees200101.

"Speech by PM Ariel Sharon at the Herzliya Conference," 4 December 2002, www
.mfa.gov.il.

"The Geneva Accord," www.geneva-accord.org/mainmenu/english.

"The Official Summation of the Orr Commission Report," as printed in *Haaretz* Online
English Language Edition, 2 September 2003, http://www.jewishvirtuallibrary
.org/jsource/Society_&_Culture/OrCommissionReport.html.

"Summary of the Opinion Concerning Unauthorized Outposts," 10 March 2005,
compiled by former prosecutor Talya Sason, www.mfa.gov.il/MFA/Government/
Law/Legal.

"Address by PM Ariel Sharon at the Fourth Herzliya Conference," 18 December 2003,
www.mfa.gov.il.

"PM Sharon Addresses the UN General Assembly," 15 September 2005, www.mfa.gov.il.

"Address by Interim PM Olmert on Presenting the New Government to the Knesset," 4
May 2006, www.pmo.gov.il.

"PM Ehud Olmert Speech at the Special Knesset Session on the Condition of the Gush
Katif Evacuees," 27 June 2006, www.mfa.gov.il.

"Address by Vice Prime Minister and Minister of Foreign Affairs Tzipi Livni at the
Annapolis Conference," 27 November 2007, www.mfa.gov.il.

"Address by Prime Minister Ehud Olmert at the Annapolis Conference," 27 November,
2007, www.mfa.gov.il.

"Rabin Memorial: Address by PM Ehud Olmert at Special Knesset Session," 10
November 2008, www.mfa.gov.il.

"Prime Minister Benjamin Netanyahu's Speech at the Begin-Sadat Center at Bar-Ilan
University," 14 June 2009, www.pmo.gov.il.

"Prime Minister Benjamin Netanyahu's Speech at the Opening of the Knesset Winter
Session," 11 October 2010, www.mfa.gov.il/MFA/Government/Speeches.

"Prime Minister Netanyahu Addresses the General Assembly of the Jewish Federa-

tions of North America," 8 November 2010, www.mfa.gov.il/MFA/Government/
Speeches.

"Excerpts from Prime Minister Netanyahu's Statement to the Knesset," 1 December
2010, www.mfa.gov.il/MFA/Government/Speeches.

Ehud Barak, "Israel 2010: Strategic Threats, Strategic Opportunities," lecture at the
Washington Institute for Near East Policy, 26 February 2010, www.washington
institute.org/templateC07.php?CID=515.

"General Debate of the 65th General Assembly on 28 September 2010, Speech by
Deputy Prime Minister and Foreign Minister, Avigdor Lieberman," http://www
.israel-un.org/statements-at-the-united-nations/general-assembly/315-ga65gd
28092010.

Ephraim Ya'ar and Tamar Hermann, War and Peace Index (September 2009), Steinmetz
Center for Peace Research, Tel Aviv University.

Settlers Opinion Poll, March 2010, by Truman Institute for the Advancement of
Peace, Hebrew University, Jerusalem, in www.truman.huji.ac.il/poll-view.
asp?id=327.


PALESTINIANS

"PLO Charter (al-mithaq al-qawmi) of 1964"; "PLO Charter (al-mithaq al-watani) of
1968," www. fatehmedia.net/ar/m-t-f.

"Al-barnamij al-siyasi al-marhali li-munazzamat al-tahrir al-Filasiniyya" [The Phased Political Program of the PLO], approved by the PNC on 8 June 1974, www.fatehmedia
.net/ar/m-t-f.

"Speech by Salah Khalaf at the 17th PNC, 22–29 November 1984," full text in Shu'un
Filastiniyya, November–December 1984, pp. 174–184.

"Wathiqat i'lan al-istiqlal" [Declaration of Independence], 15 November 1988, www
.fatehmedia.net/ar/m-t-f.

"Mashru'al-bayan al-siyasi sadara an al-majlis al-watani al-Filastini" [Political Statement
of the 19th PNC], 12–15 November 1988, in Filastin al-Thawra, 20 November 1988,
pp. 6–9.

"Mulahazat wa-as'ila Filastiniyya hawla al-afkar al-Amrikiyya" [Palestinian Observations
and Questions on the American Ideas (The Clinton Parameters)], text as in
al-Ayyam, 2 January 2001.

"The 44 Reasons Why Fatah Movement Rejects the Proposals Made by US President
Clinton," January 2001, Jerusalem Media and Communications Centre, www
.jmcc.org/documents.

"Palestinian Paper on Refugees," Taba, 22 January 2001, in Le Monde Diplomatique,
English Edition, http://mondediplo.com/focus/mideast/palestinianrefugees
200101.

"Ayalon-Nusseibeh Declaration," in Journal of Palestine Studies, vol. 33, no. 2 (Winter
2004), p. 158.

"Wathiqat al-wifaq al-watani" [Document of National Reconciliation, or the "Prisoners
Document"], 28 June 2006, www.falasteen.com/article.

"Al-tasawwur al-mustaqbali lil-Arab al-Filastiniyyin fi Isra'il" 2006 [The Future Vision of the Palestinian Arabs in Israel 2006], The National Committee for the Heads of the Arab Local Authorities in Israel, www.arab-lac.org.

"Barnamij hukumat ra'is al-wuzara' al-mukallaf Isma'il Haniyya" [Program of the Government of Prime Minister Elect, Isma'il Haniyya], 17 March 2007, www.al-jazeera.net/News.

Al-barnamij al-siyasi liharakat al-tahrir al-watani al-Filastini, "Fath" [The Political Program of the Palestinian National Liberation Movement, "Fath"], Sixth General Conference, August 2009, www.fatehconf.ps.

Sa'ib Ariqat, The Political Situation in Light of the Developments with the US Administration and Israeli Government and Hamas Continued Coup d'Etat: Recommendations and Options (The Center for Democracy and Community Development, Jerusalem, December, 2009). Arabic version: Taqrir hass, al-mawqif al-siyasi ala du' al-tatawwurat ma' al-idara al-Amrikiyya wal-hukuma al-Isra'iliyya wa-istimrar inqilab Hamas: al-tawsiyat wal-khiyarat.

Palestinian Center for Policy and Survey Research, PSR—Survey Research Unit: Joint Palestinian-Israeli Press Release, 20 March 2010, www.pcpsr.org/survey/polls/2010.

Palestinian Center for Policy and Survey Research, PSR, Palestinian Public Opinion Poll No. (35), 23 March 2010.

Palestinian Center for Public Opinion, Poll no. 168, 4 November 2009.

Speech by Mahmud Abbas, 11 October 2009, as in al-Ayyam, 12 October 2009.

Speech by Khalid Mash'al on 11 October 2009 on TV-Middle East, as in Mideastwire, 14 October 2009.

"Program of the 13th PNA Government (The 'Fayyad Plan')," Maan News Agency, www.maannews.net/eng/Print.aspx?ID=238206.

JORDAN

Official Arabic text of Husayn's speech at Algiers Summit, 7 June 1988 (Moshe Dayan Center Archives).

"Treaty of Peace between the Hashemite Kingdom of Jordan and the State of Israel," 26 October 1994, www.kinghussein.gov.jo/peacetreaty.html.

"Letter from King Abdallah to Prime Minister Adnan Badran," 16 June 2005, in Royal Speeches and Letters, www.kingabdullah.jo.

National Agenda, 2006–2015: The Jordan We Strive For, http:www.nationalagenda.jo.

"King Abdallah's interview with Randa Habib," AFP, 16 May 2009, Press Room, www.kingabdullah.jo.

"King Abdallah's interview with La Republica," 19 October 2009, Press Room, www.kingabdullah.jo.

"King Abdallah's interview with Ghassan Charbel in al-Hayat," Part 2, 10 November 2009, Press Room, www.kingabdullah.jo.

"King Abdallah's interview with Fareed Zakaria on CNN," 29 January 2010, Press Room, www.kingabdullah.jo.

UNITED STATES
"Speech by Colin Powell at the University of Louisville," 19 November 2001, full text in
    The Guardian, 20 November 2001.
"Letter from US President George W. Bush to Prime Minister Ariel Sharon," 14 April
    2004, www.mfa.gov.il.
"Speech by Senator Barack Obama at AIPAC Policy Conference 2008," 4 June 2008,
    www.aipac.org/Publications.
"Text of President Obama's speech to the UN General Assembly," New York Times, 23
    September 2009.
"Press Statement by Secretary of State Hillary Clinton," 25 November 2009, www.
    state.gov/secretary.
"Secretary of State Hillary Clinton, Remarks at the 2010 AIPAC Policy Conference," 22
    March 2010, www.state.gov/secretary.


UNITED NATIONS
"UN Security Council Resolution 1397, 12 March 2002," www.un.org/Docs.
"Annex VII: Treatment of Property Affected by Events Since 1963," in the Annan Plan for
    Cyprus, www.hri.org/docs/annan/.
"UN Security Council Resolution 1515, 19 November 2003," available online at http://
    www.un.org/Docs/sc/unsc_resolutions03.html.
"Text of Quartet Statement on Israel/Palestine," 19 March 2010, www.themajlis.
    org/2010/03/19/transcript.


EUROPEAN UNION
"Text of Statement by the Foreign Affairs Council of the European Union," 8 Decem-
    ber 2009, www.consilium.europa.eu/ueDocs/cms_Data/docs/pressdata/EN/
    foraff/111829.pdf.


## Collections of Documents

Abdul Hadi, Mahdi (ed.), Documents on Palestine, vol. 1 (Jerusalem: PASSIA, 1997).
Geddes, Charles (ed.), A Documentary History of the Arab-Israeli Conflict (New York:
    Praeger, 1991).
Lapidot, Ruth, and Moshe Hirsch (eds.), The Arab-Israeli Conflict and Its Resolution:
    Selected Documents (Dordrecht: Nijhoff, 1992).
Laqueur, Walter, and Barry Rubin (eds.), The Israel-Arab Reader: A Documentary History of
    the Middle East Conflict, Fifth Revised and Updated Edition (New York: Penguin,
    1995).
Mahafza, Ali (ed.), Ashara a'wam min al-kifah wal-bina [Ten Years of Struggle and
    Building]: A Collection of Speeches by King Husayn from 1977–1987, (Amman: Markaz
    al-kutub al-Urdunni, 1988).
Palestine Boundaries, 1833–1947, vol. 3 (Archive Editions, 1989).

The Palestine Papers, as published jointly by The Guardian and al-Jazeera Television in
    January 2011; see www.ajtransparency.com.
Records of Jordan (R of J), 1919–1965, vol. 1: 1919–1922 (Archive Editions, 1996).
Rabinovich, Itamar, and Jehuda Reinharz (eds.), Israel in the Middle East: Documents and
    Readings on Society, Politics, and Foreign Relations, Pre-1948 to the Present, Second Edi-
    tion (Waltham, MA: Brandeis University Press, 2008).
Zittrain Eisenberg, Laura, and Neil Caplan, Negotiating Arab-Israeli Peace: Patterns,
    Problems, Possibilities, Second Edition (Indianapolis: Indiana University Press,
    2010), documents online at http://naip-documents.blogspot.com/2009/09/
    document-7.html.

## Newspapers

al-Ahram (Cairo)
al-Ahram Weekly (Cairo)
al-Arab al-Yawm (Amman)
al-Arabi (Cairo)
The Atlantic
al-Ayyam (Ramallah)
The Daily Star (Beirut)
al-Dustur (Amman)
Filastin al-Thawra (Nicosia)
Gulf News
The Guardian
Haaretz
al-Hadaf (Beirut)
al-Hayat (London)
al-Hayat al-Jadida (Ramallah)
The International Herald Tribune
The Jerusalem Post
Kull al-Arab (Nazareth)
Los Angeles Times
Maariv
al-Nahar (Beirut)
Newsweek
New York Times
al-Quds (Jerusalem)
al-Quds al- Arabi (London)
al-Ra'y (Amman)
al-Thawra (Damascus)
al-Safir (Beirut)
al-Sharq al-Awsat (London)
The Telegraph

Time
Wall Street Journal
Washington Post
al-Watan al- Arabi (Paris)
al-Yawn al-Sabi' (Cairo)
Yediot Aharonot


## Secondary Sources

Abunimah, Ali, One Country: A Bold Proposal to End the Israeli-Palestinian Impasse (New
    York: Metropolitan Books, 2006).
Abu-Odeh, Adnan, Jordanians, Palestinians and the Hashemite Kingdom in the Middle East
    Peace Process (Washington DC: US Institute of Peace, 1999).
Abu-Sitta, Salman, "The Right of Return: Sacred, Legal and Possible," in Naseer Aruri
    (ed.), Palestinian Refugees: The Right of Return (London: Pluto Press, 2001).
Agha, Hussein, and Robert Malley, "Camp David: The Tragedy of Errors," New York
    Review of Books, vol. 48, no. 13, 9 August 2001.
Agha, Hussein, and Robert Malley, "Israel and Palestine: Can They Start Over?" New
    York Review of Books, vol. 56, no. 19, 3 December 2009.
Ajami, Fouad, "The End of Pan-Arabism," Foreign Affairs, vol. 57, no. 2 (Winter
    1978–79).
Ajami, Fouad, "Palestine's Deliverance," Wall Street Journal, 27 June 2002.
Akram, Susan, "Reinterpreting Palestinian Refugee Rights under International Law,"
    in Naseer Aruri (ed.), Palestinian Refugees: The Right of Return (London: Pluto Press,
    2001).
Alpher, Yossi, "Green Line and Red Line," Bitterlemons: Palestinian-Israeli Crossfire, 19
    January 2004, www.bitterlemons.org.
Alpher, Yossi, "A Blow for the Chances of Peace," Bitterlemons: Palestinian-Israeli
    Crossfire, 29 June 2009, www.bitterlemons.org.
Alpher, Yossi, "The Best Option," Bitterlemons: Palestinian-Israeli Crossfire, 15 March
    2010, www.bitterlemons.org.
"An Alternative Future: An Exchange," New York Review of Books, vol. 50, no. 19, 4
    December 2003.
Amayreh, Khaled, "No Waiving the Right of Return," al-Ahram Weekly, 25–31 January
    2001.
Amayreh, Khaled, "Embarrassed and Denounced," al-Ahram Weekly, 8–14 October
    2009.
Amayreh, Khaled, "Fatah Tells Abbas to Play It Tough," al-Ahram Weekly, 2–8 Decem-
    ber 2010.
Anderson, Benedict, Imagined Communities: Reflections on the Origin and Spread of
    Nationalism, Revised Edition (London and New York: Verso, 1991).
Ariqat, Sa'ib, "The Question of Refugees Is the Essence of the Palestinian Question,"
    interview in Palestine-Israel Journal, vol. 15, no. 4 (2008) and vol. 16, no. 1 (2009).

Aruri, Naseer, "Towards Convening a Congress of Return and Self-Determination," in Naseer Aruri (ed.), *Palestinian Refugees: The Right of Return* (London: Pluto Press, 2001).

Ashton, Nigel, *King Hussein of Jordan: A Political Life* (New Haven: Yale University Press, 2008).

Barak, Oren, "The Failure of the Israeli-Palestinian Peace Process," *Journal of Peace Research*, vol. 42, no. 6 (November 2005).

Bareli, Avi, "Forgetting Europe: Points of Departure in the Debate on Zionism and Colonialism," in Tuvia Friling (ed.), *An Answer to a Post-Zionist Colleague* (Tel Aviv: Yediot Aharonot, 2003) (Hebrew).

Beilin, Yossi, "An Israeli View: Solving the Refugee Problem," *Bitterlemons: Palestinian-Israeli Crossfire*, 31 December 2001, www.bitterlemons.org.

Ben Ami, Shlomo, *A Front without a Rearguard: A Voyage to the Boundaries of the Peace Process* (Tel Aviv: Yediot Aharonot, 2004) (Hebrew).

Ben-Meir, Yehuda, and Olena Bagno-Moldavsky, *Vox Populi: Trends in Israeli Public Opinion on National Security, 2004–2009*, Institute for National Security Studies, Memorandum 106, November, 2010.

Benvenisti, Eyal, "International Law and the Right of Return," *Palestine-Israel Journal*, vol. 15, no. 4 (2008) and vol. 16, no. 1 (2009).

Bishara, Azmi, "Reflections on October 2000: A Landmark in Jewish-Arab Relations in Israel," *Journal of Palestine Studies*, vol. 30, no. 3 (Spring 2001).

Bishara, Azmi, "The Essential Agenda," *al-Ahram Weekly*, 4–10 March 2004.

Bishara, Azmi, "An Honorable Exit," *al-Ahram Weekly*, 10–16 December 2009.

Bogaard, Matthijs, "Power Sharing in South Africa: The African National Congress as a Consociational Party," in Sid Noel (ed.), *From Power Sharing to Democracy: Post-Conflict Institutions in Ethnically Divided Societies* (Quebec City: McGill-Queens University Press, 2005).

Brown, Nathan, *Sunset for the Two-State Solution*, Carnegie Endowment for International Peace, May 2008.

Brown, Nathan, *Palestine and Israel: Time for Plan B*, Carnegie Endowment for International Peace, February 2009.

Calhoun, Craig, *Nations Matter: Culture, History, and the Cosmopolitan Dream* (London and New York: Routledge, 2007).

Caplan, Neil, *The Lausanne Conference, 1949: A Case Study in Middle East Peacemaking* (Tel Aviv University, Moshe Dayan Center for Middle Eastern and African Studies, Occasional Paper 113, 1993).

Caplan, Neil, *The Israel-Palestine Conflict; Contested Histories* (Malden, MA; Oxford: Wiley-Blackwell, 2010).

Cohen, Rich, *Israel Is Real* (New York: Farrar, Straus and Giroux, 2009).

Cohen, Stuart, *Flaws in General Eiland's Alternatives*, BESA Center Perspectives Papers, No. 99 (Bar Ilan University, Begin-Sadat Center for Strategic Studies, 7 February 2010).

Cotler, Irwin, "Beyond Durban: The Conference against Racism That Became a Racist

Conference against Jews," *Global Jewish Agenda* (December 2001), www.jafi
.org.il/agenda/2001/english/wk3-22/6.asp.

Cotler, Irwin, "Durban's Troubling Legacy One Year Later: Twisting the Cause of
International Human Rights against the Jewish People," *Jerusalem Issue Brief*, vol.
2, no. 5 (Jerusalem Center for Public Affairs, August 2002).

Doumani, Beshara, "Palestine Versus the Palestinians? The Iron Laws and the Ironies
of a People Denied," *Journal of Palestine Studies*, vol. 36, no. 4 (Summer 2007).

Eiland, Giora, *Rethinking the Two-State Solution*, Washington Institute for Near East
Policy, Policy Focus, No. 88 (September 2008).

Eiland, Giora, *Regional Alternatives to the Two-State Solution*, BESA Memorandum No. 4
(Bar-Ilan University, Begin-Sadat Center for Strategic Studies, January 2010).

Eldar, Akiva, and Idith Zertal, *Lords of the Land: The Settlers and the State of Israel, 1967–
2004* (Tel Aviv: Kinneret, Zmora-Bitan, Dvir, 2004) (Hebrew).

Ezzat, Dina, "Beyond the Wall," *al-Ahram Weekly*, 24–30 December 2009.

Fara'ana, Hamada, "Two Steps Forward Leading to a Third" [*Hutwatan lil-imam
wusulan lil-thalitha*], *al-Ayyam*, 2 September 2009.

Fara'ana, Hamada, "The Fatah-Hamas Conflict" [*Al-sira' al-fathawi al- al-hamasawi*],
*al-Ayyam*, 28 October 2009.

Galnoor, Itzhak, *The Partition of Palestine: Decision Crossroads in the Zionist Movement*
(Albany: SUNY Press, 1995).

Gazit, Shlomo, *The Carrot and the Stick: Israel's Policy in Judea an Samaria, 1967–1968*
(Washington, DC: Bnai Brith Books, 1995).

Gelber, Yoav, *Jewish-Transjordanian Relations, 1921–1948* (London: Frank Cass, 1997).

Gelber, Yoav, *Independence Versus Nakba* (Tel Aviv: Kinneret, Zmora-Bitan, Dvir, 2004)
(Hebrew).

Gelber, Yoav, "The History of Zionist Historiography: From Apologetics to Denial,"
in Benny Morris (ed.), *Making Israel* (Ann Arbor: University of Michigan Press,
2007).

*Getting to the Territorial Endgame of an Israeli-Palestinian Peace Settlement: A Special Report by
the Israeli-Palestinian Workshop of the Baker Institute's Conflict Resolution Forum*
(Houston: Rice University, James A. Baker III Institute for Public Policy, 2010).

Ghanem, As'ad, *The Palestinian-Arab Minority in Israel, 1948–2000: A Political Study*
(Albany: SUNY Press, 2001).

Giliomee, Hermann, *The Afrikaners: Biography of a People* (Charlottesville: University of
Virginia Press, 2003).

Gorenberg, Gershom, *The Accidental Empire: Israel and the Birth of the Settlements, 1967–1977*
(New York: Times Books, 2006).

Gorny, Yosef, *Zionism and the Arabs 1882–1948: A Study of Ideology* (Oxford: Clarendon
Press, 1987).

Gubser, Peter, *Politics and Change in al-Karak, Jordan* (Oxford University Press, 1973).

Hafez, Ziad, "The Palestine One-State Solution: Report on the Conference Held in
Boston, Massachusetts, March 2009," *Contemporary Arab Affairs*, vol. 2, no. 4
(October–December 2009).

Hagopian, Elaine, "Preface," in Naseer Aruri (ed.), *Palestinian Refugees: The Right of Return* (London: Pluto Press, 2001).

Hamarneh, Mustafa, Rosemary Hollis, and Khalil Shikaki, *Jordanian-Palestinian Relations: Where To? Four Scenarios for the Future* (London: Royal Institute of International Affairs, 1997).

Hanieh, Akram, "The Camp David Papers," *Journal of Palestine Studies*, vol. 30, no. 2 (Winter 2001).

Hart, Alan, *Arafat: A Political Biography*, Revised Edition (London: Sidgwick and Jackson, 1994).

al-Hasan, Bilal, "Isra'il wa-khittat al-khud'a al-jadida" [Israel and (Its) New Plan of Deception] *al-Quds*, 15 June 2009.

al-Hasan, Bilal, "Khiyaran yutasari'an: dawlat al-daffa al-gharbiyya am wahdat al-qadiyya al-Filastiniyya" [Two Choices Wrestle One Another: The State of the West Bank or the Unity of the Palestinian Cause], *al-Sharq al-Awsat*, 30 August 2009.

al-Hasan, Khalid, *Al-ittifaq al-Urdunni-al-Filastini lil-taharruk mushtarak "Amman — 11 February 1985"* [The Jordanian-Palestinian Agreement for Joint Action "Amman — 11 February 1985"] (Amman: Dar al-jalil lil-nashr, 1985).

Heller, Joseph, *The Birth of Israel, 1945–1949: Ben-Gurion and His Critics* (Gainesville: University Press of Florida, 2003).

Hermann, Tamar, "The Bi-national Idea in Israel/Palestine: Past and Present," *Nations and Nationalism*, vol. 11, no. 3, (2005).

Hornstein Tomić, Caroline, "State-Building and Ethnicity in the Western Balkan Region," discussion paper presented at Brenthurst Foundation "Fault Lines" Conference (Jerusalem, February 2010).

Ibish, Hussein, *What's Wrong with the One–State Agenda?* (Washington, DC: American Task Force on Palestine, 2009).

Inbar, Efraim, *The Rise and Demise of the Two-State Paradigm* (Bar Ilan University, Begin-Sadat Center for Strategic Studies, Mideast Security and Policy Studies, No. 79, April 2009).

Indyk, Martin, *Innocent Abroad: An Intimate Account of American Peace Diplomacy in the Middle East* (New York: Simon and Schuster, 2009).

al-Jarbawi, Ali, "Hawla 'al-wathiqa al-Swisriyya': li-kai la nastamirr fi tahn al- hawa" [On the "Swiss (Geneva) Document": So that We Do Not Continue to Tread Water (Grind Air)], *al-Hayat*, 21 October 2003.

al-Jarbawi, Ali, "We Will Give You More of Us," *Bitterlemons: Palestinian-Israeli Crossfire*, 22 December 2003, www.bitterlemons.org.

al-Jarbawi, Ali, "The Remaining Palestinian Options," *The Arab World Geographer / Le Geographe du monde arabe*, vol. 8, no. 3 (2005).

al-Jarbawi, Ali, "Hawla al-ajinda al-kharijiyya lil-'islah': al-hala al-Filastiniyya" [On a Foreign Affairs Agenda for 'Reform'; The Palestinian Situation], *al-Mustaqbal al- Arabi*, no. 335, January 2007.

al-Jarbawi, Ali, "What Is Israel Afraid Of?," *Bitterlemons: Palestinian-Israeli Crossfire*, 15 March 2010, www.bitterlemons.org.

Judt, Tony, "Israel: The Alternative," *New York Review of Books*, vol. 50, no. 16, 23 October 2003.

Karmi, Ghada, "Call It a Cucumber," interview in *Bitterlemons: Palestinian-Israeli Crossfire*, 19 January 2004, www.bitterlemons.org.

Karmi, Ghada, "Where Next for Palestinians?," *Bitterlemons: Palestinian-Israeli Crossfire*, 23 November 2009, www.bitterlemons.org.

Khalidi, Rashid, *The Iron Cage: The Story of the Palestinian Struggle for Statehood* (Boston: Beacon Press, 2006).

Khalidi, Walid, "Toward Peace in the Holy Land," *Foreign Affairs*, vol. 66, no. 4 (Spring 1988).

Khatib, Ghassan, "A Ton of Regret," *Bitterlemons: Palestinian-Israeli Crossfire*, 19 January 2004, www.bitterlemons.org.

Khatib, Ghassan, "A Farcical Position on Statehood," *Bitterlemons: Palestinian-Israeli Crossfire*, 15 June 2009, www.bitterlemons.org.

Khatib, Ghassan, "Two Alternatives: Backward or Forward," *Bitterlemons: Palestinian-Israeli Crossfire*, 23 November 2009, www.bitterlemons.org.

Kovel, Joel, *Overcoming Zionism: Creating a Single Democratic State in Israel/Palestine* (Toronto: Pluto Press, 2007).

Kurtzer, Daniel, "Behind the Settlements," *The American Interest* (March/April 2010).

Lijphart, Arend, *Thinking about Democracy: Power Sharing and Majority Rule in Theory and Practice* (London and New York: Routledge, 2008).

Litvak, Meir, "The Palestine Liberation Organization," *Middle East Contemporary Survey* (MECS), vol. 17 (1993).

Litvak, Meir, "Introduction: Collective Memory and the Palestinian Experience," in Meir Litvak (ed.), *Palestinian Collective Memory and National Identity* (New York: Palgrave Macmillan, 2009).

Lunt, James, *Hussein of Jordan: Searching for a Just and Lasting Peace* (New York: William Morrow, 1987).

Main, Ernest, *Palestine at the Crossroads* (London: George Allen & Unwin, 1937).

Makdisi, Saree, "Good Riddance, Abbas," *Foreign Policy*, 6 November 2009.

Makovsky, David, *A Defensible Fence: Fighting Terror and Enabling a Two-State Solution* (Washington Institute for Near East Policy, April 2004).

al-Maliki, Riyad, "Nahwa mubadarat salam Filastiniyya" [Towards a Palestinian Peace Initiative], *al-Ayyam*, 13 May 2004.

Masalha, Nur (ed.), *Catastrophe Remembered: Palestine, Israel and the Internal Refugees* (London: Zed Books, 2005).

al-Masri, Hani, "Awdat al-wa'i" [The Return of Consciousness], *al-Ayyam*, 10 November 2009.

al-Masri, Hani, "Min al-mubakkir na'i al-mufawadat" [From the Start We Have Understood the Negotiations], *al-Ayyam*, 24 November 2009.

al-Masri, Hani, "Waqf al-mufawadat bidun badil aswa min isti'nafiha" [Stopping Negotiations without an Alternative Is Worse Than Resuming Them], *al-Ayyam*, 8 December 2009.

Mead, Walter Russell, "Israel's Strategic Failure," *American Interest Online*, 3 June 2010.

*Middle East Contemporary Survey (MECS)*, vol. 6 (1981–82) (New York: Holmes and Meier, The Moshe Dayan Center for Middle Eastern and African Studies, Tel Aviv University).

*Middle East Contemporary Survey (MECS)*, vol. 7 (1982–83).

*Middle East Contemporary Survey (MECS)*, vol. 9 (1984–85).

*Middle East Contemporary Survey (MECS)*, vol. 20 (1996) (Boulder: Westview Press, The Moshe Dayan Center for Middle Eastern and African Studies, Tel Aviv University).

*Middle East Contemporary Survey (MECS)*, vol. 22 (1998).

*Middle East Record (MER)*, vol. 4 (1968) (Jerusalem: Israel Universities Press, Shiloah Center for Middle Eastern and African Studies, Tel Aviv University, 1973).

*Middle East Record (MER)*, vol. 5 (1969–70) (Jerusalem: Israel Universities Press, Shiloah Center for Middle Eastern and African Studies, Tel Aviv University, 1977).

Miller, Aaron David, *The Much Too Promised Land: America's Elusive Search for Arab-Israeli Peace* (New York: Bantam Books, 2008).

Miller, Aaron David, "US, Israel Get Back into the Ring," *Politico*, 4 April 2010.

Milshtein, Michael, "Memory 'from Below': Palestinian Society and the Nakba Memory," in Meir Litvak (ed.), *Palestinian Collective Memory and National Identity* (New York: Palgrave Macmillan, 2009).

Milshtein, Michael, "The Memory That Never Dies: The Nakba Memory and the Palestinian National Movement," in Meir Litvak (ed.), *Palestinian Collective Memory and National Identity* (New York: Palgrave Macmillan, 2009).

Mishal, Shaul, and Reuben Aharoni, *Speaking Stones: Communiques from the Intifada Underground* (Syracuse University Press, 1994).

Morris, Benny, *The Birth of the Palestinian Refugee Problem, 1947–1949* (Cambridge University Press, 1988).

Morris, Benny, *Righteous Victims: A History of the Zionist-Arab Conflict, 1881–1999* (New York: Alfred A. Knopf, 1999).

Morris, Benny, "Camp David and After: An Exchange (1. An Interview with Ehud Barak)," *New York Review of Books*, vol. 49, no. 10, 13 June 2002.

Benny Morris, *The Birth of the Palestinian Refugee Problem Revisited* (Cambridge University Press, 2004).

Morris, Benny, *1948: The First Arab-Israeli War* (New Haven: Yale University Press, 2008).

Morris, Benny, *One State, Two States; Resolving the Israel/Palestine Conflict* (New Haven: Yale University Press, 2009).

Muasher, Marwan, *The Arab Center: The Promise of Moderation* (New Haven: Yale University Press, 2008).

Muasher, Marwan, "Jordan's Future Agenda," *Jordan Business*, March 2009.

al-Naami, Saleh, "Band Aid Proposal," *al-Ahram Weekly*, 19–25 November 2009.

al-Naami, Saleh, "Fatah Riven with Fights," *al-Ahram Weekly*, 9–15 December 2010.

Nevo, Joseph, *King Abdallah and Palestine: A Territorial Ambition* (London: Macmillan Press, 1996).

Pipes, Daniel, *Greater Syria: The History of an Ambition* (Oxford University Press, 1990).

Pogrund, Benjamin, "Different Histories, Different Futures," *Palestine-Israel Journal*, vol. 15, no. 4 (2008) and vol. 16, no. 1 (2009).

Pollock, David, "Palestinian Public Opinion: Tactically Flexible, Strategically Ambitious," *Washington Institute for Near East Policy, Policy Watch*, no. 1731, 9 December 2010.

Press, Eyal, "Israel's Holy Warriors," *New York Review of Books*, vol. 57, no. 7 (29 April 2010).

Pundak, Ron, "From Oslo to Taba: What Went Wrong?" *Survival*, vol. 43, no. 3 (Autumn 2001).

Qurie, Ahmed, *Beyond Oslo, the Struggle for Palestine: Inside the Middle East Peace Process from Rabin's Death to Camp David* (London: I. B.Tauris, 2008).

Rabinovich, Itamar, "From 'Israeli Arabs' to 'Israel's Palestinian Citizens,' 1948–1996: Analysis," in Itamar Rabinovich and Jehuda Reinharz (eds.) *Israel in the Middle East: Documents and Readings on Society, Politics, and Foreign Relations, Pre-1948 to the Present*, Second Edition (Waltham, MA: Brandeis University Press, 2008).

al-Rantawi, Urayb, "Mitchell khasara jawla . . . fama huwa masir al-harb idhan?" [Mitchell Lost a Round . . . But What Then Is the Fate of the Fight?], *al-Dustur*, 20 September 2009.

al-Rantawi, Urayb, "Fahamat 'kabir al-mufawidin'" [His Excellency 'The Chief of Negotiators'], www.alqudscenter.com, 9 December 2009.

Rekhess, Elie, "The West Bank and the Gaza Strip," *MECS*, vol. 17 (1993).

Rekhess, Elie, "The Arabs of Israel after Oslo: Localization of the National Struggle," *Israel Studies*, vol. 7, no. 3 (Fall 2002).

Richman, Alvin, "Israeli Public's Support for Dismantling Most Settlements Has Risen to a Five-Year High," *World Public Opinion Org*, 15 April 2010, www.world publicopinion.org/pipa/articles/brmiddleeastnafricara/659.php.

Robins, Philip, *A History of Jordan* (Cambridge University Press, 2004).

Rogan, Eugene, *Frontiers of the State in the Late Ottoman Empire: Transjordan, 1850–1921* (Cambridge University Press, 2002).

Roshwald, Aviel, *The Endurance of Nationalism: Ancient Roots and Modern Dilemmas* (Cambridge University Press, 2006).

Ross, Dennis, *The Missing Peace: The Inside Story of the Fight for Middle East Peace* (New York: Farrar, Straus and Giroux, 2004).

Ross, Dennis, and David Makovsky, *Myths, Illusions, and Peace: Finding a New Direction for America in the Middle East* (New York: Viking, 2009).

Rouhana, Nadim, "The Political Transformation of the Palestinians in Israel: From Acquiescence to Challenge," *Journal of Palestine Studies*, vol. 18, no. 3 (Spring 1989).

Rouhana, Nadim, "Shaking the Foundations of Citizenship," *al-Ahram Weekly*, 27 September–3 October 2001.

Ryan, Curtis, *Inter-Arab Alliances: Regime Security and Jordanian Foreign Policy* (Gainesville: University Press of Florida, 2009).

Sahliyeh, Emile, *In Search of Leadership: West Bank Politics Since 1967* (Washington, DC: The Brookings Institution, 1988).

Said, Edward, "The One-State Solution," *New York Times Weekend Magazine*, 10 January 1999.

Said, Edward, "Introduction: The Right of Return at Last," in Naseer Aruri (ed.), *Palestinian Refugees: The Right of Return* (London: Pluto Press, 2001).

Said, Edward, "Trying Again and Again," *al-Ahram Weekly*, 11–17 January 2001.

Said, Edward, "The One-State Solution," in *Culture and Resistance: Conversations with Edward W. Said*, interviews by David Barsamian (Cambridge, MA: South End Press, 2003).

Salibi, Kamal, *The Modern History of Jordan* (London: I. B. Tauris, 1993).

Sayigh, Yezid, *Armed Struggle and the Search for State: The Palestinian National Movement, 1949–1993* (Oxford: Clarendon Press, 1997).

Sayigh, Yezid, "Arafat and the Anatomy of a Revolt," *Survival*, vol. 43, no. 3 (Autumn 2001).

Sayigh, Yezid, "The Palestinian Strategic Impasse," *Survival*, vol. 44, no. 4 (Winter 2002–03).

Sayigh, Yezid, "Hamas Rule in Gaza: Three Years On," *Middle East Brief*, no. 41, Brandeis University, Crown Center for Middle East Studies, March 2010.

Schueftan, Dan, *Jordanian Option: Israel, Jordan and the Palestinians* (Tel Aviv: Yad Tabenkin, 1986) (Hebrew).

Schueftan, Dan, *The Disengagement Imperative: Israel and the Palestinian Entity* (Haifa University Press/Zmora-Bitan, 1999) (Hebrew).

Sela, Avraham, "The Palestinian Arabs in the War of 1948," in Moshe Maoz and Benjamin Z. Kedar (eds.), *The Palestinian National Movement: From Confrontation to Reconciliation?* (Tel Aviv: Ma'arakhot, 1997) (Hebrew).

Shamir, Jacob, and Khalil Shikaki, *Palestinian and Israeli Public Opinion: The Public Imperative in the Second Intifada* (Bloomington: Indiana University Press, 2010).

Shapira, Anita, *Land and Power: The Zionist Resort to Force, 1881–1948* (Stanford University Press, 1992).

Shemesh, Moshe, *The Palestinian Entity, 1959–1974: Arab Politics and the PLO*, Second Revised Edition (London: Frank Cass, 1996).

Sher, Gilead, *Just Beyond Reach: The Israeli-Palestinian Peace Negotiations 1999–2001* (Tel Aviv: Yediot Aharonot, 2001) (Hebrew).

Shindler, Colin, *A History of Modern Israel* (Cambridge University Press, 2008).

Shlaim, Avi, "The Rise and Fall of the All-Palestine Government in Gaza," *Journal of Palestine Studies*, vol. 20, no. 1 (Autumn 1990).

Shlaim, Avi, "The Oslo Accord," *Journal of Palestinian Studies*, vol. 23, no. 3 (Spring 1994).

Shlaim, Avi, *Lion of Jordan: The Life of King Hussein in War and Peace* (London: Allen Lane, 2007).

Shlaim, Avi, *Israel and Palestine: Reappraisals, Revisions, Refutations* (London: Verso, 2009).

Sivan, Emmanuel, "The Arab Nation-State: In Search of a Usable Past," *Middle East Review*, vol. 19, no. 3 (Spring 1987).

Smith, Anthony, *Nationalism and Modernism* (London: Routledge, 1998).

Sprinzak, Ehud, *The Ascendance of Israel's Radical Right* (New York, Oxford: Oxford University Press, 1991).

Stein, Kenneth, "Caplan's Contested Histories Considered," *Review Essay in Middle East Journal*, vol. 64, no. 2 (Spring 2010).

Steinberg, Matti, "Nationalism and Marxism in the Approach of the PFLP," in Matti Steinberg, *Facing Their Fate: Palestinian National Consciousness, 1967–2007* (Tel Aviv: Yediot Aharonot, 2008) (Hebrew).

Stroun, Maurice, "Permission to Return or Right of Return," *Bitterlemons-api: Discussing the Arab Peace Initiative*, Edition 4, 15 December 2010, www.bitterlemons-api.org.

Susser, Asher, *The Jordanian-Israeli Peace Negotiations: The Geopolitical Rationale of a Bilateral Relationship* (The Leonard Davis Institute of the Hebrew University of Jerusalem, 1999).

Susser, Asher, "Jordan — In the Maze of Tribalism, Jordanianism, Palestinianism, and Islam," in Asher Susser (ed.), *Challenges to the Cohesion of the Arab State* (Tel Aviv University, Moshe Dayan Center, 2008).

Susser, Asher, *The Rise of Hamas in Palestine and the Crisis of Secularism in the Arab World*, Brandeis University, Crown Center for Middle East Studies, Essay Series, February 2010.

Sussman, Gary, "The Challenges to the Two-State Solution," *Middle East Report*, no. 231 (Summer 2004).

al-Tall, Tariq, "Al-Ustura wa-siwa al-fahm fi al-alaqat al-Urduniyya-al-Filastiniyya" [Myth and Misunderstanding in Jordanian-Palestinian Relations], *al-Siyasa al-Filastiniyya*, vol. 3, no. 12 (Fall 1996).

Tamari, Salim, "The Binationalist Lure," *Boston Review*, December 2001–January 2002.

Tamari, Salim, "No Obvious Destination," *al-Ahram Weekly*, 18–24 September 2003.

Tamimi, Azzam, *Hamas: A History from Within* (Northampton, MA: Olive Branch Press, 2007).

Teitelbaum, Joshua, *The Arab Peace Initiative; A Primer and Future Prospects* (Jerusalem Center for Public Affairs, 2009).

Teveth, Shabtai, *Ben-Gurion and the Palestinian Arabs* (Oxford University Press, 1985).

Teveth, Shabtai, *Ben-Gurion: The Burning Ground, 1886–1948* (Boston: Houghton Mifflin, 1987).

Tilley, Virginia, *The One-State Solution: A Breakthrough for Peace in the Israeli-Palestinian Deadlock* (Ann Arbor: University of Michigan Press, 2008).

Traniello, Marisa, "Power-Sharing: Lessons from South Africa and Rwanda," *International Public Policy Review*, vol. 3, no. 2 (March 2008).

Tutunji, Jenab, and Kamal Khaldi, "A Bi-national State in Palestine: The Rational Choice for Palestinians and the Moral Choice for Israelis," *International Affairs*, vol. 73, no. 1 (January 1997).

Wasserstein, Bernard, *Israelis and Palestinians: Why Do They Fight? Can They Stop?* (New Haven: Yale University Press, 2003).

Whitbeck, John, "Two States or One: The Moment of Truth," *al-Ahram Weekly*, 12–18 November 2009.

Wieseltier, Leon, "Israel, Palestine, and the Return of the Bi-National Fantasy: What Is Not to be Done," *The New Republic*, 27 October 2003.

Wilson, Mary, *King Abdullah, Britain and the Making of Jordan* (Cambridge University Press, 1987).

Yaari, Ehud, "Armistice Now: An Interim Agreement for Israel and Palestine," *Foreign Affairs*, March/April 2010.

Yakobson, Alexander, and Amnon Rubinstein, *Israel and the Family of Nations: The Jewish Nation State and Human Rights* (Tel Aviv: Schocken, 2003) (Hebrew).

Yuchtman-Ya'ar, Ephraim, and Tamar Hermann, *War and Peace Index*, March 2010 (Tel Aviv University, The Evens Program in Mediation and Conflict Resolution and The Israel Democracy Institute).

Zak, Moshe, *Husayn Makes Peace: Thirty Years and One More on the Road to Peace* (Bar Ilan University, BESA Center, 1994) (Hebrew).

Zaqut, Jamal, "Wathiqat jinif adah lil-kifah al-siyasi" [The Geneva Document Is an Instrument for the Political Struggle], *al-Hayat al-Jadida*, 30 November 2003.

Ze'evi-Farkash, Aharon, "Key Principles of a Demilitarized Palestinian State," in *Israel's Critical Security Needs for a Viable Peace* (Jerusalem Center for Public Affairs, 2010).

Zittrain Eisenberg, Laura, and Neil Caplan, *Negotiating Arab-Israeli Peace: Patterns, Problems, Possibilities*, Second Edition (Indianapolis: Indiana University Press, 2010).

# INDEX

Page numbers in italics refer to maps.

# DATE DUE